PAUL
DANIELS

PUBLISHER'S NOTE

PAUL DANIELS, 6 April 1938 – 17 March 2016

On 20 February 2016, Paul Daniels, magician, was diagnosed with an incurable brain tumour, and on 6 March it was announced that he had returned home from hospital to be with his family. His son, Martin, also a magician, told the *Sunday Mirror:* 'Dad's not going to get any better. There's no treatment which can help him. . . It is unbearably difficult. He has said before, "When it's your time it's your time" and that's how he is trying to face up to things.' Less than a month later, Paul died at home, with his beloved wife at his bedside.

For a great illusionist – and, in his heyday, the most famous magician in the world – Paul Daniels had few illusions himself. Nor had his life been free from hardships and sorrow. Even at the height of his fame and success he was often mocked, while his uncompromising views on subjects from climate change to the homeless sometimes attracted controversy. Yet he remained a strong spirit, as well as a consummate performer; it was no accident that he was the first magician from outside the USA to receive the hugely prestigious Magician of the Year Award from the Academy of Magical Arts, while a special edition of *The Paul Daniels Magic Show* won a Golden Rose of Montreux Award at the International TV Festival in Switzerland.

On his death, aged seventy-seven, tributes flooded in not just from the good and the great of show business, but from thousands of ordinary fans as well. These, perhaps, form the most touching memorial to a peerless entertainer whom Louis Theroux described, in his own tribute, as 'a thoughtful sceptic, enemy of hucksterism and paranormal flimflam, and gifted magician'.

PAUL DANIELS

MY MAGIC LIFE
THE AUTOBIOGRAPHY

PAUL DANIELS WITH
CHRIS GIDNEY

JOHN BLAKE

Published by John Blake Publishing Ltd,
3 Bramber Court, 2 Bramber Road,
London W14 9PB, England

www.johnblakebooks.com

www.facebook.com/johnblakebooks ⬛
twitter.com/jblakebooks ⬛

First published in hardback, as *Paul Daniels: Under No Illusion –
My Autobiography*, in 2000
This paperback edition published in 2016

ISBN 978-1-78606-140-9

British Library Cataloguing-in-Publication Data:

A catalogue record for this book is available from the British Library.

Design by www.envydesign.co.uk

Printed in Great Britain by CPI Group (UK) Ltd

1 3 5 7 9 10 8 6 4 2

Papers used by John Blake Publishing are natural, recyclable products made
from wood grown in sustainable forests. The manufacturing processes conform to
the environmental regulations of the country of origin.

Every attempt has been made to contact the relevant copyright-holders,
but some were unobtainable. We would be grateful if the appropriate people
could contact us.

DEDICATION

This book is dedicated to the memory of Handel Newton
Daniels and with love to Nancy Daniels

And to those close to my heart. There is no order to this,
I love you all in different ways.
Debbie, the very best wife I could ever have wished for.
My sons, Paul, Martin and Gary.
My brother Trevor and all his family.
Debbie's family for putting up with me.

There are also so many people that I would like to thank and,
again, in differing ways I owe them all so much.

The Man who wrote the Magic Book.

My first wife, Jackie, for my three sons.
Mervyn O'Horan
Howard Huntridge
Johnny Hamp
Graham Reed, Barry Murray, Ali Bongo, and the late Gil Leaney.
Timothy Reed for research material.

And to my grandson, Lewis, who is the future.

CONTENTS

CHAPTER 1

BOMBS AWAY

*T*he nation is on the brink of catastrophe as World War II approaches and Prime Minister Chamberlain promises 'Peace in our time'. 1938 also sees John Logie Baird demonstrate his first colour television set in the UK, whilst fluorescent lights, a non-stick substance called Teflon and Superman are invented in the USA. The first children's zoo in London's Regent's Park opens to whoops of delight three weeks after Hitler claims Austria; Paul Daniels enters a troubled world with a shout.

A couple of years ago Debbie, my wife, and I lived in a beautiful house set in 12 acres of formal gardens and stunning woodland. We held a garden party for showbusiness people at our home. My brother-in-law, Simon, wasn't feeling too good so he went upstairs to have a lie down. While he was there, he heard some of the guests in the upper corridor going on about how wonderful the house was. 'This place is fantastic.' Another voice cut in with 'if you want to know how fantastic this place is, you should see where he comes from ...'

I was born in South Bank, a small industrial town between

Middlesbrough and Redcar in the north-east of Yorkshire. Surrounded then by steelworks and docks and later by the gigantic ICI chemical works, it was the most polluted town in the country. That didn't bother us much because we didn't know. The streets were laid out in long blocks of terrace houses with no gardens. In fact, you couldn't see much greenery anywhere except in the far-off hills. When you are a child, everywhere you travel is a great journey. The hills turned out to be about four miles away.

My grandmother's house, 51 North Street, was the venue for my opening night. The date was 6 April 1938. I was instantly lucky because I had wonderful parents and I'd like you to meet them. Before she married, my mother was called Nancy Lloyd and she is still a small, attractive, fiery redhead, although as I write the hair is lighter. Mam has always insisted it is auburn and never liked being compared to Katherine Hepburn. My dad was called Hughie and he was a small, happy man with a disposition that made everyone like him.

Hughie was not his real name. His full name was Handel (for music), Newton (for science) and Daniel (for religion). The 's' in Daniels was, apparently, caused by the slip of the registrar's pen.

Despite the threat of war, my parents were blissfully happy. Dad had certainly worked hard at his courtship. Mam was in service in Bradford and Dad used to court my mother by pedalling a bicycle from South Bank, in the north-eastern tip of Yorkshire, all the way to Bradford about 65 miles away. Just getting a bike out of the hills of the Tees valley is hard enough and there is still a long way to go after that. He must have been in love because he did it every Saturday night after he finished work.

When he arrived, he was allowed to sleep in the greenhouse until my mother was released from her daily duties. They strolled around Bradford for a couple of hours and then Hughie rode all the way back. Determined lad, my dad.

Unlike most people, who worked in the 'works' (we pronounced it 'werks'), Dad was a cinema projectionist. When my parents married, Dad had landed a job in a cinema in Mablethorpe on the East Coast and that's where they set up home. After the long terraced streets of South Bank, Mablethorpe must have seemed like heaven on earth.

As was customary in those days, they went back up North to Nancy's mother for my birth and then returned to the bungalow a few days later on a tandem with me in a sidecar that Dad had built.

The stamina of my parents, especially my mother, was wondrous. Dad, who was nicknamed Hughie, had been in training for this trip ever since he started the weekly pedal pilgrimage to see his loved one.

Of course, I cannot remember anything of this, or Mablethorpe, but I know that they were deliriously happy living in their bungalow called 'Lulworth'. The stories I know about the area are 'hand-me-downs'; the one-legged champion cyclist and the strange, very rich man whose garden was full of rubbish seem to be part of my own experience. Strangely enough, however, when I took Mam and Dad back to Mablethorpe many years later, I could remember that there was a greengrocer's shop around a particular corner with a strange metal and glass extension over the pavement. When we turned the corner it was still there, and that was my first proof that children in prams are already learning stuff.

My father was a projectionist by default. Having served his time as an apprentice electrician, the man who was supposed to sign his qualification papers made a pass at Mam, Dad got mad and the documents were never signed. I rarely saw my father lose his temper, maybe three or four times in my life, but when he did you had to watch out. He was a short, stocky man of incredible strength and I never met a person who didn't like

Hughie Daniels, but then, I never met the man who made a pass at Mam.

Another amazing fact about Dad was his ability to be able to turn his hand to anything and achieve an incredibly high standard. Whether it involved working in wood, metal, plastic, decorating, toy-making, electronics, plumbing, or car mechanics, he seemed to be a master wizard. 'If a man made it or created it, son, then he only had the same number of fingers and thumbs as you have, so you can do it, too,' was a very early lesson.

Everything was logical to Dad if you thought about it long enough. Wisdom and calmness seemed to surround him. 'Always measure it twice, then you'll only have to cut it once,' he said. 'That will apply as much to your life as it does to woodwork!'

Soon, the threat of war was upon England and my parents believed, like everyone else, that Hitler and his Teutonic hordes would attack us on the beaches of Skegness and Mablethorpe. They packed up and headed back to South Bank where Dad got a job at the local cinema and we settled into Pearl Street.

The bombs of war had already started to drop and there was a new sense of danger every night. I have vague memories of getting under the kitchen table when the sirens went off, warning of a possible air raid by enemy aircraft. Being surrounded by steelworks made us a prime target for the Luftwaffe and our town received a pretty good pasting. It didn't feel safe at home, but there was nowhere else to run when an air attack came. Everyone just prayed the bombers would pass overhead and give the town a miss this time.

One night, the prayers didn't work because the sirens screeched their deadly warning and Mam stood terrified wondering what to do with her toddler son. Then there was a shout from the elderly couple who lived across the street. They invited Mam and I to come and stay with them during the onslaught, knowing that Dad was at work. As we crossed the street we heard a loud whistle above us. Grabbing me, Mam started to run and as we burst through the front door, the couple threw themselves on top of us as the bomb hit our house. We were covered in dust and rubble but were unhurt. Bombs were smaller in those days. The Germans killed my budgie, though, so they were the bad guys. I can still, quite clearly, hear the sound of the descending whistle.

In an instant, our home and all our possessions had disappeared and we were taken to Granny Lloyd's house a few streets away. Dad had heard the bombs dropping all around him, but kept the film rolling. When he arrived in our street after work the sight was terrifying. Where there had been an entire row of houses, only a pit of broken bricks remained. Even worse was the thought that Mam and I were still buried under the rubble. The elderly couple were quick to spot him, however, and report that we were still alive. It must have been awful for him and the relief must have been enormous. Will someone explain war to me? I cannot see the glory or sense in it at all. What a waste it all is.

Several weeks later, we were rehoused at 10 Lower Oxford Street, South Bank, Middlesbrough, and it was there that I began to grow up.

* * *

There weren't many cars around. Milkmen still used horses and carts, as did the rag and bone man who collected your unwanted clothes and gave you a balloon for them. Another old chap used to come round and had a strange sort of grinding wheel attached to a treadle which made it spin round at high speed. He used to sharpen knives and scissors on it and I loved to watch the sparks fly out as he honed the metal edges.

We could play quite safely in the streets, games with milk bottle tops and sticks and balls, and cricket with the stumps marked on a wall. The rules were not exactly MCC. If you hit the ball over the back wall of someone's house you had to decide whether to be 'None and stay in or take Six and be out'. A lack of traffic made games possible that simply aren't played today. I can't remember most of them but Levo and Tag were games with cans and sticks. We used the sticks that had been chopped to start a fire in the grate, about an inch square and six inches long, and an empty food can was placed in the middle of the street. Two sticks were laid on the top of the can, then two more at right angles and finally two more again at right angles on the top. Eventually, a pyramid of tin and wood took shape and wobbled precariously. Two teams stood on the pavement edge and alternately threw a ball at the can. Whichever team knocked it over were 'it' and had to rebuild the can and sticks before the other team could hit them with the ball by throwing it at them as they ran about. Many years later, I was amazed to see the same game being played in Venice in the streets, because again, they don't have any traffic.

Our house was exactly the same as all the others. The front doors were usually painted in a simple way, the favourite colour being 'nigger brown'. Nowadays, that word is not used among white people. It is supposed to be wrong. When the fuss blew up about the use of the word 'nigger' I was confused. Having been brought up on this beautiful colour I couldn't understand why the word was supposed to be bad. Later in life, when I went to a grammar school and found out that it derived from the Latin for 'black', I couldn't see any point in changing from the same word to the same word. If the claim was that it was said in a derogatory fashion then that, too, is confusing because you can turn just about any word into a 'bad' sound. I suppose it is because I don't understand racism. I think you have to be pretty stupid to say you don't like any particular race. There really are good and bad in all races, so I just think of us all as World People. The question is never about your colour or creed, it is about whether I like you or not.

Having stepped off the street and through the whatever colour door, you found yourself in the front room, where every Friday we had a bath in front of the open grate. From the front room you went through into a scullery with an open-topped coal boiler in the corner. It was a magical thing, that boiler. It boiled the whites on washday, it heated the water for the baths and boiled the fruit when Mam made delicious home-made jams and marmalades. Just as Dad could make anything, Mam could cook anything. Her pastry is still the best I have ever tasted.

The stairs bent upwards from this rear room to the two bedrooms upstairs. I find it strange that I have no memory of my bedroom at all, only the downstairs, and I can still sense the wonderful feeling of sitting in the tin bath in front of the fire, immersed in hot water and soap bubbles.

Going further back from the scullery you went out into a small lean-to kitchen and then into the back yard. At the far end of this small yard was a toilet in a small brick outhouse and a door that went into the back alley. Going to the toilet in winter toughened you up no end. Perhaps it was just your end it toughened up. The lower part of the toilet wall, which was the back alley wall, still had the low door in it that, in previous times, had enabled the sewage men to pull the bucket-like container out and tip it into a lorry for spreading on farmers' fields. By the time I was using the toilet we had mains drains, but I often used to wonder what happened if they pulled it out whilst someone was still sitting on the seat.

At all times of the year, however, it was very, very important that, when you flushed the toilet, you had to get back into the house before the toilet stopped flushing or, according to legend, the witch would get you. I used to have nightmares about that witch. Opposite our back alley door was another door that would let you into the opposite back yard and then the scullery and eventually out into the next street. It was a mirror image of our house. This mirror imaging went on for street after street.

There was a great deal of pride to be gained in how your house looked inside and a lot of time and energy was taken by Mam to keep it spotless. The fire grate in the front room was jet black and polished regularly with black lead and the brass knobs shone brightly on the side oven doors built into the walls. These grates were another source of wonder. You could hang a kettle over the open fire, cook in the side oven and hold bread on long forks to make delicious toast. Toast was the cheapest form of food we had ready access to and Mam joked that we were so poor she should take me to the park and let the ducks feed me! I never seemed to go without anything I needed though.

Shortly after we moved into Lower Oxford Street, Dad was called up into the Royal Navy and went off to fight in the war. He finished up in India for the next four years. We were soon on rations and all the neighbours, mostly women left behind while the men went to fight, used to help each other and keep each other company. These women were amazing, making, mending and cooking with hardly anything to live off and working as one 'unit' to support each other. Their dedication and resourcefulness meant that us kids were protected from all the harshness of the conflict.

I have vague memories of seeing air-raid shelters built and filling the back alleys between the back yards of the houses. They had thick concrete roofs and offset doors to stop shrapnel flying through them. Mam, who was the size of nothing, wanted to be a part of the war effort, too, so when I was at school she would mix cement and run wheelbarrows of the mixture along the side of railway lines in order to erect fences.

For years afterwards, we would walk along the Black Path by the railway lines and see her initials in the concrete posts.

Of course, the family was bigger than Mam and Dad and I was never short of company. At that time I had two grandmas and one granddad. The closest family was on my mother's side. My mam's mother, Granny Lloyd, was very like my mother, small and dynamic. She would have a go at any ride in the fairground and was full of life. Together with her friend Mrs Gillings, later to play a very big part in my life, she managed to persuade a local benefactor to provide the funds to build the South Bank Mission Hall on North Street, opposite her house. They were concerned about the number of kids playing in the streets and the threat from some of the bullying gangs that were starting to emerge. If she could keep some of the children occupied in a safe environment whilst teaching manners, respect and morality, then that was a good reason to have it, she decided.

Managing to get the funding, she organised the purchase of the land and the building of the mission hut, which was to have a central focus for many families in the area. Every weekend I would be off to Sunday school to learn about Jesus and the Bible stories and 'right' from 'wrong'. Pastor Ingledew was a white-haired preacher who enthralled me as he could recite whole passages of the Bible from memory. I could read him a verse and he would be able to tell me exactly where it could be found. His ability was awesome and his technique of reading and memorising fascinated me.

John Fisher, another member of the congregation, was a source of wonder to us kids. He sang with such passion that when he strained to reach the top notes, his neck quivered so much that we would all look at him in amazement and think that he was going to burst. Singing spiritual songs must have made quite an impression on me as 50 years later I still remember all the words and all the actions. My wife Debbie wondered what she had let herself in for when I started to sing them one day shortly after we were married, and when working on the Isle of Man recently, I dumbfounded an evangelistic beach group when I joined in with 'sunshine corner/Oh it's jolly fine/It's for children under ninety-nine ...' followed by:

'Join the Gospel Express
Come on, answer "yes",
We're leaving for Glory soon.

The guard is so glad,
He's waving his flag
Hallelujah! It won't be very long.

Chuff, chuff, chuff goes the engine
Toot, toot goes the whistle
And we're off on the Glory train.'

Granny Lloyd lived just around the corner from us with her son, known to me as Uncle Eddie. He loved a drink and was a tough but happy man. Granny, being so involved with the Mission, asked him to stop many times, once insisting that he should say, 'Get thee behind me, Satan.' That night he came home stoned out of his brain, claiming that he had done exactly as she asked but that the Devil had indeed 'got behind him' and pushed him straight into the pub!

Next door but one to them lived my Auntie Louie and her husband Connie, short for Cornelius. They looked just like Jack Spratt and his wife from the children's nursery rhyme. Auntie Louie was very overweight and I used to dread having to kiss her, which happened every Christmas. She would engulf me in her arms, her bosom cradling me on either side and my face would vanish into her cheek. I was always convinced that I would die of suffocation in there. Years later, I found out that my brother felt exactly the same way and that we both grew up with a fear of fat women.

Granny Lloyd's concern for the community stretched well beyond her activities with the Mission Hall when she doubled as the local undertaker. Her main task was to 'lay out' bodies. When somebody died she would get a call to come and prepare the body for the funeral. It was quite a busy time for her during the war. One day she asked Uncle Eddie and Uncle Connie to help get a body down the stairs and into the front room of a house nearby. Neither of them really wanted to do this. Both were filled with a superstitious fear of the dead. Granny told them not to be so stupid. 'He's dead. He can't harm you now.' They took quite a bit of convincing but Granny Lloyd was a forceful character.

Eddie took the head end, supporting the corpse under the armpits. Connie had the feet. All was going well, albeit with a struggle, until they came to the curve in the stairs. As they struggled to get the body around the corner they bent it almost double. Wind, trapped inside the corpse, came out as a loud and rude raspberry. Connie immediately dropped his end. 'If the bugger can do that then he can bloody well walk downstairs!' Off he went and he wouldn't come back.

Connie didn't seem to have much luck with the dead, especially when he got his hands on some ducks one Christmas and didn't know how to prepare them for the oven. He eventually chopped off their heads and pegged them by their webbed feet upside down on a clothesline in the back yard to drain the blood. He came in white as a sheet as the bodies were still flapping and the heads on the floor were still quacking.

Granddad Daniels was not very tall but, like Aunt Louie, very, very fat. He was a shunting engine driver at the steel works and I used to wonder how he got through the narrow open door on to the footplate. Everyone said that he had a great tenor voice and apparently, on some works outing, had stopped the shopping in the marketplace in Richmond, Yorkshire, by singing from the hill that many years later I was to march up and down as a soldier. The entire marketplace burst into applause as he finished 'Sweet Lass of Richmond Hill'. A phenomenal voice to match his size.

Grandma Gertie, his wife, was quite the opposite. I remember her being tall and gaunt and a bit frightening. She played the piano in pubs to earn extra money; her party piece was lying down, crossing her arms above her head and playing the piano through a towel that she had laid on the keys. She got big tips doing this, though I was never allowed in the pub to watch a performance.

Her daughter Maureen was Dad's half-sister or stepsister, I was never sure. Tall, gorgeous, with raven black hair, she was in showbusiness. She was part of a double act called Kizma and Karen. Wow. Maureen tap-danced on steps that were made for her by my father. They had to fold away small enough to go in taxis and on trains, so it was quite a feat of ingenuity. Occasionally, she would come to our house and rehearse on a new set of steps that Dad had made and I fell madly in love with her long, long legs. She taught me how to do a riffle-shuffle with a pack of cards and would probably have taught me a few other things had I been a little older.

Mam didn't like Aunt Maureen or Grandma Gertie. At some time in the past there had been a major disagreement and although I never discovered what it was about, I do know that Dad had suffered a bad childhood with Gertie. He was never given any Christmas gifts and one day the man next door, taking pity on him, gave my dad a fort that his son had been given the year before and no longer played with. Gertie seized it immediately and used it as firewood. Maybe that was why Mam didn't like Gertie. She also seemed to think that her daughter, Aunt Maureen, was a bit promiscuous.

In those terrifying days of conflict, the people of the community were more than just living closely together. If any woman was sick, for example, the neighbours would take over the house. One would do the cleaning while others cooked or looked after the children. Doors were always open to everyone and visitors would make a cursory tap or, more commonly, shout a brief 'Hellooooo'.

During the war, nothing was wasted that could be recycled, especially as there wasn't a lot of money about. The wives not only did war work previously done by the men, they also knitted, crotcheted, sewed, repaired and kept households ticking along. Clippy mats were the big thing and they all seemed to make them. When the women got together every Saturday night, old clothing was cut up into strips about 4in long by about 1 in wide and then sorted into colours. A piece of canvas was stretched across a wooden frame and the material was poked through the weave and pulled back again with a small hook. It was then knotted and the next piece poked through. Eventually the pattern in this rag carpet took shape and when it was finished the 'clippy' mat would adorn the floor of someone's house.

On Saturday nights there would be a radio programme called *The Man in Black*. There was no television in those days, so radio was the number-one source of entertainment. These were horror and mystery stories told by Valentine Dyall, who had a wonderfully deep, resonant voice. The problem was that the stories would frighten the women and my mother had to walk them all back to their houses. Brave Mam at less than 5ft and playing the Great Protector.

One day, a strange thing happened in 10 Lower Oxford

Street. From somewhere, I didn't know where, someone delivered a baby to our house. He arrived just before Christmas, on 23 December and I remember my dad came home. He must have been given compassionate leave, or 'passionate' leave as they called it in the Navy!

As usual in those days, the baby was delivered at home. The bed was moved downstairs into the front room and the crib was a drawer from a chest of drawers. A member of the family had discreetly removed me until the event had taken place. Sadly for me, that was the only Christmas I remember as a child. Like most four-year-olds, I awoke very early on the day and crept downstairs to see what Father Christmas had brought me. Normally, that would have been all right as the family would have been asleep upstairs but, as Trevor, my new brother, had just been born, they were all snoring together in the front room alongside the very chimney that Santa had come down. Standing in the centre of the room, he had left me a metal machine-gun, on a tripod, with grip handles and triggers. I grabbed the handles and pulled the triggers and the gun made a wonderfully realistic rat-atatatat-atat noise as sparks flew out of the end. I was enthralled, but Dad fell out of bed half-asleep thinking he was under attack, Mam screamed, the baby yelled and I hadn't the sense to let go of the gun. I shot them all dead three times over before Dad grabbed me. Merry Christmas everyone!

The one big thing that I remember about Christmases then is that it was the only time of the year that we ate chicken. This made Christmas dinner into something very special and I feel a bit sorry for everyone today because marketing men have now given us chicken all year round so there is nothing really all that different about Christmas meals. Nowadays, Debbie and I have whisky porridge for Christmas morning breakfast and it is the only time of the year that we have it. It starts the day wonderfully and I guess, if you had enough of it, you wouldn't worry about the rest of the day.

Dad returned to the sea battle a few days later and was posted to India. I missed him the moment he walked out the door. Perhaps it was this sense of melancholy churning away inside me that made me quiet and shy. I was still involved in the street games but mostly I would stay in and read comics, magazines and books. I loved reading.

My first school was Princess Street Junior School and it amazed me. The primary room had a set of tall French windows that opened on to a lawned garden. I had never seen a garden and I honestly don't believe that I saw a tree until I was five – scrubby bushes, but not trees. The terraced houses in our part of the town just did not have the space for such large vegetation to grow. Mrs Strickland was my teacher, a warm, loving, but strict woman whom we all grew to like very much. I loved reading and I put it down to her encouragement that gave me a window through which to escape into all sorts of fantasy worlds.

One winter it snowed and kept on snowing. To us, it was wonderful. I rushed out of school into falling snow and immediately began to roll a snowball, patting it all the time to make it compact and firm. The ball got bigger and bigger and more kids joined in rolling it about. That was OK, it was still *my* ball. Eventually it grew so big none of us could roll it so a runner was sent to get more help. My Uncle Eddie came and so did more men and they rolled it and rolled it until it was directly outside our house. It was not an exaggeration to say that it blocked the street. Off we went and rolled a smaller (but still very large) one, and somehow the men hauled it on top of the other using ladders. The following day, Lower Oxford Street was in the newspapers with photographs of the Giant Snowman. That must have been my first unconscious attempt at publicity.

Early school memories are few. I can remember finding a

thousand ways to try to get out of drinking the free milk, which was always left standing in the warm sun and would go off before it was served to us. I would pretend to go home for lunch, as school dinners came nowhere near my mother's cooking. I used to use the dinner money to buy a small crusty loaf from Sands bakery and save the remainder as pocket money. Maybe this interrupted any social activity I might have had in the playground, as I became quite a loner.

Being a lonesome boy, I cannot recall having any real friends, and the only ones I enjoyed playing with were Catholics. My street and the one next to it were like a little Northern Ireland. For some reason, birds of a feather really do flock together and our street was mostly Protestants and the next one mostly Catholics.

It always amused me that on Friday night, pay night, they would all get drunk out of their brains, knock seven bells out of each other and on Monday morning all go to work together without a second thought. Many years later I noticed the same thing in Belfast when I started to appear in the clubs there. They would all have this great fight on the Friday and be back at work without a murmur on Monday. One day a newspaper reporter got hold of this story, blew it up out of all proportion and three months later when I went back they had guns on the roofs. I blame the media for a lot; it has not been used for our good and it should be. It should lead us towards a better life, not stir up trouble.

When I was seven years old, Dad eventually came back from the war. I must have changed a lot in the two years he'd been gone, but he had changed, too. He now had a full nautical beard and I didn't recognise him. Now that I am an adult I can imagine how he felt when, not having seen his wife for years, he was not allowed to get into bed with her because his young son kept hitting him and telling him to get out of his mother's bed.

Huge street parties were quickly organised to celebrate the

homecoming, with long tables stretching down the middle of our street. Balloons tied to chairs bobbed about and the multi-coloured bunting fluttered in the breeze. Jelly was the mainstay of the menu and was probably the only thing there was plenty of at the time. I wondered how those who had lost loved-ones in the war coped with this celebration.

Dad quickly went back to being a cinema projectionist at the Hippodrome in South Bank. This had been erected in 1910 as a temporary building but it lasted until the 1960s. Its exterior consisted of corrugated metal sheets with flat metal panels on the façade. As a young boy, I was never allowed to visit my dad at work because of our strict bedtime regime. Dad would already have left for work when we were washed and dressed in our pyjamas by 6.45pm ready for *Dick Barton, Special Agent* on the radio as we ate our supper. We were ushered into bed as soon as the closing music played at exactly 7.00pm. 'Early to bed, early to rise, makes a man healthy, wealthy and wise.' Did your mother come out with stuff like that? Stuff like 'You'll stay like that' if you pulled a face; 'You'll laugh on the other side of your face when I'm finished with you'; 'don't do as I do, do as I say ...' Later in life, you find yourself saying all these things to your own children.

The fact that central heating was not yet available meant that we would automatically rise early in the cold and scratch our names on the frost which had collected on the inside of our windows before brushing our teeth in the freezing tap water. I was always loosing my front teeth. As a small child I fell down some stone stairs in a cinema, teeth first. For most of my early years I had a huge gap in my smile. It seemed like I went to the dentist every other week and that meant that from the age of ten I held no fear of dentists. I would not have any anaesthetic to dull the pain and hated the thought of being knocked out cold with gas. I just gripped the side of the chair as the drill bored deeper. Eventually, my teeth grew back again.

When I was starting to display my new teeth in the playground one morning, 'Happy' Bates jumped off an old wartime shelter and leapt on to my shoulders. As my head hit the concrete, I could see pieces of tooth flying off in all directions from under my nose. My mother was devastated that my new teeth were lost once more and the dentist cried.

It was decided that the dentist should 'carve' what remained of my front teeth until they looked like tiny fangs, to wait until my teenage years before they could be successfully capped. I was so proud that my new jaws shone like the toothpaste advert. I must have been busier exercising my new smile rather than looking where I was going, because a few days later I jumped over a wall. I made it all the way over, except for my feet. They gave me a great pivot point as I swung down on to the pavement again and smashed the whole top row. Fang the Wonder Boy had done it again. Sorry, Mam!

Over the road from us lived Mrs Grant. Now she was very old, or so we thought. She was also very strange and spooky – a spiritualist. At first I was frightened of her, but she turned out to be a nice old lady. I told her I didn't believe in ghosts and she said that when she died she was going to come back and pull my ears. Years later, when she did die, I used to sit quietly at night and will her to pull my ears, which was a very risky thing to do because they were already rather big. She never did, of course.

Trevor and I shared the same bedroom and spent all night singing songs. Of course, we got to see more movies than most kids because we didn't have to pay. Even though we had our differences, we would stick together in an emergency. If, in the middle of a row, anybody stepped in between us, it would be the intruder who would suffer. Because we were brought up in such a loving, disciplined relationship, we enjoyed the stability and safety of each other's company. No one in our house ever touched alcohol except on very special occasions and it was extremely unusual for our parents to row.

Leisure times were always arranged according to what was left in the budget, but as Dad worked for a regular wage and Mam kept the family accounts brilliantly in little red exercise books, we could afford a few enjoyable trips into the country. We grew up having wonderful holidays going camping or on the Norfolk Broads, renting boats and sometimes even a converted windmill. It nestled on a bend in the river miles from anywhere and only accessible by boat or on foot through the cornfields. It was so secluded that Trevor, Dad and I would be stark naked on the front lawn, playing shuttlecock, of all things, which is particularly hazardous if you are male!

Every time a boat came round the bend we would all run like hell, only to appear moments later when the danger had passed. The other problem was the massive dragonflies. Those blue monsters must have had a breeding ground close by for they would suddenly appear from nowhere and start to dive-bomb us. We would jump from side to side to avoid being bitten, with male parts dangling like worms to a fish.

The family name for the male organ was 'cuckoo'. I never found out why, but we all had 'cuckoos'. Apparently, I had already disgraced myself at a church tea party by proudly announcing that my father had 'feathers' round his 'cuckoo'.

It was my dad's 'cuckoo' that was in jeopardy now as three or four dragonflies took a fancy to him and started to plunge and swoop at his genitalia. Trevor and I were in hysterics rolling around the floor as my dad swerved to avoid contact and disappeared into the windmill shrieking. He was a very funny man, my dad.

Visual comedy was what he particularly enjoyed and he could easily have been a performer. A regular visitor to our house was Mrs Gillings, my Granny Lloyd's friend. One scene in a Laurel and Hardy film constantly fascinated her – Stan Laurel produces a flame from the end of his thumb. Later, this was to be made even more famous by British Gas, but at the time this was an amazing miracle. Having discussed this phenomenon once more, Dad offered to show Mrs Gillings how the effect was really done, before disappearing into the yard. I don't think he had any great insight into the world of special effects; he just seemed to have the sort of brain that could work things out in a logical fashion.

Arriving back into our kitchen with a bottle of methylated spirits in his hand he carefully unscrewed it and put his thumb over the opening. With a running commentary, he explained the whole process in great detail as he tipped the bottle up to ensure a good soaking of meths on his thumb. Grabbing a match, he proudly announced, '… they stop the film and start it again after you simply set light to it like this!' With those words, the whole of his arm shot up in flames. He had soaked his thumb so that the meths had run down to his elbow. Mrs Gillings shrieked in alarm as Dad ran around the room on fire. At first I was so shocked I didn't know what to do, but the laughter in Dad's eye told me everything was under control.

What I hadn't realised was that he was in no pain as the meths burned itself off and didn't affect his skin. My father was now playing the scene for all it was worth. Once in on the 'gag', I was in hysterics as the more Mrs Gillings screamed the faster he jumped about the room thrusting his arm between his legs one minute and swinging his burning hand around like an Olympic torch the next. I'm certain Laurel and Hardy would have stolen the idea for their next film had they witnessed it. Do not try this, there is a knack to keeping it moving.

The laughter in our family increased the close-knit nature of our existence and created a sense of equality and respect between the four of us, which was special. 'Fall-outs' were few.

It also meant that bad times were shared as much as the good, but it still brings tears to my eyes when I remember one of the saddest times of all.

My brother and I were thrilled when it was announced that we were to have a new arrival in the family. Thinking at first that maybe Father Christmas was coming to stay, I soon discovered that Mam was to have a baby. Her third child, like the previous two, was to be born at home, in the front room and all the preparations were made.

It seemed like ages before this new arrival appeared, but one day when Trevor and I came home from school there was a new, pink little squeaky thing on show for all to see. Mam looked exhausted yet proud and I tried to imagine being able to play with our new family member.

As my thoughts drifted back to reality, I detected something different about the house that day. My little boy's senses picked up an atmosphere of foreboding, of something being not quite right. Apparently, my new brother was known as a 'blue baby'. He had been born with some sort of constriction around his heart that couldn't be rectified in those days and his life was threatened.

After carrying this little fellow for nine months, the joy of birth had been snatched away and replaced by a deep sense of sadness. Mam and Dad put a brave face on it all, but the perception of impending loss was too great to contain and the tears could not be hidden.

The state of sadness in our house subsided over the following weeks as baby Keith seemed to be doing all right. He had some breathing difficulties but our hopes revived as each day the tot became more energetic showing obvious signs of improvement. Mam was soon up and about and six weeks later we began to wonder what all the fuss had been about. We got used to having him in the house and playing with him and I thought his incredibly miniaturised hands and legs were wonderful. Life became normal.

When baby Daniels reached six weeks, we were sitting at the kitchen table over dinner, when a sudden shriek from my mam made my hair stand on end. She had discovered the smallest of our clan lying in his cot quite peacefully, but not breathing. Dad went rushing in to the front room to find her holding the lifeless bundle. He immediately placed the little one on the table, performing heart massage and mouth-to-mouth resuscitation on the tiny lips. Trevor and I stood with eyes wide in wonderment. We had no understanding of what was going on, only that it was serious.

Mam looked on helplessly as the repeated attempts to revive her baby succeeded, only to fail moments later as the little one's breathing stopped again and again. There was obviously some type of restriction around the heart. After further struggling, there was no movement, no breath, no life. Eventually, it was Granny Lloyd who stopped Dad continuing the life saving.

'Let him go, he's not supposed to be here.'

We were ushered out of the room and I remember hearing Mam and Dad break down. An atmosphere of pain and agony dropped like a cloud and we were all still in tears.

Consequently, I lost a brother who had only just arrived in the world before he was taken again. It was a real shock to us all, but the grief pulled us even closer as a family. Very shortly after our baby's death, we heard that the medical world had discovered the operation to cure his condition, but it was too late. I don't think Mam ever got over that.

CHAPTER 2

SIX OF THE BEST

*T*he successful Italian Torino Sportsters went down as their plane crashed on Mount Superga in May 1949 and World Champion Joe Louis retired from boxing. In the autumn of that year, the USSR tested its new atomic bomb and the first disposable nappies went on sale in the UK. The world was transforming rapidly.

Life in Lower Oxford Street continued. The housewives' custom of sitting concealed behind the net curtains, watching the comings and goings in the front window continued, and as you walked down our street you could just see a faint outline as they watched the world go by. Everybody knew what everybody else was up to. I think that this is why the first really major television soap opera, Coronation Street, became popular. The wives no longer had to look through the net curtains and, indeed, could at last see *inside* other people's houses. Having never been a voyeur of other people's lives, I still find 'soaps' quite boring. I like films and plays that have an ending.

Granny Lloyd's Mission leaders came round for tea quite regularly. Granny's Mission was still in full swing and her

Sunday school grew by the week. Mam and Dad, enjoying the famous northern gift of hospitality and perhaps trying to think of some recompense, liked to invite folk back after the morning service. I was to be on my best behaviour, of course, and was only to speak when spoken to. We had had a lot of respect for elders drummed into us in those days, something which is sadly missing today.

Sitting around the table one Sunday, I managed to disgrace myself when one of the leaders asked how I was getting on at school. I innocently replied that I was doing well and hated only one teacher, Mrs Twates. 'We call her Twatty Twates,' I added.

No sooner were the words out of my mouth, than the whole room fell silent. 'Twat' was apparently a swear word that referred to a woman's private parts and I had just dropped the biggest Sunday clanger possible. I got a clip round the earhole from Dad and left the room very red-faced without being told what was wrong. I guess it was difficult to explain.

I would easily get slapped on the backside if I spoke out of turn and certainly if I used bad language. I still don't like swear words, probably because I was brought up to dislike them and was taught that they were an unnecessary part of the English language. I suppose if you are surrounded by swearing you learn to accept it. I do know some very funny gags that use four-letter words to great effect but I wouldn't use them in public because someone might be offended, so what's the point? I don't think swearing for the sake of it is funny, and hearing four-letter words used in gags just for effect makes me cringe and I certainly don't consider it clever. I think it is childish. The question is always: 'Is this a funny gag? Does it need adjectives and adverbs that begin with "f" and are unrelated to the humour?' In all the years of doing shows, I have never had a complaint that I have not used bad language.

When we call swearing the use of 'Anglo-Saxon words', we

are absolutely right. Historically speaking, the invading Romans banned us from speaking our native language. When the men met privately they didn't want to say 'penis', 'vagina' and 'intercourse', they wanted their original language back, so words that were totally normal in those days became a secret language which eventually became bad language. It's on the way back now to being just part of our everyday life and in a hundred years' time people will probably wonder what all the fuss was about. Bad language is a strange phenomenon, because it is different everywhere you go in the world. One word in one country is not as offensive in another, but I still don't like it.

The cinema meant a lot to me, because it was where my dad worked. I was allowed into the pictures at a very early age, though only at weekends, but upon reaching nine years old I became a paid assistant projectionist. Mam and Dad probably paid me, not the cinema, but who cared? Our cinema, note that it was now our cinema, had a gently rising slope from the front to the middle stalls and then rose sharply backwards up towards the wall from which the mysterious flickering lights issued, that filled our imaginations. I was always Douglas Fairbanks Jnr or Errol Flynn or rode away from the Hippodrome on my horse with that funny sideways run that we all did, imaginary reins in our left hand as our right hands slapped our right buttocks as if slapping the horse to go faster. Everyone went to the cinema, sixpence to sit in the front on the bum-numbing wooden benches and, if you could afford it, ten pence to sit at the back on the plush seats. Saturday mornings were set aside for kids' films and cartoons.

I would love to watch Dad at work because he was such a craftsman. Receiving the film from the previous town's projectionist he read the notes giving instructions on which parts of the film could be removed without affecting the plot. This meant that he could alter the length of the feature to fit in with his individual time-scale of programming which always included a 'B' movie as well as the Pathe News and trailers. Advertising would be performed with hand-drawn glass plates that had been held over a candle and blackened. Carefully using the flattened heads of six-inch nails, Dad would etch his message on to the soot, before sandwiching it delicately against another piece of glass. This work of art was then projected and manually 'scrolled' across the screen at the appropriate moment.

Dad's assistant projectionist, 'Plonkey', was not the most intelligent man and would consistently get his scratched messages muddled – DON'T FAIL TO MISS THIS NEXT MOVIE! was not the most literate way of inviting the audience back for more. This nice, quiet young man happened to have one of the world's largest collections of Charlie Kunz records which he used to play as people came in, so everyone forgave him.

The film itself was highly flammable and the whole of the projection room, including the floor, was made of metal. This enabled Dad to place a sixpenny bit at the end of each reel, so he got an audible warning when the spool was nearing its end and he'd be ready to change over to the other projector. That's how the system worked. A movie was broken down into several reels and you had to watch very carefully when each reel neared its end so you could switch the next machine on at the right time so that, as scenes changed, the story would continue seamlessly.

As I peered out of the little window that allowed me to see into the auditorium and view the screen, I stood with my hands twisted in a very strange position. My left arm rested on a small lever while my right hand hovered over the start button on the waiting projector. Both projectors would literally 'burn' from two carbon rods held half an inch away from each other through which high-voltage electricity was fed. The spark, or arc, that jumped across the rods was incredibly bright and would have been enough to burn your eyes out had you foolishly looked directly into the lens. This same technique was adapted for use in the theatre as a 'follow-spot' and as some of the carbon rods were made of a substance containing lime, it was from here that the theatrical saying 'being in the limelight' originated.

As soon as I saw the black blob, which appeared in the top right hand of the screen, I pressed the start button on the idle projector. The film started to run through from the numbered leader, which I had set at the required place.

As soon as the second spot appeared, I switched the lever across, opening the light gate on the new projector as it closed the light gate on the other one. At the same time, you had to switch the sound across. The signal would only appear for 1/24 of a second, so if you blinked, you missed it.

When a film was properly made, the second dot would appear at a scene change on a camera cut. Light and sound would operate together in perfect synchronisation and the audience would be unaware that the film had been switched. It was a skill of which Dad was rightly proud and at which he expected me to succeed.

My first job was to take the film out of its metal storage box and place one reel at a time on the hand-geared rewinding device, transferring hundreds of feet of brittle, highly flammable film on to the correct spare reel ready for showing. As each film was delivered on at least six reels, this was a lengthy task but the faster you hand-spun the device, the quicker it would be rewound. Keeping a consistent speed was essential to eliminate uneven winding, which would cause problems during projection. I always aspired to do it like my father who was somehow able to get the film up to an incredible speed, take his hand off to scratch his face, catch the handle still furiously spinning and not drop one inch of film.

As the acetate sped from one reel to another, I was shown

how to feel the edges of the film as it ran in order to identify instantly any flaws. My father was insistent that any old joins should be re-spliced, as he couldn't bear the thought of the film ever snapping. We were proud that we never had a broken film in our cinema.

The nightmare scenario was that one reel would accelerate ahead of the other and the film would then be allowed to escape like a tangled snake all over the floor. Not only would it break in several places, but would probably be seriously scratched. I think it was poor old 'Plonkey' who had spun the film as fast as he could one day only to discover that the clip holding the spools on the spindles had been left open. Inevitably, the spool shot off the mechanism but fell straight out of the window, trailing what seemed to be a hundred miles of film. As my father and I hung out of the window frantically reeling in the film by hand we noticed 'Plonkey' chasing the escaped spool as it disappeared down the street. Amazingly, we recovered the movie without a single scratch, and passers-by probably saw it as quite a comical advertising stunt as the cinema was pretty full that night!

The British Board of Film Censors was pretty active by this time in the early Fifties and although all the films in the cinema were certified, I saw them all. If my father censored me watching anything at the time, I wasn't aware of it. Of course, when there was a film of dubious content it didn't give a lot away as pornography was unacceptable in the public arena. You would be lucky to see a bare bum.

On the other hand, horror movies were pretty rife, ever since the release of the first Dracula film *Nosferatu* in 1922, with its spine-chilling scenes that quickly terrified audiences. *Frankenstein* and *Godzilla* never frightened me, because from where I was watching, Boris Karloff was simply a picture on a piece of celluloid. It was the same for violent movies that would simply make me smile when the audience sat in shock. Maybe it was the effect of this that enabled me to look at life from a different angle. It took many years for a film to affect me and in some ways took away the fun of the movies. I was aware that it was all illusion.

It wasn't until *Schindler's List* was released in 1993 that I reacted emotionally to the celluloid offering. I'm not Jewish, but in the cold and hard reality of that film, the Holocaust suddenly came home to me and I left the cinema in tears.

When the religious film *The Miracle of Fatima* arrived at Dad's Hippodrome, a note from the previous projectionist inserted in the film warned, 'You won't do any business with this load of rubbish!' I could see the twinkle of a challenge brewing in my father's eye as he read the note again. Sending a note to all the local Roman Catholic churches, he invited all the local priests to a free Friday afternoon screening. The projectionist was right, it was a dreadful film, but with the resulting advertising from all the Sunday morning pulpits, persuading parishioners to attend, we had full houses all week.

Apparently, as a very young man, one of the first 'Christian' films Dad screened was a silent version of the life of Christ. The pianist had difficulty in deciding what piece to play during the crucifixion scene and asked Hughie's advice. Father suggested a slowed-down version of an old Scottish song he knew and the accompanist agreed it suited the mood. Little did the hapless musician know the true derivation of the piece, for on the opening night he misjudged the speed and as the actor playing Christ had his side pierced by a sword, discovered himself playing 'Stop Your Tickling, Jock'. Both Father and the pianist were sacked on the spot!

The arrival of the 'talkies' in October 1927, with Al Jolson in *The Jazz Singer*, encouraged the masses to make cinema-going a regular weekly activity. Forty-seven picture houses sprang up in Leeds alone, as the cinema boomed and movies produced the first heart-throbs and created new fashions to follow with stars like Greta Garbo and Rudolph Valentino.

Laurence Olivier was a great actor, but I didn't like him in films and once we had to remove him from our screen in mid-film. After only a few minutes of *The Highwayman,* the audience was booing loudly. By this time, Dad's growing audience was more important to him than the film and he quickly replaced it with a cowboy feature that was in reserve for the following night. It earned him a round of applause.

Hellzapoppin' was originally a 'mad' stage show that far exceeded any alternative comedy we experience today. This was one of the first films that I was entrusted to oversee on my own. Having gleefully started the first reel, I simply waited for the 'clang' of the sixpence signalling the need to switch to the next reel at exactly the right time. I had been well trained by my father and knew exactly how to change reels seamlessly.

As the final black blob appeared, I switched cameras and watched in dismay as the film jumped from a tender love scene to cowboys and Indians chasing each other across the prairie. Panicking, my mind flashed 'my father will kill me!' and I ran into the rewind room to check the other reels, expecting to find that they had been placed in the wrong order. As I rummaged through the long metal box, I was amazed to find that all the films were correctly stacked. Dashing back into the projection room, I peered out into the darkness and watched in disbelief as the film jumped back from the cowboys to the lovers once more. As the last Indian rode away, behind him appeared the couple still making love. I had been deceived by celluloid.

The same film had all sorts of 'in-gags' such as signs appearing that asked people to go to the foyer and, eventually, one of the actors on screen getting annoyed at the interruptions and asking the audience himself before going back into the movie. To a young projectionist this film was a nightmare.

SIX OF THE BEST

One night, just after World War II, a woman in the audience screamed out as she thought she recognised her missing, presumed dead, husband right in front of her, coming down the gangplank of a ship on the newsreel. Dad stopped the film and after finding out what the problem was, announced that the film would be run again, in order for the woman to identify her man. The clip was repeated three times and sure enough the woman pointed him out. From this piece of film, they were able to trace her husband to a hospital where he was suffering from serious amnesia and they were both joyfully reunited. It was a wonderful story that made me realise how useful the media could be when used properly.

By now I was doing OK for pocket money. Not only was I showing the films but I was also delivering groceries by bike for Rogers Fruit and Vegetable Shop on Nelson Street. I could balance five or six boxes on the front and back carriers if I rode leaning to the side so that I could see around them. It also increased my productivity, as I didn't have to keep going back to the shop to re-load quite so often.

When I was about ten years old, we moved to a 'prefab' in Middlesbrough Road East, number 39. Why do we remember such trivialities as a house number we will never use again? Prefabs were the Government's answer to the need for quick housing and to us it was wonderful. It had such an impact on our lives that my mother still says she would live in one again. The integrated design was very clever. Even the walls separating the bedrooms were, in reality, wardrobes, some of which opened into one room and some into the other. The kitchen, as another example, had a plate and pan rack set into the wall over the cooking area that jutted out over the bath in the normally wasted space in the bathroom. Although intended only as temporary homes, many of these cleverly designed properties were still standing 50 years later. As the Government managed the massive rehousing programme, families were shuffled from one town to another. Fortunately for us, we were not moved very far and soon found ourselves in a home that was clearly superior to our previous residence in Lower Oxford Street.

Interestingly, it was another form of 'soap' that became an essential ingredient in our new house. We now lived directly opposite the steelworks, literally a street's width away. As I meandered home from school each day, I would check out the amount of soot collected on each set of windowsills as I passed. South Bank was maintaining its reputation for pollution and a gigantic slag tip overshadowed our house.

A few years earlier, complete with bottles of water and sandwiches, some small friends and I had walked for miles and then climbed a mountain to play on the large flat grass field on the top. Now I was older I realised we had walked half a mile and climbed the sloping sides of a slag tip. To appreciate just how big it was, bear in mind that it took years, literally years, to dismantle and eventually to be used as a sort of gravel base in road making.

We lived now, as I said, on Middlesbrough Road, which was the main road of the town, running through the rapidly growing conurbation from Stockton-on-Tees, through Middlesbrough, Cargo Fleet, South Bank and Grangetown before becoming the trunk road to Redcar.

A lively town of about 150,000 people, Middlesbrough was proud of its industrial heritage. In 1830, the tiny hamlet of less than 30 inhabitants changed dramatically when the world's first railway was opened in 1825. It was used for transporting coal from the South Durham pits to Stockton, the port on the River Tees, which was then shipped to London. When the larger coal ships arrived, the Tees was not navigable so far inland and so in 1830 a group of Stockton businessmen decided to build another port around the village of Middlesbrough. As a result, the area rapidly developed and prospered as shipyards, coal works and iron foundries sprang up, to be joined later by engineering works, chemical plants and oil refineries.

It was a pretty busy place to be and consumed more beer than any other part of the country because of the heat from the steelworks. The labourers in the smelting plants had to have some way of putting the liquid back in their bodies after sweating buckets in temperatures of over 100°F all day long.

The unique Transporter Bridge spans the Tees and passengers and vehicles are carried across the river on a large platform suspended from an overhead gantry mechanism. It's probably the only one in the world. The Bottle of Notes sculpture outside the town hall commemorates the area's most famous inhabitant, the explorer Captain James Cook. A short distance away from the town, you can cross the rugged beauty of the Yorkshire Moors where there are medieval abbeys, a white horse carved into the hillside and several picturesque villages nestling in the dales.

We had our own explorer visit us at home one day, when we all jumped in surprise as a terrific 'thump' hit our front door, followed by frantic banging on the knocker. Dad went to the front door and found a man trying with great difficulty to speak English. He turned out to be a large Dutchman and he was so animated that Dad thought there must have been some sort of accident. After calming him down, Dad discerned that his emotional state was not due to fright, but to excitement. Slowly and in faltering English, the Dutchman explained that he had been trying to grow black tulips for many years without success. Driving down our road, he had noticed with great surprise that we had some in our small front oblong of a garden. That's how well we were doing now in South Bank – we had a garden. Dad quickly destroyed the poor man's hopes of a new discovery by pulling one out of the ground and running it under the tap. The black soot washed off the flower and it was yellow. Now that's pollution!

If we ever mistakenly left the small quarter-window open for any more than ten minutes, the top of our net curtains would be sporting a large rectangle of black grime. The air was that quick to contaminate everything around it, including us. Our clothes had to be washed constantly, not to mention our skins, but at least we had a proper bathroom now.

Besides a real bath, our new home had all manner of new aids to living, including a fridge. When our fridge eventually broke down one day, my dad, as resourceful as ever, dug a hole at the bottom of the garden. Into this he lowered a biscuit tin containing our milk, finally covering the opening with a paving slab. It's a fact that even in the height of summer, our milk was always icy cold.

Not that I liked milk, in fact I hated it. I am still unable to see any gastronomical pleasure to be gained from milk churned into a block and passed off as cheese. Why does anyone enjoy eating solid sour milk? The only curdling I experienced was that of my stomach rejecting the stuff. You probably like it but I can't stand cauliflower cheese.

Come to think of it, being ten and eleven was a major time of my life. I changed house, changed school and found magic. Way to go, Paul, although I was still Ted then.

I always had an affinity with words and as my education led me to the end of my junior years, I took an exam to see how big my brains were. To everyone's surprise and joy I was the only boy in my year to qualify for Sir William Turner's Grammar School in Coatham, a seaside suburb of Redcar on the North Yorkshire coast. Not only this, but I was also one of the first boys to enter this prestigious school on a scholarship as previously all the other parents had emptied their pockets to provide this privilege for their sons. I was confused, and still am, when these institutions are referred to as 'public' schools which means they are private!

Nevertheless, with Grammar schools regarded as the best form of secondary education, and they are, the ability to declare that I went to Coatham became something of a status symbol for myself and the other boys and I wore the uniform with some pride, but not in South Bank where they thought we were 'pansies'. Although compulsory, I enjoyed dressing up in my grey shorts, replaced by long grey flannels in the winter or when reaching your second year. A smart black blazer complemented a black and red striped tie and, being in Inghams house, one of four school groupings, our uniform was finished off with four red pennants surrounding the little silver lion on the front of my cap, all of which Mam had patiently, and very proudly, sewn on.

Memory tells me that I went off to Mrs Gillings in Old Byland, near Helmsley, just before I started my new school and for some reason I was there without the rest of the family. I wonder if someone was ill, or perhaps I was getting over some illness. All I know is that I found myself in a completely strange environment of fields and cows and hens and eggs in haystacks that had to be collected. Mrs Gillings herself kept house for someone rich in a beautiful converted mill on Kaydale Beck. The old mill wheel had been sawn in half and carved by the famous 'mouse man', Thomson, into two semicircular fireside seats. He carved a mouse on everything he did and on these seats the mice were warming their paws by the fire. Lovely.

Replacing the old mill wheel was a metal one that spun in the water and generated electricity in this dwelling far removed from any kind of electrical services. Mrs Gillings and I would walk along the top of the hill from her little stone cottage and follow the long pathway down to the mill. Once, when I was on a world tour and flying over Japan, I saw that the mill was for sale in a magazine I was reading and was surprised at the power of the emotion the picture generated in me.

One day it rained. It sounds strange to say that, but all I can remember of Old Byland is glorious sunshine and sitting on grass. On this day, however, it was not just pouring, but bucketing down and, looking up into the black skies I accepted the fact that an outside visit would not be possible that day. For a 'townie' kid, there was nothing to do and somehow, my entertainment had to come from within. The obvious answer to my problem was books and with the rain still battering against the windows, I began to explore the house and came across an old bookshelf containing a number of volumes. One title immediately caught my eye and my imagination. In Victorian times, families entertained each other instead of letting television do it for them. This book was all about puppets and plays, mime and magic.

The old leather-bound book was swiftly removed from its position and, after a quick thumbing, was deemed good enough to read. Settling down on to the huge sofa in Mrs Gillings' front room was like taking my seat on a magic carpet of discovery. As I devoured each page, my eyes grew wider at the seemingly unattainable feats this book was suggesting were possible: making one playing card disappear from the pack, only to appear elsewhere in the room; being able to predict which card the spectator would choose; or with the use of a set of numbers, having the ability to guess correctly the age of a member of the audience; all were skills now within my reach. That, in fact, was my first trick – the Age Cards. I copied it out number by number because, when I had tried it on myself, it worked first time. I still, from time to time, carry a set of these cards and the trick is still a good one.

As it was, I didn't actually have an audience. It was Mrs Gillings herself and then some of the locals in the village. From the moment I set eyes on this book, I was captivated and entranced. There is no other way to describe my feelings at that time other than to say I was totally hooked. A rhythm within my life had 'kicked in'. I had seen my first magician at one of the Sunday school Christmas parties, but the strange thing is, I can't remember anything about him. It obviously didn't have much of an effect on me, maybe because I never imagined such skill to be within my grasp.

After that, I was grateful for any rain as my holiday crept slowly by, giving me the excuse to indulge in my readings and rehearsals from my manual of magic. This new art was an attractive antidote to my shyness and the insecure part of me had found a 'bridge' that would enable me to communicate with people in a way that I would not have found possible by any other means. When I got back to South Bank, I was in the public library all the time and the librarians were wonderful to me as they embarked on wide searches for magic books for me to borrow. I really must get around to taking them back.

It soon occurred to me that my audience did not want to know the secret. I instinctively knew that those to whom I revealed my technique would be far from delighted and would even be disappointed. They were much happier allowing themselves to be deceived and walking away with the puzzle still active in their minds. People need to have some magic in the world. Seeing the look of absolute wonder in the eyes of a local villager after witnessing one of my tricks filled my little boy's heart with such gladness and from that moment on, all I ever wanted to become was a magician. I was just 11 and I had to go to my new school.

That meant a long journey each day on the bus, but it was worth it. Mam and Dad hoped that my attendance there would open the doors to a proper profession as an architect, solicitor or even the medical world, and I tried not to disappoint them.

Small, quiet and shy, I still tended to hide behind books and this opened the way for plenty of ribbing on being a very short 'bookworm'. Despite trying to explain the positive side of being short, 'When it rains, we are the last to get wet,' tall boys continued to point out what they saw as my inadequacy. Kids are cruel.

Accepting bullying as a natural part of school life, I avoided it as best I could, but some days were particularly painful. It was probably my church background that was responsible in disarming my ability to fight back against this discrimination. I took the Biblical principle of 'turning the other cheek' literally one day when a group of boys surrounded me and one of them hit me across my face. I honestly believed that I should sit there and do nothing, even when one by one they proceeded to deliver their best swipes and I was left battered and bruised.

I refuse to believe that the 'do-gooders' will ever eradicate this problem as, in my view, it's all part of growing up and an essential ingredient in the young animal's training for life. However, I don't underestimate the value of being able to talk about the subject openly at school, as I believe happens in many places today.

Coatham had ancient traditions. One of these was that at the end of the first sports afternoon, new boys were thrown into the shallow pond at the bottom of our cricket field. I hated cricket. I could see no excitement in it and would stand there wondering why I was there watching those guys run up and down a strip of grass.

'Oh goodie, an hour has passed so it must be my turn to touch the ball!' I think cricket is the slowest, most boring game on the planet. Even as a spectator, I could never understand its attraction, as one is always too far away to see the nuances and subtleties of the match anyway.

SIX OF THE BEST

My main concern was my hands. I was starting to play around with a hobby that was to have the most significant effect on my life. I was worried about having the tools of the trade, my hands, damaged by a rock-hard cricket ball. I wasn't viewed as a 'pansy', though, because I loved rugby. I played in a position at the time called wing-three-quarter because I was one of the fastest sprinters in the school. Not that I was particularly fit, but I was scared of the other guys catching me and tearing me to shreds! I never had any bones broken.

So, having finished playing the most boring game in the world and being unaware of the school's strange rituals, I stood aghast as several of my peers were grabbed by hand and foot and hauled into the mud. I tried to make a run for it, deciding that there was no way I was going to let them throw me in, particularly after my parents had skimped and saved so hard to buy the uniform. Dressed in gleaming white flannelette trousers, jumper and shirt, I was not exactly camouflaged for the great escape and was soon spotted by two boys who put me in a head and arm lock. As I fought back, they called for their mates to help and I was eventually dragged away by half-a-dozen boys while I screamed and struggled every inch of the way. Once out of the mire and looking like a wet mud wrestler, I knew I would be in even deeper trouble when Mam saw the state I was in.

At school, bullying was sometimes dished out under the respectable guise of punishment as Prefects and Monitors could exercise their right to 'tan' other boys using a gym-shoe. This piece of innocent-looking rubber and cloth could cause immense pain in the wrong hands and was often wielded in the name of 'retribution' rather than 'education'. Offences such as talking in the lines; having your hands in your pockets; not wearing your cap or uniform properly; and eating sweets in public were all considered un-gentlemanly things to do and being caught would result in 'six of the best'. Prefects had made their journey up through the ranks of the earlier years and it was their job to help maintain the discipline of the school.

In our present-day, free-thinking society, 'discipline' seems to be a forgotten word and 'respect' part of a lost language. Do-gooders and freethinkers have changed the world but they have only seen one side of the coin. If you haven't experienced both discipline and lack of discipline how can you possibly know? I have had both and I know which one I prefer. Discipline. It's certainly helped me to control myself. We all need some sort of moral framework to keep us in check.

Being thrashed by a gym-shoe was nothing compared to the instrument of torture that the Masters wielded. Mostly, the Masters ruled by respect, not by capital punishment. It was an inbuilt reverence for their wisdom that kept me away from the cane. They had earned the right, through the education system, to wear their own particular uniform. Those black mortar-boarded and cloaked figures demanded respect for an insight and knowledge that we didn't have and offered a visual reminder that they were more intelligent than us.

The Masters, including the Head, exhibiting their obvious superiority, kept the school to a very high standard of discipline and achieved terrific academic results for the boys under their care. I cannot understand how a teacher today can wear a floppy sweater, frayed jeans and dirty shoes and expect the same respect from the pupils.

Every Master was distinct with his own special character. Pietrowski, Polish by birth, French by education and English by choice, walked with a kind of hunched shoulder. One of the boys took the mickey out of his physical condition as he followed him down the corridor one day. Pietrowski happened to glance behind him and saw the boy copying him. The Master swiftly grabbed the pupil, ramming him against the wall and quietly explaining that as a member of the French resistance he had been shot and buried alive. Having waited hours for the Germans to leave, he had then dug himself out from his own grave. His wounds had festered and had resulted in a deformed shoulder. We all stood in horror as, having finished his gruesome description, he dropped the boy and carried on walking down the corridor.

Our Art Master had been 'hung' at the National Gallery and the legend surrounded him of having painted his daughter in the nude. Our little boys' minds thought that he must have kept his socks on, or where else could he have kept his brushes!

Little Billy Pearson was the most loved of our Masters. It made a great impression on me, that despite the fact that he was so tiny, whenever he came into the room, all the boys immediately stood up. We also shut up. Upon entering the room he would walk over to his high stool, put his feet on the desk and speak slowly. We all thought he was in danger of falling off, but leaning on our wooden desks, we listened to every word he uttered.

'I am William, known popularly amongst you as little Billy.' He then turned in my direction and snapped, 'You! Tell me the square root of 64.'

I soon realised that the maths Master was loved because there was no malice in his abruptness and chose this technique to keep his lessons interesting. And he was deadly accurate with both the chalk and the blackboard cleaner when he spotted you talking in class.

Maths was a difficult lesson to keep lively and the homework was even worse. Once more I fell back on my dad's ability to overcome hurdles. Even though Hughie had left school early in order to work and help support his family, he was able to help me with the most difficult of homework problems. The oddity about him was that he would solve the puzzles by using logic.

Even algebraic equations were answered in this way, without him having to follow the correct mathematical formula.

'Shiny' Williams sat for an entire term building a strange unidentified object, which turned out to be a television set. As he sat there fiddling with the intricate mechanism, he would expound all types of wondrous and outrageous concepts.

'Today I will tell you how to get electricity for free,' announced the Nutty Professor. 'First of all, you must rent a flat in a high-rise building. Buying a generator, you connect it to a battery, which will give you all your lighting for free. Attach a four-bladed paddle wheel to the generator and place this outside your high-rise building, just underneath your lounge window.

'Next, you write away to all the brick companies for samples. When they send you their bricks, the postman will carry them all the way up to your door. As soon as he delivers them you throw them out of the window one by one.'

We sat staring at him in stunned silence.

'Make notes, boy! Make notes, or you will not be able to take advantage of my intelligence,' he suddenly announced glancing up from his mass of wires and knobs.

'The bricks will hit the paddle, which will generate the electricity and recharge the battery. When the postman arrives at the bottom of the building, he will think that another lot of parcels have been delivered for you and he will pick them up and carry them back upstairs when you simply repeat the process.'

This strange, round-faced, mad scientist would give a repeat performance each week. 'Today I will tell you how to get gas for free.'

We all sat in wonderment, notebooks at the ready.

'First of all you have to buy a gas fridge and some plasticine,' he began. 'Now what you do is this: locate your gas meter, probably found in your understairs cupboard. An oddity of these meters is that they all "dimple" down at the bottom of the coin-collecting box. Find the lowest point and drill a very fine, pinpoint hole, in the bottom of this metal box.

'Take your plasticine and, after warming it up, place your shilling coin into the surface, press it down to make the shape of the coin. After carefully removing the shilling from the plasticine, fill the mould you have made with water and place it in the freezer part of your gas fridge. Let it freeze for several hours before easing the ice shilling out of the mould and quickly place it in the coin slot of your gas meter. Once inside, the ice will melt, leaving no trace as to how you got your free gas.'

We all sat with eyes wide open.

'Finally, I will give you some additional advice. Put the shilling mould underneath the hole you drilled in the meter, so that when the ice melts it will drip into the mould and you won't run up your water bill!'

We left the lesson in stunned silence and how many boys actually went home and tried to put his ideas into practice I shall never know.

I think our woodwork Master had the right idea, when he showed us how to turn, carve and create wooden items, which he then used to furnish his own home. As I lathed knobs for his dressers, other boys would be working on another part of the project and it all reminded me of a construction factory. It was a good way to teach, simply because we were all involved in creating something that was going to be put to good use. I hated the thought of spending time making something just for the sake of it, only for your item to be thrown away or sat in a cupboard. Construction lessons were such fun, that I began to consider training as a woodwork teacher. It would certainly be following somewhat in the footsteps of my greatest hero, my dad. But then he was good at everything!

English Literature was my favourite subject and essays were

my favourite homework. I just rattled them off, almost without thinking, and somehow managed to balance them into correctly sized paragraphs. Reading this book you may disagree, but remember, the young are always cleverer. Just ask them.

We got a new headmaster at the school – Mr Barker – who came from the military education system, or so the rumour had it. He gave the appearance of being a big, strong man, although in retrospect I think he was just one of those wide men. Not fat, just wide.

After a few weeks of his lessons and his giving me full marks on every essay, he was giving a lesson on Shakespeare and was discoursing on how Shakespeare rewrote his works and honed them down to make them perfect in metre and tone and balance and so on. To my amazement, I heard my voice saying, 'I don't think so.' The world around me faded away into total silence as Mr Barker, interrupted in full flow, slowly turned to look at the minuscule, newly professed genius on Shakespeare. I did my best to become even more minuscule under his gaze but I didn't manage the disappearing act I longed for.

'And how, Daniels, have you arrived at this observation?'

My mouth went to work again. 'Well, that's more or less what you said I had done in an essay a few weeks ago, and I didn't. I just wrote it that way first time because it felt right. I think that sometimes academics try to discover too many hidden meanings in what people like Shakespeare just felt like saying at the time and just felt it was right to write that way.'

Total silence and then, 'Interesting. You may well be right.'

What a teacher. No put-down in front of the class. He let me think and later I admitted he might be right as well.

My love of English led to early appearances in front of an 'audience'. One of the competitions between the school's houses was for selected members of the house to sight-read from books chosen by the Masters. You were assessed on your ability to understand instantly the words on the page at the exact moment you opened the book. You had to speak clearly and with meaning in such a way that the entire school, sitting out front, would be able to appreciate what you were reading about. Despite being timid, I somehow enjoyed the opportunity to stand in front of the school and communicate the written word. There was even applause at the end, and somehow these few moments gave me a sense of achievement.

Some lads, of course, decided to start smoking, hiding around corners and in the toilets and pretending to be grown up. I tried it. For the life of me I couldn't see any sense in setting fire to money to get a taste of old smoke in your mouth and on your clothes. It didn't seem very grown up to me and, now that science has shown us the odds against you living a full and active life as you get to old age, it seems the silliest of things for young people to do.

Notwithstanding my admiration for the teachers and the system at Coatham, I generally disliked school and yearned to escape into a world that seemed to offer much more fun and usefulness. One of the main problems was that most of the teaching was performed by rote. Mechanical repetition of a subject in no way interested me. If I had been given the reason why I should learn logarithms, trigonometry and geometry, I might have learnt them, but I failed to see what use any of these skills would be in my life. I wish their usefulness had been outlined, as I would have grasped their importance and perhaps would have become something better than I am today.

Equally, I am astonished at the incredible amount of 'man-hours' that are wasted in school teaching children things that are never used again. By all means acquaint them to just above the basic level, but if their chosen occupation requires them to use these 'fringe' skills, then let their employer teach them and in so doing save the nation money. Even back then

I used to think, about many things, 'I'll never use this; why am I learning it?'

It's rubbish when parents suggest that our schooldays are the best years our lives. Life is much fuller and far more interesting in later years.

Even in early teens nothing got under my skin faster than a demand that was morally unfair. When I came across a situation that I felt was unjust, I simply dug my heels in. One such occasion happened on one of the few days when Mam was unwell and I had to join the other boys for lunch in the large boarding house hall attached to the school. The following story is like a mirror of a scene from the film Oliver.

'Red Barns' had long wooden dining tables at which 20 or so pupils sat waiting with a Master at the head of each table. We sat in silence as waitresses arrived with stacks of plates, which we passed down the line from one boy to the next and back up the opposite side. I wondered how long everything would stay hot if this long process was repeated with the arrival of the food. My fears were to be proved even worse when a huge dollop of fatty stew suddenly arrived on my cold plate. My stomach started to retch as I stared down at the globules of fat that were bobbing around in the thin liquid. I knew that if I tried to eat any of it, I would vomit. I hate fat more than I hate cheese sauce.

Trying to work around the mess on my plate, I ate the vegetables and even the occasional piece of meat, but I was acutely aware that the Master's eyes were viewing my struggle. He who shall be obeyed was sat on my immediate right and was the most unpopular teacher in the school. Now, out of the corner of my eye I could clearly see him frowning at my attempts to avoid further embarrassment and hoped his fiery attention would not be awakened.

I continued to navigate my fork around the six-inch cubes

of solid fat which looked up at me from the bottom of my plate when two words were abruptly shot into my ear: 'Eat them.'

Looking up at his harsh face, I was acutely aware for the first time of what happens to me when I'm in danger. I felt icy cold and everything seemed to slow down.

'No, Sir. I am not able to, Sir.'

'Eat it,' came the cold reply.

'No, Sir. If I eat that I will be sick,' I reasoned.

'You will eat everything on your plate!' came the demand, now raising his voice a little.

'No, Sir, I won't eat it.' During the unfolding drama, the table had been cleared in readiness for dessert, but I was left staring at my plate with the lumps of fat floating like white boats on a brown pond.

'Your parents have paid for you to eat it.'

To which I calmly replied, 'therefore I am responsible to my parents and not to you.' The whole table was instantly enveloped in a deathly hush as the Master mentally reviewed his options.

'You will eat it!' came the increasingly agitated response.

'No, Sir, I cannot.'

Just at that moment, a large tureen of rice pudding arrived in front of him, ready for him to serve it down the lines of nervous-looking boys. 'If you do not eat it, you will not have dessert,' he announced.

My response was quick, sharp and justified. 'My parents have paid for me to eat the dessert.' With the words now out of my mouth, I resigned myself to the fact that I was about to die.

'Don't you dare talk to me like that! Eat your dinner this instant! If you don't you will have no rice pudding!' he screamed.

'In that case,' I retorted, moving incredibly slowly, 'neither will anyone else.' With that, I stood up, grabbed hold of the edge of the bowl and tipped it into his lap.

The Master screamed. The rice pudding was hot. So was my

backside when I immediately received six of the best cane strokes he had probably ever delivered in his entire career. It stung severely and made my eyes water, but I didn't care. For a while, I was a hero amongst my mates.

★ ★ ★

I spent most of my time at school minding my own business and getting on with my work, but there was another occasion when I felt I was being treated unfairly. It happened when a tall prefect walked down the morning assembly line and falsely accused me.

'You were talking, Daniels. Six of the best in the break!'

'But, Sir, I wasn't ...' I spluttered.

'Shut up! Six of the best,' he threatened angrily.

Having already experienced 'six of the best' for a 'crime', there was no way that I was going to bend over a chair and allow this big kid to strike me on my bottom for being innocent. I had honestly not talked in the line and felt it quite reasonable not to go to his room at the break. So I didn't. At lunchtime the prefect came looking for me and, by the look on his face, was obviously not a happy bunny.

'Straight after school, you will come to the Prefects' room, Daniels!'

'But, Sir, I wasn't...'

'Be quiet and do as I say, Daniels!'

The same scenario was repeated without giving me an opportunity to speak and, instead of visiting his room after school, I went straight home. Upon arriving back at school the next morning, a very hot, red-faced prefect pulled me out of the line and shouted for me to go straight to his room. I was aware of 100 eyes following me as I walked down the corridor to the sound of my own footsteps. Instead of turning left into his room, I turned right, made a short cut through the cloisters, picked up my satchel from the form room locker and strolled straight out of the gates. I boarded the next bus home and arrived while Mam was in the middle of the washing.

Extremely hesitant to tell Mam at first, she eventually persuaded me to give her the full details and I held back the tears as I made my way through the story.

'Do you mean to tell me that other boys are allowed to smack you?' was her first comment. I had assumed that this was normal and acceptable.

'Yes, Mam.'

Despite being 4ft 10in when her socks are wet, my red-haired matriarch could have an extremely fiery temper. 'What?!' she shouted. With eyes widening, she immediately ran to get her coat with my appeals to calm down completely drowned by angry mutterings. We travelled the six miles back on the bus together, with steam coming out of Mam's ears. Every inch of the way I tried in earnest to dissuade her from taking up the gauntlet, but it was pretty obvious that nothing would stop her now. My pleas fell on deaf ears.

Once through the school gates, she dragged me in her wake as she burst into the school via the door that was out of bounds to me. Storming straight past the astonished male receptionist, she stomped her way down the echoing corridor until arriving outside the headmaster's office, whereupon she did a wonderful impression of Arnold Schwarzenegger (who hadn't been heard of yet) by kicking the door open. The headmaster, who had been quietly studying some papers, stood up as if a bomb had been placed under his backside. Barker had never seen such a small woman make such a big entrance!

By this time, I was in a state of nervous shock, but Mam proceeded with her mission which I was convinced would end with even more retribution being meted out upon me. All I could think of was that this man Barker was ten times as big as the prefect and probably had a strong right hand to match. Now, as his tiny visitor, trailing an even tinier boy, moved up to his desk, he calmly and politely greeted her with, 'Yes, Madam, how may I help you?'

'Are you aware of the fact that my son is allowed to be publicly beaten by another boy?' she bellowed.

'Well, Madam, you see, I have only recently joined the school. There are certain traditions here and although they have been here for over 100 years, I don't entirely agree with them either, but they take time to change.' I was flabbergasted at his apparent acceptance of Mam's position and listened as he continued. 'However, I'm sorry but your son has to be punished.'

My heart sank again as vastly exaggerated pictures of his ability with a cane flashed through my terrified mind. I stood incredulous, as Mam not only proceeded to agree, but suggested the worst thing my small boy's mind could have imagined. 'You can punish him, but the other boys must not touch him.'

The words didn't reach my lips, but my face must have read like a book. 'Mother! This is a stupid decision; he's bigger than the prefect! This guy has just come out of the Army, just look at his muscles!'

As I started to shake, Barker turned to me and looked me straight in the eye. 'Daniels, you must be punished. You will write me an essay on what is wrong with this school.'

Shock, astonishment and relief must have been written across my forehead in the beads of sweat that had begun to drip on to my collar. I wrote my essay and over the next two years everything that I had suggested was changed. Discipline and respect, including touching your hat as a Master walked past, I felt should remain, but many of the other 'traditions' should not. I had discovered that standing firm for fairness eventually brought its just rewards.

CHAPTER 3

AN AMAZING DISCOVERY

*A*s 1953 approached, Europe quietly celebrated the demise of one *of its most infamous dictators, Stalin. As well as the Russian leader, country singer Hank Williams, composer Sergei Prokofiev and poet Dylan Thomas also died. Even as 1953 was a year of death, it also heralded the key to life as two scientists at Cambridge University unlocked the mystery of DNA.*

My days were filled with catching buses to and from school, reading magic books and struggling with homework that would have been easy if I hadn't spent so much time on magic.

I tried to avoid sports as much as possible and looked like the skinniest white wimp of all time, well, at least to me. One of my worst fears was of going to the swimming baths. I couldn't swim. Some people can't and some people have negative buoyancy. I have it, my dad had it and my brother Trevor has it. We could sit on the bottom of the pool with lungs full of air with no problem at all, as long as we could stand up when we ran out of air. Dad should have been able to swim – he had six toes on one foot and they were webbed. Really.

Anyway, not being able to swim was a real pain. One day, in one of those small advertisements that you get in the Sunday papers (Are they still there? I haven't taken a newspaper in years. I've read so many lies about me I can't believe what they write about anybody any more. Shame, isn't it?) I saw an advertisement for a 'SECRET SWIMMING AID – Your Friends Will NEVER Know'. Wow, that's for me! I sent off some of my earnings, and eventually a smallish, brown paper parcel arrived. What I told my mother it was I can't remember, but I got it up to my room and opened the package.

This thing *might* have been secret when Victorians wore full-length bathing suits, but it certainly wasn't going to be very secret now. It was a very wide rubber belt that came from above my waist to half-way down my thighs. Running up and down around the belt was a rubber tube, with a non-return release valve at the rear in the middle of your back and a mouthpiece that came up from the front.

God help me! I went to the beach with this thing rolled up under my normal bathing costume. 'Your Friends Will NEVER Know' – if they were blind, perhaps, because here was this skinny white kid with the most bulbous bathing costume ever around his loins. I walked out into the sea. The North Sea is very cold, even in summer. I walked out further. I had to get this thing underwater. Once the grabbing iciness had got to my waist I turned my back to the shore, rummaged around down the front of my briefs. I wonder what my friends, who would never know, would *think* that I was doing. I found the pipe. No, not that one, *that* one. I pulled it up and, still standing facing the sea, bent my head down and started blowing.

The sensation under the water was very strange. Very strange indeed. As the tubing filled with air it straightened itself out, pulling the belt both upwards and downwards out of my costume. 'Flip' up on to my stomach. 'Flap' down one leg, up my back, down the other leg. I wonder whether the guy who designed this ever used it. He was selling this contraption and risking a manslaughter charge if it didn't work and I got drowned.

With one sudden, last big blow into the mouthpiece, which of course emptied my lungs, the belt became fully inflated and lifted my backside clean out of the water, thrusting my head under the waves. I was very aware that my Friends Will Never Know. They might have looked out to sea and wondered what the large black bum was bobbing about on the water, but I could rest assured that they would not connect it with me.

The advertisement was true! I was swimming! Well, I was flailing my arms around under the water trying to get my head back to the surface before I drowned but I couldn't argue with the fact that I was afloat. A lucky wave arrived at the same time as I moved my arms in the same direction and I flipped briefly above the water, grabbed a breath and went under again. It might be of great interest to the designer to know that now I was bent over backwards, legs and head underwater, crotch floating upwards, and that the waves were carrying me nearer the shore. Again, that was lucky because I was able to grab the sea floor and stand upright. Fighting the gadget's desire to flip me again, I found that the only way to get it off was to take off my swimming trunks, something that I was loath to do, so instead I fought my way around to the release valve situated in the middle of my back, grabbed it and pulled. The air started to come out in bubbles. As the bubbles rose in a direct line from my arse I can only assume that, although My Friends Would Never Know, they might well have got the wrong idea altogether as to what I was doing. I never used the SECRET Swimming Aid again.

The learning of magic continued and I could think of being nothing other than a magician. The problem was that I had no idea how you became a professional magician. I shared my thoughts with my parents who tried to dissuade me with the old argument about getting a 'proper', secure job. Their brushes with showbusiness had all been through my father's stepsister, the infamous Auntie Maureen. The family rumour was that apparently she had had eight husbands, and none of them were hers! With my parents' insistence that magic should remain a hobby, I had to content myself with showing my tricks to school friends.

I had left the Mission Sunday School by now and joined the Normanby Road Methodist Chapel for the highly religious reason that it had a better youth club facility. On my very first visit there, I watched other members running up to a vaulting horse and diving head first over it into a forward roll aided by a springboard.

'I'll try that,' I thought. I ran. I hit the springboard. I flew through the air. I forgot to roll and landed right on the top of my head and invented the ramrod landing. What a natural athlete I am.

One evening I could not attend the club and that was the meeting when they organised a concert. Various members were assigned to perform and, in my absence and because I was always doing tricks, they put me down to do a magic show among a few other acts.

In true Variety style I was to appear singing as one of 'The Bold Gendarmes' and then dressed as a baby with 'Sisters, Sisters' before my solo six minutes to prove my conjuring worth. I was determined to do well and spent several weeks sorting out what to do, rehearsing and honing my craft. Up until this time, I had only performed magic from the pocket. Now I was being asked to do a spot in a hall, which was quite different. Being able to purchase props was out of the question, so everything I used was created from cardboard boxes and steel coat hangers. A lot of searching through notes and magic books helped me choose what to do. I had stopped reading any other books by this time anyway. Looking back I am amazed at my choice of magical effects. The act would work for me now, if I chose to do it.

Then, nervously standing in front of the mixed crowd, I began to perform the multiplying billiard ball manipulation routine. The balls appeared and disappeared between my fingers and I was delighted as the mums, dads, grannies and granddads laughed and clapped in all the right places. My assistant, complete with fishnet tights, was Margaret Dawkins, a young girl who had been cajoled into helping me. With a hat in one hand and a pack of cards in the other, Margaret went down into the audience and invited a member to shuffle them and throw them into the hat. Bringing the hat back on-stage, I did a routine called 'Seeing with the Fingertips' and with the hat held above my head, pulled out the four Aces.

My grand finale was the production of a full goldfish bowl from an empty box, complete with two goldfish. By the time I was 14, my mind had already started to extend the tricks in the books and look for ways to make them more entertaining. I also wanted to adapt the tricks to my own style of presentation. I had bought the plans for what was called 'the Inexhaustible Box' for one shilling and sixpence from the Boy's Own Magic Club in Prestatyn, North Wales. My dad made it for me and I produced the goldfish bowl from that. I was to use this box in all shapes and sizes for the rest of my career. What an investment that was!

Once the applause had subsided, I reached inside the bowl to grab one of the fish by its tail. The audience looked on in wonderment as I held the wriggling orange fish in my hand and quickly slipped it straight into my mouth. I ate it. The audience grimaced and groaned.

'Ladies and Gentlemen,' I announced. 'Because there are

children in the audience' – remember, I was only 14! – 'I will show you how this trick is done. What you didn't know was that I had swapped the real goldfish for a piece of thinly sliced carrot.'

I showed them a carrot and took a small slice off it. I shook it about to make it look real.

'This was what I swallowed.'

The audience laughed. I then dropped it into another bowl *and it swam away*. A gasp of surprise superseded the applause and I left the stage as high as a kite.

Twenty years later, I did a fund-raising show in the same hall and a young woman came up afterwards and said she remembered that I was 'the man that had swallowed the goldfish'. We stood there for a moment and between us worked out that she must only have been two years old when she saw the show. This demonstrated to me yet again the power of the entertainer and his medium. When people say that violence in films and television doesn't affect kids to a degree they are right. It doesn't affect all kids, but it affects quite a lot. So why bother affecting them badly?

I went on to perform lots of shows in that club room, not only for the Youth Club, but also as a guest on the Young Wives Concerts as well. I can only remember what I did on the very first show, however, and none of the dozens of tricks that followed.

My parents continued to voice their concern at my seemingly addictive hobby. Doing my homework was an unavoidable evil that had to be completed before I could spend the evening developing a new routine.

Grammar school held a natural audience in the form of my peers who began to respect me for what I could do. I never bullied friends into watching my tricks, but developed the knack of drawing a crowd in. Sometimes this was done simply by practising an effect which others would be inquisitive enough to watch, and even Pietrowski, our Polish war hero, loved magic. If he walked into a classroom while I was finishing a trick he would join in. On more than one occasion, we did magic for the rest of the lesson and didn't bother learning French. I became a linguistic ignoramus.

Mam and Dad were not all gloom and doom and were concerned not to discourage my love of magic. They took me to see the famous Australian illusionist, The Great Levante, who was on tour and visiting the Middlesbrough Empire for a few days. I can't remember much about the show. I know that he vanished a nun in an organ pipe; he did the 'One Thousand Pound Trunk' trick which most magicians know better as the 'Substitution Trunk', and one of his great claims to fame in those days was the disappearance of a kangaroo. It would lie in a suspended net hammock with Levante's beautiful assistant Esme one minute, and then they both instantly vanished as the net fell to the floor. This amazing illusion was always rewarded with a great ovation, to which Levante would make his exit.

This great magician was not only a master of his craft, however, but a clever manipulator of the press as well. Each time he visited a town he gave the local newspapers the story that his kangaroo had escaped. There was an abundance of free publicity to be gained from this story, but no one ever seemed to 'twig' that the animal was always found just in time for the first house on Monday night, accompanied by a whole range of celebratory articles in the press once again. I thought he was wonderful.

A strange thing happened during my early teens. Do all children have nightmares? I certainly did. There was the witch who chased me from the back yard toilet and, in my dreams, caught me as I woke up in a sweat. Another involved being chased by a lion and it pulled the skin off my back in one piece, again at the moment of waking. There weren't too many lions in our area so maybe the Tarzan films were getting to me.

The most persistent of the nightmares were completely different to those two. In my dream, I was 'floating' along a lane and seeing everything through my eyes, rather than watching myself. When I got to the top of the lane on the left there was an old lych-gate that led into an old churchyard. Ancient, leaning gravestones surrounded the old church and, as I floated towards the main door, the L-shaped church offered another door on my right. I knew, in my dream, that the door in front of me led into the church and I knew, with increasing horror, that the door on my right hid Death. I could not stop myself. Against all my wishes I opened the door and woke up screaming. I never got to see Death but I knew it was there. This nightmare was with me for most of my young life and continued into my early teens.

One beautiful summer's day a friend, Colin Mason, and I decided to go for a bike ride. We set off out of the Tees Valley and headed south. A car would do the trip nowadays in half-an-hour but the climb out of the valley is steep if you are only using your legs and bikes were not as light as they are now. We came to a village and Colin, who had been there before, told me that he wanted to show me something really interesting. We turned off the main road and set off up a lane. I stopped. I knew this lane. This was the lane of my nightmare.

Colin could see that something was wrong and I told him about the lych-gate at the top. He asked if I had been there before and I said 'no'. I just couldn't tell him about the dream and I couldn't stop myself from seeing this through even though I was icy cold and terrified. We went up the lane and there was the gate, exactly as it was in the dream. We went through the gate and walked along the narrow church path to the building. I wanted to go in the main door, of course, but Colin said that what he wanted to show me was in 'here' and headed for the side door. I wanted to scream and I don't know how I didn't.

He pulled the door open and ...

NOTHING happened.

Colin wanted to show me a narrow wheelbase bier. This, he explained, was used to wheel the coffin from the hearse in the lane along the narrow churchyard pathways to the grave.

As I pedalled home, my head was full of wild thoughts; was I a reincarnation, for example? Was my former body buried somewhere in this village graveyard and did I have some strange mental connection with my previous life? How else could I have known the lane so well and dreamed my dream?

I got home to the greeting that all young people get when they have been out for hours. 'And where do you think you've been 'til this time?'

I explained that we had been for a ride to a village called Swainby. There was something in the way my mother started to say, 'Ah, Swainby,' and I burst in with, 'We've been there. We were on holiday there in a caravan on the bend of a river and Cousin Ada was with us and Dad came in the middle of the night and ...'

Mam looked at me in amazement. Apparently, all this had happened while I was still being pushed around in a pram. According to her, I couldn't possibly have remembered it at all, being that young.

It is my belief that the gliding up the lane came from the view from the pram and, over my head, the grown-ups had talked about the bier and what it was used for. At that age I didn't understand in detail the word 'death' and somehow later in my young life my brain cells had put it together with something horrible and created my nightmare. Ever since this realisation, I have always tried to talk in a positive manner to babies and young children. We learn at a very early age.

* * *

Meanwhile, back at the cinema, I was still showing movies and bobbing out of the tiny trapdoor of a door at the back of the 'circle' to watch them from the back row. I was sitting there one night, minding my own business, when a young man several years older than me, reached out and put his hand on my thigh. I never even thought about what happened next, it just happened. I can't remember being told anything about homosexuality or warned, so what I did was just a reflex action. There was no fear, no excitement, no thought at all, I merely reached out with my left hand, grasped his wrist and with my right hand snapped his little finger. It cracked and he screamed, causing everyone to look round as he ran down the stairs and out of the cinema. Dad came running up the stairs and asked what had happened and I said I didn't know, the man just ran out. Years later, in a working men's club after a performance, a drag act sat next to me and ran his spectacles up and down my leg. Again, without thinking, I reached out, took them and broke them. I guess I wasn't destined to be gay.

Dad decided to learn to drive with the help of my Uncle Eddie. The only problem was that Uncle Eddie had not been taught how to drive a car. His qualifying claim was that he had owned a motorbike sometime in the Twenties and the licensing authorities considered him to have the necessary road experience to enable him to teach others. He was, therefore, the proud owner of one of the new driving licences being issued by the Government. Dad was pleased to surrender his tandem bicycle with sidecar attachment for an old car that he had picked up from a friend for just a few pounds. With manual dexterity beyond any textbook, Hughie would discover the secret of what was wrong with any part of a car and repair it. This mastery of mechanics was to be something my brother and I relied heavily on in later years, but for now I was content to see him transform the ordinary car into a smooth-running, luxury vehicle. Well, perhaps not luxury, but it was to us. He even re-upholstered it, Mam and him cutting out the foam and leatherette shapes and gluing it all together.

On his first trip, we all gathered outside our house and watched in amazement as Eddie and Hughie ran the coughing, jerking vehicle around the streets as Dad tried to come to terms with the clutch. A few moments later and they reappeared from the opposite direction with smiles and laughter echoing around the tiny saloon. Dad had obviously passed his first lesson, but would still have to wait for an official driving test in order to earn his licence. Dad decided that he needed more time than Uncle Eddie could give him for practising. He sat Mam in the front seat and told her to look as if she could drive. Off they went to Stockton, a nearby town, with Dad driving carefully, red 'L' plates mounted front and rear and Mam trying to look serious. These were the days of hand signals by drivers of cars and vans. You want to turn right? You stick your right arm straight out of the vehicle. You want to turn left? You stick your right arm out of the vehicle and make forward circles with your wrist and hand. Well, that's the theory. If you are a young man in a bit of a state because you shouldn't be there anyway, with an unqualified companion next to you, maybe you lose control a little. Dad did.

At a left turn in Stockton, Dad's brain suddenly flipped back to being on the bike and nearly knocked Mam out as he signalled left by sticking his left arm straight out. Poor Mam. Amazingly enough, when it eventually came to his test, he passed first time. After that we were quite posh really. We had a car.

It was the coronation of Queen Elizabeth II that started the serious decline of cinema. Television sets became the thing to own. Millions watched her crowning on the new-fangled machines, which could transmit pictures directly into your home. No longer did you have to brave the inconvenience of queuing in the cold and wet to get a good view, a front row seat was instantly available in your living room.

The coronation gave television a kick-start as millions of eager viewers bombarded their local radio shops in an attempt to purchase the new machine of the century. It didn't seem to matter that the latest technology meant swapping a giant 20ft screen for a tiny 6in of black-and-white fuzziness. People thought they were getting the cinematic experience in their own homes, but they weren't.

As local cinemas faced a slow, painful death, they did their best to fight back. Big-budget epics and monster movies were full of special effects, while 3-D movies offered one of the craziest gimmicks whereby the audience wore special red and green glasses to see the image burst from the screen. Unfortunately, most people left with a blazing headache. The pumping of scents into the building with 'smellovision' never really caught on either. As movie producers used the huge Technicolor screens of Cinemascope and Cinerama to tempt audiences back, it was obvious that the battle was already lost when viewers still preferred the black-and-white pictures of the miniature screen. The Hippodrome hung on for a long time and I can remember an interview in the *Evening Gazette* where my father was quoted as saying that the cowboy movies were keeping the cinema alive. It was a long column interview. The only problem was that no journalist had asked my dad the questions. Nothing changes.

Thanks to Mam's careful housekeeping we somehow managed to save up enough to buy a TV set of our own. The new technology was still in its infancy and, as a result, was extremely expensive. I sometimes wonder what personal sacrifices they made in order to purchase one for us.

Our Mullard TV was soon part of the furniture, literally so, as it was designed in such a way that the doors at the front of the cabinet could close, concealing its true identity. Its imposing size symbolised the dominance this new technology was to have in the home. Little did Dad know the consequences that this new medium was to have in the later years of my own life.

Transmissions were intermittent and programmes only aired for a short while – something we should consider reverting to today! It needed a lot of tuning with four huge dials sandwiched between the tiny screen and the metal grill, which protected the loudspeaker. The choice was focus, volume, brightness and contrast, with a huge brown bakelite knob on the back operating as the tuner. Why they designed the tuning system to be on the back of the set, when you needed it on the front to see what you were doing, must be one example of the quirkiness of being a British invention.

The engineer came and tuned it all in using the test charts that were transmitted all day long. He left telling us when the first programmes would be on air. We gathered around, switched it on and sat in hushed silence as the set warmed up. Suddenly, the screen burst into life with none other than a puppet show, *Bill and Ben,* the flowerpot men. They talked in gibberish. As the sounds of 'flobalob', 'Er, Lubbalub' and 'little weeeeed' filled our front room, Dad looked aghast at the screen.

'All this money I've paid out, and they don't even speak English!'

When the Hippodrome cinema finally waved the white flag, I was humiliated and angry as my dad went from Chief Projectionist to WonderLoaf deliveryman. The cinema that had given thrills and spills to thousands was eventually demolished and bulldozed to the ground. It was a very sad day for us all.

Once again it was my father's optimistic approach to life that moved us forward. I admired the way in which Dad never complained and immediately threw himself into his new job – so much so, in fact, that when turning sharply in his delivery van one day, the side door flew open and all his bread and cakes shot out into the road.

My time at Sir William Turner's Grammar School was also coming to an end. As English had been my main subject at school, it wasn't surprising that this influenced the direction I took when considering a career. Exams had never bothered me much and I managed to get five 'O'-levels which was pretty good considering I had a kidney infection that intermittently kept me off school during the latter years of my education.

The opportunities for work seemed endless; perhaps the Grammar school grind really had paid off. One problem seemed to be which path to choose, which way should I go? Mum and Dad never pressurised me and, being a 'werks'-based society, nothing artistic was ever considered. The local *Evening Gazette* offered me a job as a junior reporter on the basis of my school reports regarding my ability in English; a firm of accountants offered me a place as an articled clerk; a solicitors department considered me to be a suitable recruit; and as my technical drawings at school were regarded as high quality, a draughtsman's role was proposed down at Smith's Dock, and this was considered the 'bee's knees' of an opportunity.

To be honest, I wasn't interested in any of them. I wanted to be a magician. Magic was all that I was interested in, wanted to read about or do. For a while I considered going on to teacher training college to try to become a woodwork teacher. Instead of getting the boys to make furniture, I wondered whether I could get them to make tricks, even illusions. After thinking about all the options, I decided that becoming a teacher would have been too great a financial burden on my parents. So for no other reason than because it was just around the corner and I could come home for lunch, I took a job at the local council offices.

It was about this time that I experienced my first kiss. A gang of us from Coatham used to hang around South Bank together and some girls from the local girls school used to join us. We would sit for hours on the wall of another local school and talk the evenings away. I can't remember sex being a topic of conversation and, looking back from this great distance, I wonder what the devil we did talk about. Cars and bikes, I guess.

My big moment came after going to the Empire cinema, also in South Bank. The drama took place in the back alley behind Munby Street near the town centre and, as we walked hand in hand in the darkness, she made it obvious that she wanted me to kiss her. We had sat for a couple of hours with my arm around her on the back row, but I hadn't plucked up the courage to do it then. Even having seen a great deal of osculation in the movies, I still had a bit of a hang-up about the art of joining two lips together, for I couldn't figure out what happened to your nose. It's further forward from your lips, so how could your lips meet when her nose would touch my nose and stop us moving any closer? Pondering the puzzle of being a double-nose width away from kissing used to keep me awake for hours.

The chance to kiss Pauline was a surprise, as she was a good friend and nothing more as far as I was concerned. As I tilted my face to the left so did she. I turned my head to the right and so did she. It was like meeting someone in the street who you can't get past. Eventually I took her by the head, kissed her on the lips and waited for the sparks to arrive. They didn't and I wondered what all the fuss had been about. Seeing a kiss on film with the orchestra and strings playing in the background, accompanied by heavy breathing and an audience in tears, I was somehow expecting more.

Once the deed was done we tried it a couple more times but

it did nothing for me at all. We went home. Maybe I was with the wrong girl. At the time I was carrying a big torch for a girl called Irene Hewitt who was a member of the youth club. Madly keen on Irene, I would watch her avidly as, together with her friend Mandy, they would sing at the youth club concerts that I did. Miss Hewitt was extremely voluptuous and could easily have led me astray. In my dreams she did, many times, but in reality I obviously didn't stand a chance.

In an age that talked openly about death, but never sex, the facts of life had never been properly explained to me. Today, it's the other way round, but when I was 16 I had to unearth the meaning of life for myself. It's extraordinary to consider the fact that I seemed to be a late-developer as far as my knowledge went, but in those days children had no real chance to grasp the truth. Sex lessons at school were remarkably bland and made no sense at all. Nudie magazines like *Health and Efficiency* had all the pictures of genitals removed. 'Polished' flesh remained where things were supposed to be.

The confusion of pre-puberty led me to experience a recurring erotic nightmare. Me and my nightmares! Having been told at school that the man simply placed his penis inside the woman, without giving us any other important details, my dream was of a lady (faceless) who would lie on the bed patiently waiting with her feet stuck up in the air. It must have been because I was so good at woodwork that in my vision a perfectly drilled, round hole was centred between her legs – an inch-and-a-half diameter of turned wood awaited the entrance of her man. I knew exactly where it was, but didn't know what it was. And for certain I didn't know what to do with it!

Having discovered a little green hard-back book in my dad's wardrobe entitled *The Techniques of Sex*, I realised I had found the true object of my quest. I was sure that Havelock Ellis's book would reveal all. Thumbing through the strange technical drawings, I would regularly lock myself in our toilet and study, for this was a subject to be learnt. Once, having exhaustively examined the mysterious cut-away diagrams of genitals for the umpteenth time, I made my way downstairs and hoped Mam didn't notice my sweating.

'Ted!'

As soon as I heard Mam's call, I realised I had accidentally left the book on the lavatory windowsill. Mothers can say your name in so many ways and convey a whole paragraph in a single word. As her voice floated down the stairs, fear instantly clutched me from within.

'Have you been reading this book of your father's?'

There was no point in lying; I was the only one in the house at the time.

'Yes, Mam.'

Then came the sentence that has struck terror into many a boy's heart.

'Just you wait till your father gets home!'

I was scared sick. Ashamed of the sexual awareness and the invasion of my father's territory, I couldn't imagine what was to come and the hours that passed as we waited for him to return from work were the longest in my life.

Only having experienced a beating from my father once, it was something that I hadn't forgotten and was anxious not to repeat. He'd slapped me on my bottom all the way up a street when I was about seven years old. It was fully deserved of course, as I was being a little shit.

'I wanna go to the fair; I wanna go to the fair; I wanna go to the fair!' I'd repeated incessantly until my father gave in. Having got to the fair: 'I wanna go home; I wanna go home; I wanna go home!'

Dad got mad, really mad, and belted me all the way back down the street. Once inside the front door, he picked up a shovel and threw it at me. I knew that I was going to 'get it' good and proper the moment I arrived back, so as soon as I got through the front door I was off like a rocket, straight through the back room, turn the corner and up the stairs. I was very small, but boy was I fast, one of the big advantages being that I could run straight under the table. The shovel just missed me and years later Dad told me that he'd frightened himself enormously when he realised how much he had lost control. A clip on the back of the head or the backside was the most I ever got after that.

This was different though. I was a young man now and I should have known better. They say that the waiting is the worst part but I dreaded what was going to happen. Sitting in the front room wondering what the punishment would be for my latest crime, I heard the arrival of my father at the front door. As he came in and smiled my heart started to beat so loudly, I couldn't hear the voices as he went through to the kitchen and started to discuss the latest situation with my mother. I got closer to the door to hear what was going on.

'So what is it?'

'He's had that book of yours out of the wardrobe.'

'Well that's good, it'll save me telling him, won't it?'

I love my father. I love my father. I love my father.

CHAPTER 4

'ORRIBLE LITTLE MEN

The late Fifties gave birth to a new type of musical experience — rock 'n' roll. Elvis Presley, Chuck Berry, Bill Haley and Buddy Holly were all exports from the USA and held the nation's teenagers in the grip of their unique brand of music. Nearer home, the tiny Morris Mini is launched and master of suspense Alfred Hitchcock keeps audiences in their seats with his new film Psycho.

Still fascinated by the art of magic and illusion in all its forms, I reluctantly agreed to leave all thoughts of show- business behind and live in the 'real' world. I suppose it was the right decision. Looking back, I do believe that everybody would benefit from having another job before the one they are going to do for life. Most passionately, I believe this about teachers, as I don't think you can teach about life unless you have left school and gone and worked in the big wide world — most teachers never have! Teachers, vicars and Members of Parliament live in a very protected environment and are sheltered from the trials and tribulations of a commercial working life. Perhaps no one should be allowed into teacher training college until they are at least 25 years old. By then you really want to be a teacher and it is, after all, one of the most exciting and important of all possible jobs.

Having joined Eston Urban Borough Council as a junior clerk, one of my first tasks employed my mathematical skills in balancing the rates books. The problem was that I had spent the last few years of my life doing algebra, trigonometry and geometry. Accountants add up and take away and, occasionally, do a bit of multiplication. I had forgotten how to add up. Computers were unheard of in 1954 so each one of the thousands of rent and rates records were kept by hand and, without the use of a 'magic' wand, were accurate to the penny. Each page was self-balancing so you couldn't move on until you had balanced that page. As each page only had about twenty entries it was easy to spot an error. The totals of all the pages were transferred to the next set of records, again self-balancing, and so on until a final total was reached.

Not many people were employed to do this, considering the numbers involved, and at the end of the year all the records were filed together for future reference. I don't think computers have improved on that. When our new machinery came into the office, using punched cards, it was supposed to be able to speed everything up, but I'm not sure that it did and it cost a lot of extra money for the mechanics and service charges. It seemed to me that the hand-written system was working perfectly well and I couldn't understand why it wasn't left alone. 'If it works, don't fix it,' I remember my dad saying.

So I found myself sitting on day one at work next to Mary Livingstone and trying to add up the columns of figures. Of course, she thought me very slow and I was. Miss Livingstone could add up the columns of hundreds of thousands of pounds, shillings and pence all at the same time. She didn't do the pence, then the shillings, then the pounds, she did them all at once. A couple of years ago I came across a book on mathematics that taught you how to do this and it turned out to be easier than the way I was taught at school. I wonder why they taught us the wrong way round?

I also had to make the tea and coffee. This I did in the old kitchen. The building had, at one time, been a very large house and the kitchen was typically Victorian. At some time, someone had left behind some very large models of steam engines and trains. I wish I had taken them home as they were wonderful in their glass cases with external connections for pumping the steam in to make them work. They were probably dumped when that set of offices was closed down.

As a job-starting-cum-birthday-present, my mother and father had got me an NSU Quickly. That's a bike not many will remember but it was the epitome of mopeds and I was the envy of my pals. Late in my school years we had all messed about on those powered bicycles. Some had an engine fitted inside the back wheel. Others had an engine on the back of the seat and, having pedalled the bike up to speed, you literally dropped the engine on to the back wheel where a cog drove the tyre around. Tyres wore out quickly on that model.

The Quickly was the first fully integrated design for a moped, not that I believe you could have pedalled it far as it was heavy. It had a two-speed gearbox and was very streamlined. I picked it up at the shop, Uptons, on Nelson Street and they showed me how to start it. Off I went under the loving gaze of Mam and rode along the street with everyone watching me. They had never seen anything like it. I approached the end of the street where the market was in full swing when I realised I hadn't a clue how to stop it. Weaving amongst the customers in the open marketplace I tried everything I could and eventually I stopped it by switching it off. It had back-pedalling brakes. No wonder I couldn't find them, I'd never heard of them.

The machine was very useful, however, for collecting rents. I was enrolled as stand-by for rent-collecting duty, if any of the officers were on leave or off sick. I really enjoyed collecting rents. I was young and fit and used to jump the fences between the houses to save walking up and down the paths. I ran everywhere once I had ridden to the estate. The other rent collectors used to tell me off for making short work of their hours. 'You just wait till it's raining or snowing and then you'll find out.' I didn't care. I was having fun. I had a couple of surprises on the job though.

It was quite usual for council tenants, or anybody, to leave their front door unlocked and open for visitors. The records book I took with me would often give instructions to walk straight through the front door and into the front room where the rent would be left ready for collection. People were very trusting in those days, but then again, most people didn't have much worth stealing!

It's a strange phenomenon but you can tell if there's someone in a house or not. It was certainly possible to feel the 'vibes' of a body upstairs, or even detect if someone was hiding. When rent was in arrears it was pretty common for the tenant to try and avoid the collector and I saw more than one figure duck down behind the window as I approached. Even if you didn't see them duck, you would sense they were in there. An empty house feels different. If the occupant was having a tough time financially, we would often turn a blind eye for a while, but if they were simply skiving we would do all we could to collect the money from them. My 'sixth sense' of 'feeling' whether the house was empty or not came in very useful. That is, until one day, when I got it totally wrong.

In one of the houses, following the instructions in my book, I entered and yelled out my customary 'Hello'. No answer, so I headed for the front room. It was the darkness of the room that confused me as the curtains had been closed, yet the envelope containing the cash had been left on the sideboard as usual. I picked up the money and started to enter the money into the rent book. As I stood there in the darkness, my eyes began to adjust to the lack of light and various outlines began to appear. Suddenly, to my absolute horror, I spotted what I thought was a man lying on a table. Against my better judgement I moved closer, hoping he was all right. He wasn't. There in the middle of the tiny front room was a corpse laid out in its box. I fully understood how Connie felt when he dropped his end. I was out of the house much quicker than I went in and I was shaking like a leaf.

Another house but the same instruction, the rent is on the front room table. 'Hello, hello.' And no reply. In I went, saw the money and I was bending over the table filling in the book when from under the table came a nasty, low, growl. My testicles went back into my body of their own accord. Never in the history of rent collecting has anyone backed out of a house more slowly. Nice doggy.

All the cash from the rents and the rates was kept in a huge safe fitted into the wall and was secured each night. Just before leaving for home one Friday, I happened to glance around and noticed that the chief cashier had left his bag full of bank notes on the floor by the safe door. He must have forgotten to secure it in the safe and when I opened it there must have been several thousands of pounds in there. It was an extraordinarily large amount of cash in those days, so, thinking quickly, I decided to take the bag home with me. After all, I couldn't leave it there all night and I had no key to the safe.

Placing the bag of notes on the wire clip on the back of my NSU Quickly, I arrived safely home and put the package under my bed. When Monday morning arrived, I happily sailed into work, only to find police cars and policemen everywhere. The place was lit up with flashing blue lights.

'What's going on?' I innocently enquired of one of the clerks who wore an expression of complete bafflement.

'All the rent money's been stolen,' came the swift reply.

'Oh, that's OK, I've got ...' but they wouldn't listen to me.

' Please, son, we're very busy. Just get on with your duties,' was all I got.

Several attempts later, I approached someone else. 'Excuse me. Are you looking for this?'

The official's eyes nearly rolled out of his head when he caught sight of me holding the bag open with notes stuffed to the top.

'Where on earth did you get that?' he bellowed, as all hell broke loose.

I explained the whole predicament and defended my actions reminding him that I was only a junior clerk and didn't have anyone's phone number to contact them in an emergency. I was briskly thanked and told to get on with my work. Somehow I felt it was all my fault and yet I had tried to help.

When the council offices were eventually moved to new premises, a new security vault was built which was burglar, blast and tunnel secure. There was no way anyone could rob this safe we were proudly told, as we were taken on a tour of this new protection system. Walking past the double-skinned, triple-lock metal door, we were then led past a floor-to-ceiling grill with one-inch steel bars. Once in this impressive chamber, the safe itself stood on a raised platform and the council officials were delighted with the solid walls and floor. Looking up, I asked what the ceiling was made of. They hadn't thought of that and gave me a very dismissive glance to hide their embarrassment. Anyone could have just gone upstairs, lifted the floorboards and dropped down into the hyper-secure safe-room through the ceiling tiles. Whoops!

Councils seem to have the reputation for incompetence, but

'ORRIBLE LITTLE MEN

I don't think they are any worse than any other major organisation. Local government is there, complete with all its little by-laws, to keep some sort of order in your district. You have to have your rubbish collected, your sewage removed and your pavements made safe, but because the council deals with so many people, a few problems are bound to slip through the net. These are the ones that get the publicity, ignoring all those who were perfectly happy.

I tried to pre-empt a few problems myself with all sorts of moneysaving ideas, which I thought were helpful. Some of my suggestions were even laughed at, but looking back they would have worked.

One thought was to place large tunnel-like tubes under all the roads in the new estates we were building. Each large tube would have a walkway along the bottom, above a tube that carried the sewage. Along the walls of the tube would be smaller tubes that carried all the services, electricity, telephone lines, gas and the like. There would be no need to ever dig up a road again. Each service would be able to access its own tube easily. If this had been taken up, it would have saved the nation millions, but then where would we be without our beloved roadworks!

At that time, and perhaps it is still the same now, we as a Council had to borrow the money to build anything, whether it was a swimming baths or council houses. Then the money we borrowed had to be repaid over a very long period of years, adding millions in interest rates. I could not for the life of me see why we couldn't levy a rate that would enable us to save up for a few years to build public amenities and that would have been a lot cheaper than the current system. Their argument was that you could not levy a 'rate for something in the future as a ratepayer might die and not benefit'. As it was, we had ratepayers paying for buildings that had long been pulled down, so what was the difference?

By now I was 17 and living two lives. Since the non-excitement of the first kiss I had practised a bit more and, of course, I was filled with the knowledge of my dad's sex manual. In the Co-op Chemists on Lorne Terrace there was a blonde goddess (well, she was to me) called Jean Pagel and I used to go in there as often as I could. The cheapest things to buy were Horlicks tablets at nine pence a packet and I bought them by the hundreds. Eventually we dated and spent many a happy hour rolling about on her front room sofa. Nothing serious happened, damn it, only kissing and fumbling but I raged with passion. Meanwhile, from the Methodist Youth Club I had moved into the pulpit. On Sundays I was a lay preacher, the rest of the week I was a young man raging with lust. Things are different nowadays, of course – I am no longer a lay preacher!

To be honest, I wasn't a lay preacher for very long anyway. I had run the service in most of the chapels on the local circuit. It was a bit like working in the clubs and theatres later; you could do the same 'act' in front of the different congregations and then you would have to come up with a new 'script' for the next tour. My main problem came in my own chapel and from my sense of observation. There was one lady who never came into church in time for the start of the service. She was always about five minutes late and the other women in the congregation would then all be whispering about her new hat. Imagine, a new hat every week. So when it became my turn to run the service in the chapel I didn't start the service. With the brashness of youth I announced that we would all sit quietly as the lady would be waiting in the foyer of the chapel and when she arrived we would admire the hat and then get on with the real reason we were supposed to be there, worshipping and thanking God. When the woman did come in, she was livid. As she was the wife of a church elder I more or less got the sack. Neither did they like my idea of not doing the service in the order it had been done for years. My idea was that if you didn't know what was coming next you might pay more attention to the words. It's funny that it was the old people who objected and the young people who liked the improvisations.

In my mid-teens, Dad and I would sit up at night after he came home from work and just chat. We would discuss life and the universe and, naturally, put the world to rights. Motorways were under discussion; these new wonder roads that would allow everyone to travel easily great distances with no delays. Yeah, right! Dad had an idea that has stayed with me – at the same time as they were building the motorways, they should put large tubes alongside them, possibly underground, maybe two to three feet in diameter. These tubes would join all the major cities of the UK and belong to the Post Office. Inside the tubes there would be, for want of a better word, torpedoes. In London, a torpedo for, say, Leeds would be filled with post and loaded into the tube. The tube at that end sloped downwards slightly and as the torpedo went in it would activate a sensor switch that activated an electro-magnet. The head of the torpedo would be magnetic and it would be pulled, aided initially by gravity, towards the magnet, picking up speed. As it approached the magnet another switch would de-activate electro-magnet number one and switch on number two and so on. After a very short time the magnets could be well spaced out as the torpedo would be travelling at very high speed. As it approached Leeds some 20 to 30 minutes later, the electro-magnets would be switched on *behind* the magnetic head to pull it back and eventually stop it at the Post Office. No train delays, no traffic jams, nothing would stop our postal system. Like so many ideas, we did nothing with it.

A long brown envelope awaited my return home one evening. It wasn't a surprise as I had been expecting the communication, though I wouldn't have been disappointed had it not arrived at all. It contained my call-up papers for National Service. Every 18-year-old, if they passed a medical, was expected to train in the services for two years in order to keep Britain's fighting strength at its maximum potential. World War II may be over, but problems in the Far East, the Middle East and the Cold War with the Soviet Union were still threats to be taken seriously.

Registering at my local army offices, the choice was Army, Navy or Air Force. I didn't have any knowledge of the military system at all. My father warned me not to volunteer for anything so I didn't. When asked about going on OTC (Officer Training Courses) or whether I wanted to be an NCO or a WO or any of that stuff I just said 'no'. I should have asked what it meant but I didn't. The rumour was that whatever you volunteered for would be ignored. Not only that, but the famous joke based on truth was that you would be sent to the entirely opposite type of service you proposed. It was all part of the early 'break-down' procedure that was to turn us young boys into brainwashed recruits, so I waited for the date of my departure to be confirmed and details of where they would send me.

By now I had been working on pay systems so I expected to go into the Pay Corps. They put me in the infantry. I was to join the Yorkshire Regiment, The Green Howards. 'Collection' day, Thursday, 7 February 1957, was an unhappy day as I prepared to leave family, friends and home behind to become part of Intake 5703, whatever that was. Worst of all, I had to abandon all my beloved magic equipment and books. My props were gone and I was on my own again. Little did I realise that once in training, I wouldn't have enough time to go to the toilet, let alone perform.

As I piled on to the train, along with 100 other pasty youths, I looked at Mam trying not to cry. Dad's voice was ringing in my ears, 'there are some things in life that you can do something about and some things you can't. Don't waste your time worrying about the things you can do nowt about.' As the train pulled away, I surrendered myself to the next 24 months and it was a good job that I didn't realise then just how tough it was going to be.

I suppose I should have had some idea of what lay in store after arriving at our destination and being quickly pushed into the back of an old, green army wagon. We rattled, banged and swerved our way up the steep incline of Richmond Hill, bruising each other's arms as we did so. I am sure that the Army specially designed the open-backed truck, so that, as it travels along, it sucks the exhaust fumes into the back, making all the occupants extremely nauseous. It was winter and extremely cold, so by the time we arrived at the barracks in Richmond, Yorkshire, we all had heads spinning, stomachs churning and teeth chattering.

This was just the condition that the Sergeant Major required. No sooner had the truck stopped, than the pins at the back were removed, the metal flap banged down against the truck and a terrific roar filled our ears:

'GET OUT OF THAT TRUCK THIS INSTANT, YOU 'ORRIBLE LOAD OF PANSIES!'

There had been no preparation at all for what were to become some of the hardest days of my young life. As the voice continued to shout at us, I wondered where on earth I was.

'GET YOUR FEET DOWN 'ERE, YOU 'ORRIBLE LITTLE MEN!' I noticed that no matter how tall you happened to be, you were still an ''orrible little man'.

We were pushed and shoved into some sort of line before the next command thundered forth:

'LEFT TURN!' came the scream, only to be followed by a complete scramble of panicking youths, uncertain at which was the left or the right way to go. After a few bumps we somehow fell into the rattling rhythm of 'LEFT, RIGHT, LEFT, RIGHT...' fired off in such quick succession, that none of us could keep up.

We were led to a freezing cold, concrete barracks with rows of beds stationed along the side of each wall. It's OK if you have been brought up to share a bedroom with a lot of other men, but I hadn't. Neither had most of the others, I guess. The shock of all that I was experiencing began to sink in and I didn't like it. As I sat on my allocated bed, it hardly gave way under my weight. The thin mattress sat on a metal tubular frame and wire base, covered with several sheets and blankets.

Without a moment to think, the voice screamed again and we were ordered into another room to collect our kit. None of this fitted, of course, which was all part of the plan. One pair of boots was issued for parades and the other for work.

Twenty minutes later, Private Daniels 23370053 stood to attention. What a wreck. Did England really think I could defend it? I was now part of the elite Green Howards Regiment. Well, they were elite until I joined them.

Learning the history of this regiment was a first priority. Apparently, the Green Howards got their name when, long ago, regiments were named after their commanding officer. In the British Army at the time, there were two 'Howards' families – one wore buff colours and the other green, thus creating the name, the 'Green Howards'.

'NOW THAT YOU ARE IN THE BRITISH ARMY,' the Sergeant Major blasted (they never talked), 'YOU WILL BE TRAINED TO OBEY A COMMAND WITHOUT QUESTION. WHEN YOU ARE GIVEN AN ORDER, YOU WILL NOT THINK, YOU WILL JUST MOVE.' Somewhere inside me, the little boy who had questioned the accuracy of his teachers was saying, 'I will believe this when I see it.' I soon saw it. The next eight weeks introduced me to the most horrendous military conditions I could ever have imagined as we began our basic training.

From the moment I was shouted out of bed at 5.00am to the last seconds of climbing into bed, I was active. If not on parade, I was cleaning something, shooting something, learning something. I became a natural marksman on all the weapons, perhaps because of my hand-to-eye coordination. I put no real effort into learning this; I just understood the logical mathematics of the techniques. There was no time to be lonely, to be homesick or grieve over lost magic. There was simply no time for feelings of any kind and barely the space to write home at the end of an exhausting day when I would collapse into bed and be asleep within seconds.

We buffed and polished and did keep fit and marched and drilled with rifles in a non-stop, high-speed way, day in and day out. For one hour every evening we would sit on the hard floor of the barrack room, backs against the wall and polish our parade boots. Polishing your boots was an art form. You used a lit candle, a spoon, a lot of spit, a duster and boot polish, of course. Army boots come covered in little bumps. Using the heated spoon you had to iron the bumps flat on the front toe cap and on the heel section. This took for ever. Then you burnt the polish into the leather again using the heated spoon. Then you spit and polished. Over and over again. You could get shaved in the reflection of those boots. This time each evening was called Shining Hour. When I wrote home and mentioned this, Mam thought we were having Sunday School lessons again. I wished!

The second weekend we were told that we were allowed visitors, but they also decided to give us our 'jabs' at the same time. As I took my place in the long line of men, I could see two army doctors standing on either side of the queue. When each man passed, both doctors would inject needles into the man's arms at the same time. As I made my way to the front of the line, I kept my eyes firmly ahead so as to avoid the sight of needles simultaneously piercing my skin. Several of the lads had already passed out and I didn't want to succumb to any possibility of needle phobia.

The pain was acute and some suggested that the Army filed down the ends of the needles deliberately, so I was proud to have emerged from the ordeal without disgracing myself. As I was leaving, I overhead one of the nursing staff state that the pay books, in which all the inoculations were recorded, had not been collected. I offered to collect them, went next door and did so. I turned to come back and fell unconscious to the floor. Remember, I could have been defending you in times of trouble!

Waking up in my metal bunk, the room was swimming, but I knew immediately where I was. I felt like, and apparently looked like, death. The NCOs hauled me up into a sitting position and I was handed my boots together with a lit candle, a spoon and some polish. Understanding the order was one thing, carrying it out was quite another, as my arms had engorged and looked like balloons. Nothing but nothing matters in the infantry like the shine on those boots.

In the middle of all this: 'GET UP, DANIELS! YOUR MOTHER'S 'ERE, YOU NAMBY PAMBY LITTLE MUMMY'S BOY!'

My parents had arrived at the camp to collect my civilian clothes. Poor Mam took one look at me and burst into tears. 'What have they done to you?' she sobbed.

Dad thought it all hilarious. Thanks, Dad. I remained ill for the next few days, but I was still expected to continue training. Sick leave was definitely not on the agenda.

The grilling and drilling made one day merge into another

and for some it was too much to cope with. There was only one way out of National Service – pretend you were mad. Several of the chaps tried this, but no one ever succeeded. When one guy was ordered to 'Blanco' his kit, he used it as an opportunity to 'prove' his insanity. Blanco was a sticky, paste-like substance used to provide a waterproof covering on the surface of our belts, gaiters and straps of our uniform, which, once applied, dried to a greeny/brown polish. The lad got hold of several tins and Blanco'd not only his kit, but his bed, blankets and his locker in his dormitory. When the officers were greeted with the extraordinary sight of what he had done, the poor lad started jumping up and down on his bed as if he had flipped. Being used to this type of con, it was the officers who flipped and the lad was sent back to the start of his basic training, where he stayed for a very long time.

There seemed no end to what lads would do to try and get out. We had one man who went home for the weekend on leave and shot his trigger finger off, thinking the Army would dismiss him. They merely moved him back a couple of training sessions and taught him to shoot with his middle finger.

Not all of our platoon was from Yorkshire. One of the lads came from the heart of the Black Country in the Midlands and I felt sorry for him because he could not make himself understood. His accent was so thick and we had to spend a long time training him to speak our version of English. He couldn't read or write either, so I used to read his girlfriend's letters to him and write letters back to her in his name. Her letters were better than my dad's book, I can tell you that.

'Jankers' was the term for serious punishment that would consist of extra-hard duties that would make you feel you had indeed died and gone to hell. I was hauled in front of the officer in charge on many occasions and given three days and, in one case, seven days 'Jankers'. My transgression was a dirty rifle barrel.

I had been shown how to clean my rifle with a piece of lightly oiled lint attached to a cord, which was then passed through the barrel. The inside of this was 'rifled', containing a groove, which spun the bullet and made it more accurate. Opening the breach, you would put your thumb in it when commanded during an inspection. The officer would come along and look down the barrel at the light reflected up the barrel off your thumb. According to the officer, if your thumb was dirty, your rifle was dirty and it would be three days 'Jankers'.

I cleaned toilets and scrubbed floors before the sun rose and painted white lines after all my colleagues were in bed. It was possible that you would be ordered to march up and down the parade ground by yourself for several hours at a time in the middle of the night. If the tasks set before you were not dealt with in the most efficient manner, your 'Jankers' could be extended to any length of time seen fit.

On one occasion, the Sergeant Major inspected our dormitory toilet block, entered our barrack room during Shining Hour and marched slowly up and down.

'I HAVE FOUND A FLECK OF BROWN ON A URINAL STAND.' Actually what it sounded like was 'HI 'AVE FOUND HAY *FLECK* OF BURROWN ON HAY YOURAINAL STAND...'

He went on, savouring his discovery and the impending doom he would unleash on someone. 'IT IS AT LEAST ONE-EIGHTH OF AN INCH LONG AND A SIXTEENTH OF AN INCH WIDE. WHICH OF YOU PATHETIC CREATURES WAS SUPPOSED TO HAVE CLEANED THE TOILETS?'

One of the lads, I think he was called Tut Brett, continued concentrating on polishing his boots as he came out with, 'I was, Sarge.' The Sergeant moved in front of the sitting soldier and bent over at the waist to address him. We all kept very quiet.

'WELL, IT IS PAINFULLY HOBVIOUS THAT YOU HAVE FAILED IN YOUR DUTIES, 'AVEN'T YOU?'

The reply was either unbelievably stupid or amazingly brave, I'm still not sure. Again, without looking up and continuing to polish: 'Well now, Sarge,' spit, polish, 'the thing is,' spit, polish, 'I look at it this way. I'm going to piss in it, not eat out of it.'

They picked him up, dragged him off and we never saw him for another week.

Gym was far removed from anything I had experienced in a school PE lesson. The leather vaulting horse was enormous. Each one of the new recruits had to run forward at speed, jump on the spring-board placing two hands on the top of the horse, and do the splits over the top before landing on the other side, hopefully with hands in the air. The whole episode was carefully choreographed as the officer shouted the commands to keep us equidistant. Unfortunately, the boy behind me over-anticipated his cue and ran forward too early, hitting his head against my back just as I reached the top of the wooden horse. I'm not very lucky with vaulting horses. As I fell forwards with the impact, it twisted my right hand over on itself and, unbeknown to me, dislocated the joints in my fingers. In the Army, however, you just keep going and, despite the agony, I scrambled out of my gym gear into battle-dress in readiness for drill parade.

With the PE trainer's shouts of 'You bloody idiots' following us on to the parade ground, we assembled in a strict line as quickly as possible. Standing at ease, with feet apart and rifles angled forward, we waited for the Sergeant Major's bellowed orders.

'ATTENTION!' was the signal to bring the left foot up and down hard next to your right followed by the rifle coming upright.

'SLOPE ARMS!' meant lifting your rifle with your right

hand whilst your left arm supports it. My right hand came up, but the rifle fell forward, committing one of the worst crimes known in the Army. I had dropped my rifle.

The officer stared in disbelief at my sin and, as he made his way slowly towards me, I glanced down at my hand. It had swollen up like a balloon and was incapable of holding a toothpick, let alone a rifle. I showed my predicament to the officer who was now staring me straight in the eye. With little sympathy, he ordered me off the parade ground to the medics who drove me straight to the local hospital, several miles away and my hand was put into a splint for several weeks. It wasn't the pain, the shock, or the lack of compassion that upset me; it was the fear of having my hand damaged to the point where I could no longer perform my magic.

Assigned to lesser details back at camp, I noticed that the pain and discomfort of my hand was not subsiding. I really panicked when they took all the dressings off. Why don't they tell you your body wrinkles up and gets dirty inside plaster? What a shock that was. After a few hours I went back to my normal shade of light pink and my skin straightened out. The problem was that my knuckles were still swollen and wouldn't bend. The Army gave me a weekend pass as compensation.

I was back home, but really anxious. Looking at the swelling and bruising, I was pretty sure that I might lose the use of my hand. I was normally good at being able to control any fear that engulfed me, but now I was truly frightened. Willing to try anything to save my hand, I decided to see a local osteopath. Considered a 'quack' at the time, this kindly but authoritative man asked me to show him my hand. The knuckles were still all swollen and I couldn't bend any of them. He seemed to be holding it gently. I woke up on the couch. Apparently he had pulled them all back into position and my brain decided that I shouldn't be there while he did it.

'ORRIBLE LITTLE MEN

He must have relocated the bones in my hand back into their rightful sockets. Within 24 hours, I had made a full recovery and was back at the army base able to do everything within a couple of days. Although my right-hand knuckle was to remain bigger than my left for the rest of my days, I was extremely grateful that my fears of never performing again were unfounded.

In the ninth week, we were awoken at 5.00am to prepare for a set of exercises. Marching up the several miles of Richmond Hill, one of the steepest inclines in the country, we marched down the other side and through a river. All day we repeated this route at the height of the Yorkshire winter. That evening, the company slept in the open on the bare, freezing ground, before being woken up for night exercises.

Before allowing the time and space for a moment's kip, the Army had served up 'bad' stew. Surprisingly, the food was not as bad as I had expected, with chips served at most meals and even once at breakfast. The rest was average stodge, apart from on Christmas Day when it was brilliant. How the army cooks managed to switch from school dinners to French cuisine overnight I shall never know.

On exercises it was quite different and I chose not to eat the mess they were serving. I was the only one who did not get the 'squirts'. Despite the pain and the agony of where we were, the difficulties of diarrhoea provided much humour and relief in the darkness of the countryside. When a flare went off, lighting up the ground below, all that could be seen was a row of bright white arses squatting in the hedge. The thought of camouflaging backsides had not been considered.

The exercise was called off and we were led into a barn where we were lectured on how stupid we had been. What happened that night could well have occurred in warfare, we were told. The men who had suffered from diarrhoea had given away their position, not only by the reflection of the flare on their white arses, but also (can you believe that an officer of the British Army would point this out?) by the rustling of leaves as they cleaned themselves off.

It was difficult for any of us to keep a straight face, as the unbelievable scenario was unfolded before us. Even more astounding was the young squaddie who stood up and announced that he had indeed thought this problem through:

'Sir! I gave this some consideration, Sir!'

'Go ahead Jenkins!'

'Sir! I did not use paper, Sir! I used my regulation handkerchief, Sir!'

As he spoke, from his pocket he pulled out a filthy brown slip of material that at one time had been used to wipe the opposite end of his body, to which he was now referring. The men either side of him fled and the rest of us were left in hysterics.

We were not let off the hook, however, and the following night the exercise was repeated with the task of capturing or defending a set of lamps strategically placed in difficult areas of the North Yorkshire moors. Sitting in the pitch-blackness of a dugout, I couldn't control a single part of my body. I don't think that I have ever been so cold since that night. My teeth were hammering together, my rifle was shaking and I couldn't stop it because I was so cold and wet. It felt like my uniform had been frozen to my body. I was jabbering.

I heard a noise behind me as a sergeant slithered down into my pit and ordered me to go and get the lamp. Instantly I jumped up, crawled over the lip of my hideout and crawled on my belly towards the light. As I approached my goal, I remembered what had been said on the first day about obeying orders without thought. That, I believe, is why the British Army was the best and most powerful in the world. I had gone from being a frozen wreck into a non-shivering, smooth-moving soldier at one command.

A few days later, part of the testing process was running a mile in full kit carrying your rifle. I was the first one over the line. Damn right I was. Was I the fittest? Was I the best trained? Nope, I was just more scared of the Sergeant than anyone else. Damn right I was.

Apart from the obvious asset of National Service for the country, there was a secondary benefit. It turned boys into men. It made us fitter than at any other time in our lives. Any 17-year-olds will argue that they are already men, but they are not. This process takes time to build competence and to gain the knowledge and experience to tackle anything in life.

Those weeks of training turned out to be the most demanding, yet productive, time of all. They laid a grounding that was worth more than any money and gave me a firm foundation to stand on in difficult years to come. I *know* I sound like an old man when I say today's youth has lost its focus and value in life and I would like to see National Service back on the agenda because it would change bad attitudes in a radically quick way. The only thing is that I don't believe we should bring back National Service as it was.

I shared my thoughts at a recent dinner party at which several top politicians were invited. I explained my reasoning and showed how it could be done in a different and possibly more beneficial way. Sadly, teachers have had all their powers of discipline and control removed by a politically correct society. Pupils have no fear of, or respect for, their elders, so they can choose to run wild if they wish and no one can control them. The 12 months of training would be for girls and boys, placing 'townies' in country environments and vice versa. They should not be trained to fire a weapon, but instead go through all the drilling and the spit and polish that we went through, alongside learning the art of survival and aspects of advanced first aid. Being shown how to react in any form of emergency situation such as a car accident or a fire, they would learn what the human being is perfectly capable of achieving. After a year learning how to save a life, it would be very difficult to go out and 'mug' or knife somebody. Young people would be of great use and value to the society in which they live.

The politicians thought it would be an excellent scheme, but would be a political bombshell. Did this mean they weren't really in the job for the benefit of society as a whole, I enquired? My question was met with a dry smile and a forced laugh. It took me a long time to realise that politicians are not in the job for the good of the country.

I do not agree with the arguments allowing women in the same regiments as men. I am certainly a fighter for women's equality, but I do not think that mixed companies are a good thing. Neither do I believe in allowing homosexuals into the Army. It has nothing to do with being anti-women or anti-homosexual, because I'm not. It is simply the vital need for that command to be obeyed without question. If I am in love with the person next to me and we are instructed to go over the top, I might feel compelled to resist if my partner was in danger of getting hurt. Love is a more powerful instinct than any amount of training, but it could get in the way of winning a war.

As a result of military training, I watched as a shoddy group of guys from all walks of life became self-disciplined and controlled. Thickos and geniuses, boffins and brickies, rich and poor were turned into confident people who were fitter than they had ever been in their lives.

As I said, not everybody was from Yorkshire and at a time of little transport, we were able to hear tales about life in Wales, Scotland and Birmingham. We sorry bunch of stragglers had become a much more likely fighting force and as we marched into the local town after our night exercises, we felt like real men.

Something else happened almost without us noticing it. We

developed great pride in being Green Howards. Towards the end of the training, we went on a long march. We were tired as hell when we reached the bottom of that damn hill up to the barracks. When the band of the Green Howards struck up to greet us with the Regimental March as we turned the corner, it was amazing. Our shoulders went back, our chests went out and we just about flew up the hill. I am convinced that it was the rousing sound of the military band playing our march that enabled us to conquer the steepness of Richmond Hill that day.

My platoon was going abroad to Hong Kong. I went off to training with one other soldier from our Regiment, Peter Schollick. We stayed on in England to train as army clerks and were sent down to Chichester. It was there that I was shown how to touch-type and work with Queen's Regulations in two weeks. The Army had a great system for teaching typing and it was the best and most useful thing that the Army ever taught me.

With the little extra freedom we now had, my mate Peter and I discovered that the local girls had not heard of the Green Howards. We told them that we were trained jungle fighters and that is why we were called 'green'. We could instantly melt into any tropical forest. Well, of course we could. To our amazement, they believed us. How they imagined this was true of the two pasty-faced Yorkshire youths who had never been abroad in their lives I shall never know, but they did.

Maybe we lost credibility about our 'toughness' when I happily agreed to try the local cider. Having been a Northern lad, I was not used to the strength of the West Country's scrumpy. After only one pint it felt like my head was leaving my shoulders and I relied on the generosity of my friends to carry me home.

We left the course as qualified clerks, were given a week's leave and told we were going to Hong Kong.

CHAPTER 5

HONG KONG

Although women's liberation had begun its long journey 50 years previously with Emily Pankhurst, the late Fifties began to give rise to the modern female. Seventeen-year-old Marilyn Bell was the youngest person to swim the Channel and US tennis star Althea Gibson was the first black female to win Wimbledon. As the Barbie doll began mass production, screen goddess Brigitte Bardot shocked America with her sensual role in the Hollywood film And God Created Woman, while Marilyn Monroe's poster showing her skirt rising up her legs advertising The Seven Year Itch was banned in New York.

Let me go back in time a little. Throughout my time at Eston Urban District Council I had dreamed of girls as well as magic tricks. I had dated but it never went much beyond kissing. Since time began man has constantly tried to get woman into bed, or on a grassy knoll. I'm not sure that I would have known what to do in either case. I had read about it and talked about it with my mates, but when it came to the real thing it was still a frightening prospect. I could easily chat up the opposite sex; it was taking it to the next stage that seemed to elude me. I had a strong hunch that my colleagues boasted about escapades that were based more in their minds than in reality. Men, gathering in groups, have always claimed more than they have ever done. If we were to put a tax on sex, maybe we wouldn't collect as much as we think we would, I thought then.

In an age when the 'pill' was unavailable and the female revolution in its infancy, sex was indeed a very risky business. Pauline had come and gone, as had my dreams of Irene. I had met a nice girl on a trip to Luxembourg but I didn't want to know her when I got home again. Margaret Dawkins had been nothing more than a magician's assistant to me and finished up marrying another friend, Don Freary. On the other hand, Avril was somehow special. I'm not sure where we met, maybe at the college I went to in preparation for accountancy in Middlesbrough, but I fell in love with the pretty blonde sufficiently to become engaged just before I joined the Army. Inviting me round to her house one evening, she deployed all those tactics women use to lead us lads astray. Well, maybe not astray, but to pop that question. What an innocent I was. Playing a record announcing it was dedicated to me, called 'Mr Wonderful', it was all too much for me and I dived in with a proposal. We nearly had sex but didn't because the awareness of having to go away for two years was stronger than my desires. The last thing I wanted was to get this girl pregnant just before I marched off. Sex could wait, I thought, but sadly Avril didn't. By the time I returned from the Army, she was in another man's arms.

So I sailed for Hong Kong in July 1957 on the *Empire Fowey* still a pale-faced virgin. Hundreds of soldiers were on board heading for the Far East. There was a lot of discussion as to whether we were going around South Africa. If we did, we would visit Cape Town and legends had drifted back to the barracks about the incredible hospitality shown to British troops passing through.

Some of the lads on board were seasick while we were still tied up waiting to sail, and as we cleared Southampton Water, the ship started to rock and roll. Heading for the Bay of Biscay, more and more men started to head for the 'head'. This 28-day journey to Hong Kong was not going to be a luxury cruise. I was fine, not even queasy, until I needed to go to the 'head' for normal purposes.

The 'head' is nautical terminology for the toilets, located at the front, or 'head' of the ship. They were originally round holes cut out of the overhanging deck, positioned there since early Navy days. The British Navy had come on a long way since Trafalgar and it was once inside the 'head' I discovered that the Forces think of everything. Bolted alongside the walls of the latrines were metal troughs expressly for the purpose of vomiting in. A long metal rail ran the full length of this over the centre and was fixed at the perfect height for the men to hold on to and lean over as they brought up their insides. The sight of the deep steel canal filled to capacity with what seemed like the biggest collection of warm vegetable soup was too much to bear. As the ship rolled so the stuff sluiced one way and then the other. One whiff of the disgusting stench and I swiftly joined the row upon row of my colleagues at the 'bar'. By the end of the day, my stomach was still 'on fire' because there was nothing left in it and yet I was still retching. When you are seasick you pray for an early death.

It turned out that we were to be the first ship through the Suez Canal after the recent Suez crisis in which Colonel Nasser had seized control of the thin strip of water that ran through his country. This waterway was an essential oil supply route for Europe and fortunately urgent diplomatic efforts short-circuited the seriousness of the situation. It cut our journey by weeks but we missed out on seeing Cape Town.

It didn't matter. My Northern eyes saw sights that were hard to believe. From the Mediterranean and into the Red Sea, out into the Indian Ocean and across into the Pacific – it may all sound glamorous and, at times, the sight of the ship cutting through the glass-flat water was a spectacle, but the Army still held drills and shooting practice and all that jazz. Arriving in the Suez Canal provided its own entertainment with 'bumboats' crowding around the ship trying to sell souvenirs. I guess the closing of the canal had hit their business hard. Negotiations were made by shouting down the side of the ship and baskets were lowered on ropes to raise and lower the goods and the money. A failed deal, or even a bad deal, resulted in the locals mooning us. Maybe that's where the name of their boats comes from.

On our journey through the canal we could see Russian MiG fighters standing on the horizon. We considered them a threat until I looked at them through a telephoto lens and I could see quite clearly that they had no engines in them.

The *gulli-gulli* man came on board at Suez. This character was an eastern magician who was allowed on board to entertain the troops and hoped to receive something in reward. It turned out that there are a lot of *gulli-gulli* men. The funniest thing was, that having looked forward to seeing this master of oriental trickery, I was surprised to noticed that all his props were from a magic dealer in London! Davenports, the magician's paradise, was renowned throughout the world, I knew, but this seemed too far-fetched.

He had other exceptional examples, however, that were simply wonderful, including performing the cups and balls routine with tiny live chicks. Having arrived with several eggs, which he carefully placed in the heat of the ship's engine room, by the time we had sailed down to the end of the canal, the chickens were hatched and our mystic conjuror had his props! He was an extremely adept performer and made such an impression upon me, that I was to use this classic effect to open my act for years to come – minus the chickens, of course!

Borrowing a coin he would immediately throw it overboard and after pronouncing his magic words: 'Gulli-gulli, gulli-gulli,' he would ask the spectator to look in his pocket, whereupon the same coin was produced.

When the *gulli-gulli* man, nicknamed after the magic word he used, left the ship at the next port, he would take the chickens with him and sell them at a profit, to buy more eggs. Apparently, he ship-hopped in this way all year round.

All in all, I didn't think he was particularly brilliant, but my shipmates did. It was then that I realised the benefit of a foreign accent: if he'd been British, he would have been booed off. Later in life, I was to meet quite a few *gulli-gulli* men and some of them are extraordinarily good at the art of magic.

The sleeping arrangements on board were interesting. The lower decks were filled with rows of upright poles that supported three bunks on each side one above the other, six in all, but the rows went on for ever. How many men were on our ship, I couldn't imagine, but there were hundreds, possibly thousands, from all the differing regiments and corps of the Army. All I knew was that you really didn't want to be in the bottom bunks during the time people were getting used to the sea.

Amazingly, as I made my tour around the Navy's pride and joy, I came across another magician. He was also experienced in hypnosis and was able to cure my seasickness problem almost instantly. Hypnosis is a combination of voice and rhythm, but you need a quiet room for it to take effect. All we could find on board this heaving hulk was a shower cabinet. As I sat in there, hoping the showerhead wouldn't drip on me, I let myself relax under the calming influence of my new friend. Having read up on the subject, I realised there were many different levels of hypnotic states. I had no fear as the technique really involved self-hypnosis, realising it was often a case of needing a voice to guide you along. I also knew I had reserved, in spaces in my mind, the right to refuse what he would suggest to me. For the chance that this awful condition could be removed from me, I was more than happy to 'let go'.

I could hear his gentle voice drifting into the background of my mind, but I was awake the whole time. He finished with a smile and I apologised saying that it hadn't worked for me. 'But you're not feeling sick any more, are you?' he enquired. I agreed with a 'Wow!' and from that moment enjoyed every minute of our four-week voyage.

Chatting afterwards, I found out that he was a manipulator and an expert with cards, coins, balls and cigarettes. He could make them appear from the most impossible places and I'm sure if he was completely nude and in a glass fish tank, somehow he would have been able to produce a set of billiard balls. He was also in the medical corps, where I felt his magic skills would probably come in quite handy.

The performance of our various skills became invaluable tools on the long haul across the ocean. Any magician should be able to work without proper equipment and be able to entertain using the things that surround him. A pack of cards was always available and is probably why so many tricks have been devised using this common 'toy'.

Pocket Magic, as it was called, was my forte so I was in my element on board ship, as we astonished crewmen with the many effects we created. I thought he was a brilliant magician but he performed in the then quite common style of being very serious during the act. It was probable that my friend had been brought up in an age where this type of magic was akin to a juggling act. Manipulators would even reveal how the effects were done because the dexterity in performing them was greater than the trick itself.

Despite his excellent abilities, he had respect for me, too. Strangely enough, these impromptu shows were an essential ingredient in laying the foundations for future presentation techniques. Although I was obviously not as skilful as my magic partner, it was the comedy and my enjoyment of what I was doing that brought what I did to life. As a result, there was a strong awareness that the audiences on-board ship liked my magic better. I couldn't understand this at the time, but later I was to have a greater appreciation of the power of laughter.

Nevertheless, there was a surprising interest on board and word of my own performances must have got around for I was soon summoned to appear at a party in the Officers' Mess. It was an early taste of a sort of on-board Royal Command Performance, for none of the other soldiers were allowed in these quarters. Not keen to disobey an order, or miss an opportunity, I prepared as best I could for the evening's work ahead.

The Officers' Mess was luxurious compared to the grey metal surroundings that the rest of us had. I began by presenting an adaptation of the *gulli-gulli* man's coin trick, which I had logically thought through that day, point by point, eventually making it more baffling. Again, but without deliberately heading for it, comedy was an important element, as I borrowed a coin and had it marked by pencil. Another officer chose a card, which was again marked, this time with his name. Me being me, I then gave the coin, which had been wrapped in the card, to the Padre. We had both a Roman Catholic and a Church of England Padre on board, and I asked them to take the coin and card and throw them overboard.

'Would you please go together,' I joked, 'as I know you don't trust each other!' and got my first laugh. Just before they left through the door, I asked them to check the card and coin, which were deemed to be correct. Upon their return I even got the pair to swear on the Bible that they had indeed thrown the whole package overboard. When we opened the Bible, there was the card and the coin inside. The night wore on with me doing impromptu magic around the Mess.

Next day, I woke up at three o'clock in the afternoon with a head that thumped like *HMS Victory's* cannon and a very furry tongue. An officer passed by, saw me and said, 'Daniels, you're a bastard.' Despite my pounding head and very unsteady feet I knew the correct military response. 'Yes, Sir. I'm a bastard, Sir.'

'On the other hand, you were quite amazing. Quite brilliant,' he went on.

This I didn't agree to because I hadn't a clue what he was going on about.

'Sorry, Sir, I've got a headache.'

'I'm not surprised, boy, the amount you drank last night emptied our bar! You said you didn't want any. You said you didn't drink but we commanded you. We had a plan you see. We had decided to get you totally pissed, so that we would see how you did it all. The frustrating thing was that the more pissed you became, the more baffling you were.'

'Sorry, Sir.'

My dulled and throbbing mind could not remember much of what I had done. The officer gladly went on to remind me in detail.

'Finally, you amazed us all by having a card chosen, replacing it in the pack and then you threw the whole pack at one of the porthole windows. Damn me if the chosen card was there, stuck to the window. On the outside! That's when you said, "Sort that one out, you bastards," and passed out. We had you put to bed.'

As the previous night's antics slowly returned to my brain, his final words hit me like a blow to the stomach, when I realised what I had done. As the officer walked away, I looked over the side and felt my face turn white. There is no such thing as magic, only acting, and at some point in the evening I must have stuck the card on the outside, but when and how I couldn't remember.

As I leant over the bubbling water below, I could see a painter's hammock suspended over the side from one of the davits. I realised that during the evening, I must have gone to the toilet and seen the hammock that gave birth to the idea. Horrified, I imagined how in the pitch darkness I must have climbed down the ropes as the ship cut through the Indian Ocean and stuck a duplicate card on the outside of the Mess window. It had obviously made a big impression on the officers, but it made a bigger one on me when I remembered that I couldn't swim! The thought that I could so easily have been swept overboard in the blackness stopped me drinking for the next 20 years.

My magical friend laughed uproariously when I told him what had happened and we continued to swap ideas and tricks. He taught me how to do a classic coin roll, in which a coin is manipulated across the back of the hand with the fingers acting like a conveyor belt. Juggling a coin from your thumb to small finger is a very difficult task to achieve, but I was determined to master it before we arrived at port.

As the ship continued on its way to Hong Kong, my magician friend got off at Singapore and I never saw him again. I wonder if he is still doing magic? The coin roll eluded me for most of the way. I just kept dropping the coin. I had to find a way to increase my concentration and I did. I stuck my hand over the side. Two shillings and sixpence, the value of the half crown coin, is a lot of money when you are a soldier on a total of 17 shillings and sixpence a week. As I practised with my hand projecting over the rail, I was amazed at the increase in my concentration. All the way to Hong Kong, I only dropped it twice and, by the time we docked, I had it mastered.

As the boat pulled into the enormous harbour I got my first

taste of the colony. This place was beyond anybody's wildest dreams. The port churned with activity. Hundreds of ships, big and small, were constantly on the move. *San-pans* were tied up in their hundreds, as well as plying their trade to and from Hong Kong island to the mainland. I was told that there were people who had been born on those tiny boats, lived on them and finally died on them without ever setting foot on dry land.

One of Hong Kong's unique fascinations was the seamless way in which ancient traditions still thrived, even after 150 years of British colonial influence had been woven into 5,000 years of Chinese culture. Adventures to more than 260 remote islands, breathtaking hikes over rolling green hills to stunning white beaches and treks to charming Chinese fishing villages beckoned. Sadly, I had to pinch myself through my uniform to remind me of the fact that I was not on holiday.

The heat was the first thing that struck me as we disembarked. Already, one guy had been flown back home with severe sunburn. He had inadvertently fallen asleep on deck and had suffered 30-degree burns. The poor red-headed lad looked like one huge blister and it was the best warning we could have had against the effects of the sun.

The first advert I saw on dry land was for a shop called the 'Wan-key' and wondered if they had known about the frustrations of being on-board ship for a month. I was soon to find out that sex was just about the number-one commodity in this area.

We were marched to a waiting truck, which took us across this most beautiful island, to the fine-looking garrison of Fort Stanley. Hong Kong was the most awesome and colourful place I had ever seen, with its bright lights and garish reds and golds and the girls wearing their *cheongsam* dresses split almost to the waist – I was constantly having to push my eyeballs back in.

We had hardly settled into our new barracks before a crowd

of soldiers were around us asking us about Blighty and the weather and any news. As usual, I pulled out a pack of cards and started playing with them on the bed. One of the lads who had travelled over with me asked me to do a trick and others soon gathered around to watch. One very flash cockney lad, I have no idea what he was doing in a Yorkshire Regiment, kept shouting out things like, 'I know how you do that! I know how you do that!'

I ignored him but he became more and more of a nuisance. Best way with a nuisance, involve him in a trick. I let him shuffle the cards, take one, show it to someone else in case he forgot it, put it back and shuffle them again. He agreed that I couldn't find his card.

I placed the whole pack face down on the bed. 'Now I am going to deal the cards on to the bed. As I take them off the top of the deck, I shall place them face up on the blanket. Just watch carefully and when you see your card think of the word "Stop", but don't say it out loud, just *think* it.'

I started to deal the cards face up on the bed until I hesitated with a face down card in my hand.

'The next card I turn over will be your card,' I announced.

'I bet you it won't,' he grinned.

'If it's a bet, then how much?'

'One hundred dollars?' he offered.

I didn't have $100. I didn't have ten! I could not afford to lose and wondered if I should accept the deal. Fortunately, a crowd of squaddies whom I knew declared their backing for me and they seemed to dislike this guy.

With the offer of being covered by my mates and knowing that I could not fail, I made sure of the bet. I even knew that the lad had already seen his card go past.

'For one hundred dollars, you are on that the next card I turn over is yours?' I asked.

'Sure thing,' he smiled.

With that, I put the card in my hand back on top of the deck still face down and took his card from the face-up pile and turned it face down. He never bothered me again.

Life started to roll along in Stanley Fort. I got a job in the office of Headquarter Company directly below my barrack room. This was the first time in my life I put weight on. We had chips with every meal, including breakfast. Those cooks knew what to feed Yorkshiremen. The snacks were also wonderful, made from the softest bread rolls that I have ever tasted, along with the best cups of tea that I have ever had. The *cha-wallah* served them on the balconies of the barracks. His cheese and tomato 'banjos' (the name for the bread rolls) were fabulous. The tea was kept in an urn that had the tea, the sugar and the milk all mixed up inside and constantly heated at the base. I don't know why it never tasted stewed. There were quite a few *cha-wallahs* all working for an Indian.

Apparently, back in England this Indian man had arrived at Richmond barracks one day and asked to see the officer in charge. In that wonderfully fruity, sing-song voice he explained how he was used to organising the *cha-wallahs* and *jadu-wallahs*, providing the food and laundry services for the Army, and could he please have the concession for Hong Kong.

'But we are not going to Hong Kong,' replied the officer, who had just had his regiment fitted with the gleaming white 'topes' uniform of the Bahamas.

'I believe you are, Sir,' smiled the astute businessman.

'I can assure you, my man, that we are not departing for Hong Kong. I'm sorry.'

'Well then, Sir, may I ask for the concession just in case you do go to Stanley Fort in Hong Kong?'

'Of course, if you insist, you bloody fool.' The officer, having already received his orders to sail to Bermuda within a couple of weeks, happily agreed to sign the Indian's document, probably just to get rid of him.

As the Indian entrepreneur walked out through the barrack gates, a motorbike dispatch rider passed him carrying an urgent, top-secret message for the Commanding Officer. The orders contained the command that the regiment would now be going to Hong Kong. 'Stop that Indian!' screamed the officer.

The little man was hauled back before the commander and asked to explain himself. How had he got access to top-secret information that even the Commanding Officer knew nothing about?

'It's easy, Sir,' came the gentle reply. 'May I show you?'
The Indian walked behind the desk and directed their attention at the huge world map that was displayed along the wall. He pointed out all the previous tours of the British Army and said where each regiment and corps had been over the last ten years. Summarising a complex set of patterns he finished by saying, 'so, by simple deduction, Sir, it's obvious that the only place you are going to would be Hong Kong.' He won his concession and made complete nonsense out of top-secret information.

I don't think that I will be breaking the Official Secrets Act if I tell you a little about how the Army is organised. I've always admired the army clerical system and with the inside information gained from my stint in Chichester, had a useful general knowledge of the workings of the military. The Army is run by Queen's Regulations known as 'QRs' which contains the ruling orders for the services. This single book covers every peacetime and wartime eventuality and is altered practically every day by the War Office to become a 'living' set of rules. As part of my clerical exam, I had to find the correct answers to a series of questions within the allotted time, using the latest set of QRs. It's a wonderful system, because although I was very familiar with its rules, they could easily have been changed in some way without my knowledge. It is never wise to assume you know and I realised how important it was to keep up to date with the latest directive. We always checked the book and the skill was in being able to find the correct law quickly and easily. The officers of the British Army never stop training and even a colonel is still prepared to learn new skills.

News of my magical ability had been picked up once again, this time by the locals. How they found out I have no idea; perhaps it was word of mouth from one of the officers from the ship. I was soon taking bookings to appear at people's homes up on the 'peak', on my days or evenings off. This was where the rich businessmen of Hong Kong lived and the English, Chinese and American residents were extremely fond of their parties. It was the first chance in a long time to be able to entertain out of uniform and in my shirt and slacks. All my clothes had been locally hand-made and cost less than six shillings. Everything in Hong Kong was so cheap and even more so when you bartered. Why are the English so loath to barter?

On one particular evening I had spent the whole night amusing the guests of an extremely wealthy Chinese gentleman, when he asked me to show a special friend some tricks. Sitting at a huge dining table was Sir Robert Black, the Governor of Hong Kong. I baffled and bemused them with a whole series of my best effects. The host was extremely grateful and gave me a generous tip for my efforts. What a nice man.

About a week later, we had an important parade at which the whole regiment was on show. The Governor of the colony was to inspect the troops. We practised like mad to get the drill right. The order was always to remain still and silent unless referred to, at which time the only answer should be 'sir!' And it had to be yelled 'SAAAH!' Even if you were responding to a question, the answer could only be 'SAAAH!' At the same time, you had to present arms by a series of moves that positions the rifle vertically in front of your body.

The sun shone brightly that day as 600 men, including myself, stood to attention on the parade ground, eyes firmly front.

Sir Robert Black, the man I had entertained, led the inspection, hands behind his back, very much in the manner of the Royal Family whom he represented. Two paces behind him was the Commanding Officer, walking in what is known as the 'slow' march where the foot hovers a few inches above the ground. He has his sword held vertically and glinting in the sunshine. Two paces behind him was the Second-in-Command, sword held in the same way. Then there was the Adjutant and following him the Regimental Sergeant Major, a most immaculate man with dark grey hair cut very short and steely blue eyes that could cut through you at a glance. He carried a swagger stick under his arm. He was also totally unbiased. He hated everyone.

To read RSM Calvert's citation was incredible. Apparently during World War II, he had walked into no-man's land and dragged his injured men out of the line of fire. He carried on even when shot himself. I had already decided that if I went into battle, I wanted him beside me.

He had the loudest shout of anyone I knew. Watching him control his men on the parade ground was fascinating. Having let 600 men march off the ground in files of three and move up the hill, I could see him tense himself up before screaming: 'BATTALION! ABOUT TURN!' The sheer noise was incredible and 600 men would simultaneously change direction. As NCOs – by now I was a Lance Corporal – we had all been trained to shout commands by standing 6ft apart in a row with another line of men standing 80 yards away also 6ft apart. Your job was to make your opposite number understand

and carry out the rifle commands, amongst a row of other soldiers all doing the same with their own comrades. This practice fortifies the voice and its ability to project and it helped me no end later on in clubs when the microphone went off.

Suddenly, Sir Robert Black stopped in his tracks, looked behind him and walked back to me. There is nothing in Queen's Regulations about how officers should walk backwards. Each of the officers behind him fell into each other like skittles, began shuffling about, and the whole parade was in disarray.

My heart was banging and my mind was panicking as, with disruption all around him, Sir Robert Black looked me straight in the face, smiled and said, 'Hello, Ted!'

'SAAAH!'

'I didn't know you were in the Army.'

'SAAAH!'

'How extraordinary. You must come up to tea sometime.'

'SAAAH!'

He turned and walked away followed by the CO, the 2IC and the Adjutant, all glaring at me with the utmost incredulity. As the RSM walked past, from the corner of his mouth came, 'my office.'

Immediately after dismissal, I handed my rifle to the soldier next to me and ran to the RSM's office. As I stood to attention, he slowly looked me up and down, got up from behind his desk and very slowly walked around me three times before saying gently in my ear, 'Hello, Ted,' and I knew I was going to die. When this is over, I thought, I was going to find every way possible of avoiding parades.

One more trip round my quivering body and then, 'I didn't know you were in the Army, Ted.'

Another slow walk around me and, 'You must come and have tea with me sometime.'

Then he exploded, 'HOW THE BLOODY HELL DO YOU,

YOU 'ORRIBLE LITTLE MAN, KNOW THE GOVERNOR OF THIS COLONY?!!'

'I ... I ... I showed him a card trick,' I stammered.

'YOU DID BLOODY WHAT? WHAT THE HELL DO YOU THINK YOU WERE DOING?' he yelped.

I explained my moonlighting misdemeanours, which I knew went right against Queen's Regulations.

'YOU ARE NOT ALLOWED TO TAKE OTHER JOBS WHILE YOU ARE A SOLDIER!' he snorted with a mixture of astonishment and disgust.

'You, you 'orrible little man, will serve your time showing what you are worth to the rest of the Army on this island. Now get moving!'

I couldn't believe how lucky I was when he doled out the punishment.

He sentenced me to perform in the Sergeants' Mess at their next function the following month and I nearly put out my arms and kissed him. Nearly, but I decided against it.

From this developed other offers to appear in other messes and I was even paid a little extra to do the local army hospitals, the NAAFI and many of the ships in dock. This included the massive USA warships and aircraft carriers, which were like floating towns. We went up the side of one American aircraft carrier on a huge lift and when we went inside we got into a Cadillac to drive up to the other end of the ship. Their military seemed to live a little differently to us. Then I joined a concert party and from then on not only had a great time but never seemed to stop doing shows.

The buzz I got from performing was in danger of reducing my regular job to a boring day-to-day monotony of moving papers. The one thing that I had to do, I decided, was to avoid parades. I used my Orderly Room job to look up various courses open to me.

HONG KONG

Not every application to join a course was accepted, the Army must stay in control at all times, of course. Finally, I was enrolled into fencing. To my amazement, this involved swords. I thought fencing was something that would be useful when I got home to put around the house! No I didn't, I'm just kidding.

One of the reasons I had applied for this was that it took place in a WRAC camp on the other side of the island and I thought I'd be surrounded by girls. I still hadn't enjoyed the sexual experiences that I longed for and, although I had been in many of the local bars where the girls were cheaply bought, I often stood there like a little boy in a sweet shop. Perhaps an instinct deep inside me wanted to be introduced to the eroticism of life in a more natural way, without having to pay for it.

As it turned out, the girls in the WRAC were nowhere near as desirable as the Chinese girls in the cheongsams, and they were pretty tough-looking, too. With muscles that bulged in places I didn't know existed, all thoughts of getting one of them between the sheets soon evaporated.

We soon found out that we were in no fit state to deal with them in any case, when on our first day the CSMI (Company Sergeant Major Instructor) proceeded to humiliate our manhood. This guy had just failed to be a professor of fencing, which ironically showed how good he was. A professor of fencing was a very rare thing, the qualifications are incredibly demanding and after years of intensive training, if you fail your exam on a technicality, this has no real reflection on your ability. This guy was mind-boggling.

CSMI Kirby was a pretty fit-looking chap, a bit on the short side, and was much tougher than he looked.

On day one of the course, wondering why we hadn't been issued with the normal protective gear and standing only in our shorts, he made us stand with our feet at right angles, slightly apart, with the right foot pointing forward. While bending our knees, we were shown how to lift our left arm and bend the wrist, which put us into an extremely camp position. I laughed; my pose held connotations I was not prepared to go along with. Having chuckled to the soldier next to me, I turned to see CSMI Kirby staring me in the face.

'Name?' he spat.

'Daniels, Sarge!'

'Come here.'

He motioned me to stand a few paces away from him and I looked back at the group of 20 other soldiers wondering what was coming next. CSMI Kirby took up a foil. This was a very flexible piece of metal with a quarter-inch stud on the end, and taking one look at my stiff body, lunged straight at me.

The force that hit me was unexpected and powerful. Feeling I had been hit in the bare chest by a champion boxer the wind went out of me and I fell backwards on to the ground gasping for air. Lying on my backside catching my breath, I touched my chest expecting to feel blood pouring out.

'Get up, Daniels!' came the retort.

As I struggled to my feet, the laughter of the group rang in my ears.

'Now stand as I told you, because I'm going to hit you again!'

'Errrrrr, no, Sarge! That's all right, Sarge. I understand now, Sarge.'

My words were not sufficient to deter Kirby from his mission.

'Stand as I told you! Feet at right angles, knees bent.'

Whoof! He hit me again. The impact, best described as a rock of ice hitting you at 50mph was enormous. This time I found that I had remained standing. As he sent me back to the ranks with my head and body reeling, he explained how the

legs act as a spring, taking the impact out of the thrust. I knew
I would never forget it! I had also learnt how powerful a sword
can be when it is used correctly.

We spent the rest of the day lunging at one another, with
right arms going forward and stiff first; your left leg pushes your
right leg forward; you go into a low lunge as your left arm drops
and then raises to bring you back up – it was like being
choreographed for a theatre show. Eight hours of lunging later,
I had never been so grateful to see my bed.

Early next morning, I awoke with the reveille and a shout
from our beloved CSMI, who marched straight over to our
bunks and started to pull the sheets off. Every single man's legs
were bent into the shape we had kept them in all the previous
day. Mine were so stiff I couldn't even move them. CSMI Kirby
grabbed me roughly by the ankles and yanked them straight. The
pain was excruciating. It was absolute agony. His continued
shouting and bawling was interspersed by the desperate screams
and cries from men having their legs cracked back into position.
Having had a quick wash down and a smartish breakfast, we
were back on the parade ground where the first thing he said
was, 'lunge!' I don't think I'd heard men groan like that before!

Slowly, we learnt the art of the foil which is a touch-sensitive
weapon. To my horror, CSMI decided to use me as the role
model once more. Wisely, I decided to play along every step of
the way this time. With sweeping movements around my bare
skin, he demonstrated just how fast a sport fencing is. This is the
reason why it has never taken off on television, as the viewer
would not be able to see the incredibly fast reflex actions.

When you push against somebody else's sword, their natural
instinct is to push back. One of the many secrets was to use
their impetus at that moment and taking the tip of your sword
under theirs, move it over the top and strike them. As CSMI
demonstrated this, he hit me again.

He also demonstrated that, if the opponent does react quickly and their foil starts to come back then you must, as you are moving forward, dip your foil under theirs and continue the attack.

He came at me in a lunge, I tapped his sword out of the way, he pushed my sword away and started to go under, I came back, he started to retreat, I hit it the other way, rolled over the top of his foil and struck him. This was totally instinctive on my part. I didn't work it out. I didn't have time to work it out.

Without a moment to rejoice in my success he lunged at me again and with an instantaneous sweeping motion flipped his sword in the air, caught the tip of the foil, flicked it in an arc and the metal handle came down on my head. What a crack!

'Don't get clever with me, son!' was the answer to my attempts to defeat him.

I finished the course with plenty of bruises, a lot of experience and a certificate in fencing that said I had ended up top of the course.

CHAPTER 6

CASUAL SEX

*E*ven Elvis was drafted into the Army. He received his call-up *papers in March 1958, but managed to postpone the big day so that he could finish his latest film* King Creole. *The king of rock 'n' roll saw his wage package drop from $100,000 to just $83.20 a month. When Elvis sang, he captured the hearts of millions of teenage girls around the world and this exercise was similar to that which many young recruits still had in mind.*

Taking the stage at every possible service party now ate up most of my spare time, but I was still awaiting the chance to put my other undeveloped skills into practice, too. Surrounded by constant boasting from my mates and with the lack of natural opportunity, I finally decided to see if what they said about the girls on the colony was true.

I saw a beautiful Chinese girl while I was walking the streets of Victoria, the main town of Hong Kong. I was instantly in love. I'll rephrase that – I was instantly in lust. This was the girl for me. I followed her for about an hour, trying to pluck up the courage to speak to her. This was the ultimate girl of my dreams. Eventually she headed for the Kowloon Ferry. I had no reason whatsoever to go to Kowloon but I followed her on to the boat. Now or never. I decided to sit next to her and ask her the way to somewhere in Kowloon and that would break the ice. A deep breath and I moved to the seat next to hers. Just as I was about to speak she made that peculiar hacking noise in her throat, as you do, and spat over the side of the ship into the water.

I never said anything, I just moved away again.

Bars in Hong Kong were certainly the easiest places to pick up a girl, but several parts of the island were out of bounds for security reasons. There were gangs hiding in these areas that were keen to take on English army boys, or so we were told. The truth was probably that these were the red light areas of the capital and the Army didn't want us straying off into forbidden territory.

We had been fully instructed in the dangers of casual sex and had watched the most grotesque film I have ever seen. Much worse than Boris Karloff or *Frankenstein,* these extended movies showed the end results of all the known venereal diseases available to mankind. With horrific close-ups of a man's penis going black and festering, I wondered who on earth would have allowed a camera crew to film their shame in such detail. Staggering out of that lecture, I was determined that if that's what could happen to you, I would never have sex at all. I'll stick to card tricks, I thought. My resolve didn't last, though, and with all the pressure from without and from within, I needed to prove the state of my manhood once and for all.

Hong Kong's high level of prostitution was caused by the poverty that existed on the island. The bars were full of girls trying to make a quick dollar, though I didn't really frequent them, as I am not drinking man and I am still not at ease in bars.

In the late 1930s, a female English MP returned from Hong

CASUAL SEX

Kong determined to stamp out the legal prostitution that existed there. The British Government would not condone legal prostitution on one of its colonies and immediately outlawed it. The result was that it continued underground and unchecked by doctors. Within two years, venereal disease was rife. The Army stance at that time was that all soldiers should abstain from sex. The story was that they put something in your tea called bromide. A classic gag was the two very old soldiers sitting on a park bench and one said to the other, 'do you remember that stuff they used to put in our tea when we were in the Army?'

'Oh aye,' says the other, 'what about it?'

'Well, I think it's just starting to work!'

Preventing soldiers from having sex was an almost impossible task. The irony was that contraceptives were freely available from the medical centre. I discovered that the condoms were so rough, thick and long that it was like wearing a rubber glove over your willy. They were more of a laugh than a practical solution and came in very useful as balloons for parties. Nevertheless, the serious fear of contracting VD remained deeply ingrained in every soldier and even more vividly so after viewing that ghastly film. Each one of us would daily and secretly inspect every part of our bodies for the slightest sore, just in case.

The slowly rotating fans did nothing to cool the effects of the hot tropical weather and vulnerable parts of everyone's anatomy were constantly sweating. Underarms and between legs were the worst, where the wetness caused all manner of soreness. I got heat rash and tried to avoid the medical centre but I finally gave in one day and covered my embarrassment with bravado as I showed the nurse the red patches of skin all over my privates. The nurse smiled knowingly and left, returning a few moments later with a huge jar containing a

115

thick purple cream. This he slapped straight on to my testicles, his smile unbroken as I yelled in pain as the stinging cream took effect. Leaving the surgery, I ran up the road flapping my shorts in an unsuccessful attempt to cool the fire. I had seen men performing this ritual before and often wondered what they were doing; now I knew!

One night, the sexual urges got too much and I left camp with the express purpose of endorsing my maleness. I knew exactly where to go, as the bars were not the only places where a female body could be purchased. Strolling slowly down the forbidden avenue, I was quickly approached by a young, thin Chinese girl. She hardly spoke any English so I just nodded when she asked, 'You want some fun?' Excitement and embarrassment churned away inside me. Fear, too.

Finding myself being led into a discussion over services and prices, I really wasn't sure what was what. Her English was so bad and some of her offers contained words I had never heard before and some I was happy never to discover the true meaning of. A *gam* was apparently a very old French word for one form of quick relief.

Finally agreeing a price, I followed this girl, who would have been in her mid-twenties, on a half-mile walk to the place of paradise. Reaching a high-rise dilapidated tenement block, we began climbing the stairs. The paint was peeling, paper hung off the walls, parts of the ceilings were hanging down and as the stairs creaked I wondered if we would reach our destination without a serious accident. The excitement of the unknown became mixed with the fear of being found by the military police who toured that dubious district.

Several flights of stairs later, we had climbed so high that I thought about the need for some extra oxygen to help me through the task ahead. The sex drive must be a very powerful thing to have got me this far. Eventually, she led us through a broken door and out on to a flat roof where an old wooden hut awaited. Never having seen a shed like this in anybody's garden back home, let alone in Hong Kong, I was taken aback to see that it contained several rooms.

Motioning me to lie on the ramshackle bed in one corner, she ceremoniously stripped off and disappeared into another room. Waiting silently in anticipation, but unsure whether to get aroused or not, I heard laughter and chatter coming from the room next door. Her family lived there!

Moments later, she returned with another very, very young girl, who, she explained, was her sister. This poor girl was clearly in training for the job, as she apparently wanted her to see how it was done. For a first-timer like me, it was the ultimate turn-off and, protesting, I prepared to leave. Shooing her sister back next door, the Chinese girl was clearly not keen to lose her client and calmed me back down on to the bed.

Lying motionless on the blanket, the naked streetwalker awaited my attentions. I knew what to do, but not how to do it. It was awful and there were no emotions whatsoever. The hooker just lay there because it was simply a job to her. I was in a strange state of mid-arousal, apprehension and awkwardness, but managed to make contact with what felt like a roll of sandpaper. I can distinctly remember thinking that this was not as good as card tricks!

It was over awfully soon and I fled thinking that now my curiosity was assuaged, it would be the last time I would attempt that. I thought sex was awful. The knowledge that I had used a condom did not arrest the abject terror of catching VD and I spent the next few weeks searching my body for the tiniest pimple. Nightmares in which my male organ went black and dropped off during a parade haunted me for weeks.

Having made a contract with myself not to go alone into the run-down areas of Hong Kong again, I took little convincing that filling a weekend's leave with two other mates would do me the world of good. Macau was a tiny island off the southern coast of mainland China and could be easily reached by a short ferry ride. It was known as a place of fun and excitement and would surely prove to be an excellent choice for a mini break.

I'll change one name here to protect the guilty. Peter, Jack and I arrived after a long ferry ride, at 2.00am. The hour of the day apparently didn't matter to the islanders on tri-shaws and rickshaws who immediately surrounded us with an invitation to see a wrestling match. The concept of watching this sport at such an early hour was ridiculous and we asked to be taken directly to our hotel. We were going to make the most of our break and seize the opportunity to escape the army life as much as possible and the Grand Hotel was the best available.

Each floor had a floor-boy who was responsible for the wellbeing of the residents under his charge. Providing us with details of his room service he also asked us, '... you been see wrestling match yet?'

'No,' I said, becoming puzzled, as this must be a very famous local sport. Making a mental note that this was evidently something not to be missed, we bade goodnight to one another and I soon climbed into my luxury bed and almost immediately sank into the beauty of 'never-never-land'.

Being a tropical venue and not having the benefit of air conditioning, the walls stopped about 18in from the ceiling, so that the ceiling fans could circulate the air across the entire floor of the hotel. It also meant that you could hear everything going on in every other room on your floor. I must have been tired to have fallen asleep in that environment. Shouts and giggles coming from the hallway brought me back to consciousness and my watch told me it was 10.00am. Breakfast was over, but something else was going on. I opened my door only to see a long line of women outside. The queue, consisting of black, white, Chinese, blondes, brunettes and redheads was snaking its way into Jack's room. Reaching the front of the column I could see Jack sitting up in bed like merry Old King Cole as each girl filed slowly past.

'What the hell are you doing?' I demanded.

'I'm auditioning for some company for tonight,' came the reply and a knowing smile.

With the help of the floor-boy extolling their virtues, Jack was openly auditioning for some 'extra' services to spice up his visit to Macau. Party-pooper me stopped the proceedings and the girls were ushered away, as we prepared for our first day of sightseeing.

Sixty-four kilometres across the Pearl River Delta from Hong Kong, the visitors' guide explained, Macau had derived its name from a Chinese goddess. It had a distinctly European flavour with winding narrow streets and alleys peppered with churches, colonial mansions and elegant inns. Throughout 400 years of history, Macau had been a Portuguese stronghold and a centre of culture in the Far East. Strangely, the beliefs, arts and customs of traditional China thrive in Macau, where a devout, conservative community somehow managed to compete in the rat-race while celebrating their responsibilities to their ancestors and gods. Tree-shaded country lanes, wide sandy beaches, lush pine forests and modern hotels all reminded me of the holiday I had always dreamed of. Macau was obviously a unique blend of cultures, people, aromas, flavours and styles and I was sorry I wasn't staying there longer

We took excursions to the town and surrounding countryside, but found ourselves constantly being pestered to go to a wrestling match. At the end of a tiring day as a tourist, I returned to the hotel early for a well-needed rest. The ground floor consisted of a huge casino and seemed to continue its wheeling and dealing 24 hours a day. Even though I've never been a gambling man, I was still interested in the concept, mathematics and skill of the procedure. Cautiously entering the unexpected hush of a busy room, I was strangely aware that 100 eyes were watching me. A huge, fat, 'Buddha-like' man sat operating the dice cage which would be rotated to decide the result of the bets being placed.

Standing by the table, watching every move and looking like a flash and confident British lad, proud of my newly acquired manipulation skills, I waited for my moment to declare my 'oneness' with the overweight croupier. I began to perform my coin roll under his nose and wondered if he was impressed. Turning his head towards me, the 'Buddha' hit a stack of ten-cent pieces with his finger and split them perfectly in half, with the top pile dropping alongside the bottom half. He grabbed the two piles and riffle-shuffled them back together with one hand. With my eyes nearly popping out of my head, I was bowled over with the skill he had just demonstrated and instantly felt incredibly stupid having shown him my pathetic little coin trick.

I was about to leave when I was halted by the arrival of a huge black limousine outside. An enormously obese Chinese man alighted and came straight into the room, carrying a large black suitcase. Placing a mammoth pile of paper notes on to the number nine in silence, the skilled 'Buddha' swung the dice cage and, miraculously, number nine was shown. This really was straight out of the movies, I reckoned.

Still in a complete and still silence, assistants pulled all the money off the other tables and put it into their client's suitcase. Every person around the table received a large-value note, as the eminent guest walked straight out, got back into the car and vanished. We were obviously being encouraged to keep the experience to ourselves. I didn't know what had happened and I was wise enough not to ask.

CASUAL SEX

Once out into the street with a pocket full of money and at a loose end, I was once again a vulnerable target.

'You wanna see wrestling match? Velly cheap.'

Having been accosted all day by the eagerness of the locals to display their national sport, I reluctantly agreed. The rickshaw man took me to a block of flats, which seemed an extremely unusual place for such an important competition. My curiosity having been aroused, I would see this through to the end. Marching up several flights of stairs, with worrying echoes of my last experience of an apartment building, I was led into a dimly lit room where on the floor was a pile of mattresses. Having sat on a seat and paid my dues, the equivalent of about half a crown, an adjoining door opened and in walked three women and two fellas completely naked. Without one look in my direction they got straight down to business with one another. The wrestling match was in fact their word for a full-blown orgy. I was so stunned, my initial instinct was to fall about laughing, whereupon the rickshaw man said that for another one-and-three pence, I could join in!

'Get me outta here,' I stammered, with thoughts of the other girl still fresh and a strong sense of unwillingness to play this unreal game.

'You no wanna stay?' questioned the little rickshaw man, who in the end agreed to take me on to other sightseeing adventures.

He wheeled me down to the coastline and we peered across the water into the pitch-blackness of the night. Suddenly, there was the sound of faraway thunder. The distant noise sounded like fireworks, until my escort pointed out that it was, in fact, gunfire.

'People try to swim river to get to Macau from China,' he attempted to explain in pidgin English. 'Soldiers shoot men, women and children, no problem.'

I stood aghast and imagined the women with children strapped to their backs being used as target practice. As a young man of 19, a million questions filled my mind. What was so horrible across the water that would make people want to take that risk? What was it that so frightened that country's system that would cause them to shoot innocent people in order to stop them leaving? From that moment on I became strongly anticommunist.

'No many get here,' my guide sadly whispered, as we walked away. Lessons to be learnt here, I thought.

Lessons also needed to be learnt by the third member of our party who had all but deserted Peter and I. Jack was a serious drinker and was in constant danger of being thrown out of the Army because of it. He was getting worse. Having seen Jack spend almost every moment of his holiday propping up a bar, I decided that his problem would ultimately destroy him and we had to intervene.

On the last night, Jack got so intoxicated with the chemical beers they served on the island, that we had no alternative than to carry him up and into bed. I had an idea.

I went back out in the street looking for an ugly prostitute. In any country street girls do not have a good life. In fact, they probably have the worst kind of life, but in the Far East you could multiply that a hundredfold. They don't have an easy or a long life at all. They have no protection and are extremely susceptible to disease. By the time they are 30, it all catches up with them; they have become wrecks. I wandered around the streets looking for the worst one.

In due course, I found the one I was looking for in a doorway. She whispered to me as I walked past her dimly lit doorway and I motioned for her to come out into the light. She resisted my demands at first and soon I saw why. She was the most awful, pitiful creature I had seen. With no teeth, her face was collapsed and scarred and looked 90, though I suspected she had hardly reached middle age.

I felt sorry for her and I handed her the equivalent of several weeks' wages and explained that I had an unusual job for her. She nodded some sort of agreement and I hoped and prayed she would understand what I wanted her to do.

Back at the hotel, the floor-boy looked at me in astonishment as I led the old-looking woman into Jack's room. The floor-boy obviously thought I was totally insane having arrived back with this little treasure, compared with the beauties he'd managed.

Instructing the woman to get into bed with Jack, it was vital that she didn't touch him, only sleep with him, I explained. I spoke my most fluent Chinese, 'No touchee, just sleepee.' She nodded once again and off I went to bed.

It must have been at about 8.00am the next morning that I was awoken by a scream that shook the entire hotel. Naked, Jack burst into my room and grabbed me.
'Tell me I didn't! Please tell me I didn't,' he yelled.

'Well, we tried to talk you out of it, but you wouldn't listen,' I lied. 'Last night you said she was the most beautiful thing on the planet. It's not our fault if you drink like that,' I reasoned.

Back at base and in a permanent state of terror, Jack went to the medical centre daily for the next three months and took all the penicillin jabs he could get. It cured his drinking problem, too.

* * *

From the moment of joining the Army, I had started a demob map. This would be a two-year countdown showing the number of days left before I was released. As departure day neared, the atmosphere of fun among us increased. We called our state of euphoria being 'demob happy'.

Just before I was due to go home, the Commanding Officer called me in and wanted me to sign on '… for another three months, to fence for the Green Howards in the Far East Land Forces Fencing Championships'. I said no. There were two reasons for this: first, I knew that there was nothing in QRs about a National Serviceman signing on for an extended three months. Three years, yes. Three months, no. And second, I knew the Regiment was going to Germany and, although I had enjoyed most of my time in the Army, I had been to Germany on holiday and it was cold. My old job still awaited me at home and it was time to leave.

In the meantime, I got a 'dear John' letter from Avril breaking off our engagement. We must have both changed in the time we were apart and trying to maintain a relationship several thousand miles away from each other is an impossible task anyway. I often mused over the fact that Mam would write to Dad every other day when he was in the Navy. She loved corresponding and that is what kept their love alive over four very difficult years of separation. Mam was a great letter writer but not a very good speller. She would begin her communication each time with 'Dear Sweatheart'. I suspect that, in the heat of India, it was an appropriate title anyway! Dad kept those letters for a long time but didn't tell her about the mistake until several years later. In our house, 'sweatheart' is an oft-used word of endearment.

Of course, Mam and Dad were already married when he went away, whereas Avril and I had only just started a relationship and we were probably too young to be so committed. A tinge of sadness filled me when I received Avril's note. It wasn't a surprise, but it was still a loss.

I returned to the UK on the *Oxfordshire*. The atmosphere on board was one of great excitement, tinged with a sense of melancholy at leaving Hong Kong behind. Once basic training in the UK was over, my time in the Army had been one of great benefit to me in so many ways and I looked back with fond memories as the ship pulled away from the island for the last time. As we sped out into the Pacific once more, I wondered if I would ever return and pondered on what lay ahead. I've always been a fella who looks forward and I find looking back pointless. It's done, you can't change it and so long as you have learnt from your past, it's time to move on.

Christmas Day 1958 came while we were on the way home. The ship was in Colombo, taking on water and fuel, but they would not allow us ashore. Some of the lads took umbrage at this and bombarded the tugs with bottles. Don't you just love the British abroad?

They must have got their own back somehow because as we got nearer home, most of the lads on board went down with Asian 'flu. There was general panic as discussions went on with Southampton as to whether they would allow us to dock. They did. We were home, but no sooner were we back in Richmond than we were told we were being sent to Northern Ireland to see our full time out. Another panic. Then some wise and wonderful person decided that would be a ridiculous expense so we were demobbed three weeks early.

It was 15 January 1959, and I was a civilian again. Mam and Dad came to meet me when I stepped off the train back in Middlesbrough and were clearly pleased to see me. Behind them ran this young man who grabbed me and, with a face full of smiles, embraced me. Stiffening with confusion, I hadn't recognised my own brother Trevor. In the time I had been away, he had grown from a boy I'd given ten bob to as a farewell gesture into a man, and I was astounded at the difference in him.

There was no sense of anti-climax in being home, realising that although I had seen another part of the world, there were areas of my own locality which still awaited discovery. I had a week off to transfer my life from the army barracks back to the terraced streets of South Bank and back into my old job with the council. It was quite a short time to get used to the everyday reality of life once more and to catch up with all the family news. By now we were living in Windsor Road, Normanby, in a lovely semidetached corner house. I was really glad to be back and to be welcomed home by all the neighbours, especially the next-door neighbour Mrs Goldswain.

She was a real Mrs Malaprop. 'Princess Margaret is getting married, it's on all the blackguards in town ...' and 'my husband's gone out to buy a dog. I think that he is getting one of them Sensation dogs.'

A huge new housing estate had sprung up, changing the whole town and I was amazed at how fast things change and time is swallowed up. I noticed on leaving the barracks that our empty places were not being filled and Dad told me that National Service had ended while I was away. Trevor had escaped the ordeal by a whisker, but undoubtedly, I tried to convince him, it would have done him good.

Some things never change and it was back to Eston District Council in the same old building. Apparently, they had installed a special machine that measured pollution and with the results were able to establish what the residents had been saying for years; that it was still the most contaminated place in England.

Nothing seemed to have altered at the council building; even the paint on the inside hadn't changed, but the staff had. I chose to do a tour of all the offices in the block to say, 'I'm back!' to those who knew me and, 'Hello!' to those who didn't. An older lady, known as The Dragon, didn't even look up until I started to pester her a little with the result that she chased me out of the door. Maybe she didn't like my sense of humour? Unperturbed, I entered the next office and immediately my eyes fell on a most stunningly good-looking brunette. Fashions had changed during my absence, too, and the girls were starting to become more liberal in their dress. It had become the era of tight mini-skirts and sweaters and gave all the blokes an opportunity to see exactly what shape a girl was in.

I gave my best Colgate smile and, to my delight, Jacqueline Skipworth, a grand northern name, seemed to like my attentions. It was not enough at the time to make a difference, but something stayed with us. That first evening I had a chance meeting with my old friend Irene, who had also grown up quite dramatically and proceeded to go out of her way to prove the depth of her welcoming devotion. She invited me back to her place for tea and we ended up making love in front of the fireplace. It was wonderful and after the experience in the shed, I suddenly understood what all the fuss was about. I was also enlightened by the fact that obviously girls were supposed to enjoy the experience as well. Now this *is* better than card tricks, I thought!

Our relationship didn't go beyond the passion of the moment and I soon found myself back at work, chatting up Jacqueline Skipworth. I made sure I bumped into her as often as I could and literally so, if possible. She was special to me, recognising how I dreamt about her and when we were together, she made my heart tick faster. I got so excited around this girl. A very strange phenomenon.

She seemed to find all my wisecracks endearing and it wasn't long before we agreed to a proper date. The only problem was that her hobby was ballroom dancing. Against all my natural instincts and for the sake of getting as near to Jackie as possible, I tried my best to share her interest. Failing miserably, I was not designed to be a dancer and felt like a lemon on the dance floor. After several efforts where I stood on her toes more often than the ground, I began to wonder why people did it anyway. I suppose my deep, inner shyness didn't help and, stretching my face into an apologetic smile, I eventually backed off and waved the white flag.

Fortunately, her interest seemed to go beyond dancing as we continued to go out together, to the cinema and occasionally for something to eat. Our friendship blossomed, but her grandmother's preferences didn't. An only child, Jacqueline had been brought up by her mother and grandmother, a formidable woman who took an instant dislike to me. Maybe she was right, I don't know. On the days when I could visit Jackie at home there were two hurdles to overcome. First, there was this old woman who was extremely protective of her granddaughter and would make sure she never left us alone together. Watching us every second with her beady eyes, she constantly weighed me up and down as if comparing me to some other, more preferential suitor.

The second obstacle was Jackie's cousin, David. This little toddler was a classic terror who had earned a reputation for biting people. There was no discrimination as to his choice of victims and he would suddenly run into the room and sink his teeth into any readily available flesh. As he was pretty small, this meant it was usually a chunk of someone's leg.

Having been instilled with a reverence for my elders, the idea of a child behaving in such a way appalled me. There is nothing wrong with discipline so long as it is administered with love. There will always be some who break the rules, but this should not stop us from making sure our kids grow up respecting others.

On the first day I met him, David introduced himself by gnawing straight into my ankle. It was sufficient to draw blood and I was not a little shocked, so the next time I was ready for him. When the human Jack Russell dashed into the room upon our arrival, he sank his teeth into the back of my leg and I grabbed his hand and returned the compliment by biting him on the arm. He let out a yelp and ran straight to Granny who started to sympathise with his misfortune, whereupon he bit her, too. After that he never came near me again, but the rest of the family spent a fortune on sticking plasters.

Despite having found girls, I was still passionate about magic. Jackie was also happy to share my interest and we spent hours getting all my old props out from their box under my bed and reviving my act. Well, that's what we told the parents.

At the Methodist club one night, it was advertised that a Doctor Hebblethwaite was going to give a lecture on the History of Magic. I couldn't wait to hear it and booked my place well in advance. Having just turned 20, I felt that I knew everything there was to know about the art. Like many youngsters, I was the bees' knees, a god-like creature sent to walk upon this earth and I found my place in the hall knowing that I knew it all.

The lecture was good. Towards the end of his talk he began expounding the future of magic and the modern face of the art. Picking up a large, solid billiard ball and a magic wand, he placed the full-sized red billiard ball on his open left palm, closed his fist and extended his arm well away from his body. Spinning the wand around his left fist, he opened his hand to show that the billiard ball had vanished. I suddenly woke up and sat there enthralled with my jaw hitting the floor. I didn't have a clue how he had achieved this. I didn't know everything.

I just couldn't believe that, with all my knowledge, I had been fooled so easily. As my mind drifted away from what he was saying and concentrated on solving the problem, his words abruptly caught my attention again. He mentioned 'the Middlesbrough Circle of Magicians', which despite living in the area for more than 20 years was something I had never heard of.

Declaring my serious interest in the craft at the end of the evening, Doctor Hebblethwaite gave me the address of the society and suggested I apply. This was something that I was determined to do, but upon reading their literature realised that it was a very exclusive club. Having witnessed the superb quality of the doctor's skills, how could I ever hope to be enrolled in such an Elite group? I had nothing to lose so I finally worked up the courage to apply. I went to the Secretary's house wearing all the gear that I had worn for my shows when I was in Hong Kong – a white tuxedo with a black velvet collar, a frilly shirt and dicky bow and, wait for it, a short black cloak with a red lining. I'm sorry. What a lemon I must have looked. I pretended I was on the way to a gig, just to impress the Secretary, Martin Marshall.

Several weeks later, I was standing in front of the audition committee and, feeling extremely nervous, began my routine. I was in awe of these gentlemen and thought that they must all be far better than I was. They treated it all so seriously and I came away thinking that I had not been good enough. They said that they would let me know and it was a couple of weeks before I got the letter that said that I had been accepted as a member. I wish that more societies would make it this tough to get in. Now it seems that if you can afford the fee you can be a member, and I still think that the Theatrical Art of Magic, forgive the capitals, should be worked at to make you appreciate what you have got. Years later I found out that, because I had developed into a magician without the influence of a magic club, I had apparently fooled them successfully in a couple of the tricks that I'd done. I didn't go to the Middlesbrough Circle of Magicians for over a year after I had been accepted because I really didn't think I was good enough and I didn't want to show myself up.

I persuaded Jackie that we should make love. We did and she fell immediately pregnant. Out of the blue, my life, which had been totally within my own control, was in turmoil.

CASUAL SEX

Telling our parents was the worst thing about the affair. Gathering together as if for a wake, the whole family sat together in one room, while I explained our state of affairs. It was awful. There was a stunned silence at the end of my short speech and at that point I would happily have used some form of magic to open up the floor and quickly disappear. Then, as anyone who has been in this situation will tell you, I actually felt invisible when they started discussing the circumstances without me or Jackie being consulted. I cared greatly for Jackie and despite my father making it clear that I didn't have to do the honourable thing, I proposed to Jackie and she accepted. In my mind there was no option and we were married four weeks later in the Methodist Chapel on Normanby Road, home of the Youth Club. That was the way it was then, and although the marriage was not to work out, I am glad that we did it. If not, I would have missed out on Paul, Martin and Gary, my sons.

Modern society is not as glib about this subject as it claims to be. The shock of discovering that your girlfriend is expecting a baby is as big now as it was then, certainly among educated and caring people. The shame of the situation in the moral climate of the late 1950s, however, was quite acute and I was eager to reduce the degree of embarrassment as much as I could.

So many things were happening at this time, that it seemed as if I had been caught up in a whirlwind. I bought my first car for £15 from a local scrap heap. Destined for destruction, my Dad saw its potential and with me as labourer, somehow managed to get it running smoothly. The bodywork was something else, though. The 1938, wooden-floored Standard Flying Nine was rebuilt completely and had 15 coats of hand-rubbed cellulose applied to it, turning it into a gleaming black and red sports car. I was offered £150 for the car the day we finished it. Not a bad investment, but I didn't sell it.

It was also about then that the Hippodrome cinema had to close. It simply could not compete with television. The public imagined that the little screen in the room gave them the same experience as the real thing. It didn't and it can't. There is nothing like having your imagination filled by the movies or the theatre, where everything else is blacked out and only the vivid images fill your mind. We all gathered in the cinema for the last night and, after the audience had left, played frisby with the 78rpm records and shot the foam from the fire extinguishers all over the place. Dad got a job driving a bread and cakes delivery van for Wonderloaf but he must have missed the magic of the cinema enormously. He didn't work for them for long and went on to work for ICI at their Wilton works. He stayed there for years, working in hazardous conditions. Occasionally, the plant had some sort of explosion but he was lucky that it was never on his shift. The chemicals also played havoc with his health and, years later of course, I considered that one of the best things I ever did was to give him a permanent job making props for me. All that was in the future, however, and having recently had concert party experience in the Army, I persuaded Trevor to do the Working Men's Club circuit with me. We got a booking at The Club, Peterlee. This was a brand new town and had built the most superb working men's club, a new trend occurring in the north. This was the first of many truly luxurious clubs.

Industry required their workers to work around the clock in shifts: six 'til two; two 'til ten; and nights. It's a generalisation, of course, but I believe this was the main reason that the North initially escaped the ratrace that was taking place in the South, as everybody went to work in the same direction. In the South, everybody scatters across the metropolis. Northerners all went to the same type of work and all knew how much each other earned, because it was the same. There was simply no point it trying to 'keep up with the Jones's' because everybody was in the same boat financially.

Somebody, somewhere, came up with the plan to turn the workmen's institutes, rough red-brick clubs, into places of entertainment. Approaching the breweries, committees asked to borrow money to build a new type of club, which would provide the workers with a new leisure experience. Owing to the fact that the breweries stood to make a fortune by selling their beer, they agreed and these new clubs sprang up everywhere with snooker halls, lounges, bars and huge concert rooms. Variety shows were available six nights a week, with up to eight different acts on, as well as Bingo.

The Club in Peterlee was the biggest of these. Arriving there with Trevor, I thought it was very funny that the architects had had no idea what was required in a concert room. The floor of the stage had been carpeted and the first act on was a tap dancer. He still did his six-minute slot, but the audience, sitting at tables, thought he was rubbish because they couldn't hear him.

On this occasion, Trevor and I had been asked to do three, six-minute spots and would receive the grand sum of £3 for our efforts. We had carefully planned and rehearsed our routines. Trevor went on first with his accordion. He was a natural on this instrument and had started to play when he was very young, without lessons. He'd developed like this for a long time and then Mam and Dad paid for lessons, which put him right back at the beginning, but eventually he became a better musician. We had wired him up with small lights around the accordion to give him a finale to his act. This was closely followed by Bingo. For some, this game was the highlight of the evening and sometimes the acts got the impression that they were just filling in between games, rather than being the main attraction.

Once someone shouted 'House', half of the audience would disappear back to the bar in order to refill while I did my magic act. Sometimes Jackie would act as my assistant. More Bingo and then Trevor and I did our comedy spot. While in Hong Kong, I had heard these wonderfully funny American records by a comedy singer called Stan Freeburg. We performed a routine of miming to these records, which, because they had not been heard in the UK, went down really well. What was really funny was the fact that we stuck an old Dansette record player on stage with a microphone up against the tiny speaker at the front in order to amplify it over the rest of the venue. It must have sounded awful but we got a lot of other bookings so maybe we were funnier than we were awful.

By this time, Jackie and I had moved into a first-floor council flat, over a bank, on Normanby High Street. Lenny the Lion was a very popular ventriloquist act and his mother got married to a local councillor and moved in below us. The council offices also moved away from the grime and the smoke of South Bank, but I noticed how many office workers who'd moved there became sick because they were so used to the pollution, while the fresh air was killing them off. I guess you get used to your own environment and I read recently that the medical profession thinks that we are now so protected that we are not building up immunities in the way that we did when, as children, we played in the dirt. Funny old world, isn't it?

I had made several things for our new home because, on £4 10s a week, we had very little money to spend on furniture. We supplemented our income from the little we got from the clubs, but with a new baby on the way we had to be very careful.

One night we went to bed and suddenly heard strange footsteps outside our room. From the lounge-diner-kitchen, a corridor ran past the bedroom, through to the back end of the old house and down a few steps into the bathroom. The corridor ran past a frosted glass partition outside the bedroom and this is where we heard the footsteps coming from. Leaping out of bed and opening the door, I looked down the corridor only to find it empty.

After several nights of this, during which it was becoming more and more difficult to get some rest, Jackie became convinced the corridor was haunted. If there was no other explanation, then it had to be a ghost, she decided. I didn't believe in ghosts, but couldn't figure it out either, so I decided to sit in the corridor one night and 'ghost watch'.

I was used to ghost watching, in a way, because in Eston Cemetery there was a tomb and, according to legend, if you ran around it three times in the dark of the night, the devil would come out and talk to you. I tried that. It didn't work. Maybe you had to do it at midnight. I would love to meet a ghost, even though I don't believe in them. The reason is that if I met one, I would ask it some sensible questions about the afterlife and nobody seems to do that, do they?

With Jackie safely tucked up in bed, I took my seat in the passage complete with a favourite book and waited in the dimming light. About an hour later, I heard footsteps approaching rapidly, walk right through me and vanish off down the hallway. Although there was no sense of coldness, or draughts, it was the most peculiar sensation I had ever experienced.

A blast of inspiration encouraged me to go downstairs and ask if I could look around the downstairs flat. It had exactly the same layout as ours, including the partition and hallway. Then I discovered a clue. Their bedroom had a 'sticky' door, which took some effort to open and close properly. I asked if they would open and close this for me, as I dashed back up into our hallway. Sitting in the corridor, the strange sensation happened once more and this time I noticed how the opening of their sticky door caused the floorboards in our hallway to move. As their partition was supporting the floorboards of our hallway, it set off a chain reaction that sounded just like some phantom walking along it. I went back, eased their door, put some long nails diagonally into our floorboards and that was the end of our ghost.

Paul was born, taking us by surprise as he was premature. Jackie had been to the doctor with stomach pains that had interrupted her sleeping and caused acute tiredness. The doctor assured her it was not the baby and gave her some sleeping pills. That night the pains came back and she took a pill. The pains grew stronger so I said, 'Well, have another pill.'

After about three pills, with no easing of the pain and losing all hope of slumber, we realised it must be something more serious. After a quick warning telephone call, we beetled along to the hospital several miles away in our little car and were told that the arrival had indeed begun. With all the pills Jackie had been taking, apparently they had to keep waking her up in order to deliver the baby.

'Wake up and push! Wake up and push!'

It must have been one of the most relaxed births of all time. As it was not fashionable for the husband to be present, I was kept outside in the corridor, waiting anxiously for some news. I was everything that you'd expect an expectant dad to be. Nervous, worried, anxious, pacing the floor. When I was called in to see our little boy, wrapped in a sheet, with his tiny little hands and feet, it felt awesome. I was filled with immense love and protection for the little bundle in my arms and I didn't want to put him down. It was 9 September 1960 and I was a dad to Paul Newton Daniels. Then, a typically male thought entered my brain: 'I've got to pay for this!'

Families gather round as grandmas knit and mothers provide prams, and with our new house, we were the proudest and most contented parents on the planet. It's a good thing that I didn't know how short-lived our happiness was going to be.

CHAPTER 7

AGONIES OF
THE HEART

The Sixties exploded into the new century like an international firework. Cars, furniture and fashion all pointed to a new era that was desperate to leave the dowdiness of the past behind and embark on a new future. Labour-saving devices now provided more time to relax and encouraged the age of the leisure boom. With the new designer denim jeans heading up the fashion front, the birth of the package holiday was soon bringing up the rear. Even the packaging of everyday items on the shelf became more vibrant.

Soon after Paul's arrival, the council offered us a brand-new semi-detached home in Nightingale Road, Teesville. It was much bigger than the flat and we had our own garden, although the laziness of the builders meant that we grew bricks in the borders. At the end of our road was another street of similar houses and, driving past one day, I saw a lady pushing a pram. I hardly recognised her but it was Irene, the girl with whom I had shared my first real passion. Irene was now a very large woman, not tall, just large, and remembering the fear I had of fat ladies,

I was relieved that our one moment of enthusiasm hadn't led to anything more serious.

It's funny how little things stay in your memory. A man called one day to allow us a free one-month trial of a brand-new design in vacuum cleaners. In fact, he called on the entire street selling from the back of a large van. We all signed up for the free trial, gave the carpet cleaner a good workout and enjoyed clean carpets for months to come because he never came back either to collect it or to collect any money.

Our neighbours thought we were quite barmy. It wasn't the magic or the comings and goings at strange times, it was the gadgets. My father, supporting his new family, especially his grandson, as much as possible, was always bringing new labour-saving contraptions around for us to try out.

Imagine a slatted wardrobe door made from big chunky wood, laid flat, with two paving slabs on top to make it heavy and connected to two ropes. This was Dad's super-duper garden ploughing device. By dragging it along the ground it would break down and turn over the top surface of soil extremely effectively. The square plough should be dragged one way, then dragged the other, until your garden was in the right state for sowing your seeds. Even the stones would be removed, as they would come up through the slats and gather on the top. It was a clever gizmo, but to anyone watching over the fence it must have looked pretty silly.

What made them talk even more was when I marked off the area of lawn and grass-seeded it, before unrolling what looked like a thin strip of fibreglass sheeting around the edges of the lawn. Having placed these sheets on the ground, I covered them with a thin layer of soil and watered it. The neighbour's curiosity became too much and I heard his voice over the hedge, 'What are you doing?'

'I'm planting my borders,' I replied, trying to keep him in

suspense as much as possible. Within an amazingly short time, up came a perfectly measured out, fully flowering 'frame' around my lawn. I had found these 'instant' edgings in some magazine where they incorporate the plant seeds within the fibreglass. Once the sheeting rots away, it automatically plants the seeds in symmetrical rows. My neighbour couldn't believe his eyes. Don't you just love gardening with no work?

Eighteen months happily passed with every normal aspect of family life imaginable. I had been able to afford our own television, telephone and run our own car on family day trips into the beautiful surrounding countryside.

You don't have to drive far from Teesside to find some of the most glorious views in the world. I went to work which once again was in an office around the corner. On Monday evenings I went to the Middlesbrough Circle of Magicians and Jackie went to ballroom dancing classes. To me, everything inside and outside our garden was rosy, which makes the following story seem even more incredulous. I really never saw it coming. I am not the first to say that and I know I won't be the last.

Arriving home from work one evening, I sensed that something was seriously amiss. The house was very quiet and this was so alien to our normal timetable that a premonition dawned that something was not right. As I stood in the front room wondering what had happened, I remembered that I had seen something I thought was odd that afternoon. While out delivering the staff wages, I had seen Jackie's mum pushing Paul in a pram long after the time Jackie should have collected him and taken him home. It was an odd sight and I can remember somehow feeling very strange about it as I continued with my work.

Looking around the front room, my eye caught sight of a note on the mantelpiece, next to a photo of our wedding. As I saw it, I started to go cold and, as I took it in my hands, my skin began to turn to ice. Reading the letter only made things worse. It was from Jackie, saying that she had left me. Her words hit me as if I had been punched in the stomach and I gasped out loud for air. I had no idea, not an inkling that anything had been off-beam between us. The previous night we had made love. How could this be?

One hint gave the real truth away, when she wrote, '…When we are settled down, we'll come back for Paul.' At first I was stunned, as the reality of the situation began to sink in. She had left us both. The room started to spin. It was as if all my emotions had been frozen. I sat on the floor. I didn't know what to do. I felt sick, dizzy and the world really was spinning away from me.

In the middle of all this, very suddenly, I thought about Paul. I had to get Paul. The last time I had seen him was in the street being pushed by Jackie's mum. I got into the car, almost out of my mind with worry and confusion and was not really in any fit state to drive. Screeching and swerving the few miles to the next town, I miraculously arrived in one piece and knocked on the door of Jackie's mum and tried to act as calm and as normal as I possibly could.

Her mother answered the door and I told her that I had come for Paul. 'Where's Jackie?' she asked and I managed to act as if everything was OK and I had agreed to pick him up. I didn't mention the note. There was a danger she would have kept Paul had she known and I wasn't willing to risk that. I wanted him by my side, where I knew he was going to be safe.

I was desperate to get the tot in the car and frantically threw my 'goodbyes' over my shoulder as I walked away. Once on the road again, I drove straight round to Mam and Dad's and sat with my face in my hands, as Mam rocked Paul back to sleep. Oddly, Mam and Dad told me that they had already suspected that Jackie had met someone else. They were both there for me at the moment I needed them most, offering comfort or practical support, but it was one of the worst times of my life.

Determined to carry on as much as normal, I took the little 18-month-old back home with me later that evening, where he slept in his cot. I lay awake all night in a cold numbness, unable to think clearly and unable to stop thinking. I just couldn't imagine what tomorrow would bring.

I took some time off work initially, making some feeble excuse about there being sickness at home, but when I was alone in the house with Paul, I felt so isolated I just thought I was going to go crackers. Mam took over the regular day-to-day bringing up of Paul, while I went to work, returning each evening to take him back home. Although I tried to carry on as much as possible, it was a really difficult task and I was in a state of bewilderment for several days. I didn't know which way to turn or what to do. What I didn't realise at the time was the care my father had shown, when years later he admitted to having parked his car outside our house on that first night, just in case we needed him. That's fatherhood! Until you have a child you never realise that, no matter how old they become, you never stop worrying or caring about them.

Coming somewhat to my senses one day, I decided that I had to find Jackie and sort it all out once and for all. My first port of call was Phil Whitcombe's dancing school. As I sailed in, he looked up and smiled nervously.

By this time, my anger had taken over and I was mad.

'Where is Jackie?' I demanded.

Phil was quite a nice guy, dressed flamboyantly and was easily the campest man in town. He had known me from the days of trying to dance with Jackie until I suggested that she did the dancing and I did the magic. His effete reply came as no surprise.

'Her dancing partner, Ted. I did warn her. I could see it happening,' he stammered.

I got his name and swept out as fast as I had arrived, leaving a very white-faced Phil gazing after me. I knew this dancing partner to be a guy who had tended to use women and decided to find out all I could about him before making my approach.

In local government we had a system for identifying and finding bad payers. I used the process to hunt down the man who had stolen my wife and found the address of a flat they had rented in Saltburn. Taking legal advice, I telephoned my friend Martin from the Middlesbrough Circle of Magicians and asked if he would accompany me. To my relief and despite the tremendous imposition I was placing on him, he agreed.

We drove up to the block. It turned out to be part of an old Victorian house that had been converted into flats. It had a round tower window on the corner and this style was to haunt me for the rest of my life whenever I drove past a similar feature. We found the number on the first floor and I knocked loudly. When they opened the door, they were extremely surprised to see me, but I just marched straight through the open door with Martin behind me.

Jackie was sitting in the bed-sit, smoking. I had never seen her smoke before and the scene seemed unreal because of this. I just thought it all looked so sordid. The guy started to speak and, in very clear terms, I immediately told him to shut up.

'I want to speak to Jackie,' I announced. Standing in the silence, looking directly at her, I asked her the question I wanted to know more than anything.

'Are you coming back?'

'No.'

The emotions churned around inside like a giant washing machine.

'Well, I'll ask you again. Are you coming back?'

'No.'

Something really odd happened. As soon as she said the word

the second time, I went icy cold. Shutters came down inside me. I couldn't have cared less about her. I guess there is some safety mechanism inside us to protect us from trauma. It certainly protected me. Now I can't even remember the guy's name, so I'll just call him Bob.

'What are you going to do then?'

'Bob has a job in the Middle East and we're going to live there.'

A moment's pause. 'No, you're not,' I said.

'What do you mean?' she enquired, as I tried not to make it obvious that I was watching him out of the corner of my eye.

'His contract in the Middle East forbids him to take a woman with him.'

He couldn't argue. I opened up a file I had been carrying and showed them both the information I had collected on Bob.

'You'll also find, Jackie, that he is still married and has children and two more with another woman.'

I didn't hit Bob, I didn't strike her, I was seemingly so indifferent to the situation, I became a 'nothing' person. As I revealed the dossier, the guy's eyes narrowed as I calmly pointed out the maternity suits and court orders that pursued him. Bob began to get very defensive and did his best to make excuses, but the mud had stuck.

Spinning round to Jackie who sat speechless on the bed with two inches of fag ash hanging from her cigarette, I coolly said, 'so you haven't done yourself any favours, chuck!' And with that, knowing there was nothing left to either say or hear, I turned to leave.

Martin, who had met Jackie on many occasions and was becoming a family friend, spoke for the first time.

'I would like to have a word with Jackie alone, please.'

Amazingly, Bob and I went and sat in the car. After a few moments of stillness, I started the engine and drove off down the road, out into the country and towards a cliff top. I had no thoughts of suicide in my head but I knew Bob wasn't too sure; I was just driving aimlessly and dangerously. I just couldn't have cared less what happened to us.

I drove back to where I had left my friend, who was waiting on the doorstep on our return. Martin drove me back home and worried for me, asking if I was all right every few minutes.

'It's over, Martin,' was all I could say. I sat in a trance as the street lights flashed past and I really felt that part of me had died. From that moment on, I was going to get on with my life and make sure Paul was OK. That was all.

Mam agreed to look after Paul during the day, giving me time to work out a more permanent solution for him. Work got back to normal and after a week of washing, cooking and cleaning, I felt that we were making some headway. Then there was a knock at the door.

She stood there looking as though she had been in a wrestling match. With hair unkempt and traces of tears in her eyes, she spoke first.

'Ted, I'd like to come back.'

They say you think very quickly. I did then. A million thought processes instantly wrestled within me as we stood staring at each other for a moment. Paul needed a mother. I had no one else. Did I want a wife? Paul came first. I invited her in, feeling nothing much at all, really.

I have tried to work out whether that was a mistake. I will never know. It would never be the same as it was before, not because of her, but because of me. I couldn't forgive her. Everything I felt had been betrayed, abused and destroyed to the point at which I couldn't accept her at face value. I had changed so much in that couple of weeks; it hardly seemed true, or possible. As far as I was concerned, Jackie had decided that our marriage was over and I had reluctantly bitten the bullet and let go. On the other hand, it is impossible to live with someone for a long time and not have some kind of friendship. I guess that's the most I can say. We settled down into a life again. Jackie never ever said that she was sorry.

We lived together for the next seven years. A kind of falseness pervaded everything we did together. She said she wouldn't go dancing any more but, on consideration, what difference would that make? The damage had already been done. My family life became strangely detached from my career and despite the fact that we soon had two more beautiful boys to join us, Martin in 1963 and Gary in 1969, home life was never to be the same again.

An even stranger phenomenon was that Jackie took a keen interest in my magic and became a very good magician in her own right. I threw myself into magic and the clubs. Trevor went off to Loughborough Teacher Training College with the aim of becoming a teacher and I started to put together a new act with a lot of help from Martin Marshall, one of the judges who had watched me at the Middlesbrough Circle of Magicians.

Using an anagram of 'Daniels', I gave this new act the horrendous title of 'The Eldanis' (it sounded exotic at the time) and crafted it purely for magic convention competitions. There were many opportunities to enter, as there were so many. The Middlesbrough Circle was very good in that its members tried constantly to perform magic, unlike other clubs where they seem to just sit around and talk about it. This is really where I started to move towards a professional career, even though it was still a few years away. Each time I gave a performance in front of my fellow members, they would carefully take it apart with their own thoughts and suggestions on improving it. This way it was possible to hone and refine my act in a way that was impossible elsewhere. There was no sense of jealousy or maliciousness among my colleagues. It was just good, honest, constructive criticism and we enjoyed encouraging one another in this practical way. Martin Marshall, known as Martini (we thought it was exotic at the time) was of particular help and became such a good friend that, later, I was to name my second son after him.

The fine-tuning meant that when the club produced a public show, everyone knew it would be of the very highest quality. We would spend weeks designing, building and painting scenery, props and illusions and I tried my hand at everything. These annual performances in which a whole stage show was built from scratch in the Middlesbrough Little Theatre, were always a great success, as were the competitions. Martin was the driving force behind the shows.

One night, Martin told me a story 'against' himself that still cracks me up to this day. I can be driving along the road and suddenly burst out laughing as I replay what happened in my mind's eye.

You have to understand that Martin was not a young man when this happened and used to wear those drawstring pyjama trousers that tie off at the front. It so happened that a company called G-Plan had created the latest fad in furniture design. Martin decided to buy a dressing table in the new design and showed it off to everyone who came to visit.

'Look at this,' he would say, and demonstrate that the 8ft-long single drawer would pull out at the corner without hesitation. 'That's real craftsmanship.' I admit I thought it odd at the time that it also had a long, low, horizontal mirror the whole length of the cabinet when everybody knows the human body is vertical. I was such an innocent and never connected the horizontal mirror with the bed in the bedroom. I don't think Martin or Freda, his wife, did either.

One night, Martin was about to climb into bed next to Freda when she asked, 'is that a boil on your nose?'

AGONIES OF THE HEART

Martin went to the dressing table with its low mirror and saw a spot on the bridge of his nose.

'No, I don't think so, I think it's just a spot,' and with that he bent over the dressing table to squeeze it.

As he bent over, his balls (sorry, Mam) swung out of his pyjamas and into the very long top drawer. Not only that, but his body weight, leaning forward, closed the drawer with his thighs and he was literally 'trapped by the balls'. He yelled, as you would, and tried to open the drawer but the handles were too wide for him to reach. Freda would have helped but she was screaming with laughter and rolling about on the bed. Women are funny like that.

The Will Fleet Trophy, an in-house competition held over several evenings each year, was named after one of the best-known magicians in the north-east and awarded for excellence in all categories of magic. Each competition evening was given over to a different aspect of the theatre of magic. One night would examine the use of silks, another card magic, one liquid magic, another tricks from a book or spherical objects and a night of illusions. Each act should last more than four minutes, but no longer than six, so timing was a good discipline to learn. All the magicians were examined for what they could do in each grouping, with points awarded for first, second, third and even just for competing. The magician who accumulated the most points at the end of the year won the trophy.

It would have been useless simply to perform stock tricks that everybody knew and bought from a magical dealer. What really appealed were the tricks that were different in approach and presentation and thinking up new ways of achieving miracles was the challenge I enjoyed the most. I wanted, needed and took pleasure in being different and something inside me suggested that this was the only real way forward. I soon developed the ability to pick up a trick and practically convert it to my own style. This was to become an essential ingredient in the television work that was to follow, where rehearsal time was limited. In television, I was to learn, anybody could do the act they have done for years and sparkle with it. You know your regular stuff so well. It's when you come to do something that is not your act where it counts. I've always believed that it was the Middlesbrough Circle of Magicians that trained me and laid essential foundations for my future career in television.

At that time, however, magic was still a hobby and any real thoughts of earning proper money from it were just an illusion. I was so involved with magic, however, that it wasn't my relationship with Jackie or Paul that suffered, it was Eston Urban District Council. The time spent on magic became very detrimental to learning about accounting, which in turn prevented me from climbing the 'real' work ladder and maybe I should be grateful for that. I soon moved to Redcar Borough Council as an internal auditor.

We formed The Eldanis as a couple and rehearsed until we had it perfected, with a few jobs dropping into our laps here and there. Having gained a little publicity about the colourful and unique nature of our act, we had been booked to appear at the Fiesta Club in Stockton. Supporting 'Little Miss Dynamite' Brenda Lee on the Sunday and the great Frankie Vaughan the rest of the week seemed like a dream come true, but we never anticipated our potential and saw each gig as purely one-off.

What made this magic act different was that we abandoned the old 'waltzy' kind of dreamy music that magicians usually worked to and replaced it with rock 'n' roll. Soft rock, yes, but it was a million miles away from what had gone before. For its time, it was also quite sophisticated with both of us wearing matching lurex outfits (yes, folks, I was in lurex before Elvis!) and a good lighting plot. The heart of the act consisted of a selection of small to mid-size trickery, big enough for a good-sized room, but not like illusions where you have the daunting task of packing and travelling them each night. We worked the magic both together and separately throughout the act. One of the better conventions, Blackpool Magicians' Convention, booked us to appear in their gala show at the famous Blackpool Pleasure Beach and a gentleman approached us immediately after the act and asked us if we had a Summer Season.

To be honest, I was so ignorant of the real workings of showbusiness that I didn't know what he was talking about. I said 'no' and he invited us up to his office where he produced a contract and said, 'sign here.' The light slowly dawned on me and I blurted out that he didn't want us, he wanted one of the professionals who were still working downstairs.

We were just a couple of amateur artistes having fun, and despite being the owners and originators of a very good act I felt like a summer season was right out of our league. How could we ever give up our day jobs? I was still an internal auditor at Redcar Borough Council.

'I'm offering you a glittering contract for a 20-week season in the Mecca of showbiz,' he repeated.

I turned it down. I wonder what and where I would be if I hadn't. Despite the fact that Jackie and I could still work together, that deep-down friendship, that I longed would return, still eluded us. The loving relationship had gone and the bare shell of an acquaintance was all that remained. A solid steel wall of hurt had cut us in two and this time there seemed to be no escape.

Jackie's affair had had a deeper impact on me than I had first imagined and I felt it was some kind of a failure on my part that had caused the split. Maybe it was. I had a sense of utter and total rejection. It never went away.

The way I dealt with my own rejection was to have a series of one-night stands, to prove to myself, I suppose, that I was able to attract and arouse women and in the process somehow claim back my lost masculinity. In retrospect, I am not proud of this period of my life at all. At the time I never even thought much about what I was doing, I just did it. Those scenes in the back of cars and in tiny flats had nothing to do with what I really wanted. Why none of the woman said 'no' I do not understand. Here was I, unable to believe in myself and, despite my obvious insecurity, nobody said 'no'. A sequence of affairs with varying degrees of success followed, though none of them lasted.

All this only served to drive a deeper wedge between Jackie and myself and it was clearly inevitable that we were on the downward slope and gradually drifting further apart. As much as I would have liked it, I didn't have whatever it took to 'bridge' that ever-widening gap. I still have many regrets, but I am resigned to the fact that the wounds of this chapter in my life may never be healed.

As our marriage went gradually downhill, I not only threw myself at women, I also transferred my energies more and more into my magic. Ironically, it was a woman who unexpectedly gave me the opportunity to put my skills to better use. When Betty Hygate knocked on my door, she struck me as a very forthright but honest businesswoman and I was interested to hear her proposals. Her son was something of a local celebrity, having won the Stubby Kaye Silver Star Award on television. Now, in his mid-teens, Billy was still working in the clubs as a guitar vocalist and seemingly making some good money out of it.

Betty must have been eyeing up my Ford Thames Dormobile-style van parked outside our house, for it was this that had obviously caught her imagination. Betty dived straight into the point of her visit.

'How do you feel about doing a joint tour of the clubs in your vehicle?' she offered.

AGONIES OF THE HEART

To be honest, I wasn't all that bothered. My life had settled down into a circle of work, playing with Paul, Martin and, of course, my magic toys. Us men never grow up, you know.

'I'll get the bookings, but not charge you commission as an agent might, and you drive the show round in your van. Billy will be the star and do his guitar spot; there'll be an opening singer called Gladys Ford; and you do a magical comedy spot in the middle.' Betty reminded me yet again how Billy was destined to be a star and was sure that he would remember me when his name was finally up in lights.

By now, with the enormous help and support from the local magic club, I was used to winning endless competitions and my skills had broadened and expanded enormously. I had subtly grown in my ability to entertain with magic but I said that maybe we should try a couple of nights out and see how it went.

They went well and we started to do more and more working men's clubs around the north-east. There was one small problem – I finished up being the roady for the show and humped the gear in and out. Well, that wasn't too bad because by now I was 28 years old and had given up local government. Mam had bought a shop in Uvedale Road, South Bank, and I worked for her. Lifting sacks of potatoes was building my muscles. I had taken the job as it gave me more flexible working hours and was also 'insurance' in case the club work collapsed.

It was also a good time to change my name. Ted Daniels never rolled off the tongue successfully and was misinterpreted in a number of different ways. When it was announced by the concert secretaries it either had a stutter in the middle ('Ted-d-d Daniels') or it became one word ('Tedaniels'). It could have been worse, I suppose. A very good act called Les Pollux I heard being announced as Les (as in Leslie), and Bollocks (as in need I say more!) When the compere had his attention attracted by the band, they tried to tell him that it was French, 'Lay', and that there were two of them. He turned back to the microphone and announced the Two Bollocks.

On another occasion in another club, Les Aristos became Harry Stowe, and so on. This last act did mind-reading and in Sheffield one lunchtime he predicted the tote double numbers for the night-time draw (a sort of lottery) and left his prediction in an envelope pinned to the wall of the stage. That night, when the envelope was opened and the prediction found to be correct (it's a trick, folks), a man in the audience stood up and claimed that the only way he could have known was if the tote double was a 'fix'. Another man stood up, said he was on the committee, and that it wasn't. The first said he was a liar and all hell broke out. I think everyone in the club, male and female, was fighting. Throughout it all, Peter Aristophanes stood on the stage, bowing.

Having tried several name variations, I chose that of my first-born son, Paul, and it just stuck as if it was meant. Paul Daniels was a mellifluous name and easily rolled off the tongue in any introduction. Encouraging everybody around me to use my new name so that I could get used to it, Mam still called me Ted, but then mams are special anyway. Nowadays, though, even Mam calls me Paul and the only time Ted turns up is when I send birthday or Christmas cards to Mam and Trevor.

Our mini concert party spent the next two years doing one-night stands within a couple of hours' travelling distance from home and the biggest miracle was always that the dilapidated Ford got us there and back in one piece. At one point, I was driving the van with my hand inside the engine to operate the accelerator. This old van did us proud as we slowly rumbled our way across Yorkshire and Durham to reach our destination. The fact that the engine was contained in a big lump of metal between the two front seats was extremely useful. In the freezing winters I would lift the metal top off the engine and it would quickly warm the interior, so we always arrived snug and warm even when the van's regular heater broke down.

Our portable concert party proved to be a big hit in the smaller clubs where our offering of a whole evening of various entertainments must have proved very economical for them, but there was change afoot. The working men's clubs were developing into large and glamorous institutions, although it was still the working lads that were running them. There were hundreds of clubs, probably thousands. In Barnsley alone, a small market town, there were 27 venues you could work as an entertainer and two of them were for full-week engagements.

Out of these developed the nightclub scene where entrepreneurs were keen to capitalise on the trend towards this new form of entertainment. The nightclubs, however, made a decision that they wanted more than just a ten-minute silent act, forgetting that those acts provided the variety between the singer and the comedian. You can't juggle for 45 minutes. You can't throw knives or spit darts or do any of the other wonderful things that the speciality act does for more than six or seven minutes. Those acts condense the excitement and really make a difference to a show. The result of this was that we lost all the thrills and spills of our speciality acts to venues abroad. My answer to this was to provide some of the missing speciality within my own act and I split my Eldanis act into two, put patter in the middle and went back to the music for the finale. The patter grew and grew and eventually I dropped the music. That was a major breakthrough for me. I looked carefully at myself and decided that I wasn't tall enough to look good in tail suits and that my hard Northern accent did not lend itself to posh, patter. I read everything I could on comedy and, like the magic, tailored it to make it fit me.

Far and away the most successful TV presenter at the time was Bruce Forsyth. For me he still is the greatest presenter of a game show that we have ever had, getting more out of the participants than anyone since. His style was 'pleasantly insulting', taking the mickey out of the players but doing it with no nastiness at all. There is a very old theatrical poster of a magician and the by-line says 'All done by kindness'. So that was the approach I decided to adopt. I would poke fun, but never with malice.

The act worked fine, but it was the clubs themselves that were a bigger stumbling block to the acts than the audiences. The local club committees had seen their authority grow enormously, with many becoming power-mad little Hitlers, but having no idea at all about showbusiness. Three stages of bureaucracy operated in the venues: the committee (these words were always said in a way that implied mysterious power and total control – the COMMITTEE were to be revered!) consisted of a dozen guys who appointed a Concert Secretary who dealt with the agents and booked the acts. Often, if he had got his own act together, he would take back-handers from all the agents. The final member of this team would be the chairman who, with no experience in appearing before an audience, would be master of ceremonies and compere the evening.

This job was a throwback from old-time music hall where the chairman would sit in a little box at the side of the stage and announce each act with wonderfully effusive English and a bang of his gavel. The concert chairman still had his own box somewhere in the room, but his use of the English language left a lot to be desired:

'Ladies and Gentleman, we've got an act here that I don't think is going to be any good, but we've paid for it so we'll have it anyway,' could easily be your entrance speech. Half-way through a song would come the announcement from the corner, cutting off the singer's microphone, 'Pies have come and are on sale at the bar.' Girl singers who were not going very well would have the audience quietened with 'Come on now. Give ORDER. Give the poor cow a chance.'

They also knew nothing about staging, lighting or sound. They had saved up and bought the equipment, but they didn't know how it worked. Why should they? They were steel workers and lads from down the pit.

For me, each new arrival at a club was like being thrown into a battle with the system and, with up to eight acts a night treading their boards, I realised that they had 'seen everything'. With the notion that 'if you want something doing well, do it yourself' firmly established in my head, I would arrive early at each venue and focus the lighting, adjust the curtains and tweak the sound to help it reach its full potential. The lights were invariably pointing at the drummer's feet, while the loudspeakers would be aimed into the roof. The amplifier would be set to full bass. Often, I found that the lights hadn't been cleaned for years and contained enough dust on the lenses to emit about a candle-worth of power. After my efforts, I may not have been the best act they'd ever had, but I was certainly the brightest!

The concert chairman walked around with an air of false dignity and knowledge but in reality was usually no help whatsoever. Telling one girl singing act in the interval how lousy they were, he threatened to pay them off. This meant only giving the act half their agreed money and was often used as a way of getting cheap acts. The leader of the girl troupe suggested that the wonderful harmonies they were producing were going over the audience's heads.

'OK then, lass. I'll let you have another go and this time we'll lower the speakers.'

It was the period when the Labour Government had lost control over the industrial areas of Britain, giving in to every union demand and pricing us out of the world market. The unions were running the marketplace and electricity strikes, among many others, were frequent. On two occasions the lights went out in the middle of my act, but I continued with the use of some candles and torches. Believe me, working in those conditions, with no microphone and cigarette smoke down to floor level, really kills off your voice. At one point, I announced the next trick, clapped my hands and all the lights came on. It was pure coincidence, but the audience thought I was a real wizard.

Another chairman proudly showed me his gas-run, an emergency stage lighting system. From a huge orange gas canister, borrowed from a set of roadworks, ran a rubber pipe, which went across the ceiling and was connected to a lamp hanging precariously over the stage on a metal hook. I am not very tall but even I had to duck every time I passed this ingenious lighting device. The Concert Chairman had resolved not to be outdone when faced with a power cut.

Despite the fact that the gas lamp, had it been lit, would probably have quickly set the stage on fire, I asked how the electronic organ would work.

'That's easy, he can just unplug it and play it like a piano.'

The awesome 'wisdom' of these men kept us acts amused for hours, and the tales would be told over and over again in the digs at night when we all assembled with our take-away Indian and Chinese meals. We always had the last laugh, as we could earn in one night what they earn in a week. The average wage before 1970 was £20 a week, so for them a whole shift would bring in as much as we got in half-an-hour. This caused some Concert Chairmen to view us as 'over-paid ponces', but they forgot the expenses involved. I had to have a car, a telephone and the clothes and equipment for the stage, alongside the agent's commission and the high rate of taxation, all of which soon ate into the fee.

I got away with the tough audiences because they admired

the skill, particularly with a pack of cards. I could do things with a pack of cards that they definitely couldn't do, but they would have loved to have the ability so I grabbed their respect one way or the other. If I didn't astonish them, I would make them laugh and vice versa. Unfortunately, I witnessed how a lot of comedians quickly 'died' in places like this where they had no choice but to wage war against the stage facilities, the badly designed rooms and the Concert Chairman before they even reached the stony audiences. Some comedians had it written in their contract that they would never play Sunderland, the most feared of all the areas for clubs. One of the clubs on a Sunderland estate even had gravestones drawn on the wall of the only dressing room, with the names of the acts that had 'died' there, with a few blanks reserved for 'new members'.

'Just look who's died here!' they would proudly point out as they showed you to your room. It wasn't the best way for any act to prepare for a night's performance. The clubs were different to any other entertainment venue in the universe.

On my first appearance at a particular Sunderland working men's club, Redhouses, whose name still strikes terror into the hearts of comedians who played there, I was booked alongside a comedian I had admired ever since I saw him at the Windmill Theatre in London. Known during the war as 'We never closed', it was later adjusted to 'We never clothed' on account of the strippers, who were not allowed to move. It was also the birthplace of most of the period's top comics and I had sneaked into this world of wonder as a pimply teenager to sample both delights.

There was obviously something seriously wrong with me at the time as I really enjoyed the comedians and found that the girls, for me, were the 'intervals' – all except one girl who was absolutely stunning. Remember, I was still a teenager when I saw her and I was greatly upset that she never waited for me and while I was in the Army she married Tommy Steele. Why should she wait? We had never met. This is very similar of course to the 'affairs' that I have had with Goldie Hawn, Jodie Foster and Meg Ryan. It's OK. Debbie knows about these 'other women' in my life and smiles sympathetically at me. Wives do that, have you noticed?

Meanwhile, back at the Windmill the performances would run all evening and into the night, with a rolling audience that would arrive and leave as necessary. The men around me had their coats rolled up into a bundle, so that as soon as a seat became vacant in front, they would hurriedly throw it down to reserve the space. Thus, over a period of hours, a man could work his way into the prized front row to ogle directly at the box of delights.

Spending two hours suspended somewhere between arousal and laughter, one comedian really stood out, although he never became famous. This guy was experienced at holding such a distracted and constantly changing audience and I was very impressed with his skill. His rapid-fire songs and gags hit the audience between the eyes and he survived each one of his 'slots' with a good round of applause.

Years passed and this same comedian now faced a Sunderland audience. The weekend lunchtime gig is the one at which the men decided whether to bring their wives that evening. You were always booked for the noon and night shows. I had gone well. I was on first and opened with my usual fancy shuffles all performed to gags. My act went well. May I be allowed more than a little conceit here? My manager says that I am the only act who he has had over the years who has never 'died'. I think it is because I have such a good time being on stage that it is contagious and the audience come along for the ride. As soon as I finished I decided to stay on and see the comic that I had enjoyed in the Windmill Theatre all those years beforehand.

AGONIES OF THE HEART

That lunchtime the whole of the bar counter had been covered with half-filled pint glasses. There must have been several hundred or so and I don't think I had ever seen so many lined up in one place. At about ten minutes to opening time, the bar staff began frantically filling the glasses to the top, making sure each one had the customary 'head'. As the doors to the club opened, the rush of men's bodies was astonishing and could only be described as a Northern man's Harrods sale. Making straight for the bar, these men bought their pints and downed them in seconds before purchasing the next.

'You ready now?' asked the Concert Chairman with a strong Geordie twang, as the comic put the finishing touches to his make-up.

'Yes, mate. Now what I need you to do is go out and introduce me, at which point I'll stick my head through the curtains and shout, "Hiya, fellas!" You hit the music and we're off.'

The Concert Chairman, on this occasion, did exactly what was required of him and introduced this great comic. The comic stuck his head through the curtains and shouted as planned, 'Hiya, fellas!'

Now there's no way you can account or prepare for what happened next. As one man, 800 voices shouted, 'FUCK OFF!'

The band played and as the curtains began to open at the top, the poor guy hung on to the bottom shouting, 'don't open these curtains!' Too late. He's dead. Within ten minutes the room was empty.

On one of our touring concert party events, Gladys made her exit to no applause, I survived with laughter but no applause and poor Billy Hygate ended his 'star' spot in complete silence, except for the clinking of beer glasses. As we made our way out through the audience, which, as usual, was the only way out, one of the lads we passed said, 'Well, ya the best concert party we've ever 'ad 'ere.'

I couldn't believe it. I thought he was taking the mick and asked, 'so why didn't you clap?'

'Why, ya canni clap wir a glass in ya 'and.'

One evening, a guy from an audience in Yorkshire shouted out, 'Arr don't like thar suit!'

'That's a shame,' I replied. "Cos I like yours. Not a lot, but I like it!" The contrast made the audience laugh and I used a very old comic technique going back to the line a few times in my act: 'You'll like this, not a lot, but you'll like it.' By the end of the act I had a catchphrase and it was one of the major factors in my later climb to fame. This catchphrase was well known all over the North of England long before I made it on television. So much so, that other businessmen in Doncaster would say to Mervyn, my manager, 'Paul must be in the area again, my workers are saying "not a lot" all the time again.' Years later, this catchphrase, credited to me, was put into the *Dictionary of Colloquialisms and Common Language*. I thought that was better than getting a Royal Variety Show!

The amount of work I was now involved in was incredible. Not only did I own and operate a successful grocery store and a mobile shop, but was adding several gigs to my bulging diary each week. Almost every weekend I was out, increasingly now on my own, as Martin and Gary, our newest family additions, needed Jackie at home full-time. The mobile shop was fun, although, to be honest, I have always liked selling things, whether it be in a shop, at a trade fair or even on stage and 'selling' the act.

It wasn't built originally as a shop. It had been a bus going around the Isle of Wight and used as a shop with very little alteration. Mam bought it first as a going concern and as an 'add-on' to her general store. We took it off the rounds and Dad and I rebuilt it and I ran it for her. Being Dad, he insisted that we gutted it completely and levelled the floor. By the time it was finished it even had a potato store in the boot and a freezer box for the frozen foods. The sides were shelved and we carried an amazing array of goods. This was pre-mobile phone days, so if we ran out of anything we had to find a phone box and either Mam or Dad would bring it out to us.

When the refurbishment was finished, we stocked it up and off I went. The first corner we came to I couldn't get the steering wheel to turn at all. I obviously wasn't strong enough for this job. So I developed the knack of coming to the corners and taking the bus down to first gear. At the corner itself I would stand up, leaving the bus in first gear, stand to one side of the wheel and heave the top of the wheel towards me using my body weight. Thankfully, the bus had plenty of room on both sides of the wheel. This went on for months and I built up muscles that I didn't know I had. Lynn, Jackie's cousin, who worked on the bus as a shop assistant, used to laugh at my antics as we went around the estates of Grangetown, Dormanstown and Redcar.

One day, trundling from one stop to the next, I gave a man a lift to the next stop as it was raining. He watched me in amazement. 'What the hell are you doing?' he asked. I explained that I wasn't strong enough to drive the bus round corners and he asked what pressure I had in the tyres. 'Well, now, it's funny you should ask that. I couldn't find out so I added about 10lb of pressure to what I have in my car tyres,' I replied. He laughed like hell. Together we trundled into a local garage where he put at least another 60lb of pressure in every tyre.

At the next corner I shot up on to the pavement and nearly ran into a lamp-post, the bus was so light to drive. You learn something new every day. After that, even Jackie drove the bus.

Mam and Dad thought I was overdoing it a bit and insisted that we take a holiday. The only thing available that we could afford at such short notice was a week at Butlin's Holiday Camp at Filey. Off we went and, after such a busy schedule, I was twitchy at having nothing to do. I think it was the Monday afternoon I wandered past one of the theatres, heard a noise and went in. They were trying to cajole people into entering the talent contest and no one wanted to play. Just to help them out I went on stage and did a few tricks with the pack of cards that I always carried. By the time I had finished and broken the ice, a queue of hopefuls had formed and the audition was under way.

A Redcoat asked me my name and cabin number and said that I would definitely be in the show that night. Crikey! I went off and checked my clothes and put together a few tricks from the stuff I had with me. I won the heat in the talent contest that night and was automatically put into the next heat the next night. Blimey! I spent the next day putting together an act for the next night because I didn't want to do the same stuff. It's funny how people will listen to the same songs over and over again but always want the comics and the magicians to keep coming up with new stuff.

I won that heat and was put into the semi-finals. I won again and now I was in a panic. A telephone call to Dad to bring some more props and he thought that I was mad. He reminded me that I was supposed to be on holiday. Well, he was right but I preferred having something to do. He brought some props and I put together an act for the Grand Final of the talent contest for the week. I won, but as it was the last week of the season, they were to hold the Grand Final of the talent contest for the season the next night. I was on again and this time put together an act that finished with the World-Famous Bullet-Catching Trick. Well, nearly. This was a comedy version where it was announced that as the marksman had failed to turn up, I would shoot the gun at myself.

This was, believe me, a very funny routine. I had done it

before and I knew it was a killer. The gun is very tiny when you take it out of the very large pistol box but it fires with a huge bang. As the smoke clears a huge steel bullet is seen in your mouth and you spit it out 'for examination' on to a plate. The plate smashes and, for some reason only known to the Gods of Comedy, this situation is so ludicrous the audience fall about laughing.

That night I worked with more great talent in one place than I have ever worked with since. All the acts were great entertainers. What a show. My turn and the act went like a dream. Everything worked, the audience laughed in all the right places. I came to the finale, the World-Famous Catching the Bullet in the Teeth trick. The laughs were still coming. The smoke cleared and I spat the bullet out on to a Butlin's dinner plate and it just sat there. The plate didn't break. The audience just sat there waiting for the punchline that would never come. I had nothing left to do. I walked off. This was before Mervyn was my manager, so his claim that I never died is true, for him. This was the only time that I ever walked off to the sound of my own feet and the feeling is still inside me. I walked out into the car park and threw the plate as high as I could. It landed without a scratch. I should have checked the prop before I went on stage and everything has been double-checked ever since.

This work overload did not overawe me and, indeed, had the opposite effect as I found how much I enjoyed my new, frantic lifestyle. It conveniently enabled me to escape from the problems at home and my busy routine helped repair some of the holes in my self-esteem.

Finishing a series of engagements in Manchester, I got involved in some arguments between Betty and a landlady in one of our regular digs and this had started a spate of rows between us. With this awkward relationship bubbling underneath, I later overheard her extol the virtues of her little

Billy to a Manchester agent. Having left the door open, I heard the dialogue erupt into a full-blown argument when the agent suggested that although her son was an excellent guitar vocalist, he could pick up the telephone and within an hour have 100 others standing in his office. He went on to try to explain to her that what was really unique was the guy outside. This is the truth – I honestly was looking around to see who he was talking about and it turned out to be me. Understandably this can't have gone down well with Betty.

After a few days of working under the intense tensions that had now pervaded our team, I said I would leave. Sadly, although explaining that I just couldn't work under such a bad atmosphere, we parted company on bad terms.

Not only was I left with a bad taste in my mouth, but a hole in my pocket, for I had now begun to rely on the extra money the shows were bringing in. No matter how much you earn, your expenses increase to match the income. Glancing through my address book at the names of several agents I had bumped into over the last two years, I telephoned Joe Vipond, a Middlesbrough agent. Explaining my predicament and tentatively enquiring whether there was a possibility of any work in the next few weeks, he replied, 'How about tomorrow night?'

Astounded, I accepted the gig for more money than I had received with the concert party. From this moment on, I got so much regular work on higher fees that I soon put the grocery shop on the market, convinced that I was now able to support the family single-handed.

The reply to my offer of a sale came in the form of a large Indian family who arrived on my doorstep the next day.

'Excuse me, sir? Most important question: is it right you are selling the shop?'

'Yes, that's right.'

'Well now, the most important question: can we look round?'

'Yes, of course.' I watched as all his relatives trundled courteously around from potatoes to plums.

'Well now, the most important question: can we be selling other things beside this?'

'I presume so, it's not for me to say. The local council will no doubt advise.'

'So, the most important question: can I be opening longer hours than you?'

'I'm sure that's fine,' I said, becoming more bewildered at the friendly interrogation by the moment.

'Well then, most important question: how much?'
Explaining that the price should include the shop with the stock, the rates and the licence on top, I disclosed my figure.

'One moment please,' he smiled, as he disappeared out of the door, returning moments later with a suitcase.

'Here you are, sir,' he beamed, as he plonked the case on my little counter and opened it to reveal several stacks of crisp notes. 'Goodbye.'

'I'm sorry?' I said slightly stunned.

'You sell shop, I want to buy and here is money, goodbye.'

I explained that in England it was important to get solicitors and agents involved but his excuse was that they cost money and we didn't need them anyway, we had struck a deal on our own. For the life of me I couldn't think why not, but I persuaded him that I had to do it legally and it was only a matter of weeks before our little corner shop had a new manager and a new identity.

The bus-cum-mobile shop had to go as well. Lynn and I had built up a good relationship with most of our customers and it was a bit of a sad day when we made the last tour. Mind you, it was not all sadness. In Dormanstown we had one lady who'd clamber aboard and used to point at everything with a long, bony finger. 'How much is that?' and 'How much is that?' and

'How much is that?' Whenever she had got off the bus in the past Lynn and I would do 'parrot' impressions as we drove away: 'How much is that? Who's a naughty boy?' It was a regular routine. The last day she climbed up and went into her regular routine. It just so happened that we had some of those cream doughnuts with the hole in the middle on the counter. As she pointed at them and started to ask 'How much ...' I upped with one of the doughnuts and jammed it on to her pointing digit. As she gaped, Lynn and I were rolling about laughing. I told her that one was free.

At the next estate, a lady came on board who, particularly when the bus was full, would say that something was much cheaper on Andy's bus. He was our 'competition' and what she was saying just wasn't true. I pointed out that she should go and shop on Andy's but she never did. We used to sell some lovely custard tarts. About 6in round they were, and about 2in deep. Lovely. She bought one. She stood there as I scooped up the tart with my right hand, careful not to break the light pastry that surrounded the custard. My left hand flicked open the white paper bag. 'In the bag or in your face?' I asked. Without moving (silly girl) she started to say, 'You wouldn't d...' and she had a face full of custard. Lynn wet herself. Luckily, the woman laughed as well and I said that I would run her to the end of the road where she lived. As I set off she came alongside me in the bus holding a custard tart in her hand. Until this moment in my life I had never laughed at slapstick comedy. I started to laugh so much that I could hardly control the bus. I knew that when I stopped I would get it. I drove slower but eventually got there. I stopped. I got it. Getting a custard pie in your face is one of the funniest things that can happen to you. Don't believe me? Go on, bake some. Have a party!

We bought a new terraced house with a garden in South Terrace, still in South Bank. Jackie and the boys moved in. So did I, but not for very long. Jackie fell pregnant with Gary and he was born in 1969. I missed so much of his growing time, diving home whenever possible to see him and Paul and Martin. The decision to turn full time pro meant that I dared not turn down any job that came my way.

With no shops to run I was now free to move anywhere within clubland and I did so. My first full week as a pro was with a rock 'n' roll star called Vince Eager. Over hundreds of performances my act had sorted itself out into, dare I say it, a unique and entertaining style. The manner in which the tricks were delivered was so very different that I suppose I was the equivalent of the alternative comedians that came along later.

That first week with Vince we were in South Wales and I think that Mountain Ash Conservative Club was the first gig. I remember that because Mountain Ash had the cleanest public toilets I had ever seen. Things like that leave an impression on a travelling man.

On one of the gigs that week the backing was, as usual, organ and drums. The problem in most clubs was that the musicians could not read music. The COMMITTEE who listened to them as they played their repertoire of learnt-by-ear music, magnificently pounding out the 'Dam Busters March' and the like, would have nothing bad said about their band because THEY employed them. 'The finest in the Valleys' or, in the North, 'You'll get none better, Ah'll tell you that, none better.'

At this Welsh venue, Vince had talked the 'dots' (music) through with the 'musicians' and on they went. There was a balcony and I went up there to watch the spot. As soon as they had started it was obvious that the organist had no idea what was going on. Vince decided after the first song to lose the organist and go ahead by accompanying himself on the guitar and just use the drummer. The organist took the hump at this and went off stage to the right. The second number started and slowly, ever so slowly, the right-hand curtain started to close. It was obvious to everyone except Vince that someone was pulling the cloth nearer and nearer to the organ. A hand came out and picked up the cigarette that had been left burning on the end of the keyboard and it and the curtain went back to the right. Clouds of smoke came out from the wings where the organist was obviously doing his impression of the famous cigar advertisement.

The song finished and I should explain that most organs had a squat oblong freestanding speaker. Not this one. It had a tall, upright speaker between the organ and the drums and as Vince was doing his link to the next song, the drummer shuffled in a crablike movement sideways behind the tall speaker. His bum suddenly appeared on the right side of the speaker as he bent down and, when he straightened up, the bottom of a pint glass appeared on the left side as it described an arc in the air as the drummer got a drink. He bent over again (we could see his bum) and then he appeared in the same peculiar, legs-bent-facing-the-audience-crab-like-movement back to his drum stool.

The next number was heavy rock 'n' roll and the drummer laid into it. Suddenly, his head started twitching to his right as he looked into the wings and he also kept gesturing with his head to his bass drum. Nobody was listening to or watching Vince. We were totally hooked on the pantomime going on behind him, particularly when, with fag dangling from the corner of his mouth, the organist appeared on his hands and knees, crawled behind the organ, crossed behind the speaker and knelt sideways in front of the drumkit, holding the drum with his hands to stop it 'crawling' forward. As Vince rocked he stayed there, nodding and smiling at the audience who were failing about. Vince's face was a picture when he saw him. I don't know what was said but the kneeling drum holder left in an even bigger huff than before.

AGONIES OF THE HEART

Vince had a manager who took me under his wing from his office in York. He went to Rowntree's and got them to sponsor the printing of a brochure for me. They said they would as I featured Polo mints in my act every night. Someone in the audience would lend me some money in exchange for a packet of Polo mints and, having checked the number of his note, would find it later in the hole in the middle of the mints. I also did a routine where the mints linked together, chain like, so the brochure was made very cleverly with the mints separate on my hand and when you unfolded the paper they had joined together. You will probably find this hard to believe but I am a collector's item. There are people in the world who collect anything to do with me and they search diligently for these brochures. The reason they are so eminently collectable is that not many of them were sent out.

Something else had happened that shocked me into the full realisation of what I was up to with women. In the midst of travelling the clubs, and the haze and fog surrounding the break-up of my marriage, a blinding awareness had come in the middle of making love to a girl in the back of a car. I had realised that I wasn't actually enjoying it; I was just doing it for the sake of it. I remember I actually apologised to the girl and drove her home. A few years later, on a long train journey, I started to doodle the names of the girls I had made love to in my 'mad' years. I got past 300 and gave up. Nowadays, that would have been a suicide mission.

From that moment on, I was very choosy about my relationships. Yet there were still a couple of times when I was on the road and intensely lonely when I tried paying for a prostitute but found I couldn't follow it through. It was all so sordid and dirty and twice I just walked away from it without 'getting my money's worth'. I'd never do that again. Many years later, I was accosted by a pro near King's Cross station in

London. Debbie had only just that minute left me to walk across to her car when a very young cockney girl in a full-length coat asked whether I was looking for a good time.

I laughed because nothing was further from my mind and pointed out that my wife might object and pointed to her. The penny dropped and the young girl said, ''Ere. You're 'im off the telly, aincha?'

I agreed that I was 'im.

'Give us your autograph, dahlin', for me mum.'

'Sure,' says I. 'Have you got a pen?'

'You gotta be kiddin',' she said, opening her coat. 'Where would I keep a pen?'

She was starkers. I didn't say the obvious!

Early on in the never-ending cycle of gigs, I met one of the greatest stage hypnotists I had ever seen, Peter Casson, who became my manager. I never had any problems with Peter, although he had the strange hobby of suing everyone and was always in court representing himself in some case or other. We met because I got a week at the Club Ba-Ba at Barnsley and the Club Ki-Ki at Kirk Sandall and he owned them. I learnt a really big lesson on my first night at the Ba-Ba. I didn't think that I had gone down very well at all and I fully understood the large sign that Peter had put up backstage: 'Will all Artistes please refrain from asking the audience whether they are having a good time or enjoying themselves as the lack of response is invariably embarrassing to both parties.'

As soon as I came off stage, the compere said that I was one of the funniest men ever to appear in the club. I said I didn't think so and he said that the only thing I ought to do is slow up. Around Barnsley, the rhythm of speech is much slower than in the north-east and I ought to give them more time to get used to the sound of my voice before getting faster towards the end of the act. Great advice. Fabulous advice. From then on I did that, and I also learnt to clip my words in Scotland and take my voice up a little at the end of the sentences in Wales. It's not making fun of anyone, it's enabling them to be able to 'hear' me better. Where this tip really came in handy was years later when I appeared in Las Vegas.

That experience was still a long way away. I still had a lot more to learn.

CHAPTER 8

FACING DEATH IN THE CLUBS

The international space-race began in earnest when American President Kennedy challenged the USSR to be the first nation to place a man on the moon. Managing to launch the first cosmonaut in 1961, the smiles on the faces of the jubilant Russians soon faded when the USA followed eight years later with the first human landing on the moon. The Apollo command module touched down on 21 July 1969 with Neil Armstrong making his 'giant leap for mankind'.

So turning 30 was a significant time for me, not for all the commonly depressing 'Oh my God, my youth is over' reasons, but because I was at last a full-time professional entertainer. Well, I hoped I entertained 'em. Looking back, I suppose it was an inevitable journey given that all I did in my spare time was magic, magic, magic. Plus my kind of entertaining with magic was different, thanks to Bruce Forsyth, although he didn't know it. I treated the audience as though they were at a party. I would be cheeky to them, they could be cheeky to me and together we had fun. There was a particular market for this, as no one else in the country presented magic in the way that I did and I enjoyed the audience's enjoyment.

Although the applause felt good, it was not the reason I did the job, I just enjoyed being on stage. Years later, the best description of this came from Voronin, who was the artistic director of a theatre in Kiev. In his clipped English and struggling to find the right words, he said, 'Paul, I lorv to vatch you in the stage. It is liking vatching the fish in the water.' He was right, I am very much at home when the stage lights go on. And any performer savours the nice things people say, it protects you from the critics' cruelty. Lord Delfont once said that I had the ability to turn the Opera House in Blackpool, which seats over 3,000, into a living room. Isn't that nice? Thank you, Bernie.

The reason I had decided to turn full-time professional was because I had an offer of a summer season show at the Cosy Nook Theatre in Newquay, Cornwall. I had more than enough club dates in the diary and I thought the summer season would carry me through until the autumn and by then I would have picked up more dates.

With all the showbusiness work that was coming in, it was increasingly difficult to get home. In fact, home didn't feel like it belonged to me any more, merely a place where my three sons, Paul, Martin and Gary, stayed with their mum. I visited them as often as I could and they were well loved by Jackie and myself, but our marriage had now drifted so far apart that we had to face the truth that it really was over between us. Now we prepared to cut the final cords that tied us.

On the last day that I said goodbye to Jackie and the family, I had more than a lump in my throat. Admitting it was over was the hardest thing of all. Of course, I would see them all again and again, particularly the boys on a regular basis, but even though Jackie and I were not happy together, somewhere deep inside I still wished it wasn't happening.

It took the most enormous effort for me to leave the house and the kids behind and I tried to hang on to myself and not show the lads how upset I was. As I got into the car, I couldn't hold back any longer and I drove around the corner only to stop a few hundred yards later as the tears flowed. Sitting alone in the car, I cried my eyes out and it took some while before I composed myself enough to drive away safely. That happened every time I visited in the years to come. I really missed those lads.

It would have been miserable for the boys if we had stayed together, as they would have been subjected to us rowing all the time. I also had a belief that I could earn more money 'on the road', although for the first couple of years I frequently slept in the back of my car to save on digs money so that I could send more home. It was several years before I stopped living out of a suitcase and found a permanent home I could really call my own.

So it was the failure of the marriage that drove me into showbusiness and not, as in many other cases, showbusiness that ruined the marriage. It was at exactly the same time that I closed the door on my marriage, the door opened with the summer that now lay before me.

The billing for the theatre, neatly built on the side of the promenade, included the singer Monica Robbins, two comedians, Don Mundy and Alan Mills, a high-speed roller-skating act called The Skating Valentines and me. Casson was a great believer in old-style variety and insisted that we did four different shows a week, with a complete change the following week as well. He thought that holidaymakers would come to the theatre more than once during their two-week break. They didn't, but the show was very successful.

I also had to present 'Uncle Paul's Children's Showtime' on several afternoons as well as the evening performances. It depended whether it rained or not.

I got a shock when I joined the production. In the world of

the amateur you rehearse all year and do a week. The 'pros' rehearse a week and do a year! Well, a season. The difference is that everybody arrives knowing their acts and their requirements so well that the only thing you have to learn are the links. In this show I was also in the comedy sketches, behind Monica with the other guys singing the backing and working as a stooge for The Skating Valentines.

'You just walk across at this moment in the act and, as you are walking, we'll both pick you up under your arms and whiz you round,' they nonchalantly explained. 'As you are going around you climb to the top of us looking as though you are trying to get off. Just make sure you don't look down, or out, but that you just keep your focus on one of us. Then you won't get dizzy. But when you do get off, act dizzy as it will get us all a big laugh.'

I didn't have to act. I spent the whole summer nauseous. I knew I could go up and down on roller-coasters, but I found I couldn't go round and round and I got very sick. Unfortunately, there was no one else in the show that could do the job for them, so I was stuck with it and lived in constant fear of throwing up on stage all season.

My own spot hadn't changed over many years of using simple, everyday household items, which I knew the audience could relate to. My act involved using a box of tissues, odd bits of rope, a couple of eggs, lemons and some walnuts. The cleaners threw my act out three times during the season thinking it was a load of old rubbish. Who am I to argue? I then had to go round Woolworth's to buy my props again.

The other surprise was Monica. I wasn't looking for a relationship but we hit it off straight away. Well, perhaps not straight away. I had taken to wearing all black at this time of my life. Black shoes, black socks, black trousers, black roll-neck and even (what a prat) black leather gloves all day long. To those who had been in the business for some time I must have looked a right wally. I thought I looked mysterious! Monica decided to take me down a peg or two and, in doing so, we became more than the best of friends. She also found me digs and generally looked after this showbusiness virgin.

By now, the shop had been sold but there had been a mistake in the transaction and somewhere along the line the stock had not been sold at the value it should have been. The stock was included in the sale price of the shop and I owed a lot of people a lot of money. The show at Newquay only paid me £35 a week and I was in a deep depression. It was Monica who telephoned everyone I owed and worked out repayment deals and, although it took a couple of years, she really sorted me out and put me back on my feet.

The show had comedy sketches. These were great. They were really mini plays with gags all the way through and were the theatrical equivalent of television's sitcoms. I was in all of them but then I was written out of most and finished up in only one. More depression. I was obviously no good. Monica came to the rescue again.

'You don't know much about showbusiness, do you? You're out because you're funny. You can't be funnier than the comedian.'

When, in my final sketch, my lines were dropped so that I had nothing to say, I turned my 'silent' policeman role into the campest, most effeminate copper of all time and still got laughs. Don't you just love showbiz?

Newquay itself was a real culture shock. I had spent all of my life in the North and did not expect to find the weather so mild and the coastline so beautiful. Even the flowers in Newquay opened at least a month earlier than they did up North. I loved to go on long, early-morning walks to watch the seals as they dipped and dived through the waves. I actually felt a tinge of resentment towards my parents. Why did we live in the North when there was so much natural splendour in the South? Then, of course, I felt guilty about the resentment. On the other hand, are you like me? I can't for the life of me understand why anyone wants to live in the Arctic Circle or in the shadow of a volcano or on an earthquake fracture line.

It was just after I started working in Newquay that I got a letter inviting me to come to an *Opportunity Knocks* audition. That was the major talent show on TV at the time and I had no idea how they had heard about me. All the letter said was that they had heard I was 'different'.

The famous Hughie Green, who had enabled a lot of artistes to become television stars, presented this ITV networked show. The Skating Valentines had lent me a stretch lurex suit to wear so that I would look 'professional' but I never got into the gear. The whole affair was so badly organised that I just wore my jeans and sweatshirt. Note I had dropped the all-black gear.

The room was full of other hopefuls and one wall was stacked high with guitar amplifiers. A row of magicians in tailcoats had coo-coo-ing noises emanating from under their clothes. Having previously explained that I had only a few moments as I had to get back to the theatre to work, I went to the front of the queue with the letter that the production company had sent me. It seems that they needed some professional acts to fill out the programmes between the amateurs (or was it the other way around?) to get a cheaper show.

The receptionist, hassled about the utter confusion of several hundred acts, all desperate to be picked, wouldn't listen to me, gave me a number and told me to return to the queue. Then I spotted the long table with Hughie Green sitting in the middle, with his assistants Doris and Len on either side. A very young girl was standing with her hands clasped in front of her, singing in an incredibly beautiful soprano voice. Having finished, Hughie called her over to the desk and, congratulating her on her superb voice, handed over his business card.

'In the next 12 months,' he instructed, 'I want you to go out and sing for people, for up to now I think you have only sung at school?'

She nodded.

'Well, my love, you are still a bit stiff and proper. When you have more experience of audiences, you will have learnt to relax. Then come back and see me.'

Next up was a guy who couldn't sing to save his life, but he was beautifully dressed. It was awful, out of tune, out of tempo and the worst thing of all was that the singer thought he was wonderful. Hughie couldn't stand more than two verses and stopped him in his tracks.

'Excuse me, do you sing in the clubs?'

'Yes, Mr Green, I do.'

'Well, do showbusiness a favour and get out of it.'

Harsh words and the room was more than a bit stunned. Hughie was a hard, but fair man and he was right. This man should not have been taking other people's money when he was so bad.

It was almost as if no one dared to go on next so I took the opportunity to walk to the middle of the floor and started my act. Hughie stopped me.

'Who on earth are you?'

'I have this letter, sir, and I'm short for time as I'm on stage tonight. Just let me show you what I do and I'll be out of your way.'

As the panel watched my short collection of tricks, they laughed and clapped along the way. Four minutes later and I was preparing to leave when one of the panel said they liked what I did and I would be getting an invitation to be on the show.

FACING DEATH IN THE CLUBS

True to their word, I received their letter a few days later, stating the date that I would be on the show and that I would come in second place. Fees and expenses were to be paid, and as it was one of Hughie's special programmes for the forces, it was to be done on an aircraft carrier. Of course, with my army experiences on the aircraft carriers in Hong Kong, this was the perfect location for me.

What an eye-opener that show was for me. I got changed underneath an aeroplane. The make-up was done from a suitcase. I learned that television is not all that well organised. *Opportunity Knocks* was famous for the contraption at the end of each show that recorded the audience's level of clapping and thus produced a studio winner. The 'clapometer', which occurred to me probably meant something completely different to the boys in the Navy but I didn't do the gag, would go up and down on a sliding scale. I had always assumed it was some sort of electronic device. It turned out to be a long cardboard box with a slot in the side. The needle was attached at one end to a rubber bungee and at the other to a piece of string. The 'engineer' pulled the string and made the needle go to the numbers on the list supplied by the production company. As per my previous information, I came second.

The whole affair added nothing to my career other than experience, although for years afterwards, Hughie Green and *Opportunity Knocks* constantly claimed to have 'discovered' me, whereas I was paid to come second! The power of the media was also underlined when a lady in a sweet shop recognised me the following day. She was the only one who did. For a long time after that, I used to ask the audiences, 'Put your hands up if you ever voted for anyone on *Opportunity Knocks.*' For years nobody put their hands up and then, one night, a man did. I continued, 'For somebody that you didn't know ...' and his hand went down again. Was it all a fiddle? I don't know. What it did provide was a vehicle for new talent to be seen so I suppose that made it all worthwhile.

Later talent shows, to avoid having to pay Hughie Green royalties I guess, had panels of people criticising acts on air. I found that to be a sad way to show talent. If the acts were no good then why put them on in the first place. And they were being viewed by 'judges' who, in some cases, had no talent themselves *and* were watching the acts live, not on TV as we were, so they saw and felt a different performance. I wonder why they can't just put new acts on television and build them up without having to resort to judging and voting?

Watching myself on *Opportunity Knocks*, I learnt how the sound that comes out of a television has nothing to do with what is happening in the arena of the show. A recording engineer sat there and rather than listening to the show, watched little meters. If a big burst of laughter sent the needles towards the red section, he would grab his little knob and turn it quickly down. If a gag got a small titter, he would turn it up. This was why television laughter always sounded so fake. This meant that while I was working in the aircraft carrier, I'd get a big laugh and wait for the laughter to die down before continuing. When I watched it on TV there were big silent gaps where the laughter had stopped because the man had turned his button down. It sounded odd. It was little observations like these that prepared me for television appearances to come. Don't wait for the laughter to stop, keep going. Ken Dodd is a master at this.

Jackie and the lads came down and spent some time with me but Jackie and I lived apart and I spent the days with the lads. It's a great place for children and I hated it when they had to go back North.

The season ended and I was back in the clubs and living with Monica. We lived in a small caravan, which I altered to make it a little more habitable. Looking back, I can't believe that we both lived in a van that small, but we did. For a while it was in the garden behind the home of a bouncer from the Ba–Ba. He was also a professional wrestling match referee. These were not the sort of wrestling matches I had seen in Macau. These were the ones where big butch fellows pretend to knock each other about. Pretend? Well, all I know is that our landlord would not be able to referee one of the later bouts because it was the one featuring the Masked Mauler. The referee *was* the Masked Mauler who 'would only remove his mask when he was defeated'. He was never defeated.

Peter Casson was too busy to be my manager and so I moved on to another agent called Bob who worked for a company called Artists Management. This Doncaster-based group contained a couple of directors, one of whom was Mervyn O'Horan. More of him later.

A bit later we moved the caravan to Cawthorne, on a farm. I was amazed at how little work farmers did. They did have to get up early to milk the cows but then there wasn't much to do until it was time to milk them again. They just seemed to potter around doing odd jobs. Those early starts used to upset me because we used to work very late. Then we would drive home through the night rather than spend money on digs. One of the farmers would come over and hammer on the door with the early post. Unknown to the farmer, I came home late one night, unloaded the amplifier and the speakers and did a little work. The next morning, very early as usual, he came with the post only to discover a new doorbell right in the middle of the small caravan door. He pressed the doorbell, which activated the tape, which was connected to the amplifier, which was connected to the huge speakers lying under the van. Big Ben BOOMED out across the countryside and I would have loved to have been awake in time to watch him. He never delivered early post again.

The closest we ever got to owning a less temporary residence was when I bought a burnt-out mobile home which I then restored. I put a lot of time and effort into renovating the metal hulk and was quite pleased with the result, but had to leave it behind for several weeks when Monica and I went away for a season. Upon our return, we heard a strange, humming and buzzing noise coming from within. I carefully opened the door, not knowing what to expect and was pushed back with the force of huge bluebottles trying to escape. The whole interior was covered; it was wall-to-wall, floor-to-ceiling flies. I went down to the local shopkeeper and bought his whole stock of fly killer, which I then sprayed through a hole in the door. Two days later and I had to go back in and shovel the corpses out, selling the home soon afterwards.

We usually tried to book ourselves out together into the clubs. Monica would sing and I would do the comedy magic and so provide a whole evening's entertainment between us whenever we could. That couldn't happen all the time, of course, and over the coming years, as I 'took off' we drifted apart. In the meantime, we had a wonderful time and I remember Monica with nothing but fondness. Years later, when I hadn't seen her for a very long time and I was married to Debbie, she turned up on my doorstep and, when I opened the door I didn't recognise her for the first few seconds. Don't hate me for that.

Ali Bongo, my good friend and brilliant magical adviser, tells a story of when he was at a party with David Nixon. David was the 'famous-television-magician-before-me' person.

Apparently, David called Ali over and, over the top of his glass and without moving his lips as he smiled around the room, said 'Ali, there's a woman in a red dress in the corner who keeps smiling at me. Should I know her?' Well, we've all done it, haven't we? We've tried to look around the room casually without looking at anyone in particular to find out who a friend is talking about? Ali did just that, even pausing, smiling and raising his glass to the lady in question. Then he turned back to David.

'Yes, you should really ... she was your first wife.'

Against Ali himself, at another party, he was deep in conversation with a young woman whom he knew he should know, but he could not recall where he had met her. It wasn't until her husband, Prince Andrew, the Duke of York, came over and said that it was time to go that the thunderstruck Ali realised he had been talking to the famous 'Fergie'.

The clubs continued to offer the most readily available source of work. Trevor, who had by this time left the teaching profession owing to the bureaucracy, had gone back into the clubs as a Musical Director. A brilliant backing musician, Trevor was popular with acts because of his ability to sight-read their music quickly and play it with great feeling.

On one occasion, I answered the phone to Trevor, who asked if I would come and appear at the opening ceremony of a new club he was going to work in as resident MD. Having made a bit of a name for myself in the clubs, they had asked Trevor if he could get me, as I was a 'bit of a draw'.

The new venue was very impressive if not completely practical for its true use. It had been designed with an entire wall made out of windows, which made it impossible to provide the right sort of atmosphere for daytime or early evening shows. The band was split in two, with the organist, Trevor and the drummer facing each other across the full width of the stage, a very difficult layout for musicians to work in.

Seeing the daylight conditions, I knew it would be hard work. Just before I went on, the Concert Chairman appeared backstage to check that I was ready. Giving him the thumbs up, he told me that he had one short announcement to make and then I would be on. Even though I had enjoyed the luxury of a resident season where the audience had come to see me, my faith in working the clubs remained undaunted, but I was always ready for any unforeseen eventuality. When I heard the announcement that followed, I froze on the spot. In what follows, the name has been changed, not to protect the innocent, but because I can't remember it.

'Now then, now then, give order, please!' The clink and clatter of the glasses and the excited shouting of the crowd subsided at the sound of the Chairman's voice.

'Now you all know Jack Higginbottom.'

A deathly hush fell over the room.

'As you all know, this is the first day of the new club,' he continued in his broad Northern tones. 'And as you all know, it would not exist if it hadn't been for Jack, our beloved president. It was Jack, who only a few years ago, went to the breweries, got the money, arranged for the architect and got the plans for this *fantastic* building we are now in.'

I listened from the side of the stage as the pin-drop quiet continued as his audience sat in silence, wondering what was coming. Somehow, I knew.

'It was Jack who also organised us to have raffles and keep kitties going so that we could afford bigger and better equipment. It was Jack who arranged fund-raising outings and coffee mornings for the women. And, as you all know, Jack took sick about nine months ago.'

'Oh no!' I groaned from behind the curtains. Trevor, who loves it when I'm in trouble, started to laugh. The Concert Chairman continued. 'So, as you all know, Jack never saw this building as he got more and more sick and I've got some really bad news for you,' he said. 'I have just been informed that on this day of the grand opening of our new club, Jack Higginbottom passed away this morning.'

Pick a card ... Paul Daniels as millions will remember him.

Above left: Some of my early career was spent doing seaside resorts and summertime specials. Even my sons got into the publicity shots – from left to right: Paul, Martin and Gary.

Above right: A promotional picture from my days on the books of Artist Management in Doncaster. See what I mean about hairstyles And it was all mine!

Below: One of Debbie's early publicity shots. No wonder I fancied her.

Above: No, it's not a trick photograph. I was trading in the Bentley on the left for the one on the right. Now there's posh!

Below: My dear friend Ken Jones, who sadly passed away whilst I was on honeymoon with Debbie. Here he is being saved from falling in the river by his wife, Ruth.

Above: My favourite photograph from all the series we did. I'm with Debbie and Ron Moody in a Christmas special.

Below: In the workshop, trying to work out where to store more stuff.

Above: Working on an illusion to pass a camel through the eye of a needle. The camel didn't want to play.

Below: Performing a card trick at close range on the best of all theatre critics, the late Jack Tinker.

Above: The wonderful home by the river that Debbie and I share.

Below left: Performing in one of the many slots in my TV series, *The Greatest Show the World Has Ever Seen*. Why did I give up wearing trousers like that?

Below right: A snapshot from our wedding day, Debbie looking stunning in her dress, which was designed by a BBC costumier.

Above: My son Martin with his beautiful wife, Joanne, and their son, Lewis.
I don't think he liked the font and the water.

Below: Mafia boss with moll? No, it's me and Debbie at the races.

Enjoying the tranquillity of the garden at our previous house, Sherwood. It had once been owned by Roger Moore of 007 fame. I think there is a similarity, don't you?

FACING DEATH IN THE CLUBS

Men are now crying. Women are sobbing.

'It is normal in this club, that when a member passes away, we have two minutes' silence. But for Jack, we're going to 'ave three.'

I am now sat on a chair at the back of the stage with my head in my hands. Trevor is in hysterics. The architect has thoughtfully provided the club with a hard floor and plastic chairs that squeak and bang as the whole audience stands to attention. For three solid minutes, all I could hear was people crying.

At the end of which: 'Thank you. Paul Daniels will now entertain you,' and he walked off.

The curtains opened to the sound of people sitting down, talking about the passing of their friend, all interspersed by sobbing. I was still sitting with my head in my hands but I stood up and walked very, very slowly downstage to the microphone, thrust my hands in my pockets and spoke.

'I never knew Jack Higginbottom.'

At the sound of the name the room fell silent.

'But if he helped to build this place, he must have been an extraordinary fella. He wouldn't want us not to enjoy it, or sit here crying over his memory. He would want us to make the most of what he has achieved here. So, I'm not doing this show for you today, I'm doing this show for Jack Higginbottom!'

As the applause burst forth, I glanced across at Trevor who was mouthing the words 'You b*****d.' I was on to a winner and the show went like a bomb.

★ ★ ★

It was the days when footballers played for the Cup and everybody knew what you were talking about. Now there are that many cups and trophies and championships they're playing

185

for, it's lost its impact to a big extent. When you played for the FA Cup in the late Sixties, it was the championship of championships. My introduction on stage in Manchester one night featured such an event:

'Ladies and gentlemen, I have some bad news. After tonight's replay, Middlesbrough have just knocked us out of the cup.'

Moans and groans from the audience.

'So will you please welcome a comedian from Middlesbrough ... Paul Daniels!'

The place started to scream and yell so I dropped on to my hands and knees and crawled from behind the curtains up to the microphone. It made them laugh and Middlesbrough won again, though I didn't mention it at the time.

Always going on with the idea of having a good time, I was always prepared to turn a situation to my favour. After all, that's what I was paid to do. I never went along with the idea that audiences were different. In the main, the vast majority are made up of the same kind of people – happy, thin, fat, sad, in love, out of love, plumbers, decorators and accountants. I found myself losing friendships in the clubs when other acts would come off and say, 'Boy, they're a tough audience!' I'd whisper half-jokingly that Sammy Davies Jnr could entertain them. It was a case of giving your audience what they wanted.

I could never understand why a singer would turn up with a huge portfolio of music and enquire as to their tastes in a particular club. I'd say I was sure that Shirley Bassey would never ask that question. She sings what she sings best.

Manchester was the most amazing place for clubland. This city was sensational and you could do six a night if you were daft enough. I tried doing four a night for one week when I opened at Bernard Manning's Embassy Club for a 30-minute spot before driving on to the Broadway club and then the Candlelight at Oldham which was really tough. I finished the evening with a drive back into Manchester for a visit to the Del Sol sited on the roof of a hotel. On the Saturday night, I was half-way through, the act at the Del Sol when I realised that the 'volunteer' from the audience who was standing on my left only spoke French. I don't know how I had got that far without noticing except that having done 28 performances that week I was on automatic pilot.

It was there that I met a strongman called Tony Brutus who carried an enormously heavy Roman short sword. Dressed as a Roman gladiator, he would bound on stage and offer a fortune to anybody who could lift this length of solid steel, fashioned like a Roman short sword, above their head. Incredibly strong, there was a very funny element to his act, as the incredible feats he carried out had made him cross-eyed. He turned this to his advantage in his act and created a lot of laughter. Tony hated the Del Sol because it was at the top of a tall building and the only way he could get his weights into the club was to hump them up the stairs by grabbing the handles and walking backwards. One night, determined not to carry the sword down again, he heaved it out of the window into the car park. It sank so far in the ground that it took him hours to dig it out again and had strong echoes of The Sword in the Stone. My laughter echoing around the car park as I left didn't impress him!

The constant touring of the clubs did not shake my immediate shyness. I was still not a socialiser, as I didn't drink with all the other acts after the show. I just arrived, did my bit and left. It never occurred to me to drink as my parents weren't drinkers and I was certainly fearful of going down the route of some of the performers who did. I had seen several great talents become dependent on booze to the point that they were no longer able to be themselves. I had also been shocked by the state of several magicians whose hands shook with the effects of alcohol. If that's what it did, then I didn't want to know. Some comics thought they were funnier drunk, but they weren't. The apparent exception was Jimmy James who was the archetypal drunk comic, but was never really sozzled at all! I remember an interviewer who asked him why he was such a good drunk comic when some of our greatest actors couldn't act drunk at all. 'The reason is simple,' said Jimmy. 'Like all drunks, I am desperately trying to act sober.'

It was the drunks in the audience that were always the real problem. Jack Sharp, a Northern agent, who had settled in Essex, booked me in London to perform in an East End pub. Arriving early as usual, I got out of the car and was suddenly enveloped by an avalanche of noise. It was coming from the pub where I was due to perform. Gritting my teeth for what I would find, I grabbed my magic box and suit bag and entered the lion's den. Trying to make myself heard above the cacophony of noise, one of the bouncers pointed upstairs.

The upper room went down into a kind of 'well' in front of the stage, with a balcony around the edge. Even though it was quite early, there was no sign of sobriety anywhere; every member of the audience was seriously sloshed. As I looked down, the floor was awash with spilt beer and fag ash, with punters sluicing their way through it as they created a constant stream to the toilets.

Moving backstage, the compere grabbed me in a panic and asked how quickly I could get on. I soon found out what the party was in aid of. West Ham and Fulham had both qualified for the FA Cup that afternoon and these men were celebrating this success as fully as possible. Was he seriously thinking I would work out there? Yes, apparently he was and, not being in the mood to lose a night's cash, I prepared myself for the onslaught.

'What's the panic?' I asked.

'I've already had two acts arrive who refused to go on,' he explained.

FACING DEATH IN THE CLUBS

'I'll be ready in ten minutes,' I smiled, trying not to turn green.

'Great. I'll give you a build-up, but don't forget you're on for half an hour. If you don't do half an hour, you won't get a penny!'

Glancing back out into the swirling mass of bodies, I knew I'd be lucky to last half a minute. The trio playing on-stage could not be heard above the din of shouting, cursing and screaming.

The compère battled his way on stage and desperately tried to get the attention of the audience in order to start the cabaret, but it seemed impossible. Way off in the distance, I heard a kind of murmuring sound and I realised that this was my introduction. The band played me on, but I still couldn't hear them. It was a nightmare.

I walked straight up to the microphone and tried to start the act, while watching the room like a hawk. A few moments in and the first beer mat came whistling across the room toward me. Rocking my head to one side, I dodged it just as an ashtray arrived from somewhere else.

I'd had a small clock inserted in the top of my box so that I could keep an exact eye on my timing. I kept this for years and gradually gained a reputation for having perfect time-keeping skills on stage. Company managers on future shows were to think that I was a genius, because when they asked me to do twelve minutes or nine, I would do exactly that. It wasn't until later that they discovered my secret.

Now, looking at my box, I could see that I still had 25 minutes left to get through before payday. Then I had a burst of inspiration. Taking the mike off the stand, I risked life and limb by going down into the alcohol-sodden audience and made straight for one particular table. Here, one man was just about capable of staying upright on his chair and I sang very quietly and purposefully to this one guy.

'I'm forever blowing bubbles, pretty bubbles in the air ...'

Out of his drunken stupor, his eyes refocused and he began to join in. His slurred tones were almost recognisable, so I encouraged him to sing louder. He glanced at his mates struggling to stay alive either side of him and they joined him until three or four were singing along. Another verse and another table joined in, then another and then another. I had picked the right football team and the right anthem. Now the whole room was singing their anthem as loud and as seriously as they could. I sang the bubble song with them over and over again for a solid 25 minutes and then made my exit with a standing, stomping ovation.

The compère immediately threw on the next act, who happened to be a stripper. She was greeted with loud boos and cries of 'Bring the singer back on!' (Suddenly I'm a singer!)

The poor girl was jeered and shouted at even though by now she was topless. Suddenly, and I swear this is true, she grabbed the mike and started to sing, 'I'm forever blowing bubbles ...'

Suddenly the whole audience stopped in its tracks and joined in with the singing once more. Twenty minutes later she, too, made her exit to a standing ovation. Don'cha just love showbusiness?

The event that really changed my life, possibly more than anything else, happened on a rare night off when I agreed to drive another comic to a gig in Essex. His car had broken down and I was happy to oblige. It was a hen party, full of women, most of whom were far filthier than men will ever be. They had booked a male stripper, and how the feminist movement can blame men for looking at nude women I shall never know. One of my jobs at Dad's cinema was repainting the toilets and we had to repaint the Ladies five times as frequently as the Men's. When I asked my dad why we had to paint the Ladies toilets so often, he said it was because the women had both hands free to write with!

FACING DEATH IN THE CLUBS

I was the only man at the hen party, standing at the bar with my usual Coca-Cola, when a Viking suddenly roared on to the stage. The women started shouting at the guy dressed in furry costume, furry boots and with horns on his head. After about ten minutes, all he had left on were his boots and horns. As he waved his chopper around, the women were screaming at such a high pitch I thought all the glasses in the bar would shatter. As I watched this man, I saw the light. Just as some people say they become born-again Christians, in a flash of light it suddenly dawned on me that no matter how tall, short, fat, thin, or bald I became, I would never look as stupid as that guy on the stage at that moment. It occurred to me that there would always be someone dafter than me in the world and this revelation did wonders for my self-confidence. I became a born-again extrovert.

Speaking of strippers, whenever I was working in the North East, my base for this period in my life was the Roker View Guest House in Sunderland. It was from there that I would travel out each day to the various clubs that, by this time, were starting to change once more. Later, when the onset of the glamorous and more popular nightclubs meant that the working men's venues descended into a spiral of seediness, the digs became home to the strippers. These girls became the normal form of entertainment, with an act or two thrown in between. I noticed that over a period of months, any new girls who moved into stripping changed from bubbly, happy personalities, to being a bit odd. Each one lost their spark and became introverted within a cocoon, which made them seem less intelligent as the jading process overtook them. I don't know why, it is just something that I noticed.

Bob Butler, who was handling my work under the Artists Management banner telephoned me one day to say that an offer of Jersey was on the table and was I interested? The timing was perfect and as long as I didn't have to spend the whole time on roller-skates I would be happy, I explained. Bob seemed like a nice guy and I got to know him well over the weeks of negotiations that followed. It was his wife who surprised me.

An act going around the clubs called 'Zareda' had a boyfriend called Johnny St Claire. Johnny would sing in the first half and help set up Zareda's spot for the second. He was a clairvoyant who did a clever mindreading act and mental manipulation and could very effectively reveal private details about members of his audience.

Unaware of how seriously some people take this stuff, I was horrified when I heard that Bob's wife asked for 'guidance' each week. I had to explain gently to Bob that Zareda, the great seer, was actually a guy named Ozzy Ray, an ex-pantomime dame. Having walked into Mac's Magic Shop in Seaton Carew, Ozzy had purchased a fake blindfold and a book on 'cold-reading'. According to Mac, whom I knew very well, he paid ten shillings for the lot. What an investment that proved to be. The book taught him the ability to be able to tell things about a person that supposedly you could not have possibly known. Clues that the cold-reader assimilates about a person include what they wear, the quality of their clothing and, in particular, their shoes; as well as their cleanliness, body language and style. Age gives a million clues as well, even being able to select names that they are likely to know because each generation has its own popular names. Having studied this book, Ozzy found he could decipher a lot of information about a person and the more he did it, the better he got, soon becoming an expert in the field. Maybe when these people have done it that long, they start to believe it themselves.

Bob's wife had difficulty accepting it, but I thought that if ever I didn't make it with my conjuring tricks, I should go in for this. If one woman was prepared to pay good money to a stranger, how many other hundreds of women were doing it too? It does make me sad, in this enlightened age, that people still believe in this over and above the fun of being entertained. I seriously think that our schools must be failing our children if they teach them advanced mathematics but don't warn them about being conned. If you are into that so-called psychic stuff, do yourself a favour – treat it as being for entertainment purposes only and get some books on how to do it yourself. It may well peel layers of belief away from your eyes.

Arriving at the Sunshine Hotel in Jersey, the air was clear and the sky was blue; what a lovely start to our season. Happily for me, the first act on the bill was Monica Robbins. The second act on the bill was Paul Daniels and the third was Bal Moane, a tough Irish comedian. The evening's entertainment was rounded off with Dougie Brown, probably the greatest ad-libber I have ever met.

On opening night, Dougie did not go down too well with the audience. The reason for this was that the audience had been laughing at me for 45 minutes, then at Bal for another 45 minutes, so that by the time they got to Dougie they were 'laughed-out'. I suggested to the owner of the hotel, who was also the entertainments manager, that I went on first followed by Bal, then Monica and finishing with Dougie. This would give the audience a break in the laughter before the star comic. The manager disagreed and simply swapped the two comics over, with the result that Dougie went very well and Bal died. This was the way it happened all summer, with the two of them alternating and each one dreading the night they were on last.

Dougie and Bal decided that I should play golf. I couldn't afford to buy a set of clubs as I was still sending money back home and there was never much left over. I therefore bought one club a week, so the first week I went and played with my 5-iron. The second week was much better because I had a 5-

iron and a putter, and so on. I was never any good at golf and I still play that way.

Dougie and I went out one day to play, not on our normal public course, but on one of the posh ones. Maybe you don't know, but when you arrive on the first tee it is standard practice to drop your ball into a tube with all the other people in the queue. When your ball gets to the end of the tube, it is your team's turn to play. We dropped the ball in the tube. We waited. Just as our ball dropped into position, a very posh team of four golfers, in plus-fours no less, moved ahead of us on to the tee. We pointed out the error of their ways and they pointed out that they were members of the club. We pointed out that that made no difference as their club had accepted our green fees and we were next. They gave in, with much ill grace.

Dougie teed up and hit the ball well down the middle. It just so happened that I had bought some new balls as well as adding another club to my set. To the members' horror, they stood and watched as I unwrapped a ball then removed a wrapped club from the bag and carefully removed the cellophane. In a moment of inspiration, I remembered that in the large pocket of the golf bag I had a new book by John Jacobs on how to play golf. I unwrapped that, cracked the spine so that it would lay open and put it on to the ground in front of the ball. Pretending to read it, I gripped the club, looked at the book, swung the club back, stopped, bent over and turned the page, then stood up with the club still raised and swung at the ball. It went down the middle. Thinking about my game nowadays, maybe I should go back to that technique. I picked up my tee, doffed my cap, said, 'Good morning, gentlemen' and went on my way, thinking, 'thank God I hit it.'

Another winter of touring the working men's clubs and I was back on Jersey. This season was spent doing the first half of the show at the very popular Tam's Hotel, and then everyone on the first half of the bill would shoot off around the island touring a different small hotel every evening and leaving, in my view, the greatest cabaret act England ever produced – Ronnie Dukes and Rickie Lee – to do the second half. Rickie was a superb singer, while Ronnie, a little, bald-headed, rotund man, drove along a superb one-hour comedy show with his battleaxe mother-in-law sitting at the piano acting as stooge.

Doing a different hotel every night, I designed portable scenery out of boxes with pipes that extended holding up glittery curtains providing a colourful backdrop. 'Tam's a-Poppin'' was the name of our 'resident' show and I could never figure out why it allowed its first half to tour the island because, if you had seen that for free in your hotel, I don't think that you would have paid to see it again at Tam's, even if you did get to see Ronnie and Rickie.

After finishing our own touring gig, we would return each night for our own entertainment in the form of the resident bandleader. This guy would provide the dance music after the cabaret, but would inevitably get slowly plastered as the night wore on. We would all watch him from the balcony, as no sooner had he got the tune going, than he would disappear into the kitchens behind the stage curtain. This was where he must have kept his supply of liquid refreshment for each time he returned he was a little worse for wear.

Each return to the stage would be in time to start the band on the next sequence or play a bit of keyboard and even trumpet. By 2.00am, his final duty would be to play the National Anthem. I wish shows still did this, as it would give us back some sense of national pride that I believe we have lost even though this guy turned it into a wonderful piece of entertainment.

As he stood to attention centre stage, barely able to keep the trumpet pressed to his mouth, the notes slowly poured forth. It was the slowest version of the National Anthem of all time. The audience, half-cut themselves, struggled to their feet and swayed in the gentle breeze. The moaning sound continued and, perhaps because everybody was in a similar state of intoxication, the fact that the tune was hardly recognisable didn't really matter.

As the final notes of the first verse struggled out of the tortured instrument and died away, the audience collapsed into their seats, only to hear the tune continue into the next verse. The indignity of a sozzled audience trying to pull themselves back on to their feet once more was all too much for us and we collapsed into hysterics each and every night we witnessed this absurd farce.

The following year, I was invited back to Jersey again, this time at the Hotel De France and without Monica on the bill. She was working somewhere else on the island and I started to chat up a dancer called Melody from our show. I'll give you a tip: if ever you are going out with two people at the same time, make sure they don't have the same initial. In my case, my mouth would get to the 'M' and then keep it going until I could work out which one I was talking about – 'Mmmmmmonica' or 'Mmmmmmmelody'.

The venue had its own purpose-built cabaret room, but the owner had decided that he would do a lot of the internal design himself. The theatre seats he designed had to be fastened to the floor in case of a fire, but the base of the seat wouldn't go all the way down. For the first week the audience sat with their heads cricked round to the side and their knees up in the air.

The 'projection room' that housed the follow-spots had been built too high on the outside of the cabaret room, so the holes the lamps came through were at floor level and the spot operators had to sit on the floor alongside the spotlights. Perhaps the manager had delusions of grandeur for instead of the normal follow-spots used for cabaret-type venues, the manager had purchased 'super-troupers' which are extremely powerful spots used at rock venues like Wembley. The high temperature from these burnt through the heat-resistant red film placed in front of the light each night. This gel, known as 'surprise pink' in the trade, prevents an artiste from looking pasty and ill in the white light, giving them the appearance of being tanned and healthy. With a little bit of make-up and one of these gels, its amazing how many wrinkles and years you can lose!

The most important thing is never to look directly into the stage lights, as the effect is like staring at 20 car headlights and can be very disorientating.

Having warned a visiting singer, Stuart Gillies, about the power of the spots, Gillies insisted he wanted it white. If you put in about six layers of red, you'd still only get a pale pink because it was so strong, I tried to clarify. No, he insisted on open white. Rather him than me, I thought, and waited to see what would happen.

As his opening music started, the stage lights swung into action and the backstage introduction announced: 'Ladies and gentlemen, will you please welcome the star of our show ... Stuart Gillies!'

He walked on and they hit him with these two white super-troupers. For a moment, he was stunned with the impact and, looking like a bleached ghost, started to get dizzy. He stumbled through his first number and did a great performance without being able to see anything other than the tip of his nose for the rest of the evening.

The resident show consisted of myself, a dance troupe called The Trendsetters, the Ivy Benson Band, and the top-of-the-bill was Michael Bentine. Although something of an oddity, I really liked Michael a lot, though I never considered him a good summer show act. He would probably have been the greatest after-dinner speaker of all time, but his style was not really suited to summer season. It was nicely funny, but it wasn't the belly laugh stuff that summer holidaymakers seek, so it was a bit of a waste of his talents.

I met a lot of great acts who admitted that they couldn't work different types of venues, particularly the clubs. The London nightclub scene is a million miles apart from the working men's; the culture difference is so great. I noticed that every venue needed its own technique to make a performance work. I don't think the London acts learnt the rules of the society that they were moving in, having tried to stick with the culture conventions they had come from. I realised early on that the social order of the clubs was incredibly amateur; the lads were not posh, though not stupid either. Hence l arrived early to set my own lights and then gave them a good, driving, funny, but technically and visibly skilful show. When I moved into the nightclub scene, the audience was full of travelling salesmen, businessmen and couples having a smart night out, mixed in with the local townies. I changed my style and my pace accordingly, with my language and gags becoming a little more ornate. On a short cruise before my summer season, I noted how the audiences there preferred the more subtle jokes.

In theatres, there was this huge chasm between me and the audience called an orchestra pit! Most club acts, me included, were held back by the distance to the front row after being used to having audiences come right up to your feet. I was really aware of this problem of bridging the gap between the crowd and me until I went to see Cliff Richard perform. As I sat in the stalls, I sat thinking, 'Wow! From down here there's no pit.' From the audience point of view, Cliff created intimacy and made his audience think he was singing just for them. From then on, the orchestra pit disappeared for me.

FACING DEATH IN THE CLUBS

When I got to television, the technique changed again. So many of my guests would be nervous because they were going to entertain about 15 million people. That's a big audience so I told them that they were wrong to think like that. On television, I had noticed that I was entertaining one to six people sitting about 12ft away from the screen in their living room. For the life of me, nowadays, I cannot understand presenters who shout at the camera as if they are in the Albert Hall!

Before the Hotel de France season started, I had already been warned that Michael Bentine was a really difficult person to get on with and this was a rumour I noticed percolated down from almost every star who existed. 'Val Doonican is a shit,' I was told. 'Don't work with Max Bygraves, he's unbearable,' another time. 'Sacha Distel is horrendous,' Everyone at the top, apparently, was nasty. I began to think that if I really wanted to make it in the business, then I had to be a 'shit' as well. Then I met Michael Bentine and he was a really nice man, so I had to re-think my understanding of this type of gossip.

As the years went on and I worked with Val and Max and Sacha, I realised that they weren't 'shits', they just wanted it right. The whole performance rests on the shoulders of these stars and if the show isn't right, they are the ones who get blamed. The audience doesn't go home saying, 'Well, that sound man made a mess of that show!' They go home saying, 'Wasn't Val's show awful!'

Consequently, the top-of-the-bill always has to push people who are treating the business as a bit of an ordinary day-to-day job, into the realisation that the audience has done us the greatest of honours and bought a ticket. They have paid a lot of money to be entertained so we should work to the best of our abilities.

During the season, Michael Bentine did me several favours, one in particular without knowing it. Before the season started, he came to see me work. By this time I had introduced an addition to my act that was a big winner with the audience. I was stunned at having seen a brilliant and powerful mind-reader called Maurice Fogel. This guy was a master of his art and, even if you knew how he did it, he would still make you believe he was reading minds. A great dramatic actor, one of the many great highlights of his act was catching the bullet in the teeth. It's a trick. Don't try it. Maurice, however, didn't need this style of trick other than for publicity. He could make your hair stand on end just with a blackboard and a piece of chalk.

Despite my admiration of the Great Fogel, another of his effects was a spot where volunteers from the audience would be jumping up and down, on and off chairs, as if driven by some invisible force. To me, and to Billy Hygate who was with me, this was so badly done that it was glaringly obvious what was happening and indeed how Fogel was doing it. I had read of others doing similar routines and always skipped past it in the magic books as being unworkable. Maybe it was only the night I saw it when it was so awful, but as I watched a light bulb flashed on in my head. In that split-second, a routine developed in my mind that was to become the major feature of my live shows from that moment on and I don't think I have changed a word of the presentation from the first night.

The performance was to become known as The Electric Chairs. They were not electric, though I do know of a frustrated magician who had some made! By the time Michael Bentine came to see me perform pre-season, this 20-minute piece was the great climax of my spot, sending the audience into fits of laughter. Michael had the wisdom to ban me from using this routine for his forthcoming season on Jersey. Top-of-the-bills have the right to say to another act on their show, 'don't sing that song, don't tell that joke.'

It wasn't so much the ability to 'top' what I had done with

something funnier, it was the fact that when I left the stage, the whole audience was talking about the chair routine. This was an almost impossible situation for any act to walk into.

I thought I was in trouble. I had grown to rely on that routine as a guaranteed closer. Talk about a panic. What to do? What I hadn't realised, and please forgive the conceit, was that it wasn't the routine that was funny. It was me. My reactions, my expressions, my surprise and my body language all created a comic viewpoint on the magic I presented. I had learnt, almost unconsciously, to be funny with any piece of business. This realisation dawned on me after a few shows without the chairs and I had a great season.

Years later, I read a book by the great close-up magician Al Goshman. As a 'table-hopper', he wrote how he thought his routine with silver dollars appearing under salt cellars was necessary for him to be an entertainer. One night, when few diners were there, he didn't do his usual routine, but found they still laughed and were baffled. He, too, discovered the secret. It is never the trick, it's never the illusion, it is never the song. It is always the performer. Ordinary singers can take a great song and it will be ordinary. Sinatra could take the same song and make it something special.

So it was that Bentine had done me a good turn without realising it. I now knew that I was a funny person and this gave me the confidence I was to need in the years that lay ahead. Oddly for such a nice man, Michael would vanish immediately he came off stage and not be available for the signing of autographs. I told the fans he was in the shower and that I would take the autograph books and pictures in to be signed. I signed them.

He had a cleverly built comedy flea circus that I carried on stage for him each night. It had no real fleas, but relied on concealed ropes, pulleys, switches and motors to make it look as if fleas were performing on tightropes and jumping across sand dunes. Years later, after the television production team had presented our own flea circus on television, Michael wrote to me accusing me of stealing his idea. It made me very sad, because we were such good friends and I never intended to upset him. I knew the idea was not original to Michael. If you are in the magic business you are virtually brought up with fake flea circuses, but I still hired a researcher to look into it. We then traced a flea circus back to the mid 1800s. You can't really put a copyright on that.

Half-way through the Jersey season, the cast was told that a legend was in the audience. It was Tommy Cooper. The hairs on the back of my head stood to attention at the sound of his name and I couldn't wait to meet him. Before the show, this 6ft 6in giant strode into my dressing room and gave me a huge grin.

''Allo!' rumbled my hero on the way through into Michael's room.

He then went and sat in the audience and I think I did the show more like an audition than a performance. That was silly because Tommy Cooper needed a funny magician like he needed another fez. After the show, a young man came backstage.

'Mr Cooper would like to see you. I'm his son.'

Following him to where his comedy genius father was sitting up on the side balcony, Tommy motioned for me to join him and offered me a drink. 'No thank you, sir, I don't drink.'

'OK then. Just give me the frog.'

The cardboard, origami-type frog was one of the items I had replaced the electric chairs with and went down very well with the audience. I used this little puppet-like creature as a comic and unusual way of finding a spectator's playing card. The green frog had a character all of its own and raised a lot of laughs along the way and I was very hesitant to part with it – even to a master like Tommy.

FACING DEATH IN THE CLUBS

'I can't give you the frog, Mr Cooper, because I can't do my usual routine and this frog is the only one I have and I can't get another one.'

'I'll show you a card trick,' replied Tommy in his wonderful bumbling voice. At which point he proceeded to show me a card routine, which I not only knew but also knew how it was done. 'Give me the frog.'

'I can't, sir. I'm sorry.'

'I'll show you another trick.'

The myth that Tommy was a brilliant magician was untrue. He was competent and had a great knowledge of magic, but if that were all he had ever chosen to do, he would never have made it into the big-time. He was a brilliant clown and I was later to discover that when I purchased his old scripts, they were covered with hand-written notes. These comments showed how well thought out his routines were, even to the point of the notes describing when he should look – left, pause; look right, pause; look at audience, pause; shrug, pause. It was all in the scripts.

'Give me the frog.'

Seeing me repeatedly hesitate, he walked down on to the stage and said, 'tell you what I'll do. I'll give you a whole routine.'

So there I am, sitting all alone in this huge cabaret room. The stage was only lit by the cold working lights that the cleaners would use the next morning. I can't tell you how funny the next ten minutes were, you had to be there. He proceeded to play the part of himself and his girl assistant. She keeps coming on too early and he sends her back, but Tommy is playing both parts. He says, 'And she runs on at the end and drops all the props! It's very funny. Give me the frog.'

I'm alone in this cabaret room and I can't breathe with laughter. The routine he did was pure Tommy Cooper. I could never have used his routine. I gave him the frog.

Years later, no one who saw it will ever forget how Tommy Cooper died in the middle of his performance on live television at Her Majesty's Theatre. I wasn't watching, but as a fellow Water Rat and magician, I was asked to do one of the eulogies at his memorial service. I explained that I felt it was impossible to remember such a great man with sadness; you can only feel sad for those of us left behind and still missing him. I made the congregation laugh and I told the story of the frog.

Two days later, my frog came home. Tommy's wife had found it among his props. I typed out the whole story and put it in an envelope with the frog. Some collector in the future will enjoy the moment again, I hope.

A year later, I attended a charity magical auction and purchased the comic robe that he died in. A friend asked if I had seen the event at Her Majesty's and I said 'no'. He offered to send me a copy of the video. Days later, I sat there watching a man who is about to die. In my lifetime, I never want to go through those emotions again. Without being disrespectful, it was well known that Tommy had lost his timing over the last two years of his life and needed a drink to build his confidence. On this last night, however, he was superb and his timing awesome. He was absolutely back on form and I know he is going to die. When he finally collapsed, I sat and bawled my eyes out.

I wrapped the tape in the robe and made up a parcel, which is still in my collection. I told my secretary that nobody would ever be allowed to look at this in my lifetime. It was just too emotional to handle. It's still there.

★ ★ ★

What you are about to read, ladies and gentlemen, is worth a lot more than the price of this book. You are about to learn how to become rich. It is an easy method and all you have to do is apply it.

The man who owned the Hotel de France was called Parker. Now, he was worth a bob or two, and yet did not seem to have much in the way of common sense, at least, not to a starving genius like me. I pointed this out to him one day and also pointed out the differences in our respective bank balances.

'Ah yes,' he mused, 'that's probably because you don't know about the FU fund.' I didn't, so he went on. 'Most people save up for a holiday, a car, or for presents, spend their money and then have nothing left. They never think of saving up to be rich.' Little lights started to come on in my head. 'In my family, we are all taught about the FU fund and it makes us rich.' I had to ask, wouldn't you?

'The FU fund is a very simple principle. All you do is put 10 per cent of ABSOLUTELY EVERY penny that you earn, find or get given, into a bank account or investment account where you can't get it back out again. You need an account with, say, a five-year notice of withdrawal. That way, you can't impulsively draw the money out and spend it. Now, you may well ask, what is the use of money that you can't use? Well, to be honest, for a few years, it's no use at all, BUT there is this magical thing called compound interest. The banks give you money for letting them use your money, it's called interest. But you leave the interest in the account and next year they give you interest on your interest. At the same time you are constantly adding to the capital sum because you must never stop paying in 10 per cent of everything you get. Even if your granny gives you a pound, you must put ten pence into the account. It has to be a habit.'

I put up all sorts of arguments. He would have none of them. 'Everyone thinks they need all the money they earn but there are a lot of people living on a lot less than you. You can do without the 10 per cent and one day, in some years' time, you will look into your bankbook and think, "I'm rich." What you also have to remember is that much more truthful than the old adage of "money attracts money", is the adage that "the confidence of having money, attracts money".'

I started to save. Try it, believe me, it really works. Just a couple of years ago I read a book from America called the *Wealthy Barber,* and Chapter Two was devoted to exactly this principle.

As I said, on the Bentine show I met a nice girl called Melody and we lived together, on and off, for the next two years. It was actually less like 'living' together and more like 'moving' together, as I still had no permanent home.

It was while I was living with Melody in Kenton that child stars Lena Zavaroni and Bonnie Langford burst on to the scene. Suddenly, showbusiness was very young. I looked at them and thought that there was no way I was going to make it now – showbusiness had become so young and I was past 30!

My hairline was receding and one day when I expressed my fears at a dinner party, a little Jewish fellow sitting opposite whispered, 'Why don't you wear a wig like me?'

I was gob-smacked. Thinking that I would always easily spot a toupee, I leaned closer, looking for a 'join'. This fellow's hairpiece looked real, not a hint of a wig. Offering to make me one, he explained how they are often made far too thick to look real. Using less hair makes the wig look real. This would do me the world of good, he insisted.

The following week, he delivered his masterpiece and I was very impressed. Initially though, rather than making me feel self-assured, it had the opposite effect. In fact, I felt pretty insecure wearing what felt like a piece of carpet on my nut and I was sure everybody would notice. Deciding to give it a go, I took it out for a test drive. While visiting my sons in the North, I took the wig for a walk on Redcar beach where the northeast wind howls most days of the year and I thought this was the perfect place to give my new top a spin. Walking at a 45° angle against the vicious gales I was amazed when it didn't blow off. My head nearly did, but the matting stayed firmly in place.

I became very fond of my new-found youth and clipping it to my head each day became as regular as brushing my teeth. It also kept me warm in the winter! Replacing it every six months was a necessity as the real hair began to go gingery after a while. My cousin Bob, naturally more ginger than me, used to get my hand-me-downs!

The first time I wore it on stage was at my beloved Batley Variety Club, and a volunteer on stage that night announced he was a hairdresser. I couldn't resist it. Unfastening the piece from my head, I whisked it off, handed it to him and said, 'Well, cut that then!' It got a roar from the audience.

The following night I had yet another opportunity when an audience member announced that he worked in the furniture business, for a company called Wigfalls. Off it came again and fell to the ground, symbolising a live logo for his company. I'll do anything to make people laugh.

I wore a wig for several years until the Sun newspaper did an interview with a wig-maker in London who revealed his list of clients. Suddenly, after years of not being noticed, I was told I wore the most obvious wig around. Every year, when newspapers haven't got any news, they run wig stories. I still get mentioned for the wig and even I can't remember it. As the years went by, I started to ease it back and have it thinner, until one day I took it off altogether and *nobody* noticed. I would sit at home watching Spitting Image poke fun at my wig, knowing that I hadn't worn one for six months.

Madame Tussaud's, the great waxworks museum, sculpted three models of me from a special photo session where I stood on a rotating platform as the camera clicked away. At the press call, one of the reporters asked if I was going to donate one of my wigs.

'I don't wear a wig,' I replied.

Chaos reigned as cameramen climbed ladders to try and take pictures of the top of my head. The next day, several of the tabloids proudly announced on their front pages the headline: PAUL DANIELS NO LONGER WEARS WIG!

This made me realise how 'intelligent' some of the press in this country are. This type of 'in-depth' reporting of similar incidents is beyond my understanding and comprehension. With the startling news of my wigless state on the front, page 5 contained the story that Chernobyl, the Russian nuclear power station, had just blown up. Where is the sense of priority here?

Incidentally, we haven't taken a newspaper in our house for years. Debbie and I have read so much about us that is pure fabrication, or altered to imply things that we haven't said, that we find it impossible to believe what they write about other people. If they go to that much trouble to alter stories about a man who does card tricks, how can I believe them when they write about important people? The press say that they should have freedom. Why only them? They say that anyone in the public eye should be open to public scrutiny and I agree with them. When I, or anyone else, is performing in public, whether it be on television or theatre, cabaret or opening a shop, by all means the press should have the right to 'cover' the story and, if that is their wish, criticise the 'performance'.

On the other hand, why should they be allowed to 'cover' my private life without my permission? If someone breaks into my home tonight I can phone the police and have them arrested. If a journalist decided to break into my private life and expose it, when I have committed no crime, there is no recourse. By anyone's standards, surely that is an invasion of human rights.

We have a free press. We do not have a truthful one.

Melody and I stayed together for the next two years as I toured the clubs once more. The problem was that I was occasionally still seeing Monica and I was in a real quandary as to which one I wanted to be with. Many an evening I had to eat two dinners as I flitted from one to the other. Melody and I split up when she went to Canada to dance. She was away for two weeks and I knew that she wanted several alterations to the flat in Kenton. I built wardrobes and did, even though I say so myself, a marvellously modern paint job in the bathroom. I worked day and night to get it finished then, together with Bonnie and Clyde, our two Pekinese dogs, I went off to meet her at the airport. As she got off the plane with another man, she said, 'didn't you get my letter?' I gave her the dogs' leads and ran to the car, drove like the wind to Kenton, grabbed all my stuff and then drove out to ask Jack Sharp if I could stay with him. I told him the story and he laughed like hell. He still asks whether I have seen 'Wardrobes'. I did see her once or twice after that, but it was all over and we are still friends who write from time to time.

These years were to lead to the most significant summer season in Guernsey where I finally decided to turn SHOWbusiness into showBUSINESS. I was top-of-the-bill now, by virtue of the fact that I was very well known in clubland and had won a lot of comedy awards. Maybe I could move up the ladder, and for that you needed a plan.

During the previous Bentine season, a thought had constantly niggled away at me. Michael was on a lot of money a week and yet he wasn't the right man for the job. He wasn't comfortable with the season and left early.

I took over the top spot but I don't remember getting his

money! Had he been placed in the right environment, I know he would have 'done a storm'. The thing was, he was paid a lot more money, because he was a lot more famous. I used my bonce and worked out that he was famous because he was on television and, more importantly, he was on regularly.

Telephoning Artists Management, I asked if Mervyn O'Horan could come over to Guernsey and see me. I was a holiday golfer by this time, never very good and I still play that way, and when Mervyn arrived we immediately set to on one of the local courses. We got to a short hole that had to be played off a very high plateau down on to a green below which was surrounded by ferns. This meant you had to be accurate. We were both level on scores and when Mervyn embarked on his back swing, I casually said, 'I'm leaving your office.'

He lost the ball and, being a Yorkshireman, has never really forgiven me for that.

I was a good act and a good earner for the agency and they had never had a complaint. This was bad news for Mervyn.

'Why are you leaving?' questioned a frowning Mervyn.
'Because there has to be something better than what I'm doing. All I do most of the year, week in and week out, is one-night stands in working men's clubs. I bet you that if I was to phone the office now, that the next eight weeks after I finish here will be Sunderland, South Wales, Doncaster and Sheffield.'

We made the call to prove my point and that is exactly what had been booked for me. Mervyn took my point and promised to talk to others at the office about how I felt.

From that moment on, Mervyn became my personal manager. This man was to become much more than that, my good friend, for the next 30 years and he still is. True to his word, Mervyn discussed the problem with a guy called Howard Huntridge, now a good friend but a heck of a hustler, who went straight to the BBC. It took Howard a lot of time and patience to make contact with the talent scout for BBC Light Entertainment who was responsible for getting new acts on television. Finally arranging the meeting, he told the man about an act called Paul Daniels and the rest is history. Well, almost!

CHAPTER 9

MAGICIAN ON FIRE

The sounds of the Seventies arrived with the super-stardom of Abba, Queen, Elton John and David Bowie. Punk rock and disco-fever spawned the Sex Pistols and John Travolta, and in the same year that the Bee Gees' soundtrack to the film Saturday Night Fever *tops the charts.*

One of my dreams was always to perform at Batley Variety Club, a new, high-tech venue, and even though it was a nightclub it really was the Palladium of the North. Batley was the biggest and the best of several huge venues that had become wonderful places to work; the audiences were looked after, relaxed and eager to be entertained. I got my chance during a winter of cancellations when everybody was falling down with 'flu except me. Dashing from one club to another on snow and ice, with only minutes to spare, I became an expert on driving safely in bad conditions. As I came off stage at the Aquarius Club in Chesterfield, I was asked whether I would 'double' up later at Batley. Would I? I was in the car in a flash, driving up the M1 in the snowed-over fast lane. I arrived late, of course, and had a very quick word with the orchestra leader. No time for music to be studied, all I did was ask him to play me on, wait a while and then have the whole band give a 'taa-daah!' when I dropped all the cards in my hands into a box. Off he went.

Batley Variety Club was the best. They had their own Stage Manager, a gentleman from the older world of theatre, who checked you over before you went on. Just as I was about to enter, he noticed a cotton thread on my jacket and tried to pull it off. Mistake! It was tied to my ear and that hurt. Magicians move in mysterious ways and that was part of a trick. He told me they had an apron stage and that I would walk out around the outside of the curtains as they opened. For the first time ever, my act box was placed on-stage without my checking it. The dressing rooms were really good. I felt that I had arrived.

When I walked on stage the volume of the applause hit me and stopped me in my tracks. I had never seen a room so well appointed for cabaret performance. You were the focal point of the sound of the applause from the audience. Someone must have gone to Las Vegas and copied the design. The act got under way and I dropped all the cards into the box. Instead of the band playing a loud chord to raise the applause, the whole orchestra stood up, waved their hands in the air and shouted 'taa-daah!' I fell about laughing. I was down to do 30 minutes and, thanks once again to the clock in the box, exactly that time later I walked off feeling as if I owned the place. I played Batley many times after that, both as a support and as the feature attraction, but I can still feel the thrill of that first time.

Howard Huntridge, now starting to arrange for the BBC talent scout to see me, telephoned the Corrigan family who owned Batley Variety Club. It was the best and most reliable place in the country to see me work and Howard wanted to know if there was a free gap in their diary. There wasn't, but the Corrigans, enthusiastic to help, offered to squeeze me in anyway. A few further arrangements by telephone and I was told that the 'man from the BBC' would be coming to see me work. Come to think of it, I wonder why television companies don't employ anyone to talent search any more? I know they do if they are producing a talent show, but this man found acts and placed them into suitable shows in the schedules.

There was one problem. I was finishing Guernsey on the Saturday night and my Batley BBC audition was to be on the very next Sunday night. It was a tight schedule, but I was confident I could do it. Knowing that this was to be my big chance, I'd packed my car on the previous Wednesday and sent it on to the ferry, ready to meet me in Southampton. My car was my hotel, my dressing room and my attic. I lived in that vehicle and managed to squeeze my entire life's chattels inside the metal shell with a mixture of art, expertise and sheer luck. Packing my car so well, any door could be opened and nothing would move, it was that solid. I even left an oblong, letterbox-shaped hole in the pile of objects on the passenger seat, so that I could look through it and see if anything was coming from the left. The final performance in Guernsey was full of the usual last-night tomfoolery. We filled Lee Clark's clarinet with talcum powder so that when it was blown, he was suddenly surrounded by a cloud of fragrant dust that got everywhere. In the interval and in front of the audience, I also taped his piano keys together along the edge so that they wouldn't be noticed. When he hit the chord for his big closing number every key went down. He couldn't see the tape, so he gradually stripped the piano down to find the problem.

The gag that was played on me centred on the fact that every night I threw three pieces of rope out into the audience and then asked for volunteers with rope to come on to the stage. Unbeknown to me, the cast had given every member of the audience a piece of rope, so that when I gave the order, the whole auditorium would stand up and walk forward. Unknown to the cast, I had changed my entire act so the gag never happened.

This was the happiest season I ever did. Every act clicked with the punters, the hoteliers and with each other. The show closed and, as we took our bows, half of the audience, who were made up of the island's hoteliers, came forward to give us flowers, gifts, wine and chocolates. Apparently, they had been so impressed with the value and quality of the show they wanted to make their appreciation clear.

The after-show party was fun. Knowing that we would not be allowed to take the stuff back into the UK, we drank all the booze (yes, even me!), scoffed all the chocolates (yes, especially me!) and put flowers in our buttonholes (well, Lee Clarke did!) I bade my fond farewells to everyone. Booked on an early morning flight the next day, my plan was to pick up the car and drive the 300 miles or so to Batley in Yorkshire. That night I slept soundly and woke sparkly bright at 9.00am. Unfortunately, that was exactly the time my plane was leaving. Grabbing the phone, I did all I could to hold up the flight, but the receptionist said that it was actually going down the runway.

There was no alternative but to charter a small private plane, which wiped out a lot of my hard-earned wages from the season. Landing on grass at Southampton, I ran across to the Customs Office in order to pick up my car. By now, I was running several hours late and was in serious danger of missing the most important gig of my life.

The fellow with the clipboard looked serious and I knew that out of all the officers available, I had the 'job's worth'.

'Is this your vehicle, sir?'

'Yes, it is.'

'Right, sir. Empty it.'

'You've got to be joking,' I stammered. 'It took me three hours to pack it! You must be kidding!'

'As a matter of fact, sir, I am,' he said, breaking into a smile. 'If you can get a five-pound note into a walnut, which is inside an egg, in a lemon, I've got no chance of finding anything in this car, have I? Sign here.' He'd been on holiday in Guernsey, seen the act and was taking the mickey. I wonder whether Customs men get checked when they come back to the UK from abroad.

I drove all the way to Yorkshire and arrived mid-evening, ready for an appearance at 10.00pm. Quickly introduced to the man from the BBC, Colin Farnell, I waited my turn to appear. I had hoped that Colin would be entertained by some good acts while waiting for my spot. Apparently, however, he had already sat there for two hours listening to drumming. The club had been booked for the entire afternoon and evening by a drummers' convention. I was the only non-drumming act on. All the audience were drummers, too, and as I went out on stage I cried, 'don't worry, I'll keep all these plates spinning,' because there were so many drum kits on stage the cymbals looked just like a plate-spinner's act.

I went down very well, thank you, and Colin liked my work. He promised to get me on to one of his television variety shows. I was thrilled, only to be disappointed a few days later when he telephoned to say that all the possible slots he had for magicians were filled for the next 12 months. I think he was being polite. I don't think that the BBC wanted me, or is this a persecution complex?

Fortunately for me, he telephoned a man called Johnny Hamp who produced a show for ITV called *The Wheeltappers and Shunters Social Club*. Staged to look like a genuine Northern club, complete with running bar, tough audience and Chairman, this programme was aired on Saturday nights from around 9.00pm. I went over to Manchester to do my first and my only real 'audition'. *Opportunity Knocks* didn't count because

MAGICIAN ON FIRE

I had been invited to do the job and I really wasn't all that bothered. This job I really wanted.

I walked into a long room and Johnny was sat at the far end with a couple of staff members. I started to talk and realised it was ridiculous to work the small 'audience' at that distance. So I picked up my act box and walked down to the other end and worked about three feet away from where they were sitting. Despite one of his advisers saying that I was totally unsuitable for television, Johnny struck a deal and I was set to appear in February 1975.

Since *Opportunity Knocks* and one or two small guest TV appearances, I had studied books on film and television techniques and direction. I was really quite well prepared for *The Wheeltappers and Shunters Club*. Seventies hit singer Alvin Stardust was top-of-the-bill but, in truth, the whole studio was full of very well-known club acts.

Comedian Colin Crompton was playing the part of the Club's Concert Chairman. ''Ere now, everyone. Regarding the notice in the Gents what says "Wet Paint". This is not an instruction!'

Bernard Manning was the top resident comic who played a strange role of compere 'added on' to Colin's Chairman. Johnny Hamp was at the heart of this clever series, which offered an incredibly life-like, genuine impression of a Northern club and even hid the television cameras so that the audience would feel the right atmosphere. It also meant that all these club acts who would have been unnerved in a television studio felt very much at home in their own environment.

During rehearsals, my name was called and I walked out on to the catwalk extension that jutted into the audience and set down my table. I have always used a solid-looking magic box, as I believe that an audience doesn't like wobbly magician's tables. It gives them a subconscious sense of insecurity, the last thing you want when trying to entertain them. All these little bits of psychology are built into the act. The audience doesn't and shouldn't recognise them, but they are vital to the success of the performance.

Being a magician, I have to be aware of audience and camera angles and asked Howard if he would check this on one of the monitors for me as we rehearsed. The floor manager listened to his earpiece and, looking up at me, said, 'Mr Daniels, the Director has told me that he would direct this show, not you.'

'Oh no, I wasn't meaning to be rude, but I am about to do a magic act and I don't want any shots that would give away what I'm doing. When I'm working live, I control where the audience looks by my body language, my words and gestures.'

'The Director says he will still direct the show, Mr Daniels,' came the reply.

'Ah. Well. Er, right. Then I'd best go and you can do the next act.'

I said this nicely. There was no malice intended. I picked up my box and headed off stage.

Howard, who had spent a lot of time setting all this up, nearly had a heart-attack. Johnny Hamp came running after me.

'What's wrong, Paul?'

'All I want to do is to make sure the magic works, otherwise what's the point of having me here? If a shot is taken at the wrong angle at the wrong moment the secret is gone.'

What I didn't know was that Johnny's father had been a magician, so somebody was smiling on me that day. We laughed later that his father had the wonderful title of 'The Great Hamp'.

I explained to Johnny that I knew that behind the back wall of the stage was a huge picture which slid to one side revealing a hidden camera, used for certain audience shots. I couldn't allow a camera looking over my shoulder in that way and the Director wouldn't know what was appropriate to see or not.

Johnny went off and a few moments later another message came down from the control room and into the floor manager's ear, 'the Director says he will not use the camera from behind, except where you say so.' That Director kept his word and, in fact, was the best I ever had. Having come into television from theatre, he instinctively knew the timing of the joke, to the cut of the person's face, without missing the nerve-ending of the trick. It was wonderful direction.

Slowly making my way through each section of the act, to allow the crew a chance to see what I was going to do, I got to the point where I was to borrow some money. Bernard Manning immediately jumped forward, peeling a note off a large roll. He is not a man known to wash his mouth out regularly with soap and water, though many have said that he should. When his money disappeared, he started laying into me, like a heckler with a stand-up comic. Amongst his peers, he obviously felt he could take the new guy apart. I met his heckling (and, yes, Mother, he was very rude) with the best returns I could and, possibly because I used to spend hours writing my own heckler stoppers, unbelievably, I won!

As I pretended to forget about the money, Bernard got worse with his shouting and bawling for the return of his money. The language got so bad I had to be rude myself (forgive me, Mother) and after one particularly virulent attack I answered with a sigh and 'Bernard, does your mouth bleed every 28 days?' He gaped like a stuck fish and Johnny Hamp still regrets to this day that he didn't have the recorders rolling at that moment. Don't get me wrong – I like Bernard Manning. He works audiences his way and I work them mine. He's a very funny man who chooses to work in a very bawdy style. I don't think he ever needed it, but he did.

Eventually we got to the bit where the money was to be discovered inside a packet of Polo mints.

'If my money is inside this pack of Polos, I will kiss your arse!'

He snapped the pack in half and his note was inside.

'Your place or mine?' I asked and walked off, leaving Bernard speechless for the second time in a few minutes.

After the recording, Johnny came up to me and said that I was either a lucky bastard or dead clever. Apparently, throughout my spot I had forward- and back-referenced all the time so the piece could not be edited at all. Johnny took the decision to air the whole twelve minutes at a time when nobody got more than four. Twelve minutes on prime-time television was unheard of. Overnight I was a 'name'. People knew who I was because, also, throughout the spot, I had kept repeating my name.

No one becomes a star on one television show. The day after the *Wheeltappers and Shunters*, the telephone was ringing non-stop at Mervyn's office and I was recognised on the street, but I knew that it would be a one-show wonder and that I could easily disappear back into clubland. If I was to climb the ladder of fame, then I knew I had to be seen regularly.

On the following Monday, Mervyn and I started to get a sense of what was brewing. The phones were going crazy with bookers and people wanting interviews. By Tuesday the fan mail was pouring in. As we sat in the office opening the enormous influx of fan mail later that week, Mervyn gasped. One of the letters was a very sexually explicit letter from a woman in Bognor Regis and made *Forum* magazine read like Enid Blyton. Mervyn, bless him, was shocked and asked if he should telephone the police, but I suggested that he book me for a summer season in Bognor. That same day, Johnny Hamp telephoned and said that the reaction to my appearance had been so good, he wanted to book me for another programme. It was on this second show, where I did about 15 minutes, that

Johnny came up to me afterwards and said quietly in my ear, 'You're not lucky, are you?' He had spotted my forward- and back-referencing technique again.

That didn't stop him giving me a 20-minute *Wheeltappers* and eventually he gave me the whole show. Thanks, Johnny.

In the meantime, odd television appearances followed, including a guest appearance on the *David Nixon Show* the same year. David was a superb television magician and I saw how he was so at home in the studio. He made the viewer feel as if they had been invited into his front room. David also knew his specialised craft intimately and was acquainted with exactly where each camera was, which way to turn for the next mid-shot and what was long shot and close-up. I went home from that one and got some more books on television direction.

In those early days of watching myself on television, it was a strange experience. It didn't feel like me on the screen. It was someone else and was a bit like when you listen to your own voice on a tape recorder, sounding different to what you expect. So, occasionally, when 'that man' on the screen did something that I knew was clever, I would talk to the screen out loud, go 'Yeah' and clap and encourage the magician I was watching. This mostly happened when a clever move, invisible to the audience, was made. I soon realised that others in the room, family, friends or other acts in digs, thought that I was being big-headed, but I wasn't. It just wasn't 'me'. Sometimes, when the 'man' could have been faster, or better, or said something naff, I was also his biggest critic. I learnt to watch myself when I was alone.

Several TV special appearances followed over the next couple of months, including a series with the strange title of *The Lunar Debating Society*. This had temporarily replaced the late-night ITV epilogue slot and featured a different entertainer each week. I was booked for a week of close-up magic and followed a week of Spike Milligan reading his poems. I haven't got a copy of the *Lunar* show and I wish I had. I thought the format was great. A one-off television special for New Year's Eve then followed for Granada, where I put the whole show together myself and the cost of mounting this was more than I got paid. It made me consider the fact that television artistes should get paid a lot of money, because they entertain a lot of people.

For this hour-long programme, I put together the whole show and had complete control over every aspect of it. This caused some to suggest I was conceited, but I just wanted it right. I'm sure my hard Northern accent didn't help and my blunt way of working probably upset people, but I was always very short of time. I came from the streets and that's the straight way in which I communicated to those around me. It saddened me when some felt they couldn't work with me, because as any artiste in showbusiness will tell you, we all need to be liked.

I designed a special rotating doors illusion that swung round each time to reveal a girl standing in the quadrant. It could produce seven or eight girls all dressed in their flowery costumes and looked very effective. Having sent the design in to the television special effects workshops, I was amazed when I arrived at the studio to discover this illusion, which was at least three times the size. The builders had misread the instructions interpreting centimetres for inches and it was so big we could have produced a hundred girls or more out of it. We still used the effect as there wasn't time to remake it, but I needed four crewmen to help me swing open the doors because they were so heavy.

An oddity in this show was an illusion called the Ghost Cabinet. This was a small, curtained cabinet and anything placed inside changed in some way. A man from the audience was invited up and he examined the box and then placed a piece of rope inside. The curtains were closed and opened and the rope was knotted. A white glove was placed inside and the man sat in front of the curtains. The white glove came out and caressed him. Immediately the dancing girls on the show came on and stripped the box down to small pieces to show there was nobody there but, of course, the Invisible Ghost. What made this so odd was that the Director shot it on the wrong lens.

Have you ever noticed in athletics or during a horse race on television the runners look very bunched up but when you see the same group from the side they are all spread out? That's because the first shot is taken from the front on a telephoto lens and that foreshortens the distances. The same thing happened with the trick. The cabinet, shot from the front on a telephoto lens looked as though it was right up against the back curtain and could have been worked from the back. The Director, when I pointed this out, said, 'Yes, I see, but it isn't worked like that, is it?' He really didn't understand that, in the studio, he was watching one thing but he was showing the audience something else.

The illusion was never shown and the girl inside, Nikki, (you didn't really think it was a ghost, did you?) was paid never to be seen in an illusion that was never seen anyway. More than that, she received repeat fees every time the show was shown somewhere else in the world. She ended up getting more money than I did.

The success of the one-hour special meant the offer of an Easter show as a follow-up and I began to design this from start to finish as I was now accustomed to doing. In the middle of all this, a friend from Granada Television appeared and asked to talk to me in private. He explained that he had been present at a producer's board meeting where my name had been discussed. Apparently, one of the directors had said that I was a bright new talent and worth hanging on to. Indeed, he had even proposed that I should be offered more money to equal my value to the company. Another director had countered this suggestion by saying there was no need to offer more money as Paul Daniels had no idea of his worth.

I don't often get angry. I find it doesn't really help so I tend to laugh at stupid situations instead. I will occasionally act angry in order to get a point across as a last resort, but on this occasion I felt so betrayed I just shrugged my shoulders and smiled. Inside, with this new revelation of what the television bosses thought of me, I decided to leave. I felt somehow very let down. I had worked hard for them and I just thought that they would recognise that and reward it accordingly. Welcome to the real world of money, my son.

The next day, Mervyn started to let it be known that I was available to work for other TV companies. I was known by a lot of people at that time, but I wasn't really a star name. The BBC expressed an interest.

They had used me in a series made in Manchester called *For My Next Trick*. The first series was taped in a deserted church in Dickenson Road and had already been written to include conjurors John Wade and Terry Seabrook with Faith Brown as the singer/stooge. I was brought in at the last moment to bring a different angle to the series, but I was horrified when I saw how the programmes had been compiled.

The idea of the series was based on *The Comedians*; another very successful Johnny Hamp show where the latest comics would tell gags which were intercut with each other. Unfortunately, not many producers or directors understand the theatre of magic, as it is a totally unique art form, and I knew before we had recorded the first programme that the idea just wouldn't work.

Each magician would be recorded doing their complete routines, but in the editing room all the effects were intertwined with each other. For example, Terry Seabrook borrowed five pounds and it was accidentally burnt; then it cut to John Wade doing a piece of origami; then a cut to Paul Daniels doing a line; followed by a cut to Faith Brown singing a song. The final cut would return to Terry Seabrook finding the fiver in his wallet. The disjointed format made no sense at all and jumping from the start of one trick, to the middle of another, to the end of another, just didn't work with magic in the same way as comedy. I used a leaf out of my *Wheeltappers* notebook and quickly developed a way of presenting very short, 30-second tricks and jokes, which stayed intact and worked on their own. Terry Seabrook was a very funny magician and John Wade a very elegant one, but I was the only performer who really survived the series because I adapted to fit the format.

Even our friend Johnny Hart had a lucky escape. Johnny was obviously getting bored with his usual act and had declared an interest in doing comedy and illusions. He had refined his original routine so perfectly, but had stayed with it too long without learning too much about the rest of the business. He seemed to think that he could just buy a trick, pick it up and do it, which was a great mistake on the day he arrived at the *For My Next Trick* studio.

Having purchased a set of 'multiplying candles', Johnny walked on to the set with a beautifully coloured silk top hat. As we watched one of the highest-paid television magicians at that time, he proceeded to produce lit candles from thin air. Unfortunately, the candle flames shot about 2ft in the air and looked nothing like candles at all. In fact they were metal tubes filled with petrol and highly dangerous.

Apologising to audience and crew, Johnny disappeared into the backstage corridor to try to shorten the flames by flicking the candles up and down, which shot the excess petrol along the backstage corridor. This time the flame was only 5in long and although it still didn't seem like a real candle, it was passable, I suppose. A few moments later and he had produced two handfuls of candles all burning away and lighting up his smiling face very nicely.

With the climax of his opening piece over, Johnny blew the candles out and placed them in his silk top hat before going into a card routine. I continued to watch the escapade on a monitor as the camera cut to a close-up on Johnny. Suddenly, I noticed that the picture was getting hazy and as Johnny produced more cards he started to drop them into his hat, and as the camera widened to reveal his top hat, we saw that it was on fire. The smoke and flames coming out of the hat were so fierce that a hole had started to appear at the front.

Johnny Hart suddenly became aware that his top hat was out of control and, frantically grabbing it, ran to the backstage corridor where he had emptied the previous lot of petrol. In seconds, studio firemen and foam fire extinguishers surrounded him. I immediately bounced on to the stage and announced that there was nothing to worry about and that it was only Johnny giving one of his more extinguished performances.

Not to be outdone, Johnny turned up again two weeks later with a stock version of 'The Zigzag Lady'. The only hitch was that every magician on the planet was presenting this famous illusion invented by the late, great genius, Robert Harbin. A new innovation in magical illusion, Zigzags were being over-exposed in every cabaret, club, TV show and could be purchased virtually everywhere and everybody was presenting it in the same way.

Having had a chat with my dad, who was becoming increasingly interested in the technicalities of my props, I proposed a new way of doing the same illusion where the middle of the girl slides to one side. Once I saw that the adaptation would work, I suggested to the producer of the programme that he wait until it was built and I would show it to him. 'Johnny Hart is booked to do the Zigzag,' he replied.

'Oh, but I think you'll be pleased with this because its different from all the rest,' I pleaded.

'Johnny Hart is booked to do the Zigzag,' came the response. In truth, Johnny's illusion was different, too. Instead of the girl's head showing through a round hole at the front, it stuck out of the top. I noticed on the instructions enclosed with this version that it proudly stated it was a 'design improvement so that every travelling magician can get one in the boot of his car'. I couldn't imagine that a magician had designed this. The balance was all wrong. What had been forgotten was that it is the essential dimensions of the box and the psychology behind the trick that actually makes it work. Consequently, the whole illusion was laughable from the moment he started.

Johnny had decided not to rehearse with the girl assistant who screamed the moment he inserted the first blade. It made contact with her boobs. No rehearsal again, you see. She didn't have a clue what she was supposed to do and found herself trapped inside a box with a mad magician terrifying her. With the girl looking terrified, Johnny carried on smiling while trying to tell the girl what to do and hoped he wouldn't be heard above the background music. He eventually gave up, but was told that he could come back the following week and have another go.

'Why don't you use mine?' I petitioned.

'Johnny will do the Zigzag,' came the echo through gritted teeth.

I couldn't wait to see what would happen the following week and, sure enough, it was as entertaining as the previous one. Same box, same girl, but this time when Johnny inserted the blade, the girl's head did something that told everybody exactly how the trick was worked. Once again, the illusion was dropped from the schedule, but now it was my chance.

My version was wheeled in the following week and I suspected the crew were wondering if all the hysteria over the past few weeks was a competition of the Zigzags. The girl got in, her head, hands, feet and belly sticking out through various holes. The blades I used were absolutely full width and I made a volunteer from the audience push the centre section out. As he pushed, I pulled as well which made him fall forward, the middle part toppled out completely on to the floor and he fell into the empty space in the centre. Feigning panic I screamed, 'You've pushed too hard!'

A head was left supported by four thin poles and it was real. The combination of laughter, surprise, drama and my dad's construction expertise had made the new Zigzag work at last. I would have loved to be in the living room of every magician in the land at that impossible moment.

The Producer of the series didn't get my sense of humour at all. That was OK. I didn't get the humour of the writer he had booked to write the shows. At a planning meeting, I told him of an idea whereby I would introduce a Chinese girl and claim that 'in the Far East, magic is handed down from father to son but, as there were no boys in the family, they had had to teach her the act. She is a genuine mind-reader, the like of which we have never seen before.' I would then introduce her, using her Chinese name and point out that, as she didn't speak any English and I had lived in Hong Kong for a while, I would translate for her. Any member of the audience could place any object at all from their pockets or handbags and I would simply say three words, to remove the possibility of any code, and they would be 'What is it?' The Chinese girl would then reply and tell us what was on my hand. This would happen and the girl would say, 'Ng luk chow,' or something similar, and I would say 'CORRECT, it is a pen,' or whatever it was.

'Amazing,' said the Producer, 'How does she know?'

Terry, Faith, John and I thought he was kidding. He wasn't.

'No,' I said, 'she doesn't know. I'm looking at the object so I just say whatever it is.'

'Well, how does she know what to say?'

'She doesn't. It's a gag. She says anything she likes in Chinese so long as it is very short.'

'Yes, I see. But how do you know what to translate?'

He never understood at all and eventually agreed to do it if we used Faith Brown in a Chinese dress.

'You can't do that,' I tried to explain. 'The gag will only work if the audience believe it is really going to happen.'

He said we couldn't do it. I went to Manchester University and paid a Chinese girl myself to do the routine. The audience laughed (I knew they would because I had done this joke for the Bentine season with an Oriental dancer from the Trendsetters troupe). The Producer came downstairs and said that he still didn't get the joke, but as the audience had laughed he would keep it in the show. Knowing the BBC they probably made him Head of Light Entertainment.

It is this constant drive to improve on what has already been achieved in magic that gives me so much pleasure. I never decry a brilliant magical invention; I'm just concerned to push it as far as it will possibly go. I had found out that my dad was able to turn my quick sketches into physical objects. He was unable to add anything in terms of the deception because he didn't know the business of trickery, but knew everything there was to know about torque and stress almost instinctively and we would endlessly debate the possibilities. He would always be saying to me that I would never get away with it and couldn't believe how simple some of the tricks were.

There are a couple of things about my business that you should understand. Magic is not just for children. Magic should be considered alongside opera or ballet, drama or comedy, because it can be any or all of those as well as its own art form. When you go to see a magic show, let's face it, the guy can't really do magic. That's OK. Stallone isn't Rambo, nor could anyone ever be; Christopher Reeves as Superman can't really fly. Magic is the same. When you go to see a magic show you go to a theatrical experience where the actor on stage, playing the part of a magician, can apparently defy all the natural laws of physics and science.

Think about it. We are taught that matter cannot be created, and yet a magician makes objects and even people, apparently appear from nowhere. Matter cannot be destroyed and yet a magician makes things vanish without trace. Solid matter cannot be penetrated without leaving some trace and yet, as seen on television, I pushed Penelope Keith through a pane of glass. Both Penelope and the glass are doing fine. Matter cannot travel through time and space instantaneously and yet magicians again make objects and people vanish from one spot and reappear somewhere else in the blink of an eye. And we have the Law of Gravity, yet magicians make people float in the air. The list goes on.

The magic show is great theatre when it is performed correctly and should be enjoyed for what it is, pure escapism and not to be taken too seriously. The presentation can vary enormously, from high drama to low comedy and sometimes you get the full range in every show. Me, I go for comedy and hide my skills behind the laughter. I love people having a good time.

Levitations were a particular project of mine and over the years I wrestled with many ways of achieving the illusion of enabling a girl to float in mid-air. Dad would get very upset every time I came home with another suggestion as to how the product he was already in the process of building could be adapted and improved.

'Oh no, here we go again,' he would sigh.

Dad had at around this time turned 60, but was in no mood to contemplate retiring. I was finally earning a substantial amount of money and was in a position to employ my own father full-time. Hughie had difficulty believing this and constantly brushed aside my suggestions that he give up his job with ICI and be engaged as my personal craftsman. His job at the plant, surrounded by and working with chemicals, was not doing him any good at all. He kept feeling very dizzy and passing out. I thought that if I could find the right place, he could come and work for me as a prop-maker. I needed a house with a bit more than a granny flat.

'I don't want to be a financial burden to you, son,' he would consistently murmur.

'But, Dad, I can easily afford to employ you,' I insisted. I showed him what I was earning and finally he agreed. He only had one last question. 'After I am 65, will there still be plenty for me to do?' There was.

One week in November 1978 was to be the major turning point in my career. Imagine this for a week in the life of a 'turn'. If you don't know that expression, it comes from the old days of Variety. Acts were called turns and even numbered. One of my earliest memories of the theatre was the red numbers that lit up by the side of the stage at the Middlesbrough Empire telling you which number turn was on stage.

Sunday – my first time at the London Palladium

I had taken a tour with Sacha Distel because it finished at the London Palladium and every act wanted to work there. For a couple of weeks, I had been driving myself all over England and Scotland. The tour went North and South and back again. Like most tours, the manager had obviously failed geography. During this tour, I was constantly in touch with Granada TV and BBC TV. Neither knew of my arrangements with the other. This was going to be quite a week but even I didn't know how big. Eventually, I arrived for my first ever performance at the Palladium on the Sunday evening. This was to mark the start of my extraordinary seven days.

The stage doorman handed me a parcel, which he said had been left by a gentleman a few moments earlier. I didn't recognise the handwriting on the package, but on opening it up I had a copy of the book *Every Night at the London Palladium* in my hands. *Sunday Night at the London Palladium* was a huge television variety hit in the Seventies and this book listed all the acts, anecdotes and stories from this great theatre.

Inside the book, the inscription read: 'Just walking by, saw your name and thought you'd like this! Yours, Graham Reed.'

Graham was an old friend from my days at the Middlesbrough Circle of Magicians, but I hadn't seen him for more than 15 years. It was a very special moment for me and was the nicest thing he could have done. I made it my business to track him down soon afterwards and we became great friends again. In fact, Graham is my oldest friend and the most generous of men. He even became one of the ideas men on the *Magic Show* television series.

With the book sitting in my dressing room and almost willing me to succeed on the greatest stage in the world, I stepped out into the limelight. The act went down so well, it was the most wonderful sensation I had ever felt and I flew all the way that night. It was almost as if I had been in training all my life for that particular 40 minutes.

After the show, John Avery, the Palladium manager, said, 'You were fantastic. Where on earth have you been?'

'Trying to get here!' I said.

'Well you're certainly going to make a return visit,' he promised.

MAGICIAN ON FIRE

Monday – a hotel somewhere near Gatwick

The next evening wasn't as grand as the Palladium but it was still very important for me. I had been booked to do my first ever 'posh' after-dinner cabaret at a corporate function. This was, of course, in completely different surroundings and conditions to the clubs I was used to and I was very happy when the show went really well. Although it was a late gig, I drove through the night to get to Manchester. I had to be in Granada's television studios the next morning.

Tuesday – Granada Television Studios, Manchester

I had been offered and accepted the host's job on *Be My Guest* for ITV and rehearsals started early in the morning. The Producer was Johnny Hamp again. The concept of this show was that it would feature guests chosen by the host. I got to pick the guest for the first show. At the end of each show, all the guests' names would be put in a hat, a name pulled out and that performer would choose the guests for the next show. Showbusiness was inviting the showbusiness it liked.

On my first presentation I chose Del Shannon, famous for his pop hit 'runaway'; The Bachelors singing 'I Believe'; The Drifters and 'Saturday Night's the Night for a Party'; and comedians Ken Dodd and Dougie Brown. Doddy was a Nutty Professor character and was one of my all-time favourite comics. He still is. Doddy can make you laugh with one twitch of his knee. I did magic between the acts and even got a sketch with the Incredible Dodd.

During rehearsals, he knocked on my dressing room door.

'Can I come in, Paul?'

'Of course you can, Mr Dodd.'

I was delighted to have any opportunity to be with the

'master', and I really wish that I could remember the exact gag we talked about.

'Just a little bit of advice, you know. It's much funnier if you say the tag-line the other way round,' Doddy suggested.

'Why?' I genuinely wanted to know.

'I don't know,' confessed the joke-smith, 'it just is.'

The genius was right of course. I went out a few moments later, changed the punchline around and the laugh was ten times as loud. Comedy is a very strange thing and Doddy knew from experience how to get the very best out of a gag. No one can explain the gut feeling of a grafting comedian, having tried it every way round until suddenly it's in the right order.

During the day in the studio, I noticed how others there were giving me surreptitious glances. People were whispering in corners and it was obviously at my expense, or so I thought. Summat was up. I grabbed Johnny Hamp and asked him what was going on.

'We've had a telephone call from the Palladium,' he confessed. 'You were there on Sunday night and they liked you so much, they are trying to fit you into the *Royal Variety Show*.'

'But that's next Sunday night!' I said.

'That's right and the running order is already set, but they still want to try and get you on board. No one wanted to tell you in case you didn't get in it.'

I couldn't believe it.

'Well, they'd better make their minds up fast because on Saturday night I'm in Spain.'

Wednesday – recording at Granada Television Studios

The next day, Johnny returned with the news that the *Royal Variety Show* was 'on'. From years of dreaming about working at the London Palladium, here I was about to appear twice in one week! Johnny explained how Mervyn was working on flights to get me back from Spain early on Sunday, but I was a little worried recalling the last time I had an important flight to catch when it had gone down the runway without me.

Determined that the transportation of my props was not going to be a problem, I hurriedly asked my newly hired craftsman to make a duplicate set of everything and deliver it to the stage door of the Palladium for the Sunday. Dad happily obliged and the twinkle in his eye showed how proud he was, although I still don't think he could believe what was happening. The show that night went well and Granada were very happy. I said goodnight to everyone and drove through the night to London. Granada didn't know I was recording the next day for the BBC.

Thursday – the BBC and The Magic Show

The BBC were doing a series of magic shows with each one being hosted by a famous magician. I remember that Fred Kaps from Holland did one and Harry Blackstone from the USA was another host. These names may not mean much to you but believe me, they were very big in the world of magic. They needed a token British host, I suppose, and I got the job. Not only was I performing but I also had other magic acts on as guests. This wasn't as loose in its format as the magic shows I was to do in the future, but it was a quality show and I had a good day, rehearsing in the daytime and recording that night. I only travelled a short way that night as I had most of the next day to travel to the next venue.

Friday – Great Yarmouth

I drove to Great Yarmouth. Having had a kip in the car, I arrived on Friday morning where the International Round

Table had booked me to appear in the biggest tent I had ever seen. Seating thousands, this was a special annual celebration and I was on the bill with Faith Brown and the New Seekers.

Sadly, Faith, though she is a great act, 'died' that night because there were too many foreigners in who didn't understand her brilliant impressions. I am fortunate that magic is able to cross all the international barriers. We stood in the wings feeling really sorry for her, as you do when a mate is in that situation. Trying to get them back, she actually over-ran which caused me some problems, as I needed to get back across country that night for my early morning flight to Spain.

If Faith reads this she'll kill me for the line I used. It isn't mine, it's very old, but it works and this audience had lost interest in the show. After the compère had announced my name, I breezed on and grabbed their attention with, 'right. The man got it right. My name *is* Paul Daniels and if you don't laugh at this lot, I'll bring the girl back on.'

I know, it's cruel, but who said showbusiness was pretty? It more than cracked the ice and the audience, as Ken Dodd would say, 'gave in'. I did 30 minutes, my allotted time exactly, and bowed at the end of the last trick. As I raised myself from the bow, I was stunned to see that the whole tent had stood up and was giving me a standing ovation. This was my first ever ovation and there's nothing like it. It was wonderful.

As I made my exit, the compère who was also the agent for the job, Reg Parsons, had tears in his eyes at the emotion of the moment. As I shot past him, I whispered, 'I know why you're crying, Reg. We should have asked for more money!'

Throwing my case in the car and not bothering to change out of my show gear, I drove through the night once more and arrived at Gatwick airport in time for a few hours' car rest. I had been so high after the standing ovation, I hadn't needed any matchsticks to keep me awake.

MAGICIAN ON FIRE

Saturday – Spain

I caught the flight to Spain to do a corporate job for Sony. Having arrived, I was then driven for hours across the countryside, to wherever this event was taking place. Another good show. I was having the week of my life. Doing the show, it amused me in that it was the worst sound system I had ever heard and yet it was for Sony! I know it wasn't their own gear, but it's always the way. Plumbers' taps always drip. I'm not knocking Sony. My house is full of their stuff.

As usual on corporate jobs, I entertained the representatives after the show. It was a very late night but I made sure this time that it would be impossible for me to oversleep, with every conceivable alarm clock and wake-up call activated. I'll give you a tip – *never* rely on hotel wake-up call systems. Ask any regular traveller. Strangely enough, despite the exhausting week, I was not tired. The adrenalin must have kept me going, but there was no way I could risk missing the morning flight back to London, which would deliver me in time for the *Royal Variety* rehearsals.

Sunday – the Royal Variety Show

A few hours' rest in a hotel bed was all I had before waking up with the dawn and facing several hours' drive back across the Spanish wilderness to the airport. We got there in plenty of time, only to discover that the flight back to London had been seriously delayed. So what else is new? Panicking and making numerous telephone calls, I eventually got on a plane and arrived in London four hours late with the possibility of missing the whole event swirling round my mind. I didn't even pick up my luggage. I just walked straight through the airport and got into the car. I'd pick up the stuff later in the week.

That particular year, the *Royal Variety Show* was in the presence of the Queen Mother, with, among others, Vera Lynn, Tommy Trinder, Harry Secombe and Dickie Henderson on the bill. It was to be an amazing lineup and I was the only one I hadn't heard of! Again!

I arrived at the stage door and ran straight out on to the stage where the entire cast had finished rehearsing and were being placed in the line-up for their final curtain calls. Every member of the grand parade was spotless, with the men looking like penguins and the women glittering and shining as they do. I stood there bleary eyed, unshaven, in a creased suit, splayed hair and breathing deeply. On stage was the very camp Stage Director placing people very carefully. He turned, saw me and thought I was a stagehand.

'Who on earth are you? Get off. Off. Off. OFF!'

'I'm Paul Daniels and I've come to do a show for your mother.'

Harry Secombe collapsed with laughter and I am probably lucky I am still in the business. The Director glared at me so I explained how I had been delayed travelling back from Spain. He stuck me on the end of the line and we rehearsed our bows.

Starting to feel a little worse for wear, I squeezed myself into the corner of a packed dressing room and tried to revive my flagging brain. The television Director arrived and asked me what I was going to do.

'Ten minutes,' I said.

'Don't you get smart with me,' he snapped.

I thought he was a bit nasty, especially as I've always thought showbusiness should be fun. I really did misunderstand that he meant he needed to know what I was actually going to do on stage, but by this time I was too 'out of my tree' to make sense of anything. So I talked him through where and when I would be in my 'front cloth spot'. That means, of course, that you are working in front of the first curtain or gauze, usually while a bigger stage setting is taking place behind the curtain.

Tommy Trinder's introduction was a big let-down: 'Ladies and gentlemen, here is a young man who, I'm told, is making a name for himself in the clubs, though I've never heard of him. Here he is, Paul Daniels!'

I didn't understand his cockney way and I thought he was being rude. In a way, I'm glad he did it because it made me angry and fired me up from being half-asleep to 'How dare he!' and I shot out on stage firing on all cylinders. Usually in the *Royal Variety*, there is a newcomer who becomes a winner, with everybody talking about them. 1977 was my year.

At the after-show party, it was amazing. Press and audience members were all over me asking where I had come from. I wasn't tired any more. The television Director walked past and whispered in my ear, 'I can still edit you out of the show completely!'

It didn't upset me too much, because after a week of two corporate jobs, two major television series, a standing ovation, a trip to Spain and tearing the audience apart at the *Royal Variety Show*, I knew I had finally made it. Once everybody else had left, I sat alone in the bar on that Sunday and there is no other way to describe the feeling. I remember thinking, 'Christ, I'm going to be a star.'

The Director still had his moment, even though the next day the press reported more than favourably on my act and I got rave reviews. He changed my position on the bill. Whether he did it deliberately I don't know, but either way there was no point to it. When the act I had followed appeared on the television programme a week later, I didn't follow it and I honestly thought I had been cut. Then I appeared a few acts later. As they say in showbusiness – bitch.

What a week. Wonderful shows, fantastic reviews and I was going to be on the television. This business doesn't half level you off, though. The following night, I appeared as the cabaret at Scunthorpe Baths!

Showbusiness does that to you, lifts you up and then brings you back down to earth with a bump.

★ ★ ★

Part of the plan laid down in Guernsey was not only to be on television, but also to do better work. The working men's clubs had been very good to me, but amateurs ran them and I wanted to do more professional venues. I moved into the cabaret clubs and then I wanted to move into theatres. At the time, the Delfont Organisation owned more of the summer season theatres than anyone else. Advertisements used to appear in the showbusiness newspaper *The Stage*, along the lines of 'Would anyone knowing the whereabouts of The Flying Waldrons please ask them to get in touch with the Delfont Organisation.' I wanted to place an advertisement that said, 'Would anyone knowing the whereabouts of the Delfont Organisation please ask them to get in touch with Paul Daniels.' Mervyn didn't think it would be a good idea. 'You may never work again,' he said, and maybe he was right.

As it was we wrote several letters to the Delfonts but received only the usual brush-off replies. We did say how much we wanted when asked, but we didn't get anywhere.

Out of the blue, we got a letter to say that one of their show directors, Maurice Fournier, would come and watch me work and asking where he could see me. The nearest place to London was a club in Essex and we told him all the details. He came, he saw, I conquered. I stole that line. He watched me work in a cabaret environment for an hour-and-a-half and afterwards did what all artists love, he came and told me how wonderful I was. Amidst the glow, however, he dropped the bombshell.

'The problem is that I am only looking for a ten- to twelve-minute act.'

'I can do that.'

'Well, I don't know ...'

'I really can.'

He couldn't understand why I would want to give up the full act just to do what was basically a 'warm-up' spot in *The Val Doonican Show*. What he really didn't understand was how much I wanted to work in real theatres.

Eventually, he arranged a meeting and off I went to meet the great Bernard Delfont and his Chief Executive Richard Mills. We met in the Prince of Wales theatre in the heart of the West End. After the general chat, the offer was made. If Val Doonican liked me, then I would be booked to do the Christmas season at the Opera House in Manchester, opening the second half of the show. Bernard stated the fee but he quoted the figure from our letter of 12 months earlier. I pointed out that since then I had risen in stature somewhat in the business but he wouldn't give in. Taking this season would mean a big drop in money. I took the season. I didn't realise until the second night of the run how much money I'd dropped!

After meeting Val in his lovely home and discussing what I would do and what we would do together in the show, I went off to Manchester and rehearsed all the lighting and music cues and all the little things that you do to get the show ready. After Val had greeted the audience, he would introduce me and I would come on and apparently teach him the oldest trick in the world, the cup and the ball trick. I worked the trick in such a way that Val got the tag, the laughter and great applause by producing a potato and everyone thought he had done the trick. Then I was off until the start of the second half when I would do some card shuffles to gags followed by vanishing some money that had been borrowed from a member of the audience. They would then find their money again by breaking open a walnut that I had taken out of an egg. The egg had been removed from a lemon. Average running time 11 minutes with laughs and good magic along the way.

Opening night, no problems. The show was performed in front of the press and hoteliers, some other invited guests and some paying customers. Val was a major star with a wonderful warm personality. Known for his rich voice, what most people didn't realise was that his show had so much comedy in it.

The second night came and I went to the theatre early, just as I used to do in the clubs, and I was amazed to see how early everyone was. All the dancers and the cast were in make-up and costumes and very, very slowly it dawned on me – we were going to do two shows a night and nobody, but nobody, had mentioned this to me anywhere along the way. They all just assumed that I knew that in theatre you did two shows a night. I got ready very quickly and even more quickly realised that Bernard Delfont had got me to agree to a deal where I thought I was negotiating a fee for six shows a week and he was getting twelve. You lives, and you learns.

The Val Doonican Show was a great show to be in, directed to the full by Dickie Hurran, an ex-hoofer, (oops, sorry, ex-dancer; Debbie will kill me) who was a real 'tits and feathers' showman. He loved it all and was as hard as hell with acts and stage crew, hassling them and bullying them to get it right, but he always put on an excellent show. We developed a great relationship over the coming years.

The Stage Manager was Roy Murray. You couldn't get a better man for the job. His parents and grandparents had been in showbusiness and Roy knew nothing else. Every scene and prop was checked three times before being revealed to the audience. I have a photograph of Roy's granddad who had an act called Casey's Court. In those days, you didn't just get the character of the pantomime dame at Christmas. 'Dames' would tour the theatres with comedy sketches. These weren't gay drag artists and they made no attempt to disguise the fact that they were men. They just parodied big-busted, blowsy women and the most famous of them all was Norman Evans, who did his act 'over the garden wall'. Roy's granddad, Will Murray, had such an act, where he played the landlady in a house full of young men. Looking at the photograph, most of them were just boys and in the play the house was full of mayhem and madness.

In parts of the North they still say, when things are all going wrong, 'this place is just like Casey's Court.' What makes the photograph interesting are the two young men sitting on either side of Will Murray. One is Charlie Chaplin and the other is Stan Laurel. What an act that must have been. Chaplin must have had one of those 'convenient' memories, as in his autobiography he talks about going into the film company's clothing store, finding a cane and a bowler and creating the character of the tramp. In the photograph, he already has a cane and a bowler. According to Roy, all the funny walks and bits of business were part of Casey's Court, so Chaplin must have learnt a lot at the school of Will Murray.

I have so many happy memories of working with Val, the totally ageless, classless, family entertainer. When he walked on you just knew nothing was going to go wrong and you could feel the audience relax into their seats. His family image almost got tarnished one night at the Opera House. Not his fault and nothing to do with him, but in the interval, Paul Burnett, the Musical Director, came backstage and asked whether we had seen the couple in the box on the stage left side (known as Prompt Side) and at stage level. 'He's all over her. It's getting very passionate.'

I said that during my act I would find a way to calm them

down by making some gags about them and on I sailed. During the gags and the card tricks, I saw, out of the corner of my eye, that Paul had not been exaggerating at all. They were 'snogging' like crazy and his hands were everywhere. Most of the audience in the circles were not watching me and I thought that as soon as I had lost the cards, I would have a go.

On a chord of music, I dropped all the cards into my box and turned to take them on. They had gone. Good, I thought and headed, thankfully, stage right to borrow some money to do the egg, lemon and walnut trick. Then I heard a strange noise. They were on the floor of the box and it became more and more obvious what was going on. As I continued with my trick, the stalls were craning their necks, the circle was boggle-eyed and the upper circle were just about giving them a standing ovation.

Suddenly, the girl let out a sort of strangled shriek and I immediately came out with 'Oh, listen everybody, it's a Punch and Judy show.' The audience roared and the spot-light operator swung the lamp around to illuminate the box. The man's head came up over the front of the box. 'There's Mr Punch,' I said and, as her head appeared, 'and there's JUDY!' Cheers and loud applause. By the time I had finished the act, the front-of-house staff had sent someone around to sort them out, but they had fled.

It was a great season and I really learnt a lot from Val, one of our finest and often underrated entertainers. Watching the likes of Shirley Bassey and Ella Fitzgerald, I asked myself what it was that made them so different from the rest? What makes them bigger and better? It doesn't matter whether the star is American or British or French or whatever. Why is it that when Max Bygraves or Val Doonican walk out on stage, the whole theatre relaxes? You can feel it. I realised it was because these big, big stars are never frightened to cry in public. They don't hold back any emotion at all. They will give everything they have to encourage their audience to come along for the ride. It was important that I learnt to do the same. Audiences work very hard for their money and if they are going to part with some of that in order to have a night out, then I should give them the very best I can.

You should never make a decision about whether you like or dislike an entertainer by what you see on television. The show that comes into your living room is nothing like the live show at all. The entertainer's performance is diminished in size (and I can't risk too much of that at my height) not only by the size of the screen, but also by the angles chosen by the cameramen and director. The editors change his or her timing. The sound, especially of laughter and applause, is unreal. So many times I have had people at the stage door who have said they didn't want to come but friends or the wife or the kids made them come along. They are always surprised at how funny or colourful the show is when it is live.

That's why I don't think politicians should be allowed on television. We had some acts who came into the studio and were brilliant, but they didn't come across on the screen. We have had brilliant politicians who have been out-voted for the same reason. It's bad for the country to pick a 'media person'. I will now climb off this soapbox and get back to the story. The following summer *The Val Doonican Show* went to the Futurist Theatre, Scarborough, and I went with it. Did you know that all acts have a nightmare? Actually, they have about two or three and they are all to do with this weird business that we work in. There's the one where you are in a play, or a musical, or a pantomime and you are the only one that hasn't been given the script and you don't know your lines. There's another where you can't get to the theatre. All the transport systems that you try, even running, can't get you there and you know you are going to be 'off' when your cue comes. A variation on that is where you are in the theatre, you can hear the show you are in through the backstage tannoy, but you can't find your way to the stage. Believe me, these nightmares recur and you wake up sweating. Being 'off' is the worst thing you can do.

During that first week in Scarborough, I was in my dressing room on the top floor, dawdling around. What I was thinking about I don't know but way off in the distance something was happening, something was coming through the tannoy. Suddenly the penny dropped. I realised that I had heard Val give me my introduction for the third time. Grabbing the props, I even stuck a metal table into my mouth and ran down the stairs that way, I was shoving stuff into my pockets and arrived on the side of the stage where Val was stuck because I wasn't there. We did the business.

For the whole of the show I was dying inside. When it had finished, I went to apologise to Mr Doonican. 'Don't let it happen again,' was all he said. I never did.

In that show, I met and fell in love with Nikki. She was different to any other girl who I'd been out with, being what I called a child of nature. Speeding down the motorway at 100 mph, she'd suddenly say, 'Oh look! The daisies are coming out.' She didn't care what kind of animal it was, Nikki would just walk up and stroke it. Over the years, I have even seen her get too close to a tiger. A truly nice person and both she and her husband Joe are still good friends.

She came from a nice family, too. At the time I went out with her, they had a really good idea, especially if you want to drive shopkeepers crazy. Have you ever noticed how commercial Christmas is? No? Which planet are you from? Nikki's family had a rule that Christmas presents had to be made, or built, or painted, or anything other than bought. Brilliant. I think it was her dad who photographed the family all year long and then gave them all annual family 'diaries'.

Nikki created the greatest photographic albums I've ever

seen. Whereas you and I normally just stick our photos straight inside, she cut them all into shapes and somehow made them look as though they were moving on the page. If her name had been Hockney, she'd have made a lot of money, for she was doing it well before him.

The Scarborough season was a happy one. My sons came for their summer holidays and the town itself is a great seaside resort. I can't remember which one of us 'lads' was the Ace on the shooting stall next to the theatre, but I know it used to close for about 15 minutes every time we were due to go past on the way to the Stage Door, just so we wouldn't win the prizes. Val packed them in twice nightly. All was right with the world.

A winter mixture of after-dinner cabarets, cabaret clubs, television shows and the usual one-night stands led once again to another Val Doonican season. 1977 and this was in Bournemouth. I consider myself very lucky to have caught the end of the era that had these wonderfully huge summer shows, with twice-nightly shows and lots of acts and girls. Any artist who worked in Bournemouth during those years will tell you that one of the strangest events in the season, and yet one of the most endearing, was an invitation to tea. This went to absolutely everyone appearing in Bournemouth and came from a Mrs York-Batley. There was tea, of course, with sandwiches, cakes and scones but the highlight was the game of croquet. This kind, elderly lady did this purely out of the kindness of her heart. She is long gone now, but remembered fondly by a whole generation of 'turns' and dancers.

During my summer season in Bournemouth, I suddenly realised that I had been living on the road, in digs and with various girls for more than ten years. Surely it must be time to settle down?

One newspaper had already published an article claiming that I was using a helicopter to travel and was living in Chelsea with six women. My sons, naturally, had fun poked at them at school and it was no good trying to point out that I wasn't. Don't journalists work out how many people they are going to hurt before they write their fiction? Among the family and close friends I told them that I *wished* I was living with six girls and a helicopter in Chelsea! OK, I wasn't too bothered about the helicopter.

We drove up from Bournemouth one Sunday morning to view a large house in a village called Water Stratford, just south of Silverstone and just north of Tingewick. We were a bit early so we went to a huge Sunday market on an airfield nearby.

One of the stallholders was selling the popular 'slinky' toy, a magical toy that apparently walked across your fingers. In his salesman's voice we heard, 'Come on, Ladies and Gents, get yaw Slinkies 'ere. Ya friends'll say "they like this, not a lot, but they like it".'

'No, they won't,' I said.

He looked up, stunned, and the Slinky dangled half-off his suddenly motionless hand.

'My Gawd! What you doin 'ere?'

'You mention my name,' I said, 'and as if by magic ...'

I knew then that the catchphrase was really getting around. When we got to the converted barn and cowshed, I knew it was exactly what I was looking for. Having been built originally in the early 1400s, it had been beautifully modernised, complete with enclosed courtyard and swimming pool. The house and the village were quite 'Old England'. Its positioning in the south Midlands was of no great concern, as I was already aware that wherever an artiste buys a house, the bookings will immediately come in at the other end of the country. Walking around it, I worked out that I could have the main barn and Mam and Dad could have the 'cowshed' end. Negotiations were started and I returned to Bournemouth.

MAGICIAN ON FIRE

Three nights before the end of the season, I walked down the bank towards the theatre only to be met by Roy Murray and a couple of the management. Val was sick and would be off. They were bringing in a comic to top the bill and we revamped the show to fit. The next night I think it was Roger de Courcey with Nookie Bear who topped. They were really stuck for the last night and I said that I would do it. I wasn't being big-time. It never occurred to them that I was topping the bills around the resorts every Sunday night. I went on and the show went fine and ever after Robert Luff, the producer of *The Black and White Minstrel Show* and who was involved in the Val Doonican production, claimed to have discovered me.

I bought Giffard's Barn for £47,000, a small fortune in those days and, having started negotiations in the summer, I got the keys two weeks before Christmas 1977. It was the first house I had really owned. I went inside this lovely, warm, stone-built house by myself on the first day, lay on my back in the huge empty drawing room and laughed like hell.

It had cost me a lot of money, but I was making a lot of money. It's an extraordinary fact that however much you earn, your costs will rise to match. I think that only the multi-millionaire Bill Gates is ahead of his expenses. When it comes to earning money, you really can't win in the UK. If you spend it on big houses and flash cars you are a show-off. If you don't, you are a cheapskate.

In my experience it is good for kids, particularly in deprived areas, to see someone 'make it'. For them there is a dream. When I lived in South Bank we all wanted to be in the movies. We all had the Hollywood Dream. Now it's *Who Wants to be a Millionaire?* It's the lottery millions. Some people say it's greed, but I don't think they have known what it is like to be truly hard up.

Having picked myself up off the floor, I telephoned Mam

and Dad. They were the ones I really wanted to share my new home with, more than anybody else.

'Let's go mad!' I suggested.

By the following week, we had all moved in. By Christmas Eve, we had the tree up and the log fire roaring. That afternoon, a Harrods van came up the drive and delivered a case of champagne. It was a thank you gift from a charity event I had performed at Buckingham Palace the previous day. Nikki had given me some superb, cut-glass champagne flutes and they lent the final touches to a real, old-fashioned English Christmas.

On Christmas Day, Mam had performed the usual annual miracle of the Christmas Dinner and we sat sipping champagne from Buckingham Palace, out of crystal glasses, in front of a roaring fire and feeling simply glorious. My brother Trevor told us that he had been in Rome the week before and in a restaurant where the background music was all Vivaldi. I started to laugh uncontrollably. I couldn't stop myself at all. The whole family looked at me in amazement.

Eventually, I got it out. 'Just look at us,' I said. 'It's a bloody long way from South Bank!'

Christmases were special at Giffard's Barn, particularly as I had Mam and Dad to spoil. At last, I felt I could give them back a little of the love they had shown me over the years. With Dad now living 'on site' to make my props and illusions, I felt it only right that I purchase the gear to make his job as easy as possible. So, just before Christmas, I went to a large hardware shop and in the middle of the store was an incredible workbench, which looked perfect. It had a central motor, which drove every woodworking tool known to man and even had its own vacuum system for sucking the muck away. A company called 'Kity' made it and I didn't bother to ask how much it was, I just wanted it for Dad.

It was delivered the next day and I got a shock. It arrived in a million different pieces and boxes ready to be built. I asked the deliveryman to put it in the downstairs toilet. The poor man gave me a very strange look, but obediently started to stack one box upon another. It filled the toilet up to the ceiling, at which point I got some Christmas wrapping paper and covered the door to seal the present inside. The deliveryman stood and stared in disbelief. It wasn't until he left that I realised why he'd looked so puzzled – I should have told him we had other toilets.

Dad's face was a picture that Christmas morning. As he opened the door, he gasped in surprise, for there sat the world's biggest Meccano set and it was all his. That was when I learnt about his childhood and the cruelty shown to him during Christmases past. It took him a month to put it together.

The following Christmas, I gave them an envelope. 'That's a bit of a comedown after last year,' said Mam.

Dad opened it. 'I think you'd better sit down, Mam,' he said when he had finished reading the contents.

It was a certificate of travel to take them to Hollywood. I was thinking of how they had been brought up in the boom years of the cinema and that maybe they would like to see where it all started. I was right; the tears that streamed down Mam's face were priceless.

It was their first ever aeroplane flight and as we waved them off, I said to Trevor, 'I bet Dad comes back in a stetson.'

I was wrong. It was Mam who came back in a stetson. They had a fabulous time and seemed very much at home. Whenever I go to Hollywood, I never meet anybody, but my parents came back with stories of having dinner with Liberace and Cary Grant. Meeting Joan Collins' chauffeur on the plane, they took up an offer to be driven around by him and cancelled the limousine I had booked for them.

Giffard's Barn has great memories. Sammy Davis Jnr had a

line in his act something like, 'Hey, look at me. I'm rich. Do you want to know how rich I am? I've got a swimming pool and I can't even swim.' When I was at Giffard's, I altered the line. 'Do you want to know how rich I am? I can't swim and I've just had the pool moved.' It was true and I know at the time there was a good reason, but I can't remember it. Maybe it came about because the bull from the farm next door jumped over the wall and landed in it. We had to get a crane to get him out again. I didn't even know bulls could jump.

I'm not someone who drives 'on the bonnet', I always drive at least two cars in front, looking way ahead of the car. I suppose its called defensive driving, then you are ready and alert for any eventuality, and it's saved me from several accidents. I enjoy driving well and taught my son Martin to drive and he turned out to be a much better and safer driver than I was. I told him that as there was always a long waiting list for tests to say on the application form that he could take any cancellations. They phoned him to say his test was in one week's time. I made him drive me one morning from Giffard's to the heart of London, travelling through all the early morning rush hour traffic. When we arrived he was in a sweat but I told him that no matter what happened from now on, it could never be worse. He passed his test first time.

On Christmas Eve, as he was still new to driving, I suggested he followed me back from the Prince of Wales Theatre to Giffard's Barn, where we were to spend another family Christmas. I warned him to keep his distance in case the roads were icy as the night sky was crystal clear and the stars sparkled in the heavens. Pulling into the driveway Martin got out and displayed the signs of being a great ad-libber:

'This is going to be the greatest Christmas I've ever had.'
'Well it hasn't started yet,' was my reply.

'I know, but I've just followed a star to a stable.'

CHAPTER 10

UP, UP AND AWAY

An illusion is defined as the creation of a magical effect that uses an animal, sometimes a human. There were an abundance of worldwide deceptions in the Eighties, where events were not always what they seemed. Diaries allegedly written by Adolf Hitler were discovered to be fakes and the inventor of modern jogging, James F Fix, died of a heart-attack whilst jogging. The wreck of the Titanic *was discovered, Live Aid raised £8 million for the Ethiopian famine and Madonna burst on to the scene as the newest American star.*

The 1970s had been very good to me. I was slowly learning more and more about television, thanks to appearances in shows like *The Club Acts of the Year, Ace of Clubs, Opportunity Knocks, Wheeltappers, The David Nixon Show, For My Next Trick, Fall In The Stars, Be My Guest, Parkinson, The Marti Caine Show, Pebble Mill Showcase, Thank You and Goodnight, The Paul Daniels Show, The Magic Show, Jim'll Fix It, Paul Daniels' Blackpool Bonanza,* two *Royal Variety Shows, Disney Time, Blankety Blank, The Shirley Bassey Show* and *Larry Grayson's Generation Game.* I was well prepared, therefore, for the start of *The Paul Daniels*

Magic Show, which ran on BBC TV from September 1979 to March 1994, for a total of 15 series.

I know that, to many people, the world of television itself is magical, so let's pick a few stories out of the list.

Club Acts of the Year was another talent competition, but this time the viewers were comparing like with like. It is a bit silly to try to make singers, comedians, dancers and jugglers compete against each other because they all have different talents. *Club Acts* made magicians compete against magicians, comedians against comedians and so on. I didn't win. All day I had been asking whether it was OK to go on screen with a box of Kleenex tissues and use it in a trick. I had brought some sticky plastic sheeting to cover the box but 'they' said to leave it as it was. A couple of minutes before I was due on stage, in fact the act prior to mine had already started, one of 'them' walked by and told me that I couldn't go on with an advertisement like that. I didn't stop to argue. I ran all the way up to my dressing room on the top floor and I stuck the plastic on as I ran back down the stairs. I got to the back of the stage, which was huge, as I heard my name being announced and I ran flat out to the wings, braked hard and walked on trying to act like Mr Smoothy. The trouble was that I had to speak and I sounded like a cross between an asthmatic and a heavy breather.

I did several shows of *Jim'll Fix It*. The Producer, Roger Ordish, is now a good friend of mine and he told me that over the years he had more requests to assist Paul Daniels, be sawn up by Paul Daniels, be vanished by Paul Daniels and so on, than for any other requests. That's nice, isn't it?

Granada TV's *Blackpool Bonanza* was a television show recorded in the Norbreck Castle hotel in Blackpool. The auditorium, in which they hold exhibitions, was huge. I was the host of the show, doing magic and introducing the guests. This summer spectacular was my first real series on prime-time and, again, was produced by Johnny Hamp. It was competing against the BBC's *Summertime Special*, which toured the seaside resorts and for years I kept a small strip cartoon about the show. There were two characters and one says to the other, 'Have you seen *Blackpool Bonanza*?' 'No, what's that?'

'It's like *Summertime Special*, but one town takes all the blame.' Lovely.

This show happened during the summer of 1978 when I was appearing on the North Pier with Marti Caine. I did the first half and she did the second. Great singer, very funny comedienne (that's what they called them in those days, using English that told you instantly whether the comic was male or female. Nowadays you have to guess, sometimes even after you've watched them.)

The theatre on the pier was at the far end as usual. This was the way they were built, to avoid paying council rates because the building was beyond the average tide level or whatever. Located at the end of a half-mile walkway, the stage door is approached by what is more akin to a wind tunnel. On one side there was a café and on the other side was the theatre. When the wind was up, I would battle my way to the end, and towards the end of the season it could be hell getting down there. Once, carrying Starsky, my rabbit, in his hutch, I really couldn't make any headway at all. I had to 'tack' like a yacht to reach the stage door. At one stage I looked to my right only to find the people in the warmth of the café rolling about with laughter at my antics, the Norman Wisdom look-a-like.

In a storm, the waves would crash up against and through the bottom boards of the orchestra pit to the extent that the musicians would put their feet up on the chair in front of them in rough weather to keep dry.

There is a story about Robb Wilton, one of the all-time great funny men, who was doing a season on the North Pier. He was a quiet comic, droll, with a biting sense of wit. One night the storms came and this one was a beauty. Robb tried to keep working although hailstones were banging on the metal roof and waves were banging up at the floor. At one stage in the act, a large pair of emergency exit doors were forced open by the wind and flapped noisily back and forth, the wind now howling into the theatre, ice cream tubs and programmes flying everywhere as the ushers ran and struggled to shut them again. As they won the fight there was a sudden lull in the storm, a moment of tranquillity. Robb, who had kept silent throughout the ructions going on in front of him, took a breath, folded his arms, did his trademark picking of his teeth in the corner of his mouth and slowly said, 'I think they're training me to be a police horse!'

Within showbusiness, the staff of the North Pier were legendary. The ushers and the stage door man did not come from showbusiness, but were hired for the season. They tended to be elderly. A stage door man, doing his job properly, protects the whole of the backstage area and the artists, from intruders. Not on the North Pier they don't.

One night I had just come off stage and, without a knock, the stage door man opened my dressing room door and pushed in an old man. He stood there without saying anything and we smiled at each other as I waited to see what he wanted. He just stood there smiling, so eventually, after what seemed an embarrassing amount of time, I asked if I could help him.

'Finest thing I've ever seen,' he said.

I though he was talking about my act. 'Thank you,' I smiled back.

'No,' he said, 'not you. Twenty years ago, when I stood on the end of the pier and watched it burn down. Finest thing I ever saw.' He was still saying it when I pushed him back out of the stage door.

On the other hand, it was raining one night when the same stage door keeper came and told me that there was someone waiting outside to see me, who said he knew me, but who, according to this guru of our business, 'doesn't look as though he is in showbusiness'.

'What's his name?' I asked, and the doorkeeper looked vague.

'It's something to do with those cages you keep birds in.' I hadn't a clue what he was talking about and then the penny dropped. Aviary. My mind took a sideways leap and I immediately knew who he was talking about. I ran out into the rain and brought into the warmth John Avery. An idiot with dreams of setting fire to the pier could get in, but not John, the manager of the London Palladium.

Towards the end of the season, two serious-looking gentlemen asked to see me in my dressing room. In their wonderfully flat north-western tones, they explained that they were from Southport Borough Council Entertainments Department.

'Now we've see your act, Mr Daniels, and we think you are very funny,' they began. 'Now you will have heard of Southport and we would like to know if you would consider coming for a summer season next year?'

'Look fellas, do you mind if I get shaved, 'cos I have a show to do in a minute?'

'Not at all, Mr Daniels. You go right ahead.'

'I don't really talk business. You need to talk to my manager, Mervyn O'Horan.'

'No, we don't like managers and agents, Mr Daniels, we like dealing direct.'

'Well, he has to make the decisions but I'll pass the message on. You can trust him, he's dead straight. How long is the season?'

'It will be as long as you'd like it to be.'

'And what are the dates then?'

'Oh, you can pick the dates.' That was very good because then I could pick only the high-paying weeks at the centre of the season.

'Who else is on the bill then?'

'Whoever you want, Mr Daniels,' they smiled.

Thoughts of whether Sammy Davis Jnr was available to do a warm up for me in Southport flashed through my mind.

'What about dancers?'

'You book whoever you want, Mr Daniels. It's your show.'

To anybody in my position, this was an incredible deal. I could pick the best business weeks and get commission off every act that I booked as well. I constantly asked them not to talk money with me. That had to be left to my manager.

I was half-way down my face with a razor when they said, 'We were thinking about £20,000 a week.'

Stopping short of cutting my throat in surprise, I turned round to look at them. They were deadly serious. This was an unheard of amount for a season.

'I think you r-r-r-really do need to talk to my manager,' I stammered. Mervyn telephoned me the next day after hearing about the proposal and asked me what I wanted to do.

Having chatted it through with Richard Mills, Chief Director of the Delfont Organisation, whom I am proud to call a friend, I understood why it wasn't such a good deal. He put in plain words the fact that I needed to see where my bread was best buttered. Delfonts could offer me several summer seasons in a row as they held a chain of resort venues, whereas Southport had only the one. It was a reasonable argument and taking a deep breath, I turned Southport down.

And so it was that in the middle of this season, I did the *Blackpool Bonanza* shows. I was performing twice-nightly on the pier and on the Sunday morning, early, I started to rehearse for the show which was recorded that night in front of a very large audience. I was everywhere, learning, watching, sorting out tricks and trying above all to remember the names of the acts. In the whole season I only forgot one name and it wasn't exactly the hardest name to remember. Roy Walker, the Irish comedian. The trouble was that I had never met him, never seen him rehearse and he was new on the scene. I had no trouble with the next act, Shakin' Stevens and Bogden Komenovski, but Roy Walker was a blank. I hope he has forgiven me and, by the way, he was brilliant.

On the Monday morning after that first *Bonanza* recording, I learnt something else about television. If you are really working at it, the strain is greater than you think. The alarm went off by my bed and I couldn't get up.

I couldn't move a muscle. For whatever reason, and I am sure it had to be the mental strain, I was completely paralysed and I was on my own in the house. It took until about 11.30am before I could move my arms and legs and I was terrified.

The following Sunday, I paced myself into an easy-going attitude and that's the way I have worked ever since.

This was quite a season. I received a telephone call asking me whether I would act as the MC for a major variety show in Aberdeen. It was to be in the presence of Prince Charles and would be on a Sunday evening. I was already doing two shows a night on the pier and, now *Bonanza* was finished, Sunday was my only night off. Add to that the distance to and from Aberdeen and I told the organiser that it was impossible.

'No, it's going to be very easy – the oil companies who are working that area of the North Sea are sponsoring each act. They are paying for aeroplanes, limousines and hotels. You will be well looked after.'

Well, despite the other 12 shows that I would be doing both sides of this one I decided to say 'yes' and put it into the diary.

I asked for a list of the acts that I would be introducing and worked out my material accordingly.

Two weeks before the show I got another telephone call. Apparently the oil company that was sponsoring me could use its company jet to get me to Aberdeen but they couldn't find a plane that would bring me back again. All attempts to charter a small plane on the following Monday morning had failed and they were asking whether I could go by train.

The railway system at that time was notoriously bad. I said 'no'. They asked if I would drive there and back. I said 'no'. They asked if they could drive me there and back. I said 'no'. I wasn't being awkward. It's a very long way and I was already working very hard. I find that when someone else is driving me I can't relax and I watch the road all the time in case of emergency. Quite what I'd do, I've never worked out, I just don't feel safe.

I explained the situation to my office and Howard Huntridge offered to come to the rescue. In the previous few weeks Freddie Starr, Colin Crompton and Howard had all qualified as pilots and suddenly the air seemed a very dangerous place to be. The first two were crazy comedians and Howard was just crazy.

'No,' he said, 'I am not qualified to fly you myself, but I have an idea how we can fly you back.'

Well, I knew the major oil companies and the organisers of the Prince Charles Trust had failed to find a plane, but Howard moves in mysterious ways. He was a truly lateral thinker. I said OK.

The trip up to Aberdeen was fantastic. The oil company provided one of those company jets that only top golfers could afford. We even had an inflight hostess who served drinks and sandwiches. Reg Parsons, a member of my management team, who was not too keen on flying (and that is the understatement of the century), accompanied me. Even Reg, however, was impressed by the service and the luxury but even so, seemed much happier when we landed.

The show that night was fantastic. The opening act was a top American star, Billy Daniels, famous, amongst many other talents, for a song called 'That Ole Black Magic'. His name and mine being the same, and the song having magic as its theme, gave me all sorts of link opportunities as the compere for the show. The only real problem in the show came at the end of his act when he sang a song called 'Melancholy Baby' so very movingly and dedicated to his friend who had written the number, but who had died that very day.

Billy was crying as he sang, the orchestra was crying, the dancers were crying, the audience were crying and I was crying but for a different reason. I knew that I had to follow this tear-jerker by introducing someone whom I hadn't seen for a few years, Michael Bentine, known, of course, to the public as one of the Goons from the radio show of the same name. This well-known idiot in the nicest sense of the word was about to enter as an Arab with a huge scraggly bird on his arm to work a zany comedy spot, and everyone was crying.

Well, I got out of that one by telling a story or two about the confusion between Billy Daniels and myself, which was strange because Billy was black and I was, and still am, white. The rest of the show ran without a hitch and was great to do. I really enjoyed myself and the audience had a great night out.

Morning came and found Reg, the scaredy-cat flier, and myself standing on the side of the tarmac at Aberdeen airport. There was no sign of Howard or an aeroplane of any type. The air was sharp and crystal clear and Reg and I scanned the skies.

'I'll kill him if he doesn't turn up,' I said, exaggerating only slightly. Slowly, we became aware of the sound of a small, light aircraft making a noise like a scooter running out of petrol. A tiny Cessna fourseater made a circuit to land.

'Well, it can't be that,' I said, 'it's far too small.' It landed and taxied to a halt.

Howard got out of it. So did the pilot, dressed like a businessman and carrying a small briefcase.

Howard started to walk faster. So did the pilot. Howard started to jog. So did the pilot.

Howard broke into a sprint. It was obvious that he wanted to get to us before the pilot.

As he went past us, Howard said, very quickly and not too loudly, 'Pretend you're buying it. It's a demonstration flight.'

I couldn't believe it. Before I could get out a 'But ...' the pilot had grabbed my hand, shook it and had embarked on his sales pitch.

'I understand you are looking to buy a light aircraft, Mr Daniels.'

'Well ... er ... er ... yes. I have been thinking of that for a little while.' Nearly the whole truth and nothing but the truth.

How little a while he'd never know. 'This one does seem to be a little small, however,' and I gestured towards the pile of stuff on the ground. There was a suitcase, a box of magic props, a rabbit in a hutch, a folded but still large table, two suit bags and some other odds and sods.

Reg Parsons came in with, 'Well, I really don't think there will be enough room for me,' but his hopes were dashed when this Super Salesman went into action.

'Oh don't worry, sir. The modern light aircraft has more room than you would think,' and from somewhere in the plane he took out a small toolkit and started to unscrew panels off the body and the wings. I was fascinated to find that a plane is mostly just skin. He got the props box in the back part of the structure, making sure that all the cables ran freely. The table went in a small space behind the back seat, together with all the more compact items.

UP, UP AND AWAY

He put the suit bags into the wings, again checking the cables before replacing the panels. Reg was terrified and totally convinced that this was all illegal. Next, this genius of packing put Howard and Reg into the rear seats and handed them the rabbit in the cage. Have you ever seen a single-engine light aircraft up close? They have a tiny set of wheels in a sort of triangle formation at the front end and the tail is unsupported.

As the hutch was grasped by the lads in the back, the whole plane tipped up backwards. Reg yelled.

'Don't worry,' smiled the salesman and ran around to the front, jumped up and held on to the propeller. The plane regained its balance and then he made me the most wonderful request: 'Could you get in now, Mr Daniels, and could you all lean forward?'

As we all sat there auditioning for a part in the Hunchback of Notre Dame, the salesman resumed his role as pilot by working his way hand over hand into the plane with us, holding down the front end until he was in his seat. 'Keep leaning forward, we're a bit tail heavy.'

Reg groaned.

'During the war, you know, a pilot took off with a plane full of paratroopers and as he took off he realised that he hadn't done his pre-flight check and that all the flaps were locked on. By commanding the paras to move around the plane to his orders he managed to redistribute the weight, do a circuit under weight movement and land safely. He was dismissed from the service which seemed a bit unfair. I think he was brilliant. I tell you this because, in a way, we are going to do a miniature version of that. First, let me check that it is all right for take-off.'

Now, I don't know about you, but I have never been able to understand a single word of what air traffic controllers are saying. The background noise coupled with tinny speakers makes it all indecipherable to me, but apparently we received the OK to take off.

'Right-oh, Mr Daniels. We are going to go down the runway now and when I shout "NOW" would you all sit up and lean back?'

Reg was more garbled than the air traffic controller. I feared for the health of the rabbit he was holding.

Off we went, the pilot shouted 'NOW', we leaned back and the plane took off. It really did. Up it went, climbing all the time. In fact, that was the problem. We were so tail heavy that we couldn't straighten up. For ages we flew along with the Cessna doing its impression of a helicopter. Finally, but after quite a struggle, he got it level and we were off to Blackpool.

The pilot explained all the technicalities to me as we flew along, and I pretended to be interested as we went from beacon to beacon. Howard flew along reassuring Reg that he really wasn't going to die.

Suddenly, the pilot looked at the map strapped to his knee and said, 'damn!'

'WHAT'S THE MATTER? WHAT IS IT? WHAT'S WRONG?' came screaming from the rear seat. Reg obviously was suddenly worried.

'Oh, it's nothing much. It's just that the radar is out at Blackpool and there is a weather report of low cloud. We'll have to go to Manchester.' Now it was my turn to be worried. If we went to Manchester the timing would be all wrong and I'd miss the show on the North Pier. Bernie Delfont would be after my blood and I said so. Our pilot considered this and then said, very slowly, 'Well, there is one way. They teach you it when you are training to be a pilot but I've never actually done it.'

Howard chimed in, 'Oh yes, you mean a ...' and off they went into technical jargon.

'What does that mean?' asked Reg

'Basically, it is what you sometimes see in the movies. The airfield talks you down.'

'How do they talk you down if they can't see you?'

'They listen and advise accordingly,' and the pilot immediately contacted Blackpool who put up very little argument as both they and the pilot thought that this was a really interesting thing to do.

So there we were, a happy band of travellers (except for Reg), about to descend through the clouds to Blackpool airport. The pilot switched on the overhead speaker so that we could all enjoy the experience. Except Reg, who was reciting strange incantations about never flying ever again.

A flat Lancashire accent cut through the noise of our aircraft. This was the first air traffic control voice that I had ever been able to understand. It gave our call sign followed by 'Are you flying a single-engine Cessna?' Upon being told that we were, the voice from the control tower said, 'Well, you've just gone over us heading south,' followed unbelievably by, 'We've got the window open and we heard you.' We were then instructed to make a circuit as we descended and that is how it went on.

Every now and again, we would be told that we had gone over in such and such a direction and all the time I was watching the altimeter showing that we were going down and down in what appeared to us to be thick fog. We were flying completely blind.

I leaned over and gently reminded the pilot that there was a very tall object that stuck up in the air in this town called Blackpool Tower. 'Oh,' he said, 'we should be well south of that.'

'SHOULD BE? SHOULD BE?' yelled Reg. Howard calmed him down as we continued our descent.

The altimeter showed that we had landed. We hadn't, but we must have been very low.

Suddenly – very, very suddenly – we shot out of cloud into

clear air. I swear this is true. A few feet away, on either side of the wingtips, were roofs. We could see people in the street with their heads snapping from side to side as we flew past them.

There was a scream, not from Reg. It was the pilot. 'WHERE ARE WE?' For some strange reason that I have never been able to fathom, I never panicked, so I was able to answer the question calmly and quickly. 'Pontins!'

We had flown into the holiday camp at the end of the airfield.

'Where the hell is the airfield?' asked the pilot and, not knowing technical terms like port and starboard, I said, 'left.'

He turned left. He stood the damn plane on one wing and turned left. How he didn't crash into one of the chalets I don't know but now he was faced with a high wire netting fence.

Amazingly, he levelled the plane and raised it just enough to clear the fence and drop the aircraft on to the grass on the other side.

Reg was no longer with us but he came to as we trundled across the grass and came to a halt.

Calm as you like, the pilot became a salesman again, turned to me and asked, 'Well, what do you think?'

I told him that I still thought it was a bit too small and that I would think about it. We unloaded the plane and just before he set off to return the plane to Doncaster, he asked Reg if he wanted to have a lift to Manchester.

I think that you can imagine Reg's answer for yourself. I'm too nice a guy to repeat it.

The season at the North Pier drew to a close and, at the final performance, the last-night gags were worse than usual. While in the middle of an appearing rabbit routine, my co-star Marti Caine entered stage right in an old trench mackintosh. With her back to the audience, she opened her mac to reveal that she was stark naked. I tried to retain my composure as she closed her mac, smiled at the audience and slowly walked off. The audience knew it was a gag but didn't know it was for real.

Taking a moment's pause, I then looked straight out into the audience with, 'right! Now I remember where I left my wand!' The audience roared and I carried on.

During the interval, I dashed out of the theatre and down the pier to the shops where I purchased a few items and ran back to my dressing room where Mam had already started stitching some bits together for me. The second half started and Marti is now on stage doing her act. During one of her loveliest songs, I walked out on stage in a full-length coat, similar to the one she had worn earlier. Smiling at the audience, I then turned my back and opened my coat. I was naked apart from a cardboard tubular striped walking stick dangling from my ... loins, with a garter belt complete with suspenders hanging all the way down to my evening dress socks and shoes. Marti lost her place in the song and, as the music ground to a halt, she fell about laughing.

I then discovered that one should never use Sellotape in your pubic area, because pulling it off was a nightmare!

Too few years later, Marti died of cancer. That's not fair.

Just before they launched the *The Paul Daniels Magic Show* as a series, the BBC asked me to guest on *The Shirley Bassey Show*. Did Britain ever produce a bigger international singing star? I certainly don't believe they have ever produced a better one. I am not talking Spice Girls or any other 'created' pop group that comes and goes in a couple of years at most. I am talking enduring star status here. Even in the rehearsals, she was sensational. Miss Bassey had, according to all reports, come through some unhappy relationships (hadn't we all?) but when I met her for the first time she was happy and in great form. She was the epitome of the word 'star' and acted it to the full, loving every minute of it. The moment came in the rehearsal where she finished a song and then introduced me. I was to do a small card trick and then Miss Bassey joined me on my part of the set and the Producer wanted me to do something with her. Unfortunately, he wanted me do to something the public could watch so I had picked out a comedy card routine that would really get her involved.

As she came over and the cameras rehearsed their moves to cover the action, I stopped and asked if she wouldn't mind going for a coffee while I rehearsed with the cameras. She wouldn't go, saying that she wanted to watch what was going to happen. I said that I'd rather it came as a surprise to her on the actual recording so that the reactions would be greater. She said she wanted to see what was going to happen. There was 'lively' discussion between Miss Bassey and me. Eventually, as it was going nowhere, she pointed out that it was her show. I pointed out that I was a guest, and as the same producer who had asked her to do the series had asked me to be a guest that maybe she should trust him. With a full Bassey glare, she said that I had better be good at what I was doing. I pointed out that I was so good at magic that if I had been a singer they would have called me Bassey. Shirley cracked up laughing as only she can. It's a great laugh. She went off to her room. The Producer grabbed me by the lapels and said, 'don't you ever do that to me again.'

When I am feeling a bit cocky with myself, I watch a videotape of me on a New Year's Eve special for Granada, where I am singing and dancing. Ugh! When I am feeling a bit down I watch the recording of *The Shirley Bassey Show*. The trick worked so well. Shirley didn't know what was coming and was so natural, especially when she folded up laughing at one of the lines. We meet from time to time and she looks as gorgeous now as she did then. Now *that's* a star.

In truth, I have always thought the term 'star' is used too easily. Once, on the radio, I heard that if Rod Stewart is a singer then there ought to be a better word for Pavarotti. Perhaps there should be some kind of international agreement or committee and representation would have to be made to them to see whether a person can have the title. Nowadays, stars come and go in months. I think that the title should only go to the likes of Humphrey Bogart, Lauren Bacall, Gary Cooper, Goldie Hawn, Tom Hanks, Roger Moore and Sean Connery. Maybe then you would also have regional, national and international stars and you would know what you were getting for your money. OK, I know, I'm meandering, but I can't be the only person who thinks this way, can I?

Funnily enough, in the world of television, the television production crews don't think that 'stars' are very special at all. They treat them like items on a conveyor belt in the fun factory. Celebrities come and celebrities go with such regular monotony that they are treated as commonplace. Add to that the number of television shows being produced on a conveyor belt system and you start to understand why so much television programming is just filled with unexciting dross.

You can't really blame the production crews. To them it's just another job, most of the time. Let's take a mental leap and consider death.

What?

Death.

To most of us it is something to be feared and we shut away all thought of it. We protect ourselves by not thinking of its coming and we are shocked and hurt when it calls.

Way back, when I was an auditor visiting the Eston Cemetery, I had to spend time in the cemetery lodge checking the accounts. Hearses were always pulling up outside and the attendants would get out of the long black cars. Half-bowing reverently to the mourners and smiling sadly, they respectfully made their way into the office, gave one last sad glance at the bereaved and closed the door behind them, whereupon they took off their hats and clapped their hands together saying, 'Watcha, guys. Get the kettle on 'cos it won't take us long to drop this one!'

To a young man this was shocking, but I soon realised that they meant no disrespect. To these chaps it was just a job. A corpse to them held none of the fear and worry that it meant to the rest of us and was simply part and parcel of their everyday life.

It's the same in hospitals. Doctors and nurses, in the main, grow immune to the cries of pain and suffering and only occasionally are jerked into a realisation of what is really happening, no matter how much they care. Maybe it is the brain's way of handling the situation. So, if such giant emotional happenings as sickness and death can become so normal, what chance has a television show got?

Nevertheless, this was a time when television meant a lot to the public. Shows were getting many more millions than they do now and I don't think it had anything to do with the fact that the viewers now have many more channels to choose from. Television was not something that we had grown up with. Nowadays, it is much more of something playing in the background while the family get on with other things.

Despite all the guesting and the small series that I had done on television, it took the mad week in my life, which culminated in the *Royal Variety Show*, to open up the prime time slots for me. As the Seventies were coming to an end, the BBC approached me with their first offer of a full-blown TV special, with the possibility of a series to follow, with my name in the title. *The Paul Daniels Magic Show* took several weeks to put together and record but was finally scrapped. The show was just like all the other variety shows, with guest singers and the like. Somehow it just didn't seem to be different enough. John

UP, UP AND AWAY

Fisher, the original producer of the BBC's *The Magic Show*, was given the job of sorting out the concept.

John flew out to Hollywood, where I was having what I felt was a well-earned holiday. I'm still not sure how he found me. I hadn't told anyone where I was staying, having picked a small motel at random on Hollywood Boulevard. Nice place, with a central swimming pool, but a bit noisy at night with a lot of people coming and going. It turned out my motel was used extensively by the ladies of the night! I didn't tell John. Coming and going? Bad choice of words, perhaps.

We agreed that the format of this new show should be given over to magic and speciality acts alone, the two elements of showbusiness in which we were both experts. Other shows on the box were offering more and more pop groups and singers, but no one was giving space for the peculiar world of jugglers, black art (a specialist form of mime and puppetry), fire-eaters, cowboys and contortionists, as well as the world's finest conjuring talent. We felt there was enough interest in this aspect of the business to grab a decent audience.

This would be the first real magic show on television since *The David Nixon Show*. David was a magical superstar who filled that early time on television, but sadly, he recently died after several months of being very ill with cancer. I was with him on the *Royal Variety Show*, where he was part of the celebrity gathering for a scene from *My Fair Lady*. I was a bit embarrassed about this and I knocked on David's dressing room door and apologised for the fact that I, Mr Nobody, was doing the magic spot, which I felt was rightfully his.

Having been lying down in the dark by himself, the gentle giant raised himself to sit upright and smiled, 'No, it's all right, Paul. I've had my time. Now it's yours.'

That was the last time I saw him. He really was a gentleman.

So, with David gone, the BBC enlisted the talents of George

Martin, David's scriptwriter and a very funny comedian in his own right, and Ali Bongo, who was David's magical adviser, for the first of these new-style *Paul Daniels' Magic Shows*. At the initial meeting we sat around discussing the format and what I was going to do.

Of course, George and Ali had a lot of reminiscing to get through, which was nice, but when it got down to actually doing the tricks they kept coming out with, 'Well, when we did it with David, it would go like this ...' or 'David would do it this way ...'

I really did try to keep pulling the meeting around to me and to my way of working but eventually I felt I was left with no choice. Knocking on the table I said, 'I'm sorry, fellas, but we really do have to get something straight. I am not David Nixon. I don't want to be David Nixon, just as much as I'm sure he didn't want to be me. We're different and, much as I loved the guy and what he did, that was then, this is now. This is going to be *The Paul Daniels Show* and it's going to be done in the style of Paul Daniels.'

If my wording sounds strange to you, let me explain. I have always talked about Paul Daniels as a product. In meetings, I often revert in my mind to being Ted Daniels in order to disassociate myself from the 'product' that is known as the magician Paul Daniels. How else can I talk about myself, or 'him', if you know what I mean?

I went on, 'if you can work with that, fine. If you can't, then it's over because I can't be David Nixon.' I felt awful having to say it, but it had to be said.

George Martin chose to leave and we parted on good terms, while Ali Bongo decided to stay. There is no way that you will ever get me to knock David Nixon. He had his own wonderful style that was right for his time. Within the secret side of magic that uses manipulation, he was a bit limited and it didn't matter one whit. He used other methods and that is as good a way to work magic as any other. I had my own way and that did include some manipulation skills (known in the trade as finger flinging!) that used to scare the hell out of Ali when I chose to do them in front of the camera. He often thought it too risky whereas I believed it would just work. His 'You can't do that,' or 'Oooh no, you won't be able to do that,' were a constant source of encouragement to me to make it work. Directors, too, used to shooting exactly what was rehearsed, took a lot of getting used to me. I like being 'free' during a routine to go where I feel like going and doing what I feel like doing at any particular time. I am a jazz magician.

Ali was to remain with me as my magical consultant for the next 15 series of *The Paul Daniels Show*, spanning 16 years and beyond. I was always astonished at how good he was. Ali is quite a unique character who, it seems, has worked with magic since time began. If you want anything made in paper, cardboard, gluing, felt or rubber bands to make something unusual happen, Ali is the man. He also sat show in and show out next to the various directors we had over the years, telling them where and when they could 'cut' the shots so that the magic could be clearly seen not to be camera tricks. That was a very important aspect of the show. We always had a live audience and performed the magic in real time in front of them. Once, we even had an audience made up of journalists to prove further that we didn't use camera tricks.

While keeping the entertainment factor as high as possible, the shows did go on subtle crusades sometimes. The Bunco Booth, one of the most popular items we did, was designed to show the people at home that they really couldn't win if they played the gambling games that you see on the streets or at racecourses. You really, really, really can't win, so no matter how sure you think you are that the 'Queen is over there' or 'the pea is under that shell' or 'this loop will catch my finger', I promise you, you will be wrong and you will lose your money.

In later shows, we would do pseudo-psychic magic to try to make people at home think that perhaps the charlatans out there should be looked at a little more closely. Once, when we were discussing a 'psychic' bit for the show, Ali told me that at one time in his life he was performing on a pier and the gypsy who normally did fortune-telling had unexpectedly died, having signed a contract for the whole summer. Why is that funny to me?

Ali was given the job and said how, after a couple of weeks, he was able to 'read' so much from the customers' ages, clothing and style that he became an adept fortune-teller. There is an awful lot about people that we observe instinctively, but never analyse, he said.

Along the same lines, when the live touring magic show was in Bradford, I remember how the members of the company all thought it hilarious that the 'psychics' from the Psychic Fair opposite our theatre kept asking us where the car park was. Didn't they know?

The moment the first series aired, it doubled *The David Nixon Show*'s viewing figures. From day one, the television show was extraordinarily successful. That first series I only did small magic, interacting with the audience, and left the illusions to the guests. For example, I would do the cut and restored £5 notes, a ring melting through a solid stick, a three-card trick and David Devant's Eternal Triangle which is a very old and amazing card trick with which the viewers at home were able to join in. Special guests included Hans Moretti who fired crossbows at a target on the trigger of another crossbow and so on until one of the crossbows fired a bolt to split an apple on his own head – all this while blindfolded. (Moretti, not me.) All that in 30 minutes. The first programme went out on 9 June

1979 and the run contained four programmes and finished with a Christmas Special.

Mervyn, my manager, used to go to his local pub after the shows aired and sit and listen to our Yorkshire audience talking about it. We learned a lot from their observations. In one show, for example, Hans was upside-down and swinging on a burning rope above razor-sharp bayonets trying to escape from a strait-jacket before the rope burnt through and he plunged to his death. Well, what do you do for a living? In the same show I did a card trick where blank cards became printed. That night and the next day, all the people in the pub talked about was the card trick. That was when I learned that the big illusions and the huge spectaculars are as big as the screen, that's all. In a much later series, we had a young American guest who became a headliner in Las Vegas – Lance Burton. He came to my house and watched shows we had recorded in the past. After hours of viewing he watched me show, in extreme close-up, a large matchbox to be empty. From it I produced a couple of mice and they, as I said, filled the screen. I heard him say, almost to himself, 'shit, you don't need tigers!'

When a new series was commissioned even before the last one had been screened, I knew we were on to a winner, but the team and I had one big worry. Where could we find all the new effects, tricks and speciality acts that were required? Did enough exist for another series, this time with eight programmes? Well, as we found enough for 15 series which included more, longer shows, as well as specials for Christmas and Easter, I guess our worries were unfounded. It became, however, a 24-hour-a-day, 365-days-a-year mental exercise to find and create the material. I would record ideas on dictaphones while driving the car; I would wake up in the middle of the night and jot down illusions that I had just dreamt up, literally. It got to the point where I would take a notebook to the toilet. Looking back, if someone had told me that I was heading for more than 600 television appearances with thousands of tricks, I would never have believed it possible.

The creative team was an essential part of the show and included my friend Graham Reed, he who had dropped the book off at the Palladium stage door and who joined the team at a later stage. Graham was in marketing and advertising and was an ideas man. He would come up with a plan for a trick or stunt but had no conception of how it could be carried through. That was for others to work out!

'Wouldn't it be a good idea, Paul, if you escaped from being tied up between two powerboats while on a raft?'

He had no method, just a plot for the play, which would get us all thinking. I liked this way of working, particularly as it would cause great laughter in the room as we invariably took the mickey out of Graham, when he confessed to having no idea if it was possible. Come to think of it, all of Graham's ideas involved me getting into danger. Maybe he fancies Debbie more than he tells me?

Over the years, the team was always Ali Bongo and me, to whom we added Gil Leaney, Graham Reed, Barry Murray and an Irish magician called Billy McComb who was with us for only one season as he never came up with any ideas. All he kept saying was 'Pigs are funny,' but never suggested how we would use them.

As I told you, Ali was great with the small stuff and the occasional illusion. Gil Leaney had been a warm-up magician for a legendary radio show starring Wilfred Pickles, and was a builder of beautiful props with an intimate knowledge of the design and construction of illusions. He had built illusions for the great illusionists in the heyday of theatres. Barry Murray was a brilliant researcher who was able to dig out information from any magazine that had been written at any time and had been involved in the pop world. A great 'dreamer', he brought a historical and musical element to the programmes.

Others would drift in for a week with an idea that we would develop and adapt to the style of the show, but mainly the shows came out of the minds of those named above.

For most of the early years, John Fisher was the producer and also the researcher. I believe that research was really his forte, as he knew so many people in the worlds of magic and circus who would feed him ideas.

Debbie, who joined the television series later, became the 'critic'. Coming from outside the world of magic, she looked at the performances with a different eye and would frequently pick up on aspects of the effects that, as magicians, we couldn't see because we were too close to the subject. We 'understood' what was going on and Debbie would point out that the viewers wouldn't even know what I was talking about.

Our team would get together for a brainstorming session once or twice a year and then practically live together for three months as we compiled the series. I spent the next 16 years of my life in a whirlwind of activity, constantly trying to think up new concepts, or unique ways of presenting old ones. Sometimes people would discover me sitting alone in a corner, ask me a question and back off when I didn't answer, thinking I was in a strange mood. They probably thought that I was rude if they didn't know me. In reality that was how I rehearsed best. I would logically working through a presentation and I would 'see' what it would look like, who would stand where, what could go wrong, what I would do if it did, and so on.

The Paul Daniels Magic Show became a major part of the nation's viewing but, because we were all so close to it, I guess we never really noticed just how successful it was. We had our personal moments, of course, when we enjoyed the success.

There was the Christmas that we became the first show to knock *Morecambe and Wise* off the top of the ratings. Now that was a mixed feeling! I loved Morecambe and Wise. They were the gods. Early in my career, I had to stop watching them because I found myself talking and timing like Eric.

I'm reminded of a charity event held one night at Grays, Essex, in a large nightclub. Prince Charles was there and a lot of star celebrities. It was a dinner and cabaret evening and the stars were sitting at one long table with me perched on one corner as a relative unknown. Do you remember how Eric had a running gag in their TV shows? He used to lift the front of Ernie's hair and say, 'You can't see the join.' Eric, this night, decided to go to the toilet, stood up from the table and, as he passed my corner, grabbed hold of my wig, lifted it a little, said, 'You can't see the join, you know,' and walked on. Nobody noticed in the dark and the noise of the club.

As he came back past me I grabbed his jacket and pulled him down to say, 'that could have been embarrassing.' Immediately he came back with, 'It was. I didn't know you wore one,' and walked on. He was just so funny.

Nevertheless, knocking them off the top spot did feel good. Another great success came when the show being repeated on Tuesday nights on BBC 2 was at number one in their charts at the same time that the new show, aired on Saturday nights on BBC 1, was at number one in theirs. This was so unique that the BBC took me to lunch. During the lunch, the executives said that there was now nowhere to go! I suggested that we should go for the Golden Rose of Montreux, which is possibly the most prestigious television award in the world.

Well, they weren't too sure about this at all. They had an 'alternative' comedy show lined up for that and John Fisher and I pointed out that to have any chance at all, the judges from all the other countries had to understand what was happening on the screen. They still weren't sure, but they eventually said we could go ahead.

Where John got the funding from I don't know, because the show was expensive to make. Good shows always are. It took three days to shoot the Easter Special and off it went to Montreux. The executives went with it and we stayed at home shooting the next series. Phone calls flew back and forth.

'We are up against specials from Bette Midler and Sammy Davis Jnr.'

'There is a lot of talk about the show.'

'The judges laughed and people have asked if they can see it.'

Eventually, on a recording day came the call, 'WE'VE WON.' The BBC went mad. Everyone was running down the corridors and shouting the news. They hadn't had a win in something like 17 years.

That same year, a show called *Spitting Image*, a puppet show that featured famous and infamous people as puppets and included me among them, won the Bronze at Montreux. If you watched the national news you would have thought they had won the Gold. ITV really blew the trumpet and the BBC hardly gave us a mention. They never did know how to publicise themselves and their shows.

It was just after this award that I got a telephone call from a friend who said he had seen the registration plate MAG 1C for sale in the Times. For the benefit of any Americans who are reading this let me point out that in the UK you can't buy any plate you would like for your car. You have to make 'words' up out of sets of numbers. Jimmy Tarbuck, for example, has a car with the number COM 1C. I had tried to buy MAG 1C years before, but was told it had never been issued.

To be honest, I wasn't really all that bothered. I had never really been much of a car man even though, over the years, I have had some really nice ones. Cars I do remember are a huge

Peugeot Familiale, which looked like something out of an Al Capone movie, and the Scout Group borrowed it for just that reason for a parade they were in. The engine blew up when I was near Newport and I had to buy a car in a hurry to do the rest of the clubs for that week. An organist in a club was getting married and didn't need two cars so he sold me a Triumph Herald, on the spot, for £150. When I got into it, I laughed at his eccentricity. It had a small racing steering wheel, a stubby gear stick, rev counters and, most peculiar, a huge lump in the middle of the car. I had never been in one before so I just put the latter down to bad design.

I trundled it around the Welsh Valleys for the rest of that week, never looking under the bonnet. The idea was to just run it into the ground while I looked for another car.

On the Saturday night, I set off for Yorkshire and hit the road out of Wales just after midnight. I was going uphill alongside a convoy of Army trucks on a two-lane highway when some prat came up behind me flashing his lights. Where he thought I would go I have no idea but I changed down and accelerated. Immediately, I was pushed into the seat as this little Triumph Herald took off like a rocket. It left Mr Prat miles behind. Top gear and it still kept accelerating. When I got to the first available stopping place I pulled in and lifted the bonnet. I was looking at the engine from a Spitfire sports car.

After that, I had great fun waiting for sports cars to come alongside me on the motorways and then pulling away to leave them standing. I imagined them going into their garages and asking for their cars to be tuned up, 'because I was left standing by a Triumph Herald'.

Coming over the Pennines one night, very late after a gig, I hit a bump in the road and the chassis snapped. I guess the combination of the weight of the oversized engine and the famous rusting of the box chassis was what did it. Somehow I nurtured and coaxed the car out of the mountains and down towards Barnsley. I pulled into a Ford garage at about 2.30am and went to sleep in the car. As soon as the garage opened, I went in and bought a new Cortina. The salesman asked whether I had anything to trade in and I pointed to the Triumph parked at the other end of the forecourt. He asked the year and we did a deal. I insisted that the new car had to be taxed and insured immediately as I was going away that afternoon. While all that was being done, I just prayed that he wouldn't go and look at the Triumph. After what seemed like an age, I drove away and I never dared to go back for a service.

When I was with Melody, she had a Citroen and I drove her in to get it serviced. Standing on the forecourt was an unbelievable car that later I saw in a movie at Beaulieu Motor Museum as the 'Car of the Future'. You have to remember that, at the time, cars were very 'boxy' and only Jaguars had any real roundness to them. This car was streamlined beautifully. Even the front headlamps were behind an all-glass front end that was designed to be part of the bonnet. The Citroen SM had a Maserati engine and was way out in front of any other car when it came to design. This was the first car I had ever lusted after. I phoned Mervyn and the deal was done. I owned my first supercar.

The first morning I picked it up from the garage and drove it out and around the London north circular road into the early morning rush-hour traffic. Everyone was turning their heads to look at this very rare and beautiful car. It broke down. Well, it stopped. It was out of petrol. What possesses a garage to let you drive out without petrol? The other problem was that it had an 'improved' Citroen suspension, the one that goes up and down. Well, when this car lost power it sat down on the road, low and heavy, and you couldn't push it. It took ages to get some juice and get it rolling again.

I had owned it for about a week when I had a show to do

down near Dover. After the show and very late at night, I set off for home. Melody fell asleep. I lowered the steering wheel on to my lap, for no other reason than because I could, and drove up the M2 motorway. 'I wonder how fast this thing goes?'

I put my foot down. At 110mph I changed into top gear and away it went. I really don't know how fast I was going when I flew past a sign that said the end of the motorway was in one mile.

'I wonder how long it takes to stop?'

Well, it slowed down and I continued on up the A2. After a couple of miles I could see a flashing blue light and a policeman waving cars past, until he saw me, that is. He waved me into the side of the road and walked around to the driver's side of the car. Well, it would have been except that the car was left-hand drive. He bent down, looked in, expressed disgust at his mistake and walked around the car to my side, where I was sitting with the lowered wheel. As he walked round, I lowered the car to its lowest position.

He bent over and knocked on my window. As I lowered the window I raised the car so he had to straighten up a bit.

'We have had a report of a car going along the motorway at very high speed,' he said.

'Well I never saw it,' I replied.

This came as such a surprise to him he burst out laughing. I lowered the car and he bent over to say, 'that's the coolest answer I've had in the ten years I've been stopping people. It was you.'

'Ah, now that's a problem,' I answered. 'I have only had the car a week and it is all in metric so I don't know how fast it is going.'

'You mean you don't know how to convert kilometres to miles?'

'No.'

'Just a minute.'

He got on to his radio system and asked how to do it and told me to divide by eight and multiply by five. I had raised and lowered the car during most of this conversation, watching him bend and straighten up all the time. I thanked him. Suddenly, he noticed he was doing aerobics. 'What the hell is going on with this car?'

'It's just come off the motorway and it's panting,' I answered. Again he laughed. I must have been working well. He stood back and looked at the car.

'I've never seen one of these. What is it?'

I told him and gave him a conducted tour of the car. He got his mate out of the parked police car and I showed them how the headlights went around the corners when you turned the steering wheel. I showed them how the steering wheel was fully adjustable and how the same went for the luxurious leather rolled bucket seats. I showed them how the car went up and down at the touch of a lever to let you drive through fords and flooded roads. I showed them how the car, when jacked up, lowered the rear wheels from under the arches. They asked if they could look under the bonnet and I lifted it to show the engine, six cylinders of pure power served by three split carburettors. One of them pointed forward to a small, single-cylinder 'engine' sitting close to the front.

'What's that?'

'That is possibly the best feature on the car. When the big engine breaks down you can get home using the small, single-cylinder two-stroke.' They were really impressed by that, gave me a warning, and I drove away. Melody asked me what I was laughing at and I told her that I was just imagining these two coppers going back to the station and spreading the legend of the car with a 'breakdown engine'.

'So what?' said Mel.

'Well, I was actually showing them the air-conditioning unit!'

When it came to the MAG 1C number plate, however, Mervyn said that as I was always buying stuff for other people, I should buy myself a present. He arranged for the seller to bring the car round. A beautiful red Ferrari pulled up outside my home. I *had* to buy it. How could you not buy it? This was, and is, the greatest car in the world to drive, and I do mean DRIVE. The owner said how glad he was to be selling it and when I asked why answered, 'Because I am sick of people asking me if this is Paul Daniels' car.'

Wow, I had some fun in that car. I loved it. Eventually, however, it spent more and more time in the garage as I toured more and more. I needed something with more boot space for the clothes and the act props so I got a Bentley. I have had a couple of those now and they are the greatest touring car for comfort. So there you have it: Ferrari for fun, Bentley for comfort.

When it got to the stage where I hadn't used the Ferrari for a couple of years, I decided to sell it. It's only a car. The advert went out and someone bought it. They came and collected it on a trailer and, as it went down the drive and out of my life, I cried. I never thought that I would do that over a car, but I cried.

CHAPTER 11

DISCOVERING DEBBIE

I *t seemed as if the rest of the world was toppling down. The Berlin wall was the first to go in 1989, uniting Germans once again, quickly followed by the dismantling of Lenin's statue in Riga, USSR, which symbolised the end of the Cold War between the East and the West. Costing £6 million, the huge EuroDisney theme park opened near Paris and Paul prepared for some thrills and spills of his own.*

Now that the BBC television series had started to roll, Richard Mills offered me the top-of-the-bill spot in Great Yarmouth. The show would be a full-blown Variety show featuring both large and small magic and lots of acts and dancers. There was a full orchestra and tons of scenery. I provided all the necessary tricks and illusions and Delfonts did the rest. So it was that on 23 May 1979, that I turned up at the rehearsal room in Shepherd's Bush, London. I was carrying a few props and, as usual, I was early. The rehearsal room was underneath a church and I was not the first to get there. Sitting on the low wall that surrounded the building, waiting for the building to be unlocked, was a very pretty dark-haired girl. I made the usual greetings and found out that she was going to be one of the dancers in the show. Waves of normality swept over me but, goodness me, I couldn't get involved. I was the star of the show and had to be equally friendly with everyone.

Eventually the others turned up and we went through the usual getting-to-know-everyone routines. The dancers got into their leotards and leg warmers ready to rehearse. This is always a wonderful moment for any red-blooded man and I noticed that the girl from the wall was not only pretty but had a great figure. She reminded me of the little drawings of a girl that used to separate the paragraphs in the Penthouse magazine, which I only bought for the jokes, of course.

We had to place some of the dancers into the illusions and I picked her out. During our brief conversation, I had noticed that she had personality and a great laugh. She was petite, lithe and a fabulous dancer. Her name was Debbie McGee. So now you know why 23 May was mentioned. She won't let me forget it!

Later, I was to find out that Debbie had been a soloist with the Iranian National Ballet and that she had been trapped in Iran when the Ayatollah returned to power. The English dancers had to hide and a friendly Iranian at the airport who fancied Debbie shoved her on a plane home. Although primarily ballet trained, Debbie had studied all forms of dance and needed a job as soon as she arrived back in England. Seeing a notice in *The Stage* newspaper, she auditioned and got the job in Yarmouth.

Thrilled at gaining work so quickly, Debbie telephoned a friend to break the good news.

'But who is Paul Daniels?' she asked her mate.

Having been out of the country for so long, she had not seen this new magician (and sex symbol!) appear on the scene.

Her friend said, 'if you switch the telly on, he's on now.'

DISCOVERING DEBBIE

Debbie, running to her TV, pushed the power button and *Blankety Blank* sprang into life. This game show, hosted by Terry Wogan, was at the height of its popularity.

I had 'guested' on several of them and asked the Producer if I could 'send the show up'. He said 'yes'. Often trying to go way over the top in being silly, on one occasion I ran out into the car park, snapped off my car aerial and ran back into the studio with it. Terry used a microphone on a long, thin stick so I produced mine and we ended up having a sword fight. Every show I did I would try to come up with visual gags.

On the day that Debbie tuned in, *Superman, the Movie* had just exploded on to our cinema screens and everybody was talking about it. Before the programme, I told Terry's scriptwriter the gag about Superman being stupid because he wears his underpants on the outside.

I had taken a bit of a gamble, hoping that the scriptwriter would tell Terry the gag before the show. I had also concealed a Superman T-shirt with a big red 's' under my velcro-attached shirt and tie. Sitting down at the *Blankety Blank* desk, I took a pair of red Y-fronts out of my pocket and pulled them up over my trousers while everyone was busy setting up the show.

Right at the start of the show, Terry picked on me. 'Oh no, it's not you again, Daniels!'

'Don't you start with me, Wogan,' and I pulled my shirt open to reveal the 'S'.

Bang on cue, Terry said, 'Superman's an idiot, he wears his underpants on the outside!'

I immediately stood on my chair, exposing my red Y-fronts and said, 'What's wrong with that?'

The huge explosion of laughter was so loud, that the sound engineer hadn't time to turn his buttons down and the sound went into distortion. Meanwhile, this was Debbie McGee's first view of Paul Daniels! Debbie's eyes widened at the thought of spending a whole season with this idiot and phoned her friend again to say so.

'No, don't worry,' said the friend, 'he's normally a very good magician.'

'Oh no,' said Deb, 'I can't stand magicians.'

What a great start to a romance.

The season started and Debbie and I just sort of got along. I was still with Nikki but Debbie and I started seeing more of each other away from the theatre and both of us wanted it to go further. Eventually we 'snuck' away for a day and I rented a boat on the river. Being the flash, splash-the-money-about kind of guy that I am, this was a small day boat with a tiny cabin. It's a good job that we are both small in stature or our love life may never have taken off. From the moment that I lassoed a small bush on the riverbank and tied her up (the boat, not Debbie), passion took over and tidal waves were announced on the local weather stations as we rocked and rolled the boat about.

From then on it was love at every stolen opportunity but it was me, however, that kept pushing her away. Yes, there was the well-hidden fear of what had happened in my last marriage but also I was 40 years old and Debbie was 20. Nikki meant a lot to me and I didn't want to hurt her. Talk about being in a turmoil. Over and over for the next few years, Debbie and I would have flings that sometimes lasted quite a while but it would be me that would keep interrupting the affair.

'You've got to understand, love. The press will have a field day if they find out about you. They'll murder us on the age difference and look how your parents, sister and brother will feel when they go to work, or school or whatever. Go and find another fellow.' So that's how we met, and parted, and met and parted, for years.

Debbie was a great assistant – one of the best, if not the best, in the world when it comes to helping in the theatre of magic. Those who have written about the 'Blonde Bimbo' who got the job on TV because of her affair with the magician have no idea what they are talking about. The Blonde Bimbo has a degree (I haven't) and an amazing knowledge of all forms of dance. Debbie got the job on the television series when I wasn't there. I had refused to go to the auditions because I didn't want the press to do to me what they had done to Bruce Forsyth when his girlfriend was a hostess on the show.

Martin, my son, was 16 while we were in Great Yarmouth. Paul, his older brother, had started to work for me in Blackpool but didn't seem to be very disciplined in his work habits. When we were doing television shows they would both help me whenever necessary and both helped out backstage with the props and the scenery. Paul became a particularly good flies man. That's the guy who hauls the scenery up into the air and lowers it to the stage when it is needed. A good fly man never bangs the scenery on to the stage but brings it to its 'dead' perfectly. Paul could land it like a feather.

In fact, every job Paul took on, he did very well. Assisting in the show, on stage, he seemed uncomfortable and had probably inherited my shyness, but again he did the job very well. He would help out solving problems with fitting up the show with a lovely sense of logic. When we put out demonstrators selling a range of magic he outsold every other demonstrator. He became a financial adviser and did well. Paul gave that up for tiling and, having seen his work, it's good. All of which made what happened to him later very sad.

Probably because, when I left school, I had taken on a job in which I had no interest, I told all three of my sons that they should do what they really wanted to do.

'I don't care if it is picking rice in the paddy fields of China; if it is in your heart then you should go for it. If you fail, that's

OK, but it would be terrible to be older and still thinking, "if only I'd ..." If you have a dream, then do it.'

My career now took on a life of its own. I would do a summer season, a television season, a run of corporate cabarets, nightclubs, radio and so on. Holidays were grabbed between all of this and I would take the lads whenever I could. Gary was a bit too young to go on the trip we made early in 1980 when we went to Los Angeles and it rained. Oh boy, did it rain. Houses were being washed away. Landslides were blocking roads. We went to Disneyland and got well soaked. I took the decision to change the holiday, rented a car and set off for Las Vegas. After numerous diversions we managed to find a way to cross the Mojave Desert. It was pale green with plants and flowers popping up all over the place. The locals kept saying, 'You are so lucky to see it like this.' But we had that stuff back home and we wanted to see a desert! We were all ill with colds and flu.

One day, shopping in Vegas, the whole of the shop shook. An earthquake. I grabbed the lads and Nikki and got them out of the shop fast. Nobody else took any notice. That night on the television they announced, in passing, that there had been an earth tremor in Las Vegas but the *big news* was that it was still raining in LA. We thought they'd got their priorities wrong.

We went back to LA over snow-covered roads. This was turning into the holiday from hell so I organised flights to Florida where at last we could enjoy the orange groves and the theme parks and we finished up having a great time.

That was the year the full summer show moved to Bournemouth. Once again, I was in the Pavilion Theatre where I had spent a happy summer season in *The Val Doonican Show*. Now I was back as top-of-the-bill and the show was called *Summer Magic*. Bournemouth has a jungle drum system of communication. It must have. How else can you account for the arrival of dozens, possibly hundreds of requests for charity appearances around the area before you even know you are going there yourself? I said 'yes' to them all. I hope I am a charitable man, but that wasn't the real reason I took them all on this time.

An act called Little and Large were 'hot' at the time and the Civic Authority let it be known to my management that they fully expected Little and Large to do the major business and that our show might break even. A summer season show extends for a few weeks before and after the main body of holidaymakers arrive in the town and that is normally a quiet time, as very few locals bother going to see shows that they believe, incorrectly, are 'just for the grockles'. That's a south coast word for tourists.

By doing all the local charity jobs, I believed that the locals would support the show and they did. There was another 'benefit' that we hadn't anticipated. They told all their friends, visitors and holidaymakers to come to the show as well and we did great business.

In the early part of the summer, I agreed to do a pantomime for Dick Condon, the manager of the Theatre Royal in Norwich. Now there was a real manager of a theatre. The whole building buzzed with excitement all day long. He had snack bars and restaurant service, photographic and art exhibitions and he sold everything he could to do with the productions that were on at any given time. He seemed to be everywhere with his lovely Irish accent, greeting people, usually by name. You would find Dick wandering around the town saying, 'Hello there,' to passers-by, 'we haven't seen you in the theatre for a while.' Way to go, Dick, way to go.

Not many civic theatre managers have that drive or initiative. As an ex-internal auditor, some of them drive me crazy, but then they are not generally appointed from showbusiness but come from other administrative jobs. Civic theatres can, and should, make a profit and not be a burden on the taxpayers. It can be done. Dick Condon proved it.

Ask any performer from any branch of the theatrical arts and they will have their own horror stories of having to work in modern theatres, designed by architects that the local council have appointed but who have no experience in theatre at all. Mind you, I have heard the same moans from hospital nurses, television workers and many others that their buildings, too, don't fit the purpose for which they are supposed to be designed.

I have been to 'theatres' that are designed as 'multi-purpose' buildings. This means that they don't correctly fit any of the 'multi-purposes'. Gymnasiums, for example, in which the seats pull out are acoustic nightmares for bouncing sound and kill the shows that the managers try to put on. We have had to walk through the corridor, where the audience is coming in, to get to the stage. That destroys the 'magic' of theatre. It also prevents you carrying and setting up props.

Let me tell you about one theatre that embodies all the errors in one design.

The local council used their own in-house architect. On the day of the grand opening, the first artist knocked on the stage door and asked to be shown to her dressing room. 'Dressing room?' asked the stage door keeper. The architect had forgotten to build any. So they quickly brought caravans down for the acts to change in. This blocked the car park completely. For the first few months, performers had to run outside in the cold to temporary caravans in order to get changed. Eventually, they stuck an ugly block of dressing rooms on to the rear of the building.

The orchestra leader turned up next and asked to see the orchestra pit, normally a long 'slot' across the front of the stage.

He was directed to two egg-shaped holes in the front apron that protruded forward of the proscenium arch.

'What's that?' he asked, and was told that was where the musicians would be placed.

'Well,' he said, 'I'm sure that it looks very nice but if I am in that hole, how can I conduct the musicians in the other hole and vice versa?'

Soon the stage management discovered that backstage was fitted with hemp ropes, which haven't been used in the theatre for decades. When it is a dry day, the hemp dries out and the scenery lifts off the stage. When it is wet, the scenery sags. Still, that was nothing compared with the fact that the grid, from which all the scenery hangs, was set above the stage at only half the height of the proscenium opening. If you are not a theatrical person, let me explain. This meant that all the scenery, when lifted to the top, would still be half in view of the audience. The crew had to fold everything in half to get it out of sight.

The ceiling of the theatre, going forward from the stage to mid-stalls, is angled downwards so voices from the stage tend to hit it and bounce back instead of going to the back of the theatre. To get over this, they put speakers at the back, which can be very confusing if you are sitting more than half-way back in the stalls. You see the show in front of you and the sound comes from behind you.

The last error is wonderful. I love this. Along the ridge at the bottom of where the ceiling dips and half-way back in the theatre, is a curtain rail. We asked what it was for and we were told that this was a brilliant idea.

'When there are not many people in the audience we can close curtains across that rail and make it into a smaller theatre, which will make it more intimate and better for the performers.'

Isn't that a good idea? Not really. The spotlights and control boxes are behind the curtain.

Wait for it folks – this theatre won a design award! Do you remember when Prince Charles had a go at architects? I'm on his side.

You'll probably think I am kidding but while writing this chapter, Mervyn O'Horan telephoned me. He is trying to book a tour of theatres and, in the *British Theatre Directory*, the Theatre Royal at Hanley does not have its telephone number listed. It actually says, 'telephone ex-directory. Please contact venue for details.' How the hell do you do that? It has to be a joke, you think. When Mervyn telephoned directory enquiries he was told, 'sorry, it's ex-directory.' He telephoned the local tourist office and they gave him the number. All together now: 'There's no business like showbusiness ...'

While I'm having a moan, I might as well have a pop at some 'luvvies' and modern directors who think that it is artistic to go back to the design of theatres in the Middle Ages. Theatres developed from the streets and marketplaces into amphitheatres and buildings where you didn't have to rely on passing a hat around, but could charge customers to come in and watch. Somebody else added scenery, but by the time you get to Shakespeare they are still working in the round. Over the years that followed, theatre slowly developed by placing drama, the musical and other theatrical entertainments into a picture frame known as a proscenium arch. Consequently, the whole of the audience's imagination was filled with the only thing they could see – the play, the musical and the comedy.

In recent years, some artistic quacks have decided to regress centuries of progress by designing and building apron stages that jut out into the audience, theatres that go back to 'theatre in the round'. Subsequently, you sit in your seat watching the actor on stage while in the distance you can also see the opposite side of the audience where a woman offers her friend sweets, or picks her nose. This is a major step backwards in enjoying a dramatic experience, because your imagination is filled not only with what is happening on stage but also with what is going on in the audience as well. Alongside this is the disconcerting fact that the audience on the other side of the room is also watching *you*. The idea of restoring Shakespeare's Globe Theatre might have been a wonderfully historic idea as a museum piece, it might make an interesting night out, but the thought that it is the best way of watching plays, even those of Shakespeare himself, is one of the silliest ideas this century.

Enough of this moaning, Daniels, get on with your story ...

As the Bournemouth season was coming to an end, I just happened to mention to Richard Mills that I was going to do a pantomime in Norwich. He gave me, as they say in the North, usually with their arms folded across their bosoms, 'a funny look'. Not that Richard has bosoms, well, not that I've noticed. The next day he came to me and said that the reason for the 'look' was that he and Bernard Delfont had been talking about taking my show into the West End.

This really was amazing because there hadn't been a successful Variety show in the West End for ages, and I do mean ages. I rarely get excited at the promise of something that might happen. So many times, when I was working the clubs, some agent, manager or television producer would promise you the earth and nothing would happen. I learnt not to look forward and risk disappointment, but to enjoy things when they happened. This promise, however, really gave me a buzz. The problem was that they already had a show in the Prince of Wales Theatre and they were not sure when it would run out of steam. I took a gamble and got in touch with Dick Condon. Without hesitation, he released me from my contract, appreciating that a season in the West End would be far better for my career. He didn't have to do that, but Dick was a really nice man.

I couldn't believe that I, Ted Daniels from South Bank, was going to open at the Prince of Wales. I even read up on the history of the place. Originally built in 1884, it was demolished and replaced with a new version, which became the envy of every other theatre owner. The reason for this was its key position, sandwiched between Piccadilly Circus and Leicester Square and was rightly described as the best location for a theatre in the West End. The foundation stone was laid by Gracie Fields in 1937 and it quickly became established as a theatre of musical comedy and Variety. Its colourful history had seen the likes of Benny Hill, Harry Secombe, Frankie Howard and Norman Wisdom appear there, as well as some of the best musicals including *Underneath the Arches*, a tribute to Flanagan and Allen.

Arriving for the first day of a three-week rehearsal schedule, I met the Company Manager who would be responsible for the day-to-day wellbeing of the cast. My two boys, Martin and Paul Jnr, worked on the backstage management of my personal props and Dad was in full-flow with all the illusion-building. Already on his hands and knees was John Short, happily painting long slats of wood with brightly coloured ultraviolet paint, which would be used in the magical opening sequence. John was the Deputy Stage Manager and had the onerous task of cueing the technical changes on the show each night. When presenting live magic, timing is essential and John later proved to be the best man for the job.

I was certainly fortunate to be surrounded by the best the business could offer including Production Manager Roy Murray, Choreographer Fred Peters, Musical Director Paul Burnett and the wonderful Dickie Hurran. This vastly experienced stage Director and ex-hoofer was not liked by a lot of people because he liked to get things right. There was even a rumour that he had thrown a brick at an assistant stage manager on his last show. A tough man, he would shout and holler at his stage management and crew one minute, but take them to lunch the next. Somehow, he was able to keep business and pleasure separate.

Needing to buy a top hat for one of the routines, Dickie and I strolled down to Dunn & Co in the Strand. While we stood waiting to be served, we watched how a young salesman attempted to sell an umbrella to an American and failed. Once he had left the shop, Dickie said to the assistant, 'that's not the way you sell an umbrella.'

Picking up the parasol, Dickie went into one of his old song-and-dance-man routines, looking like something out of *Singing in the Rain*. The umbrella flew around his neck, his arms and his body before he spun it up into the air, caught it and slid it down with the point between his crossed legs and said, 'that's how you sell an umbrella!'

Without meaning to, I apparently endeared myself to the staff and crew of the theatre. During what is known as the fit-up, when all the scenery, sound and lighting rigs are being built, we worked well into the night. They were all a bit surprised when I worked with them. I love to know where everything is in a show and also how it works. It got to about 2.00am and I left. Apparently, there were comments of, 'I wondered how long he'd stick it.' About half-an-hour later, I turned up with large trays of fish and chips, having woken up a fish and chip shop owner and persuaded him to cook the order for me. From then on I was God!

During rehearsals for *It's Magic*, I got a telephone call from the New London Theatre where Andrew Lloyd Webber's musical Cats was in preview. Wayne Sleep, playing Mr Mistopheles, was having problems in his dance routine where he had to perform a couple of lightweight tricks. I dashed in, watched the dance routine, pointed out the reasons it wasn't working, trained Wayne very quickly in the handling of the props and dashed out again. It was months later that I thought I should have asked for money. Now that's not like a Yorkshireman, is it?

The original contract for *It's Magic* at the Prince of Wales was for a one-week run with options and I was a bit miffed when I found that out. Now I understand the business side of things a little better and don't blame them for 'taking out insurance', but at the time I thought they didn't have much confidence in me. My contract also stated I needed to attend a medical, as this was what the insurance company required. Unlike a play, where you can substitute a main part with an understudy, this show, and indeed any show that features a 'variety turn' relies entirely on the featured performer. In this case, that was me, and there's only one of those!

Off I went to BUPA where I had to sit down in front of a computer screen and was asked to fill in the electronic questionnaire, which would give an automatic health check. It was a great system. Operators were trained, not in a wide range of skills, but in applying specific health checks. One would check your blood pressure, another a hearing test and so on. All their conclusions were fed into the computer to enable it to arrive at a final analysis on my wellbeing or otherwise. I thought that BUPA had it right when recognising that trained nurses were not required to conduct these simple tests. Maybe the NHS could have saved some money by adopting this procedure?

Moving along the chain of girls making all the checks, I finally arrived at the end of the conveyor belt and, having stated that there was nothing I needed to discuss with the doctor, sat having a cup of tea before leaving.

A nurse came over. 'Mr Daniels, would you mind if you did see our doctor?'

I heard the death march in my ears. I was only 41.

'No, not at all,' I said, trying to keep my voice steady like us macho types do when we are faced with imminent death.

Upon entering the doctor's room, I had visions of some horrible disease having been discovered in my veins.

'Mr Daniels, it says here you don't take any exercise,' he said, thumbing through the mile-long computer printout.

'This is true.'

'None whatsoever?'

'Nope.'

'Tennis?'

'A couple of years ago I had a game.' I shrugged.

'Golf?'

'On my holidays. Once. I've been busy.'

'Then do you mind if I do some more tests on you?'

My heart sank at thoughts of going through the whole procedure once more, coupled with an urgent desire to know what was wrong. Why was he prolonging the agony? Why couldn't he just give me the worst now?

With thoughts of knowing it was all over and silently writing my will in my head, I sat there while he conducted every single experiment again. Once again, we sat facing each other as he thumbed through the results. The only sound was of my heart thumping loudly, obviously desperate to prove how healthy it really was.

'Well, to be honest, Mr Daniels, I don't understand it. I can only put it down to the fact that it says here you don't smoke and you don't drink.'

'That's true.'

'You see, Mr Daniels. The computer takes a comparative record of everyone who comes through our clinic. And according to this print-out, despite the fact you take no exercise, you are the fittest man we've ever had.'

I could've kissed him, but I didn't. Instantly I felt so fit, I felt like cancelling the taxi and walking back to the theatre.

Later, however, I wondered whether they did that for everyone, just to make them all feel better.

I never get stage fright. Other performers say they need it. I have never understood that need. My philosophy is that we are getting paid to play with our toys. Actors have the scripts and direction and love play acting, just as singers love to sing and dancers to dance. What we do is a mere frippery, a passing shadow. We help people to leave their normal lives and enter a world of wonder, leaving reality behind. The supposedly important things of life go on no matter what we do. When asked, I always say that tomorrow Bill Clinton will still be in power, or Tony Blair, or whoever. The madness of terrorists will go on. So backstage I am Mr Cool. Sometimes Debbie has to wake me up to go on; I just fall asleep once everything is set up and ready to go.

During the rehearsals for this, the biggest show of my life, I had always parked behind the theatre and walked in the stage door. For the opening night, however, I went by taxi and the driver approached the theatre from the front. I saw me. That's not true. I saw ME. The picture of me and the title seemed to go from the floor to the sky. Suddenly, I knew what this was all about and that if I didn't go well in front of this mostly invited audience and the media, a lot of people would be out of work. My mouth started to go dry. Stage fright started to set in. When people kept bobbing in to wish me luck I must have seemed like a stranger to them.

The way that the opening was staged I had to stand alone upstage, in the dark, for six minutes. My legs went wobbly and I really had to hang on to myself. If that is what some acts and actors go through every night, then they must be barmy to stay in this business. On cue, a white doorframe floated down on to the stage, filled with smoke and I stepped through it and out from the total blackness – I suddenly appeared in a flash, as if by magic! The applause erupted, and the real magic was that my stage-fright vanished.

The eight performances a week featured brilliant singer and impressionist Karen Kay who closed the first half with a superb Shirley Bassey number. Sometimes her son would turn up, a nice lad who grew up to become the world-famous pop star Jamiroquai. Jean-Claude with Yvette managed to juggle full-size footballer puppets, plus two footballs, with his feet while lying upside down. The Philippe Genty Company presented a dazzling array of black art and ultra-violet puppets.

In a very long run, there are so many stories. We were well into the run when, as usual, half-way through the magic and after a particularly good trick I walked forward and asked, 'Any questions?' This was a regular set-up as someone inevitably would ask, 'How did you do that?' and I would answer, 'Beautifully.' OK, it's not the greatest gag in the world but it served a purpose at the time. On one show, however, a hand could be seen waving in the air when I asked if there were any questions. I pointed to the man underneath the hand and said, 'Yes, sir. You have a question?'

A Middle Eastern gentleman stood up and said, 'Excuse mee. Thees ees not *Eveeta*?'

This man had sat through the whole of the first half of the show, magic, puppets, foot jugglers, impressionist and the second half's opening dance and magic routines *in the wrong theatre*. As I explained that *Evita* was in the Prince Edward Theatre, the usherettes checked his ticket. He had been seated, coincidentally, in the only empty seat that exactly matched his ticket for the other place. The whole audience exploded in laughter as I sang 'Don't Cry for Me, Argentina' to him. I wonder if he ever got to see the real thing.

Several famous people came to see this show which was a real oddity in the West End, home of great drama and fabulous musicals. Sir Alec Guinness brought his grandchildren and when I announced in glowing terms that he was in the 'house', he wrote me a lovely letter saying that, like the rest of the audience, he was craning his neck to see who I was talking about and was very appreciative that it turned out to be himself.

I am rarely thrown but my heart missed a beat when I entered one night to see Michael Caine's so very famous face sitting dead centre of row C in the stalls. It kind of puts you off when someone you admire so much comes in to see you.

Another night you would have found me sitting in my dressing room after a performance totally dumbfounded and only able to come out with 'But I ... but I ... but I ...' like an idiot. The problem was the woman in my room who was raving about my performance and demanding to know why I had never appeared in America and so on. My problem was that I had never met a star of the magnitude of Ingrid Bergman who was in to see the show with her daughter. Eventually I found a talking point. I had met Gladys Aylward, the amazing missionary, when I was in Hong Kong and Ingrid Bergman had played her in the film *Inn of the Sixth Happiness*. Miss Bergman was such a fan I should have made her my agent.

One of the great sadnesses was to get a letter from a man who had really enjoyed the show but I never got to meet him. When I read the letter, I dashed round to the front of house and they confirmed that they had had a man in a wheelchair (not easy to do in the Prince of Wales Theatre) two nights before. They had not recognised him, so I never got to meet James Cagney, for that was who it was.

DISCOVERING DEBBIE

For a magic show to be entertaining, you don't really need big illusions and in many cases people prefer the smaller magic. As a small boy, I remember seeing The Great Levante, an Australian illusionist, use a block of wood, threaded on to a piece of rope and when it magically came off you could hear a great gasp of surprise from his audience just before the applause came. You had to be there because you can't explain why the surprise was so great. Timing, I guess. Similarly, I know I can entertain several thousand people at a time with just a cup and ball routine. Most magicians have had the trick or tried it out at some time but it's the presentation that is vital, not the size of the trick. I studied the classics like the 'Chinese' Linking Rings. With some of the tricks, when I was in a long run or a season of shows, I would actually try to lose the audience and then bring them back again by changing the timing.

It's a fact that illusions are far harder to perform than sleight of hand or close-up magic. A lot of the public would probably find that hard to believe and there are even a number of magicians who won't buy it either. The reasoning behind the thought is simple. When performing a big illusion, the audience is watching you top to toe, arm to arm, the full image, rather than just looking at your hands. The rhythm and timing of your body doesn't matter so much in close-up, the audience are looking at the trick. On stage, it's a totally different ball game. The whole scene has to be 'sold' to an audience.

Whenever I have designed a full evening magic show I have always included illusions. You 'pays your money', you should see as wide a range of entertaining magic as I can put together for you. Several illusions were featured in *It's Magic* at the Prince of Wales including a dramatic *Star Wars* levitation, which closed the show each night. Lying flat on a flashing metallic box, I was covered with a silver sheet by the chief 'space-man', one of three creating the effect. As the chief space-man raised his arms, the music intensified and my body rose six feet in the air, as the metallic box was removed.

Floating, literally in space, deep tones boomed out over the auditorium, 'ladies and gentlemen, what you are about to see, you will remember for the rest of your life!'

With this, the chief space-man pulled the silver cloth off my body. I had instantaneously vanished!

The chief space-man walked forwards to centre-stage, took his space helmet off and I said, 'ladies and gentlemen, I hope you've enjoyed my show. Goodnight!'

Originally booked for its single-week run, *It's Magic* opened on 10 December 1980 and ran for 15 months. It was the only production in the history of the Prince of Wales Theatre where every critic praised the show and it closed on 6 February 1982. During that time, I had also made several training films for banks on the recent innovation of credit cards, a couple of television series and was a BBC Radio 2 disc jockey on Sundays for six months. Oh, yes, I was also on radio with a quiz called *Dealing with Daniels*. Having appeared at nearly 500 consecutive stage performances as well, no wonder I was tired, but the bookings were still very strong. I desperately needed a holiday and asked to take two weeks out, even offering to return with a completely new show.

It was decided by Delfonts that it would not be possible to keep the theatre 'dark' for a fortnight, as it would cost far too much money. I decided to leave and handed in my notice. It had been a fabulous time of my life. Towards the end of the run, there was some discussion with an American producer who wanted to take the show to Broadway. This wasn't any old producer, this was Alex Cohen, who was about as big as you can get.

He came to see a matinee performance and out I sailed on to the stage as usual. By now a couple of the acts had moved on and I was doing a bit more magic. The show was flying. In the second half, I got two men on to the stage and I asked them where they were from and what they did for a living. One came from Yorkshire but he had a wonderful suntan, which raised a laugh and I played around with that for a while. Then he told me that he had worked in Saudi Arabia and I expected him to be in the oil business.

'No, I train Arab pilots to attack Israel.'

You could feel the audience cool off immediately and I was well aware that Alex Cohen would not be a Methodist. I didn't make any gags about it (would you?) and simply moved on with the cogs whirring in my brain trying to arrive at a way to reverse this state of affairs.

About ten minutes later in the act, I always whip out a dishevelled handkerchief and normally say something about them also making these in white. On this occasion, I said to the pilot trainer, 'You'll recognise this, it's an Arab flag.' The audience roared at the ten-minute-late response and probably thought that I had worked it out, but it was just an ad-lib.

At the end of the show, I gave a farewell curtain speech as usual and said, 'that's it, ladies and gentlemen. I do hope that you have enjoyed a wonderful afternoon with us here at the Prince of Wales Theatre. If you have, then you must tell all your friends that you have. If you have not, then you must tell all of your friends that you have.' A laugh.

'And there's something else you must do. You will remember that when I came on, I asked where you were all from. What a mixture we had today. We had Russians and Americans, Iranians and Iraqis and even a gentleman volunteer on stage who said that his job was to train pilots to attack Israel and I know that we will have Jewish people sitting out there. In other words, we have had just about every warring faction in the world sitting in this theatre. When you all go home to your various countries, will you please tell everyone, and remember for yourselves, that this afternoon you all laughed together?'

Alex Cohen was in my dressing room faster than I was.

'That was amazing, that was wonderful. Do you always give that curtain speech?'

'No, Alex, only when you're in the house.'

I went to America to have a look at New York but the idea never came to fruition because it would have meant staying in America for whole year. They wouldn't accept a shorter contract and I had big family ties in England and I didn't want to be stuck anywhere for a year. I wasn't disappointed; I had enjoyed the London run enormously.

I went to work in Las Vegas instead. The way I got the booking was interesting. Mervyn and Howard went to Los Angeles to try to see agents who would get me into Las Vegas. I wanted to go there because I wanted to find out whether Americans thought I was funny. Don't ask me why this was important to me. I don't know. Maybe it was because the BBC had said that they wouldn't sell my shows there as they had been told that I was 'too fast for the Americans to understand me when I spoke'.

Mervyn telephoned me and said they were having no success so I suggested that they go to Vegas and find the equivalent of a working men's club's concert secretary. 'Somebody in the casinos must do the booking of the acts.' They went to the Tropicana and, sure enough, there was a man responsible for booking acts. He agreed to see them and they left him a video to watch. That evening he put it on but went to the bathroom to get ready to go out. His wife watched it and called him back in. She thought I was funny so I got the job, a month in *The Folies-Bergère Show* at the Tropicana Hotel. More than that, because of my track record I got a really unusual contract for the time, I was down to do a 35-minute spot when nobody got more than ten minutes.

DISCOVERING DEBBIE

I went out to Los Angeles two weeks early with Joyce, my secretary, Mervyn and Howard. Joyce Waldeck was easily the best secretary anyone ever had except for one thing – she wouldn't learn computers. Somehow, that didn't matter and she did, very simply, point out one of the great reasons many people are frightened of the machines: 'I have never wanted to process words, I only want to write letters.'

One of the national daily newspapers sent a reporter and photographer with us to cover the trip. We nicknamed him 'scoop'. The first day's coverage was so ridiculous with a story about me leaving home in the early hours of the morning accompanied by a mysterious woman in black with black stockings. There were also two dark-jowled 'heavies' with me, obviously there as bodyguards. This was quite a description for a small conjurer, his secretary, his manager and his fixer, none of whom would have said 'boo' to a goose. Ah, the wonders of journalistic fiction.

The reason for going early was to 'learn' the language. Just as years before I had learnt that all areas of the UK have different rhythms and dialects, I knew that America would be the same. An example of this was when I used to call home.

'Good morning, how can I help you?'

'I'd like to speak to London, England, please.'

'Certainly, sir, may I have your name?'

'Daniels.'

'Could you spell that for me, please?'

Every day I would spell my name until, after a week, the operator said my name back to me after I had spelt it, and I heard the difference. The next day the conversation went almost the same.

'Good morning, how can I help you?'

'I'd like to speak to London, England, please.'

'Certainly, sir, may I have your name?'

In 'American' I said, 'Dayniyells.'

I was put straight through without being asked to spell my name.

From that moment on, I changed the pronunciation of the vowels and realised why the French teacher, way back at school, had tried to get us to create the vowel sounds over and over again. It is the sound of the vowels, not the consonants, that make the 'sound' of the language. So the Tropicahna (English) became the nasal Tropicayna (American). There were other rhythm and sound changes but I'm sure you get the idea.

We moved from Los Angeles to Las Vegas. Some acts go there and become gamblers. Not me. I took one look at the incredible display of hotels, casinos and lights with the greatest performers and shows in the world and thought to myself, 'Nobody pays for this but losers.'

Another week of language acclimatisation and the day before I was due to open, I went to the Tropicana and found my way backstage. A man with a clipboard, who turned out to be one of the many assistant stage managers, asked me to leave because the public are not allowed into the performers' area. I told him my name and that I was to open there the next night. He checked his board.

'Right, Dayniyells. Magician. Right?'

I agreed that I was and he yelled, 'OK, FELLAS, OPEN THE DOORS, WE GOT A MAGICIAN COMING IN.'

The shows in Vegas are enormous. If you haven't been you cannot begin to imagine how huge the scenery is or how much of it there can be. On his command, the tallest, widest doors that I have ever seen slid open and a line of stagehands stood looking out of the gap into the bright sunshine. Me, too. I didn't know what was happening so I stood on the end of the line and looked with them.

Eventually, 'Where are the trucks?'

'Trucks?' I replied.

'Oh, are we getting the cats?'

' Cats?' I replied.

Astute readers will have noticed that I was not holding the brightest conversation here. Then the light dawned on me. They were expecting an American-style magician, with big boxes and cages, lions and tigers. I pointed to the small box on the floor. 'My act's in there.'

The guy with the clipboard yelled again, 'Close the doors, fellas, we got us a weirdo.'

Wasn't that nice of him?

I was shown to a dressing room and went through my rehearsal. There was another act on the bill called Barclay Shaw. I had seen him before and he had a brilliant puppet act, although he was also a brilliant illusionist. He got very bitchy when he found out how long a spot I had been given and, covering that up, gave me lots of advice, as it was my first time in Las Vegas. This 'advice' made no sense to me at all and, if I had taken it, I am sure I would have 'bombed', as they say over there. I listened, but decided I would do my own thing my own way.

That night all the dancers (there must have been over 100), the other acts, the casino staff and even the kitchen staff came out and stood at the sides to see what the little Englishman was going to do for over half an hour. The stage was the widest and the deepest that I had ever been on but I was ready. I had spent three weeks learning American. I could communicate. I heard my name announced and walked on to face 300 Japanese!

Immediately I said '*Kon ban wa*', which is 'Good evening' in Japanese, and I bowed low. Three hundred Japanese stood up and bowed in response. I found out who spoke English and organised my own translation team. The job became easier because every time I said something funny I would wait for them to translate and I would bow and they would all stand up and bow. This was a great running gag for the Americans who were all seated behind them.

In all my shows I get people out of the audience and, obviously, decided to get a couple of Americans up from behind the Japanese. To the first one: 'What's your name?'

'Randy,' came the reply.

I acted shocked and then, breaking from America-speak into posh English, said, 'Well, dear boy, if you ever go to the United Kingdom, you must never say that. You must say, "Hello, I'm Randolph."'

'Now why the hell would I want to say that?'

'Let me explain. The word Randy, in England, is exactly the same as if I went up to a young lady over here and said, "Hello, I'm Horny."'

The audience roared, the Japanese translated, the Japanese laughed, so I bowed. They all stood up and bowed. They sat down.

'Well, I'll be darned,' he said.

I found out the other man's name and made something of that before turning back to Randy.

'What do you do for a living?'

Now I know you are not going to believe this, but it's true. He came back with, 'I'm a venereal disease inspector.'

The lid blew off the cabaret room. I jumped back about 6ft. 'Isn't that dangerous? You know, a HORNY VD GUY?'

Some nights you just don't have to work hard, the audience do it all for you. Barclay Shaw realised that I knew what I was doing and we became friends.

I really liked my month in Vegas and the management wanted me to stay and sign a long, long contract. That was not for me. I had just done a long stint in the West End and couldn't face what, to me, would become an office job. I have quite a few friends in Las Vegas who have signed ten-year contracts and longer. True, they earn fortunes, but I have never taken a job just for the money and so I left Las Vegas and went on holiday.

This was a really strange time of my life. Debbie and I were still in our 'on and off' stage which was all my fault. In between times, I was going out with a stunning solicitor (no, not the American version, the legal kind) but it wasn't that that was creating the confusion. I didn't want to perform any more. I didn't know what I wanted to do but I was exhausted from the long run of shows. I had been doing live shows, television and radio flat out and intermingled. It had all become too much.

How British Airways found out that photography was my hobby I don't know, but they came up with an offer to Mervyn that I leapt at. They would fly Debbie and I around the world for up to three months, all flights and hotels paid for, if I would take pictures that could be used in a book and possibly their brochures. I agreed to all of this but just before we set off, I received an invitation to a Variety Club luncheon at the Hilton on Park Lane.

On the day, I went in by taxi, and as we arrived there were mountains of photographers and television cameras. 'There must be someone important coming,' I said. It turned out to be me. Months before, someone had muttered that if the Variety Club were to offer me an award would I accept it, and I had said, 'Yes, thank you very much.' What I didn't realise at the time was just how big the Variety Club were and how prestigious was the award. I sat through the whole of the meal wondering what the hell I was going to say but I think I did all right and, of course, enjoyed the accolades. It did occur to me, however, that I had won all the working men's clubs awards and had never done one again, won all the nightclub awards and had never worked in a nightclub after that. Would I work again in theatre now that I had this?

Debbie and I packed up the gear and off we went. What a trip that was. We flew to Calcutta first and, when we landed, they came around spraying the plane and us to kill the bugs. I don't know why because when we got off the plane there were more than enough bugs to go around anyway. The city was a real culture shock. Hong Kong had poverty when I was there but nothing like Calcutta. At the time, they were building an underground system. The machines that we would use in the UK stood idle as woman after woman came out of the hole in the ground with baskets of earth balanced on their heads. Both here and in the next city we went to I found it hard to contain my anger at the cruelty and torture to children, bones broken and twisted to make them into beggars' tools. You could rent one of these poor, skinny, distorted children and take them out on to the streets to beg and make a profit out of their condition. Awful.

In the film *Gandhi*, there was a scene in which the great man takes a tray from a man serving his group with tea. He said something like, 'How can we expect to stop the British from treating us like servants when we treat our own people like servants?' and some of the people in the cinema applauded. All I could think was that I have never thought of a waiter in a restaurant as a servant. A good waiter can make you have a really good night out, for example. Italians seem to do it best. In that one action, Gandhi, an undoubtedly great man, took away a job from a man who could probably not do anything else very well. I never thought of a rickshaw or trishaw man as a slave or a servant, I just admired their fitness and strength. When they were removed from the streets, they fell into extreme poverty because they didn't know how to do anything else. Not everyone is as well educated as Gandhi. Another of his major 'reforms' was to limit imports of foreign-made goods to practically nothing. This didn't work; it only made a few families very rich.

DISCOVERING DEBBIE

Countries have to trade with each other. You can't make everything for yourself. The quality of life will go down. India was poor beyond belief. What their Government spent their money on I don't know, but it wasn't for the benefit of the people.

One of the items that I wanted to photograph was the Howrah Bridge. The driver would not let me do this. Apparently, a German tourist had photographed it the year before and had been thrown into the river by the public for being a possible security risk. I pointed out that the bridge had been made over the road from where we lived in the prefab in South Bank and that it was probably one of the things that had turned our tulips black. It made no difference. I was not allowed to take a photograph. I pointed out that there were now satellites in space that could take a photograph of the minutest detail of any part of the earth. The answer was still no. I walked on to the bridge and saw the plaque that verified Dorman, Long and Co of Cleveland had built it. The next day, an urchin offered me some photographs of the Howrah Bridge for a few rupees.

Debbie and I left Calcutta for Bombay and we had to fly on the internal Indian air service. I do hope that by now they have improved this service. As we walked through the metal detector doorway in Calcutta it bleeped. We stopped and were immediately asked to move on. We explained that the door bleeped and were told that it was supposed to bleep. As we watched, everybody who walked through it made it bleep. I guess it was set too high. We got on the plane and couldn't sit together. The plane stood on the runway for an hour-and-a-half. The only thing on offer to alleviate the heat was water and you really cannot drink the water in the East. That is not an insult. I know that when the Indian cricket team came to the UK with their wives, years ago, some of the wives got very ill when they drank our water. Our stomachs must get used to our own germs.

After what seemed ages, the plane took off and we flew across India. Debbie and I would get up and talk to each other from time to time. Night fell and in the middle of a conversation I told Debbie to get back into her seat and belt up. 'This plane is going down,' I said and I was right. The plane landed while people were still standing, shooting them forward in the aisles. Then the voice came over the loudspeakers, 'We are now landing at Bombay airport.'

When we got off the plane, there was no one there to meet us. We stood waiting by the carousel for our luggage and Debbie, tired out, took off her shoes. 'I'd put them back on,' I said. She asked why and as she did so the luggage carousel started up. Rats ran from under it and Debbie was immediately hanging around my neck. Thank you, rats! We had no contact telephone numbers so I walked out of the airport and hailed a taxi. As the driver spun the cab around at high speed to stop in front of us, I should have spotted that his turban was angled to one side and that he seemed overly happy. He threw our luggage on to the top of the car, as there was too much to go in the boot. We got into the car only to find he had a friend sitting in the front seat, equally happy. 'Where to, Sahib?' he asked and I told him to take us to the best hotel in town.

The world lost a great racing driver when nobody signed him up for Formula One. We went like a rocket into Bombay with him ducking and diving across the lanes. As he drove, he and his friend would pass a cheroot backwards and forwards that smelt awfully sweet. Then he would aim the 'bullet' at a gap that wasn't there and it would open up just before he arrived. We marvelled at people sleeping head to toe along a parapet on a bridge that we crossed. They had obviously learnt to sleep without rolling over. The pavements were full of people sleeping in the open.

Ahead of us I saw the traffic lights changing to red. We were in the third, outside lane at the time. As the cars in front of us slowed to a stop, blocking all three lanes, he went through the traffic on our left without slowing down at all and bounced the car up on to the pavement, horn blazing. People scattered and he took the car between the traffic light and a building, bounced it off the pavement again and straight into the traffic that was now moving through the lights at right angles to us. Debbie pulled her wide-brimmed hat down over her eyes and I did a bit more than cross my fingers. If only I had worn my brown trousers for the trip.

We cleared the traffic into an empty road ahead and I told Debbie we were all right. 'What about the luggage?' Debbie whispered. She was right to worry. We had shot all over the place and he hadn't bothered to tie it down when he threw it on the top. Unfortunately, the driver had good hearing. Without altering his driving style at all, he swung his left foot, which normally he would have used to stop the car, across and on to the accelerator. He opened the car door, held the side of the steering wheel and swung himself out of the car hanging on to the wheel and the door. Standing up he looked on to the roof, got back in, shut the door and said, 'luggage OK, Memsahib.' Debbie went back under the hat for the rest of the journey.

We checked into the Taj Mahal Hotel by the gateway to India. We were shown to a beautiful room and went to bed. We had actually arrived at the very hotel British Airways had intended us to be in so we had got lucky. The next morning, I used the toilet and washed my hands. As I was drying them there was a knock at the door. I opened it and there was a man outside who said, 'Good morning,' and took my towel and handed me a clean one. From then on it became a great mystery. Every time either of us would wash our hands he would be there with a clean towel. We even opened the door to see if he was there and he wasn't anywhere in sight, but if we washed our hands there he was, the Genie of the Towels.

BA gave us a driver, Joseph, to take us anywhere we wanted to go. 'Would you like to go and see the bodies burning?' was his first question. We didn't. Apparently there were trucks that went around on a morning collecting the bodies of people who had died on the streets during the night. Not my scene and I couldn't imagine that British Airways would want the photographs. I took lots of pictures that they wouldn't want to use.

One night we went to a nice restaurant with a good band. We were the only people dining. As we have found all over the world, the singers, who are native to the country, sing in perfect American but talk in their own lilting accents. It is a very strange phenomenon. Debbie and I were seated at a round table that was so large we had to shout to each other. I ordered lamb chops and asked for the wine list. This took for ever and I had to ask quite a few times. Eventually, the head waiter came over with some embarrassment and offered us the only two bottles of wine that he had. I had never heard of either of them and when we did drink one of the bottles it tasted strangely of curry. In a country where nothing can be imported, everyone suffers at every level.

The lamb came in a pastry-covered pot with the bones sticking out of the pastry. The smell was not good and the bones were as clean as a whistle and not connected to the meat at all. The meat tasted like it smelt and I didn't eat too much of it.

As we drove back to the hotel, I told Joseph about the meat. Next morning he explained, 'I went back to the restaurant because you were not happy, Mr Daniels, and they told me that they were very embarrassed because you ordered lamb but they did not have any lamb. They served you dog but the real problem was that it was not a young dog.' Somehow this explanation did not make me feel any better about the night before.

Thanks to the Variety Club Award news being sent around the world, everywhere we went on this trip either the local news stations or even the television companies themselves were always there trying to get me to work. I didn't want to work but it is very hard to say 'no' when people are being so complimentary. I agreed to do a television programme for children and went out and bought some packs of cards, tissue paper, string and the like to make up some small magic tricks for them to see.

I was taken to a small television studio where the facilities, to say the least, were primitive. The lights were the small, portable lamps normally used in domestic video making, hanging on Dexion framing. The television cameras themselves were rectangular boxes that only recorded in black and white so they decided to shoot my part on film, not tape. They found a table for me to work on and it was an ex-British Army metal desk that made a strange blump-blump noise every time you touched it and the middle went up and down. They brought in a group of small children and sat them on metal and plastic chairs that squeaked every time a child moved.

The camera was a collectable. An old German film camera with an enormous magazine mounted on the top. When it was eventually started it made a sound like a tinny machine gun.

In came a beautiful young Indian girl who was the regular presenter of the show. She sat down and the director gave the order to roll the camera. Then, and I am sorry to say, I laughed out loud, when, in the midst of the blump-blumps, squeak-squeaks and the machine-gun, he shouted, 'QUIET, ACTION.'

He hadn't a hope in hell of getting quiet in that racket, but he didn't seem to care. Then I got one of the biggest surprises of my life. The girl smiled at the camera, paused, and very slowly said, 'super ... cala ... fragilistic ... expiali ... docious. Super ... cala ... fragilistic ... expiali ... docious.' Delivered in that lovely, lilting Indian accent, these were the last words I expected. My jaw dropped and she went on, 'that is right, children ... Magic,' and she turned to look at me. It took a couple of seconds to realise that it was my cue to work. I'd love to see that film because I must have looked a right wally for the first few minutes.

We flew from Bombay to Hong Kong and the reception there was the opposite of Bombay. We were met at the door of the plane and practically jogged through the airport. Our luggage was first off the carousel and loaded into a car before we could blink. We were across the other side of the harbour before we knew it and into the hotel in about seven minutes.

As we were signing in, Barry Norman, the television film critic, said 'Hello'. It's a small world, but I wouldn't want to paint it.

From a lot of reminiscing in Hong Kong, and a trip to a monastery that painted Jesus, with Chinese eyes, on a donkey on dinner plates, we went to Japan. Tokyo was just like every other major city in the world. The hotel had the biggest foyer of any hotel I had ever stayed in and I liked the fact that none of the staff expect a tip. I got the impression that they thought it an insult. Perhaps by now, the Americans, notorious for their over-the-top tipping, have changed them and, if so, that's sad. We also experienced the efficiency of the Japan Travel Bureau. One evening, I decided that if we were really to experience Japan, we had to get out of Tokyo and at about 5.45pm went into the JTB office. They found a man who spoke a little English (in those days it was very difficult to find any written English on any of the signs) and I told him that I had looked at his brochures but did not want to go on any of his organised trips around Japan. I explained that I wanted to go to various bits and pieces of each trip and gave him my list. He was gone for half-an-hour and returned with two books of tickets, one for Debbie, one for me. All these tickets were printed with our names and properly bound in a book.

As per his instructions, very early the next morning Debbie and I went down to the foyer and the porters piled up our, by then, considerable amount of luggage. We looked around for a yellow flag and spotted a girl standing by the doors holding one up on a stick. As we approached her she asked, '*Daniels-san?*' and I said their word for 'yes', which sounds like 'Hi'. She pointed out to a line of buses where another girl was standing with a yellow flag. We walked to the bus and she tore out the first of our tickets. We got on to the bus and, as we seemed to be the last, she got on and in the international language of English started to ask where everyone was from. We were sitting in the middle of a band of Argentinians, which probably doesn't mean much to you, but you have to remember that we were at war with Argentina at the time. Debbie tried to stop me but I couldn't resist announcing that we were from England. Strange how the bus went silent, but even stranger was how we got along so well with them on the trip. Ordinary people never want to go to war.

The bus set off and I flipped. I could see that all our luggage was still standing in the hotel foyer. The guide calmed me down and told me not to worry. I worried. We were driven straight to the station without hold-ups and we looked at our next ticket. It had on it the platform number, the carriage letter and the seat number. We walked to our platform to find that it was lettered and painted so that people could form orderly queues to await their train. It was also the first time that I'd seen raised bumps on tiles to give blind people information and warnings. We stood on our letter and waited. At five to seven I thought the train was going to be late. Silly me. At three minutes to seven the train pulled in, our carriage stopped in front of our noses and we found our names on our seats. Remembering how late we had booked our seats and how early in the morning it was, this was the first of the JTB miracles. The interior was immaculate and there were flowers in little wall vases between the windows. As the second hand ticked towards the hour, the doors closed and the train moved off exactly on time. It rocketed through the countryside at an incredible speed and all I could think about was the luggage.

During the journey, our ticket was collected, revealing the slogan 'Red Flag' on the next one. As we pulled into a small country station there was a girl standing with a red flag so we got off and were pointed to a bus which took us to a small Japanese hotel, I think they are called *riokhan*, and there on the counter were two envelopes containing our room keys with our names on the outside. We had never stopped moving since we left our luggage but when we got into the room, there it was. Magic.

That was the way it was for the whole Japanese trip, incredibly efficient. Every room we went to had shaving gear and toothbrushes and kimonos. They thought we were crazy to be carrying all the luggage and I agreed with them. The televisions were bi-lingual and stereo. The first night we slept in a Japanese inn and they pulled the bed out of a cupboard and unrolled it on to the tatami matting all I could think of was that I had just paid £3,000 for a four-poster bed and this was more comfortable.

Japan ... Singapore ... Bahrain – and it was on the trip to Bahrain that I lost my fear of death. It was an overnight trip and I went to sleep on the floor. I have never been able to sleep while in the seat on a plane. What I didn't know is that you are not allowed to sleep on the floor but nobody saw me down there. There is a lack of oxygen or something and I woke up dizzy. Thinking that I must get into the toilets, I started to head through the kitchen area of the plane.

I woke up on the floor. Panicking stewards and stewardesses surrounded me. It wasn't their fault but this was one passenger they didn't want to lose. An oxygen mask was stuck on my face but at the exact moment I awoke I can clearly remember feeling fine. Some water seemed to trickling down my face and then I knew why they were in a panic. I had cut my face badly on the way down but I had felt no pain. I can remember thinking, 'I don't feel very ...' and waking up thinking only a few seconds had passed. I'd been out for a while, apparently.

The next day, by the pool in Bahrain, a man asked if I'd been mugged. I explained what had happened and how strange it had all felt. 'I think death is like that, ' he said and instantly I just knew he was right. One day, not for a while yet, I hope, I will think, 'I don't feel very ...' and then I will feel nothing ever again. There will be no pain because that is a physical impossibility. All pain and feelings will stop, so there will be nothing. You can't be frightened of 'nothing', can you? I have never been afraid of death since.

From Bahrain we went to Cairo, where we had a quick look round before going on one of the most interesting and photogenic trips of my life. We flew to join a Sheraton cruiser and cruised down the Nile. Most things haven't changed there in thousands of years. What made it even better was that there were only two English people, travel agents, on the boat and they didn't split on me. Debbie and I were anonymous, surrounded, in Egypt, mostly by Jewish ladies from Florida.

It was a truly fascinating trip and I started to call the tour guide by the name that I had heard one of the crew use. It sounded like 'Affaff'. She laughed, strangely, but kept friendly.

Apparently I was calling her 'very fat'. How to make friends, by Paul Daniels.

On one outing, I asked her about someone called King Tut. She had been talking about him and I wanted to know if he was a relative of Tutankhamun.

'It's the same man,' she said. 'At that time in history, all kings, pharaohs, and leaders were given virgin birth and called Son of God. In this case, Tut was called the Son of the Sun God. It's the same with your Jesus Christ.'

You could have knocked me down with the proverbial feather. In that moment, just as some people claim to have seen the light and found Christianity, or Buddhism or any of the world's religions, I became a Born-Again Atheist. Suddenly I could understand why we needed religion in the past, to keep law and order and discipline among primitive peoples, but for the life of me I couldn't understand why the ancient superstitions and fears were being perpetuated today. Surely by now we could teach a better way of understanding why it is not only wrong, but fairly stupid, to be a bad person, even a criminal.

As the cruise down the Nile came to an end, they held a talent show on board. Everybody had to come to the party in Egyptian-style dress and Affaff went around trying to get people to join in the show. Some said they would belly dance but only for a minute, some Belgians said they would do a sketch, which would last six minutes, and eventually she got to me. 'Put me down for an hour-and-a-half,' I said and she laughed out loud.

'Oh, Mr Daniels, you are so funny.'

Eventually, I persuaded her to put everyone else on first and I would fill in whatever time that was left at the end. I hadn't worked in months and I got lucky. In the first few minutes I got heckled by one of the guides and was able to 'attack' back. At the end, the captain looked at his table of prizes and announced that he felt I should have the lot. I explained that wasn't fair because I did this for a living, so I just took a bone letter opener as a souvenir.

Back in Cairo, on the last day of our holiday, I inadvertently polished off a drink containing ice whilst trying to design a T-shirt for the Sheraton hotel manager. For three months I had travelled the world avoiding such a mistake. The next morning at the airport, I had Tutankhamun's revenge and two elderly English nurses literally dragged me into the ladies' toilet in order to clean me up. I was grateful for these elderly ladies, who cared enough to put their concern into action. Thanks to them, I was able to make it to the plane and home.

In the last couple of weeks of that memorable trip, I had lost my fear of death and also lost my fear of eternal damnation. I felt so much better about the so-called mysteries of life and death. I was happier than ever before. To make sure, I came home and did a lot of reading. It's all there, in the books, so the guys who run the business of the churches and the religions must know it, too. I wonder why they don't tell us? Even the Roman Catholic Church, the 'founders' of the spread of Christianity, was the result of a decision in the Roman Senate so they could still rule the world when they were losing their military control. Don't believe me? Run the Time Line in Microsoft's *Encarta* and look at when military power ended and religious power began. It's the same date.

So I returned to England a changed, happier man.

I had more than a shock when I got home. My eldest son, Paul, has a lot of charm and is liked by many people. Sadly, he has never matured and taken responsibility for himself and by no means appeared to want to. He has an excellent brain for solving problems but he has never accepted the task of living and improving his lot in life.

Paul Jnr's first job at 16 was down at Smith's Docks near Middlesbrough, but the ports were closing as the industry went into decline. I offered him a job looking after a novelty exhibition and shop that I owned in Blackpool. He took the post of manager and began to oversee the company, but never put his heart into it. He would spend all day playing on the slot machines rather than run the business. When the shop closed at the end of the season, I took him on as part of my stage management team and he looked after my props.

Unfortunately, he was never honest, which I thought was odd, because he was brought up to believe in the value of truthfulness. When he started drinking heavily, this was also in strong contrast to the rest of our family history. None of this behaviour seemed to fit in.

I still kept him on as part of my team at the Prince of Wales Theatre, but money and jewellery would consistently go missing from my dressing room. You never want to think ill of your own child. With no evidence that it was Paul, I started to watch him very closely and on one occasion I saw him remove a bundle of cash. I discovered at this time that Paul lied and, in fact, lied very well. He had become a master of deception but it wasn't magical.

While I was on my three-month sojourn with Debbie, Paul got drunk and stole my Ferrari. It may be odd to say that my own son stole my car, but I was down on the insurance as the sole driver. It also had the number plate MAG 1C and was the most recognisable car in town. Consequently, the moment he took it out, the police picked him up to find out who on earth was driving Paul Daniels' car. When the officers stopped him and asked for his name, he said, 'Paul Daniels', because that's who he is. They recognised that he was drunk, arrested him and put my car back in my garage for me. That was nice of them.

Unbelievably, a few nights later, he took it again. This time he was charged and was due to appear in court. It was all such odd behaviour that we had a psychiatrist examine him. The report pointed out that Paul seemed to be suffering from a mild case of schizophrenia. From that moment on, Paul seemed to refuse to want to live in any type of normal, decent world. He certainly didn't want to be in my world at all and this was, and is, extremely hurtful to me.

There was worse to come but I didn't know it. You can't help wishing your kids are going to do better than you have and not necessarily in your own business. Paul had become a real worry.

There was a telephone call from Mervyn that gave me another jolt the first day back from the trip.

'You are doing a Royal show tomorrow night in honour of those who fought in the Falklands.'

Wherever we had gone in the world, according to all the news programmes and newspapers, we were losing the war with Argentina. We came home expecting to have to learn Spanish. The fact that we'd won came as a big surprise to me and Debbie. I found out where the show was and Mervyn had organised an illusion to be delivered to London from my stores in Milton Keynes.

'It's the Backstage Illusion,' he said.

'Really? Who's going in it?' (This trick involved two people.)

'Roger Moore and Twiggy,' came the reply.

'You've got to be kidding. Roger Moore will never fit in it.'

I altered the illusion so that I would 'present' it to Roger on stage and he would get a surprise when one person changed into another, in this case Debbie to Twiggy.

The next morning saw me in the theatre and the usual mayhem of a Royal show was going on. Bernard Delfont came and said 'Hello' to me in the stalls and asked where I had been and what I was up to, the usual stuff. Robert Nesbitt was directing the action on stage. The Royal Box was being decorated with flowers. As the work was coming to a conclusion, I leaned across and tapped Bernie on the shoulder.

'Excuse me, Bernie, it's about the flowers on the Royal Box.'

The cigar twitched in the air. 'Yes, very nice, very tasteful.'

'Yes, they look lovely, but aren't those the colours of the Argentinian flag?'

The cigar froze and then, 'Robert, Robert ...'

And off he went. It was too late to rebuild all the work so they stuck some other flowers in. Not quite as nice looking, but possibly more politically correct.

I rehearsed the trick with Debbie and Twiggy. Roger turned up later and I walked him around it without telling him the end. He went away and I never saw him again until about 15 minutes before we were due onstage. There was a knock at the dressing room door and, when I opened it, Roger stood there swaying slightly.

'I owe you an apology. I'm pissed.'

Apparently, he had had too many friends in the show and he had spent all the evening enjoying their company.

My entrance came and I did a small opening trick. Roger entered to well-deserved applause and told a slightly risqué joke. In case he had any more up his sleeve, I rapidly went into the trick and pulled him around the stage, pushing his head down to look under the table, lifting him up and practically running through the staging of the illusion. At the end we got the raised eyebrow bemused look for which he was famous through so many 'hero' roles as Twiggy appeared and we were off.

What the audience thought of the little conjurer bullying Agent 007 all over the stage I'll never know.

I had other problems of my own. I still didn't want to go to work on stage despite Richard Mills asking me to do a season at the Opera House in Blackpool. It's a great venue but I had no 'drive' in me. I didn't know what I wanted to do.

The musical *Annie* was on in Bournemouth and I went to see it with a girlfriend. As the curtain came down on this very uplifting musical, I said to her that the audience all seemed to be on a high.

'That's what happens in your show,' she said.

'You've got to be kidding.'

'No, surely you must know they all go out really happy?'

I had no idea. You go on stage and you do your thing. I knew I made them laugh but I had no sense of what happened when the curtain came down. WOW. If I could do that, then I *should* do that! That night I telephoned Richard and asked whether the Opera House was still 'on'. When he said that it was, I sat up all night and wrote the show.

Next day it was in his office for consideration with all the guest acts, tricks and illusions suggested. Dick Hurran was called in and fought with the Delfont budgets to get the best costumes and scenery. He booked the Valabertinis, who I think came from Czechoslovakia and did an act on very high unicycles. He booked Jean Claude and his footballers and an act called the Koziaks from Hungary. This act had been on my television show and caused me to ponder on the British love of amateurism. The week the show was transmitted a young girl, also from behind the Iron Curtain, had competed in the Olympics. The media had gone crazy over the fact that she had done a backward somersault on the beam. All credit to her for that but the beam is about 4in wide and bolted down solidly at both ends.

The woman in the Koziaks' act did a double backwards somersault, not on a wide beam, but on a round, flexible, pole vaulter's pole that was being held at the ends by two men. As she did the somersaults she also managed to go through a hoop that she was holding. A little later she did a forward somersault on the same pole, a much harder thing to do as you can't see the landing area coming. This woman never even wobbled on landing; it was if she was on the floor with all that space to land on. Nobody in the media noticed.

I got a telephone call from Dick.

'You know in the scene from *Barnum* that closes the first half, well, who is going to sing the "Join the Circus" number? Everyone in the show is French or Hungarian or Czech.'

I asked him to let me think about it. The ending of the first half was very important in making the show spectacular and featured illusions built around the theme of the circus. The Ringmaster had to sing the song. I got a copy of the music, telephoned Mary Hammond, one of the best voice coaches and made an appointment. When I arrived I told her that I didn't have any time for singing lessons but would she listen to me and tell me whether I could handle the number on stage.

'If I can't then tell me, because I don't want to be an idiot up there.' She asked me to sing a couple of notes that she played on the piano but I explained that the 'plonk' of a piano note bore no relationship to the sound of a voice so I couldn't do that. She played the intro to the song and I couldn't do it. I felt embarrassed and most peculiar standing there with no audience. I stopped her, took a breather, then closed my eyes and 'saw' the theatre. She played, I sang and I can remember at the end hitting a note that I had no idea my voice could reach. Mary had no doubts I could do it so I phoned Dick and told him I would do the number. It made my year! All that 'rehearsing' in the bath had finally paid off.

The show we did at the Opera House in Blackpool was the last of the really big Variety shows in that enormous theatre. It seated somewhere in the region of 3,300 people and had a huge stage. As well as the speciality acts, we had a full orchestra pit and 16 dancers. The heyday of summer seasons was coming to a close and in a large auditorium like that, even an audience of 1,500 would only half-fill the place. They loved the show, though, and that's the important thing.

One night I was asked to come down to the stage door and

this was quite a hike at the Opera House. The fly floor was very high and the dressing rooms were above that. You have to come down in a lift and pray that it doesn't break down during the show. The doorkeeper had said that there was a young girl who didn't seem very well, so down I went to see what the trouble was about. I stepped out of the lift and walked down the side of the stage area. Sure enough, there was a girl in her late teens and the doorkeeper had got her a chair. A man who turned out to be her father was with her. As I approached she seemed to go into a fit and I was really worried about her.

'Oh don't worry, Mr Daniels,' said her father, 'she even has orgasms like that when she sees you on the telly.' There's not a lot you can say in those situations so I signed her autograph book and went back to my room very quickly. See, I told you I was a sex symbol.

Another group of women started following me around the functions and fetes I attended in the area. I didn't mind them at all. They were a really funny gang and the 'leader', Karen, wrote very funny poems about their adventures following me around. Apparently, Karen's daughter had developed a crush on me and, as I parked near the offices her mother worked in, asked her to keep an eye out for me. That's how the Paul Daniels Spotters were born. They have all now left the office and got different jobs but from time to time they still turn up, hiring buses or whatever to travel the country, and I love them all.

The Opera House was the last of the summer seasons I was to do for a very long time. That side of our business was dwindling and I had been lucky enough to perform in the big ones. I talked to the Delfont organisation about the possibility of doing a production show in Majorca or somewhere similar. I had, for a while, gone out with a lovely girl who was a manager with Thomson's holidays and she told me just how many people they sent out every week. I thought that perhaps they would like a change from flamenco dancers, but the idea never went ahead.

In a way, I am glad that I didn't get involved with foreign seasons because I was able to throw myself into the world of corporate entertainment and do even more television.

CHAPTER 12

IT'S MAGIC

It's the Millennium that everybody talks about and very few can pronounce. The Nineties had seen Nelson Mandela released and apartheid ended; the information age had arrived with the home use of the Internet; and Michael Jackson married Elvis Presley's daughter, Lisa Marie. There was hope for us all.

Well, if I thought my life was busy when I was at the Prince of Wales, in the Eighties it went insane. Television, the great devourer of material, became my home. I did magic shows, game shows, guest appearances, specials and even a medical programme and *QED*. My mind was always whirring away trying to solve problems, usually related to magic, for future presentations. I exaggerate when I say 'future', it was usually for a programme that was being recorded the following day. I'm a devil for leaving everything to the last minute and rarely think things out until absolutely necessary.

There is no way, in this book, that I can cover everything that happened to me in the maddest of the television years, but I'll tell you some of the stories and maybe you'll get a flavour of my life. I hope so.

Take a week in the life of *The Paul Daniels Magic Show*. Months before recording, the team would have got together and discussed in general what was going to happen. A little later there would be another meeting and so on until we had all the tricks we would like to do with their titles on postcards.

Just before the series began, there would be meetings with designers and prop-makers, special effects men and technicians, and those postcards would be divided up into 'shows' for the coming weeks. A certain illusion would be postponed because it would take longer to build, another kept as a 'spare' in case anything went wrong.

If the show was to be recorded on, say, Saturday evening, on the Monday of that week we would all meet at the rehearsal rooms in Acton, sit around the table and discuss the items on the postcards. There would be the Producer, the Director, me, Debbie, Ali Bongo, Gil Leaney, Barry Murray, Graham Reed, the floor manager (that's the television equivalent of the stage manager in a theatre) and at least one assistant floor manager known as a 'gopher'.

The floor of the rehearsal room would be covered in long strips of coloured tapes to outline where the set would be standing as well as any permanent fixtures. This was so we could get a feeling of how much room we had around illusions or in dance routines and the like.

We would talk about the various routines that we hoped to do and the gopher would start to make phone calls to the props buyers as we expanded the concepts and brought in more gags. Sometimes, even that simple operation would lead to some wondrous errors.

I walked in one morning to find a gross of drinking glasses and, when I asked what they were for, I was told that we had ordered them. The week's programme was there in rough script form and I looked through it but could find no need of 144 drinking glasses. Slowly, an idea formed in my mind and I looked down the list again. There was a trick to which we had added a drinking glass. In case I dropped it, I had put in a request for two glasses, not to the gopher, but to a young person who was learning the job. They had gone to the gopher and, in case the fragile glasses were broken, had ordered four. The gopher couldn't get through on the phone to the buyers so asked the floor manager to do it and said that we needed eight. You're ahead of me now, aren't you? The floor manager ordered 16 but the buyer responsible for our show wasn't available so he left a message with his department. The message was passed along twice and became first 32 and then 64. The buyer, thinking that we needed 64 drinking glasses for some illusion or other knew that he would have difficulty ordering 128 and went for the round figure of one gross. We sent them back.

By the Tuesday of the recording week, you would have found us still sitting around the table tearing the routines to pieces and generally waiting for props to arrive. It was quite amazing the number of times they didn't arrive until the actual recording day so we used to 'talk' the tricks through rather than physically do them.

Wednesday, and a couple of bits would have drifted in, if we were lucky, and we would also start talking about the following week and what we might do in that recording. During the afternoon, it was common for the guest acts to have flown in and we would watch them rehearse, suggesting moves that would enhance their television appearance. Television is different to theatre, circus and cabaret and needs to be 'shot' for the small screen. That's why theatre shows, recorded for television showing, are never as good as the show specifically created for the television screen in a studio. I guess it is difficult to cross from one medium to another.

Thursday morning would see all the cameramen, lighting men, sound men, make-up and costume designers gathered round to see what we were going to do. If there was anything specifically needed for costume they would have been told well in advance wherever possible but sometimes we would pop a request in at the last minute. In those days, the BBC studios were much better served than they are now. The costume department, for example, could call on a vast range of clothing from within their own store; there were scenery and props departments, and even make-up could call on a stock of wigs and beards and even scars! When you are making creative light entertainment shows regularly you can often have a great idea at the last minute that will bring the whole programme to life. Sadly, nowadays, all those fabulous facilities have gone and I feel sorry for the programme makers.

This was the morning when the lighting man would ask about, or if he was very lucky, see the colours of the costumes and the illusions to complement them with his lights. The cameramen, working with the director, would work out the choreography of the cameras. Most cameras are mounted on huge, solid wheeled bases that can be slid across the concrete floor of the studios. One of the director's jobs, usually worked out in conjunction with the chief cameraman, is to make sure that when he is getting his shots and they are zooming around the floor, that they don't crash into each other, cross the shots in vision or even run over the cables. To see a camera's metal apron cut through a cable is quite spectacular. Sparks and cameramen shoot off in every direction.

You may have wondered at the number of people listed in the credits at the end of a programme or a film but, believe me, if they weren't important they wouldn't be there. They cost money, that's why.

On Friday we would go over it all again, and again, and

again, hopefully with props and, if the studio was not in use and our set was being built, we would go down and have a very slow walk through on the studio floor.

Saturday being the recording day, we would all be in the studios. Ali and Barry would sit by the director's chair, up in the director's box, watching all the shots to see whether I made a mistake or had the wrong angle. I would walk through the show very, very slowly in the morning so that everyone could make their notes and learn where they should be. After lunch we would do it again, a little faster, but inevitably there would be mistakes and we would all stop, go back and do that bit again. Just before tea we would do a fast run in the clothes we were using in the show, called a dress run.

During tea, I would go over any last-minute changes or notes with the Producer and then, at around 7.15pm, the warm-up man would go on to the floor, greet the audience, explain what was happening and generally whoop them up. Then he would introduce me and as I, too, greeted them and cracked a few gags, I would be eyeballing the individual members of the audience and pointing to suitable people for the participation tricks. Ali would have them fitted with microphones. I never met these people before the actual recording of the tricks because I thought it gave a more natural, ad-lib feel to the show. How did I pick them? Generally I would look for happy, cleanly dressed people aged between 25 and 35 if I could. It didn't always work out and, of course, there were exceptions but that was my general rule. In the clubs, I had learnt that under 25 they could be cocky and think that they were being funny when they weren't. Over 35 and they could develop pomposity. Not everyone fits those descriptions, thank goodness.

At 7.30pm the show would start to be recorded and it was all over by 10.00pm. You may be surprised that it takes that long but there were always stops for costume changes or lighting changes, and sets to be cleared or placed, so it takes time.

Frequently, we were back in the rehearsal rooms on Sunday morning, especially when the panic started to set in the further into the series we got. Game, or quiz, shows were different. There would be a couple of meetings before the series started recording where the production team would sit around and go over the questions a few times trying to weed out those that were too hard, or unsuitable, or with doubtful answers.

Then we would go into the studios on the morning of the show and while I was doing a final question check and reading up on the contestants, the cameraman and the director would be shooting the prizes for insertion during the recording. The computers and the lighting would all be checked at the same time.

The contestants were brought in for lunch where I would sit and meet them, talk to them and try to become a 'friend'. After lunch we would go into a small lounge where I would go over all the rules and the movements of the show and, most importantly, tell them 'why'. I would try to ensure that they were as comfortable as they could be in this weird environment and then leave them to watch a previously recorded episode of the game so that they were brought 'up to date' in their minds.

While they were watching that I would go and make notes on their fact sheets of details gathered over lunch. We would all meet up in the studios and both teams would get to play the game, but with different questions from the evening, of course. Then it was time for tea and at 7.30pm we would record the first show; I would get changed and then we would record the second show.

I started making game shows because the BBC wanted me to do more magic shows and I refused. The executives don't really think things through. To explain this, I have to take you back in time a long way, folks.

IT'S MAGIC

There were major stars of the Variety theatre, people like Max Miller, George Formby and Gracie Fields. If you haven't heard of them then don't worry, just accept the fact that they were major stars and as big as anything we have now. Even later, in the clubs, we had our own stars. Tom Jones was one example. Shirley Bassey was another. We got to see these people once a year and it was a big event in our entertainment calendar.

When television gets its hands on a great entertainer, the bosses don't really look at the long term, they saturate the screens with him or her. Russ Abbott is a fantastic live entertainer in many different fields but nobody can be fantastic 26 weeks in a row. The audience gets too used to the brilliance and it becomes too normal for them. Was there ever a better couple on the screens than the two Ronnies, yet even there, towards the end, I heard people saying they weren't as good as they used to be. I think the real problem was that they were exactly as good as they used to be and, sadly, were over-exposed.

I wouldn't do more than ten magic shows a year, with a Christmas Special sometimes as an extra. So they asked me to do a game show. *Odd One Out* was the first, later *Every Second Counts* and finally *Wipeout*. So many of the other game show hosts told me that they thought *Every Second Counts* was the finest format of all the games that were on air. It certainly built up the tension and worked towards an exciting climax. Two stories from that show come to mind.

A Scots couple walked down towards me, stood on the marks as they had at rehearsal and, as was normal for the game, I asked the wife to tell me all about her husband. She started to speak and I interrupted, 'You're not English, are you?' This was obvious from her very broad accent and I was playing the idiot.

'Och, no, we're from Glasgow.'

Taking the mickey, I came back with, 'Now that's a shame,

because I have heard that the people from Edinburgh speak the finest English in the British Isles.'

This was a red rag to a bull.

'Edinburgh? EDINBURGH? I'll tell you about Edinburgh. His mither comes from Edinburgh and they're all *mean*.'

She was totally oblivious to the cameras and her husband trying to shut her up.

'When you gae roond to his mither's hoose she always says, "You'll have had your dinner then?" just so she does'na have to give you any?'

The audience were howling and slowly it dawned on her that she was being recorded. Her face was, as they say, a picture.

Another couple came down and my information was that they came from Yorkshire. At lunch they had talked with broad Yorkshire accents and I'll change the names here to protect the innocent. He was a stocky, happy guy and his wife, slim and slightly taller, with a pretty face. I asked her to tell me all about him and before she could start, he came in with an American southern drawl, 'let me introduce myself. I am Beauregarde Johnson and ...'

I stopped him. 'What?'

His wife explained, 'He sings part time in a country and western band. He's very good.' She went on to explain what he really did and what he was really called. I asked him to tell me about his wife.

'This is my beautiful wife Sheila. She works in a butcher's shop but really she wants to be a nurse.'

'I don't,' said Sheila.

He never turned a hair. He smiled at me. 'She does.'

'I don't.'

'She does, she's even got the uniform.'

'I've got the hat and the suspenders and that's all he cares about.'

IT'S MAGIC

We collapsed – me, the audience and the cameramen.

When I started doing the game shows, I could not believe how inefficient the system was. Whether it was mine or anyone else's game, we would record two shows on, say, a Saturday evening and two shows the following Saturday and so on. The whole of the set with its electronics and lighting rigs would be erected and taken down and so on until eventually it got tattier and tattier. I asked why we couldn't do two on a Saturday and two on a Sunday, reducing the wasted time putting the sets up and down. They thought this was a great idea. I was amazed because I knew in America they do five shows a day for a week and then they have twenty-five shows in the can.

After a season of four shows a weekend, I tried to persuade them that we could do the whole series in one bash by recording day after day until it was all finished. This, I pointed out, would be more economical for all of us. I wouldn't have broken weeks in my calendar and could take on more live work and they would reduce their costs enormously because they wouldn't have to put the sets up and down all the time, wouldn't have to re-set all the lighting, and the cameramen would know all the shots.

The bosses told me that the strain on the crew would be too great. What the bosses didn't know was that I was very friendly with the crew, who were equally puzzled by the inefficiency of the system and had also asked why they couldn't do shows day after day. They had been told that I couldn't stand the strain.

So eventually we started to do shows day after day, taking a day off half-way through the recording of the 'season' to make sure everything was working all right and so that we could take a breather to check the coming questions and prizes.

In the meantime, the *Magic Shows* had developed not only a following of millions in the UK but they had also developed a reputation in the world of circus and cabaret. Video tapes came in from all over the world from acts hoping to be on the show. They knew that the BBC would make a better job of recording their performances than anyone else. At that time, the Corporation had the finest lighting, sound and cameramen in the world. They really did it better. I asked one of them about it and he commented that occasionally they would be having a drink with some of the crews from the commercial channels who would boast of better pay and conditions.

'So we have to do it better so that we can just smile and say, "Yes, but the end product is not as good, is it?" '

The commercial channels could never be as good for me, anyway. I hate just getting into a good play, or interesting show, only to have my interest shattered by the overblown sound of the commercial breaks. I don't want the show to be interrupted at all!

Once again, America came into my life. They had seen what I had done with the American game shows in the UK and they wanted me to go over there and present them in the same style. Most game shows came from America. I turned them down. My family was, and is, very important to me and I hate being too far away from them. I even get twitchy on holidays abroad. The Americans, as is their way, thought it was a money thing and upped the offer. It was very hard to explain to them that money didn't come into it and they went away, no doubt muttering about the crazy Limey.

ITV made me an offer to cross the channels and go to work for them. I considered this carefully and said that I couldn't go without my production team. They offered to take on the production team and put John Fisher, the Producer, on their permanent staff. We would all be on increased salaries. I reported this back at the next planning meeting. John Fisher said that he would not leave the BBC, believing that his future lay with them. Despite the considerable increase in money that it would have brought me, I decided not to break up the team and I stayed with the BBC. In retrospect I think that was a mistake, but I have no regrets. Spilt milk and all that jazz.

Time was flying by, shows came and went. Huge illusions and tiny tricks poured out of the studios and into the living rooms of the nation. Every week hundreds of letters would arrive asking about the various effects we created. To the general public they were entertaining. To the magicians they mostly commanded respect because they realised that hardly any trick arrived on the screen without being either a totally new invention, a totally new presentation or just twisted around somehow in the method. Some magicians copied the stuff, some got jealous. It didn't matter, that is the way it has always been.

The biggest talking points over the years were the Bunco Booth, the Magic Kettle that poured out any drink asked for by the audience, Silverstone race track with Jackie Stewart, the Vanishing Elephant, the British Library book test, the Disappearance of a Million Pounds, the Houdini Water Torture Escape, my 'death' on Hallowe'en, the chimpanzees and the Christmas Specials.

The Magic Kettle was a very old trick and we did it more than once, each time adding a new twist in method and presentation. A man called Robert Swadling, a great designer and maker of magic, had come to John Fisher with a new way of doing it and I had added a presentational touch so that four members of the audience could merely think of a drink, clean a glass out, pick up the kettle themselves and pour out the drink that they were thinking of. That made one magic magazine write that we had used stooges in the audience to do the trick. John was incensed and made them retract the statement. I hate stooges in the audience. American acts even 'plant' people to stand up at the right time and 'lead' a standing ovation. How do you ever know how good a standing ovation really is if you do that?

In series seven in 1985, I was taken to Silverstone and taught how to drive a racing car that had been designed by Jackie Stewart. The idea was that I would be handcuffed, tied into a sack and that would be locked into a large wooden crate. The whole box would be swung up into the air by a crane and lowered into the middle of the track. As this was happening, Jackie would get in this car and drive it once around the track and, as he completed the circuit, aim it at the wooden box in the middle of the track. He was to crash through the box, but to the viewers' astonishment, it was me who got out of the car and Jackie was seen to have been driving the crane. This was a difficult illusion to make work on screen because we had to make it obvious that no camera tricks had been involved. No camera trickery was ever used in my shows, because there just wasn't any point. If you use such methods, and I have seen them used in magic shows, then anybody could have done the stuff we did.

So I trained hard to drive the car at high speed. I was a genius. I could take on the world. I spun Debbie and others around the track to show off. Then Jackie Stewart, three times World Champion, turned up and drove me round Silverstone. I had been going backwards with the brakes on. He was the genius. The trouble was that Jackie burnt out the clutch. He had his own mechanic with him who refused all help but managed to replace the clutch in under half-an-hour. A few weeks later, the clutch went on my own car and the garage told me that it would take three days. I told them I would pay labour for half-an-hour. I knew about such things, you see.

As we got closer to the first real run-through, I noticed a man getting into a crash helmet and I asked him who he was.

'I'm the stunt man,' he said. 'I'm going to do the first drive through the box to see what happens.'

IT'S MAGIC

I don't think that I am any braver than the next guy, maybe just a bit more stupid, but I couldn't let him do it. Nobody knew for certain what would happen when the car hit the crate but, as it was my idea to do it, I couldn't risk someone else getting hurt. I drove the car and I can tell you that as you approach such a solid-looking object all your instincts scream out for you to turn away and miss it. What happened was that, every time we tried it, the box exploded over and under the car. So that was all right. The 'mistake' that we made, but it turned out to be a bonus, was that we used a red sack. We had never intended to tell the guest commentator, Mike Smith, what was going to happen anyway, so that we would get a real reaction from him, but when he saw the sack being dragged under the car after the impact, he thought that not only had I not escaped, but that it was me being dragged up the track. He nearly fainted because it looked like I had been thrown all over the place. It gave Mike a very bad turn and I don't think he got over it, asking that it never be shown on television again. It was good TV though.

In the great age of the Variety theatre, or vaudeville as it was known in America, one of the most publicised illusions of all involved the disappearance of a very large elephant. John Fisher came to an early prerecording planning meeting and asked me whether I could vanish such a large mammal. Of course, I knew all the methods that had happened in the past and I outlined them all. Elephants, as everyone knows, vanish in boxes or cages and usually in a theatre or even a cabaret environment.

'No,' said John, 'I want it to vanish outside.'

John had two good qualities. He was the best of researchers and he always tried to get me to push the limits of what had gone before. 'Wouldn't it be wonderful if it could vanish from a football field?'

'Yeah, right!'

The team didn't know whether to laugh or cry. I did what I usually did in such situations – let it fester away in my mind. At the next meeting, I came up with a logical, but very expensive, way of vanishing an elephant in the middle of a field, football or not.

Note the word 'expensive'. I could never understand the BBC's thinking when it came to expenditure. We were getting millions of viewers who were all paying their licence fees but we had a smaller budget than other programmes that had much lower ratings. Ah, if only I had been artistic, darling, I would have understood it all.

Off I went on my merry way, conjuring around the world, because that was what I had to do in between all this television world of wonder. The lads were growing up and I had a life outside the studios. Incidentally, it was while I was doing one gig that I was ferried in a bus from one venue to another, or maybe it was back to the hotel, I can't remember. I do remember that a young comedian called Jim Davidson got into the bus with his girlfriend and on the way I did a couple of card tricks. The Krankies were also in this minibus as I recall. Years later, in his autobiography, Jim wrote that I tried to 'pull' his girlfriend and was rather uncomplimentary. What he obviously didn't know was that I do card tricks for everyone. I always have a pack of cards in my pocket and it's good practice for me.

The other thing is that I didn't fancy her at all. Jim has his taste in women and I have mine.

I came back to the next planning meeting and, surprisingly, there were all the technical boys from the visual effects department.

'Go on,' said John. 'Tell them the details of how you want to vanish the elephant.'

Well, to be honest, after gallivanting around the world, I couldn't remember. It had been months since I had muttered my offering. Gil Leaney, magical adviser and a lovely man, offered help.

'We are going to use your method,' he said with a twinkle in his eye, peering into my face, as I desperately tried not to look confused.

'It's the one with the tent,' prompted Gil. I couldn't believe they were going to spend that kind of money.

My brain kicked into gear and I laid down the details of what would happen. The football field, I was told, was one the Gurkha Regiment used in their barracks. These lads are great soldiers and you don't want to upset them, believe me. I kept it as simple a plot as I could.

We would drive on to the field in a Land Rover. I would be with the Commanding Officer and a celebrity, Johnny Morris, the presenter of Animal Magic. Alighting from our vehicle we planned to walk over to and across the back of the tent. We could do this because all the sides would be laid flat. Volunteers would be allowed to stamp around or poke whatever they wanted, in and around the tent.

The greatest elephant trainer in the world, Bobby Roberts from the Roberts Circus, would bring on an elephant with Debbie riding on top and lead it into the tent. I would fire a cannon, the tent sides would fall down, a crane would lift the top off into the air and all that would be left would be Debbie. A spectacular vanish.

And that is what we did, exactly that. From concept to recording. Perfect. It cost a fortune to set up and rehearse. The elephant had to come overnight in a special truck all the way from Scotland and the trick was over in a few minutes of recording time.

The effect was so clean one newspaper printed that it had to be a camera trick, which it wasn't. Then they said that we had carefully chosen the camera angles to hide the elephant behind the tent top, which we didn't. What they had forgotten was that, as always, we had a live audience there on the field with us.

It was a great trick to pull off and when anybody asked me where did the elephant go, I always replied, 'Have you ever seen Debbie eat?'

The person it seemed to affect most was Bert Weedon, a wonderful solo guitarist and the author of the famous *Play in a Day* book. He couldn't let it rest. He wouldn't let it rest.

'Where did it go?' was his constant cry every time we met. Of course, I wouldn't tell him so he asked me to whisper it in his ear on his deathbed. I refused. Knowing Bert, he might recover.

The years went by and I asked Bert to come to the studio and play his guitar 'behind' a trick I was doing at Christmas called *Spirit Painting*. A member of the audience chose Marilyn Monroe from a list of celebrities and, as her picture appeared on a plain white piece of paper, Bert played 'Candle in the Wind'. Elton John wrote this famous piece of music, so we had a visual and audio link. Lovely.

The trick finished and the audience applauded.

'You think that you were only here to play the guitar, don't you Bert?' He nodded, obviously puzzled. A clap of my hands and stagehands appeared from everywhere and totally dismantled the set. All we were left with was the concrete floor and the bare walls of the studio. The audience were invited down to examine everything and Bert stood there as puzzled as a man can be.

'Look up in the air and, as you can see, we have a silk tent. As it comes down, please hold the sides and the corners.'

The audience did this and I turned to Bert.

'What's the one thing that you are always asking me? Over and over again, you want to know where the elephant went. Well, Bert, it went here.'

The tent was pulled up into the air again and standing next

to Bert was a three-and-a-half-ton elephant. The same elephant, in fact. You had to be there. Bert's face was a picture. The trouble is now he keeps asking me where it came from. And I never tell.

There is a very well-known trick where the magician, playing the part of a mind-reader, has someone in the audience think of a word in a book and the magician tells them what that word is. How do they do that? Pushing the limits again, we got permission to shoot an outside broadcast in the British Library. Magnus Magnusson and Lord Soper were allowed to pick any word in any book. When they did so, a librarian who we had in the studio opened a dictionary only to find that we had previously marked the same word. This was a good trick and full of interest. During the effect, the page from which they were choosing the word was shown in close up and we got hundreds of letters from people who had chosen the same word on the screen. That doesn't surprise me. It is how so-called psychics and clock starters and stoppers get their results. With millions of people watching, the odds are way in your favour of something happening somewhere.

On one occasion, we did a trick whereby I spoke softly and made people turn up their sound systems. Then I made them come closer and closer to the screens. Suddenly, there was a loud BANG and we transmitted a shattered screen 'effect' which we held on screen to give the impression that we had 'shot' their TV set. It was a good gag but we got half-a-dozen people claiming that we had broken their sets. Pure coincidence, because a transmission cannot break a television set.

Under the strictest security of all time, we borrowed f1 million from Barclays Bank, and got it to the studios surrounded by their security men and the BBC's own team. It was brought into the studio in a large safe, checked and counted by Barclays staff and verified by Robert Maxwell, the newspaper magnate. Then it was placed into a metal box with windows on the side, which was raised up on a table so that you could see under it. The table was surrounded by laser alarms and pressure pads on the floor. Suddenly, I activated the alarms, the box filled with smoke and the money was gone. Where was it? Back in the safe! This was a really good illusion to pull off because the people involved knew that we didn't have a second million. That would have been an easy way to do it but my current account was a bit thin at the time.

The strange thing was that my letter from the BBC, which set up the train of thought in the first place, merely asked me to vanish f1 million. Nowhere did it ask for me to bring it back again. I wonder what the legal ramifications of that would have been because I did work out a way to get it out of the building, despite all the security, while all the 'checkers' and the audience still thought it was there.

So, we vanished £1 million and, if you remember, Robert Maxwell was the man who managed to make a lot of money vanish from his workers' pension funds. Maybe we gave him the idea.

John sent someone to the Houdini museum at Niagara Falls to do research on the Water Torture Escape. This was arguably his most famous illusion and attempts had been made to copy the effect over the years. What we managed to do was to remake the illusion using the same dimensions and, more importantly, utilising the same method that the Master himself had employed. It was truly ingenious. Gil Leaney made the contraption and my son, Martin, was the performer. I don't think that I have ever taken more care over the risk factor. Paul Jnr came in as well to act as back-up safety and we spent the night before the recording going over and over the procedures should anything go wrong, particularly as Martin had hurt his ankles in the rehearsal and he had to be hung upside down to enter the water.

IT'S MAGIC

Some magicians criticised the presentation, which was very fast as a result of the injury. My instructions were, 'don't mess about in there. The pain may make you gasp and you will intake water. Get out as fast as you can.' He was out like greased lightning. The magicians thought we should have had more suspense: the public thought it was miraculous.

Some of the illusions we do can be quite dangerous, although the audience would not realise this. It's often the most dangerous-looking ones which are the safest because they are so tried and tested and rehearsed to perfection. However, I do design illusions for Debbie to vanish into very quickly, where she could easily hurt herself if she didn't concentrate fully.

I also have to look out for apparatus made by construction firms who may be used to working with scenery but not with magic. On one occasion, the head of a screw had not been removed and it punctured Debbie's shin. She still has a small scar, evidence that somebody forgetting to cut a bolt head off has marked a perfect pair of legs.

Imported illusions have to be carefully checked as well. A Czechoslovakian box was on standby for a future show, but we had to bring it in at the last minute when a guest artiste failed to appear. We normally dissect any new prop and check absolutely everything, but on this occasion we didn't have time and we used it straight out of the crate.

Debbie could fit in it, but it needed to be made a little more exciting. We decided to push long flaming torches through the holes where Debbie was supposed to be, 'proving' that she had disappeared. All the stuff we make is fireproofed and we assumed that this would be the same, but the blinds inside the box were certainly not. With Debbie trapped and bolted inside the box, the blind caught fire. I had walked forward to take a bow, looked round and saw the smoke. I don't think that I have ever moved so fast in bringing a trick to a conclusion. The flames were shooting upwards. This was OK, as Debbie could crouch low in the box, the problem was the fumes. They were filling the box rapidly and Debbie was starting to cough and retch with the plastic smoke. Fortunately, we got her out in time, she stood there smiling until the director said 'Cut' and then went into a coughing fit. Still, the audience were unaware, and that's what matters.

I've also had a few close calls myself when attempting some of the grander stunts for the series. The escape from a raft made by the special effects department at the BBC was one. Robinson Crusoe they were not, as the raft barely kept afloat and I still couldn't swim. Over the years, I had tried everything but with no success. Once I even met the coach of our National Swimming Team and I joined them for an early morning training session at the swimming baths. After an hour or so, he was sitting with his head in his hands in despair.

Despite the fact that I had a scuba diver underneath just in case I went in, I knew that I would sink like a stone. I had even made myself an undersuit created from bubble-wrap, in the hope that this would keep me afloat if it went wrong. Happily, I discovered that it also kept me warmer.

Fortunately, the stunt worked well, but I still got wet as the raft tipped and bobbed in the water. In breaks between rehearsals and takes, I sat in the back of the car and de-bubble-wrapped myself, with a car hair-dryer aimed at my hands and feet to try and get some blood circulating again.

The worst accident I suffered was while doing the Indian Rope Trick. We wanted to do it in the open air because that's where the legend says it was supposed to happen. Dressed in a beautiful white Indian coat and turban, I was given a handful of gunpowder, which I was to throw into the fire. This would give a lovely surprise bang, providing necessary atmospheric decoration. In rehearsals, it was very effective. One of the advisers thought it would look more authentic if I threw the gunpowder from an Indian-looking brass pot. I agreed to try and a small, vase-shaped one was found with a belly bottom and a narrow neck. As I flicked it with my right hand towards the fire, the gunpowder formed an arc, hit the flame and flashed back into the pot, which exploded. It took the surface off my right hand and ignited the nylon lining of my sleeve. The hot nylon melted into my arm and I thought to myself that, if I was to get it off again, now was the time to do it as it couldn't possibly hurt any more than it did. I pulled it off and said, 'Oh bother,' or words to that effect.

The costume designer was trained in first-aid. Running to the outside catering trucks, she grabbed a bucket of cold water and a bag of ice and plunged my hand into it. The shock waves that went up my arm were excruciating and I could see that the skin was hanging off. For years, I had been terrified of any risk of injury to my hands and even more so recently, during which time they had become my essential means of working. It's funny, but I never even gave it a thought that my hands were insured for £1 million. My insurance was very strange at the time, anyway, with each part of my body being independently insured, sadly some parts for a lot less than others.

For some strange reason, with everybody around me panicking, I became very calm and went into my slow motion, dream-like state again. Miles away from a hospital and half-way through a 'take', I recommended that we finish off the job and then I would get to a hospital. We could spray some white paint over the blackened parts of my costume and keep the cameras at a certain angle, I suggested. It all worked according to plan, but when it came to me climbing up the rope it was extremely painful. I tried to use my legs and left hand as much as possible, but in order to make it look correct, I had to use my burnt right hand, too. That was so painful, it was almost unbearable.

Having finished the 'take', I put my hand back in the bucket and was rushed to hospital, where they said it was the quick action of the costume designer that had saved my hand. I was very grateful to her.

The Indian Rope Trick is supposed to be a legend. Every time it has been written up it is always second-hand. Researchers liken it to the legends that we have of *Jack and the Beanstalk*. Apparently, the Japanese have a story of the cherry tree that grew to the sky and the Native Americans have something similar.

While putting on make-up, before the accident, I was sitting reflecting on how odd we are. There was I being 'browned up' and I remembered going to see the great K Lal show in India years before. In his illusion show, he and his assistants were 'whited up'. Funny old world. One of the musicians from the Indian band that we had employed for 'backing music' to the trick asked me what we were going to do. I told him and he came back with the most surprising comment, 'the Indian Rope Trick? Oh yes, I have seen that.' Note the difference here. He did not say that he knew someone else who had seen it, *he* had seen it.

He went on to describe something that I believe is the 'root' of the legend. Frequently, people have approached me and told me of tricks they have seen me do that I know I never did. I do know what they are talking about but the effect has been distorted, enlarged and exaggerated out of all proportion to the original.

Apparently, there is a troupe of magicians and jugglers travelling around a particular district of India and they do a trick whereby the magician plays an Indian flute and ropes rise into the air. This, by the way, is fairly easy for a magician to do, so don't dismiss the story yet. The ropes rise until the bottoms of the ropes clear the ground and the magician gets quite agitated, commanding people in the crowd to grab the bottom of the ropes to stop them rising into the air any further.

Again he plays the flute and suddenly commands the audience to look up and watch the ropes dance. He plays again and the tops of the ropes dance about in the air. When he stops playing he shouts, and the ropes drop to the floor *and the people who were holding the ropes have disappeared*.

That's a really good trick and the best bit is that it is totally possible using standard magic principles.

After the accident, we had to have a break from recording for a few weeks while my hand and arm got better. As soon as we could, we were out on the road shooting some more outside illusions, even though I was still having treatment. When we were in Scotland, I went for a change of dressing and was looked after by an Indian doctor who asked me how I had hurt myself. I told him.

'The Indian Rope Trick,' he replied. 'Oh yes, I have seen that.'

Unbelievable. He told almost the same story, coming from the same district, the only difference being that he had seen it when the travelling players came to his school and did the trick in his school hall. What a coincidence.

Somewhere in the middle of all these magic shows, a children's show, *Saturday Morning Superstore*, asked me to be a guest. I seem to remember that the host was Mike Read and I had to be 'on the floor' by 9.00am. That meant being in by 8.30am so that I could get changed and have my makeup done. I drove up to the entrance in Wood Lane and stopped the car just short of the car park barrier, the usual long arm that swings up and down. From the glass-walled office by the gate came the usual 'man in a cap'.

'You can't bring that car in here,' was the cheery early-morning greeting. I felt I was in an Al Read sketch, if you are old enough to remember that brilliant comedian.

I looked into the empty car park, lines all painted and not a car in sight.

'I'm here to do *Saturday Morning Superstore*.'

'I don't care what you are here to do, you can't park that in here.'

'Well,' I pointed into the back of the car, 'I've got all these props to unload.'

'You are not taking that car in there.'

He did not bother to tell me how I was supposed to get all the props into the studio. I hate people in any business who demand of someone, 'do you know who I am?' so I took another route.

'If you look on the list in your office you will find that they phoned me yesterday for my car registration number and organised the car park for me.'

'I don't care what they did, nobody is parking in here.'

I was left with no option but I did manage to find a different way to put it.

'Er, do you know what I do for a living?'

'I don't care what you do, I am not letting you into this car park.'

I gave up. 'OK, I'll go home. Would you phone the studio for me and just tell them that I was here, and I've gone home?'

I drove home.

While appearing at the Prince of Wales, Giffard's Barn had proved too far to get to on a regular basis. I lived in the Kensington Hilton for about nine months and then bought another house in Royal Crescent, a beautiful row of Georgian buildings opposite. Somehow, I had managed to buy one of the few houses in the crescent that had not been converted into flats. New bathrooms and a kitchen were installed and all the lights and curtains were voice activated. I was ahead of my time and, remember, he who dies with the most toys, wins. The house had one other big advantage – it was just around the corner from the studios.

In no time at all I was sitting having a coffee, feet up and watching the television. On came the programme and Mike said the usual greetings and then, 'Paul Daniels is supposed to be with us but he must have disappeared. Never mind, I'm sure he will be here soon.'

'Oh no I won't,' I said to the set, but he didn't answer me.

After about ten minutes the phone rang and it was the ever-efficient Joyce.

'What are you doing there? Have you forgotten you are supposed to be in the studios?'

I explained what had happened. Joyce had worked at the BBC for years and I had stolen her to work for me. She couldn't believe it.

'I'll ring you back,' she said.

Sure enough, she did. 'They are going to send a car for you,' she said.

I told her to ring them back and cancel it. I had a car and it was packed with the props. It was ridiculous to use licence-payers' money on a car when I was prepared to drive myself there and park in an empty car park.

'I'll ring you back,' said Joyce.

Yet again, she did. 'Can you be there in exactly 15 minutes' time, don't go beforehand. They are going to send him on a tea break to prevent any embarrassment.'

I went and did the show. On the following Tuesday evening, I was coming out of the Television Centre when I spotted a camera crew shooting a very strange-looking machine. It turned out to be the Sinclair C5, an attempt at a one-person electric vehicle. A little lamp came on in my head. I watched as the very low-slung 'car' went round and round the inner courtyard and found the man in charge of it.

'How much is that?' I asked and he told me that, fully fitted with the bright orange tonneau covers and the rear flash that made it much more visible to other traffic, it was £450.

'Here's a cheque,' I said. 'I'll take it.'

He argued back, 'Oh you can't have that one. That's the first one and it's our demonstration machine.'

'Get on the phone to Sinclair's and tell them that you are selling it to me and that tomorrow I will drive it right through London for them.'

They delivered it round the corner and the next day I had it charged up and ready to go. True to my word, I drove the C5 through London and the press loved it. I, and Sinclair, received full-page publicity and they never cashed my cheque.

A few days later, having made some phone calls to find out when he was on duty, I drove the C5 up Wood Lane and turned into the entrance to the BBC Television Centre. Out 'he' came to find out what my business was and I lay back and drove the machine under the barrier and into the car park. It was hysterical. He chased me round the car park and I drove it back under the barrier, raised my fingers in a 'formal' salute, and went home. Worth every penny, even if they'd cashed the cheque.

I've never used it since, other than to show nephews and the like. For a while, Dad and I considered hanging it on divots on the back of the Ferrari but we never got round to it.

I suppose the most famous trick I ever did at the BBC was the Iron Maiden escape. John Fisher had either approached the bosses or they had asked him to make a Hallowe'en magic special. John called the team together and we went over various 'spooky' concepts. Eventually, he asked me whether I could come up with something that would really 'spook' the nation, 'like Orson Welles did in America when he announced an invasion of Martians'.

Various ideas were mooted until I came up with the idea of

a trick going wrong. We worked on this show for longer than most and eventually the following went out as a live show on 31 October 1987. We shot the whole thing in a rather gothic setting and style.

As I remember, there was a version of a levitation done using Debbie and then, inside an old mansion, I performed a version of Fogel's Houdini Séance routine, with magic tricks to illustrate what happened at the last real séance held to try to contact the great escape artist. Eugene Burger, a strange-looking, bearded, dramatic magician created a couple of intimate magical moments, personifying ghost-storytelling with a twinkle in his eye. As I have always tried to be up to the minute with technology, the electronics company Panasonic provided a blank tape, still in its cellophane from the production line, and we put it into a free-standing, battery-operated video recorder, which was only attached to a battery-driven video camera. We recorded a shot of the house clock coming up to midnight, but little happened, only an ornament fell over. When we played the tape back, however, a ghostly shape could be seen to walk across the room.

Finally, I asked the invited audience to go next door, back into the hallway of the house. Standing on a large table base was an evil-looking illusion. This was a kind of iron Maiden cabinet, the interior of both the cabinet and the door having large metal spikes. There was obviously no spare space for anyone inside. A paper door covered the interior also and, when I was chained into this, a hopper of metal balls was opened, allowing the balls to drop through to another container that, in turn, was connected to the door release.

When this second container reached a certain weight it pulled the pin out of the release and the enormous door swung shut, metal spikes tearing through the paper and into me, if I didn't get out in time. This was all demonstrated, checked and in I went. What the viewers didn't know was that all week I had been escaping from this beast, bursting out of the paper door just before the spikes came swinging round. They also didn't know that until the afternoon of the recording, only the close members of the production team knew that I wasn't coming out. I had designed two illusions in one. We told the cameramen on the afternoon so that they would not over-react that night.

On the night of the live show I went in, the invited audience sat around, the illusion started and, as my foot started to come out through the paper door, the metal spiked door slammed shut. There was a stunned silence and then the director cut the screen to black. Instead of the happy music that always ended our shows, there was total silence except for the voice of the floor manager being cut off in mid sentence, 'Would you all please go to the next ...' The credits for the show rolled up stark white against the black screen and, at the BBC, the phones went mad.

In the house, which was well out in the country and cut off from civilisation, the audience went, uncomfortably, back into the lounge. The stage hands pulled the door open and tore away the paper. I was still standing, chained, in the same position I had occupied before the trick started.

'I can't get out,' I said and a stage hand said, 'Oh bugger, he's still alive so we'll have to come to work on Monday morning.'

Once released, I went in to the next room to reassure the audience and to remind them that this was Hallowe'en and we had just said 'BOO' to the nation. Anne Robinson, the journalist who now presents television shows, looked at me in amazement, total amazement.

'Get me a phone,' she demanded, knowing she was on top of one of the best stories of the year. We wouldn't let her get to a phone because we didn't want a leak to the papers before they went out for the next day. She has never given me a good write-up since, saying in no uncertain terms that she doesn't like me as a person. Amazing that she has this perception seeing as how, apart from passing her once in a corridor, that was the only time that she has ever met me. I can't tell you how that breaks my heart.

Meanwhile, the switchboard at the BBC was blocked. The telephonists couldn't give an answer for quite a while because they didn't know what the answer was. John Fisher was dancing around the house in delight that we had pulled it off and we all had quite a party after the show. The phone lines were blocked for three days and we had created an 'event' like Orson Welles and his *War of the Worlds*.

The BBC being what it was, and the schedules being so tight, despite the live Hallowe'en show being created on the Saturday night, we all had to be in the studios for a Sunday recording of one of the series.

I sailed in bright and breezy, still on a high and went into my allocated dressing room. The team were already in and waiting for me. John's face showed one of his tight upper lips.

'Well, I'm glad you're happy,' he said, 'because you might have cost us our jobs.'
I couldn't believe it. The whole event had been approved by John, I had come up with the concept, it was all built and recorded under his supervision and the night before he had been dancing on air. Now, in one sentence, it was all down to me. We had done what we set out to do, we had made a good programme. He should have stood his ground. Apparently, the BBC were not happy about the fuss and the publicity. The Head of Light Entertainment made one of his rare trips to visit us at work and started to give me a ticking off based on the fact that the *Sun* newspaper had said that our viewers had phoned in their thousands to complain. I called the BBC operators to find out what was happening and their comment was, 'Well, you've

given us a lot of work with everyone phoning to ask if you are all right. When we tell them that it was a trick, mostly they just laugh and say, "Oh no, he's fooled us again." '

They may have had a few complaints but the problem with the BBC is that it gives enormous credibility to the *few* complaints it gets out of the millions of viewers who don't.

'Be that as it may be,' said the Head. 'The Board are not very happy.' 'Then let me go and talk to them,' I said. 'Let me tell them about the operators and the people's reactions. Let me tell them that the viewers must be sick to the back teeth of plastic television and knowing what is going to happen next. What this place needs is more Hitchcocks and Spielbergs and Cecil B De Milles. And if it keeps everybody happy I'll tear this bloody thing up.'

In my briefcase, I had my contract with the Beeb.

'There's no need to go that far,' he said and the whole matter was never mentioned again.

I went to work in Naples, to entertain United Nations staff I think. An agent, and now a friend, Kenneth Earle, had fixed it all up and he had put together a mini-show. We had a guitar player who would also be our musical director, eight dancers, a comedian who worked under the stage name Geronimo Tate and me. The order would be dancers, Geronimo, dancers, me, finale with everyone. We went by train. I know that sounds like a horrendous journey, and it was.

There's something you should know about Geronimo's act. There is a very famous recording of Billy Eckstine and Sarah Vaughan singing 'Passing Strangers'. They alternate the lines, Billy's rich, deep voice contrasting against Sarah's higher, sweeter sound. These people were big stars and were known as 'singers' singers'. Geronimo had turned this into a comedy ending to his act. He had two hats and he would wear the man's hat and do Billy's voice switching hats very quickly to do

Sarah's. It was a good bit of business and would always get him off to good applause.

We arrived in Naples quite a few days early which surprised our UN organisers. They asked Kenny if we would mind doing a show up the coast a little for some troops stationed there. The UN organised transport and offered extra money for the extra show so we loaded up and off we went.

I don't know who built that place but somebody had obviously been to Sunderland and had a look at the designs of north-east clubs. It was a duplicate of a working men's club and Geronimo and I felt at home. The stage was in the corner of the room and we were to get changed in a curtained-off corridor. We had a lot of backstage visitors because the girls were getting changed in there as well.

The American equivalent of the Concert Chairman came around to inform us how delighted he was to have the Ing-glish show and that he was going to put another act on first to warm the audience up for us. Off he went and we heard an unbelievable introduction, worse than any clubland chairman back home, and this was to a mixed audience. In the UK, it is quite common to see the Chairman knocking on the microphone to see if it is on. He usually hears his knocks coming out of the speakers and then comes out with, 'Give order, I said give order. Pulleeeze. Right around the room. ATHankYEW'

The American went through a similar routine. He, too, knocked the microphone, but then he announced, 'Anow HEAR this. ANOW Hear this. Tonight ERLADIES AND GENTLEMEN,' every consonant was punched into the microphone, 'we have for you, the Ing-glish Show.' Loud cheering. 'These people have come all the way from Ingerland to entertain yew. I do not want to hear any bad language of any type. Do you understand me here? I do not want anybody shouting out f★★★, c★★★, b★★★★★★★,' and he went through the list. 'We are going to get the evening started by bringing on another entertainer to get yew all in the mood. Give a big hand to Billy Eckstine.' Our jaws all hit the ground. Out walked one of the all-time great recording artists and he sang. Geronimo was saying, 'What do I do? What do I do?' and I told him to do what he always did and it went well when it was his turn.

We went back to Naples and they asked us to do a show in a nightclub in town that was used as a club by the American Navy. More money? No problem. I'll change the names to protect me. I do know it was not a good place to be. The walls and the pillars holding up the ceiling were painted in what appeared to be black tar. The chairs and tables were cheap and nasty and the whole affair was run by two guys who I will call Max and Louie. I think they had a licence to run the place on behalf of the American government, but to us they looked as though they should have had 'mafia' tattooed on their heads. Later, they turned out to be nice guys, but one look and they terrified me.

The club had a stage in the middle of one room with an extension that projected forward into the room. This is always called a runout. The dressing room was behind the band on the stage with no other way out of it but to cross the stage. The American Navy is a 'dry' navy, or it was then. No alcoholic drinks were allowed on board. Any type of drug could be had, but no booze.

In this place, the booze was meeting the drugs and as the show continued, you could hear men sitting on the floor in dark corners, giggling in a silly, high, way. Geronimo didn't last long. Just before I went on, the girls, all dressed in black, did a routine to the music from *Shaft*. Every black member of the audience was on his feet, punching the air and chanting 'Shaft, Shaft, Shaft' in time to the music. The girls finished the routine and formed a gesturing tunnel for me to walk on, carrying my act. The black guys kept chanting even after the girls had gone. I said nothing, just started shuffling cards without speaking. As the shuffles got more and more complicated I stared them down into their seats. The final guy was huge and I thought he would never go, but he did. Only then did I start the act.

If I was to pick the hardest night of my life, that was it. Prostitutes were working the room and would take a guy out into the alley, crossing the stage area to get him there and have him back in his seat before I had finished the trick I was doing when they left. Military police would jump on to the stage, push me off the microphone (literally) and announce, 'Now hear this. Now hear this. Furlough is cancelled for USS ...' or 'Now hear this. Now hear this. A wallet has been found in the alley and...' It didn't matter one jot that I was up there. I would win the audience round and then lose them again. This happened over and over so I built it into the act and made fun of the police. The sailors loved it and gave me quite an ovation at the end.

I walked into the dressing room and nearly passed out. The concentration had been tremendous and I needed air. I asked the guitarist and Kenny to pack up the act and then I did something really stupid. Dressed in an English dinner suit, complete with evening shirt and bow tie, I walked out into the waterfront streets of Naples. It was foggy, murky and dark. I walked and walked, trying to get the show out of my head. I heard footsteps and it dawned on me where I was. I got my back to the wall and two gorillas came out of the mist. See Naples and die.

'Is youse called Daniels?'

I nodded.

'The Boss wants to see ya.' At last, I was in the movies. With one on either side I was escorted back to the club and taken upstairs where Max and Louie had a restaurant, arguably the best appointed restaurant I have ever been in. The head waiter was in tails and the contrast with downstairs was ludicrous. As they had been waiting for me before starting the meal, I explained where I had been. Max said, 'that was a very foolish thing to do, Paul. You are lucky that my guys were able to recognise you.'

How many guys are walking around Naples at 1.00am in a dinner suit?

The meal was superb and, as we sat at a long table, Max next to me and then everybody spread down the sides to where Louie was sitting at the other end, I started to do table-top magic. I did tricks and gags with knives, forks, spoons, bread rolls, napkins, bottles and whatever was around. Some were for everybody, some were for Max alone. Eventually, after a card trick, he asked if I played Poker. I lied. I said 'no' and asked him about the game. He asked me to deal five cards each to him and me so I shuffled, cut and dealt.

We picked up our hands and he explained about having a pair and having two pairs and so on.

'What's the best thing you can have?' I asked.

'A Royal Flush, that's the ten through King in one suit.'

'You mean like 10, Jack, Queen, King, Ace in Hearts?'

He nodded.

'Oh,' I said, surprised (what an actor), 'I've got that.'

Out of the corner of his mouth, Max called Louie down to our end of the table. Louie towered over us as we sat there.

'Look at that, Louie. The guy never even played Poker before and look what he got.'

Louie looked pityingly at Max.

'Who shuffled the cards, Max?'

'He did.'

SMACK. Louie hit Max across the face and it wasn't a light tap. Max hardly flinched.

'Who cut the cards, Max?'

'He did.'

SMACK again.

'Who dealt the cards, Max?'

'He did.'

SMACK.

'Of course he got the Royal Flush, you've seen him with a pack of cards. He cheats.'

I hotly denied this scurrilous attack on my honour and told Louie I just got lucky. 'You do all the shuffling and let's try again,' I said. 'I really want to learn this game.

Louie took the cards, cut them and dealt the cards to me, Max and himself. He tabled the remainder and we all picked up our cards to check them.

'Oh look,' I said (and believe me, friends, this is not good Poker to get this excited), 'I've got another one of those Royal things.'

Louie threw down his cards in disbelief, 'In Spades you ain't.' Apparently, this is a common American expression.

'Actually,' I said, 'in Spades I have.' And I laid down the 10, Jack, Queen, King and Ace of Spades.

Max stood up and smacked Louie.

Then Max raised his glass. The evening which was now morning was coming to an end. In his broad New York accent he said, 'I wish to make a toast, ladies and gentlemen. I wish us all to drink to this remarkable man. Paul, we was not expecting an arteestee of your calibre.' He pronounced it 'cal-eye-burr'. 'Tonight, downstairs, it was ... it was ...' His brain sought a fine compliment, he found it. 'Tonight, it was like watching a diamond in pig shit.'

CHAPTER 13

MY 'REAL' LIFE

In the meantime, as all this television stuff work was continuing in the foreground, I had another 'real' life, of course. The lads were growing older. Gary, the youngest, outgrew us all and became an electrician at ICI. He worked really hard and took exam after exam, climbing the ladder of knowledge. Martin, the middle one, worked in the clubs and the corporate scene and eventually broke into television, being a presenter on *Game for a Laugh* and for a game show as well as guesting on other shows. The press, of course, tried to create mayhem in the family by either saying he was better than me or not as good as me. They missed on a couple of counts here; first, we are great mates; and second, he isn't me. When he does stand-up then he is his own man and can write comedy as well as anyone I know.

One interview sent Dad into a turmoil and I had to remind him that he, Dad, had had the press publish an interview with him that never took place. It's very hard for the relatives sometimes.

Paul drifted, sometimes being with us, most times not. He married a lovely girl from Bristol and it didn't last a year.

When we went on tour sometimes we used to call it a family show. That didn't mean that it was just for families to come and see, although it was all of that, it meant our family. The show consisted of me on stage, standing in front of beautiful theatre curtains that my mother had made, using props that my father had made, being accompanied by music played by my brother, generally Martin performed as well and, occasionally, Paul assisted on and off stage. I loved those times. Later, when Debbie and I got married, I sometimes felt we should adopt Roy, our stage manager, to complete the family circle.

I needed to sort out the Daniels housing situation. Giffard's Barn was very nice but I hardly ever got there. Royal Crescent was useful and kept me fit because it had five floors and no lift. The dining room and kitchen were on the ground floor. All the great political leaders of the mid-twentieth century had dined there, as guests of the previous owner. On the first floor I had a lounge and office. Above that was my bedroom with a large jacuzzi bathroom set off it. One day I had Anne Diamond, the television presenter, in my bedroom. No, no, no – you're wrong. Anne had a flat in Royal Crescent and I was showing her round the house. She said, 'You do realise that your bedroom is my entire flat.' There was an answer but I restrained myself.

Then, on the top floor were another couple of bedrooms and a bathroom. I had the basement converted to a completely separate apartment. Martin lived there for a while and Paul lived on the top floor.

Fire worried me in this house. The whole building had only one staircase. So many houses in London were firetraps. There was an advertisement for a fire-escape device and I had one fitted to the rear of the top floor. Metal staircases were out of the question as they were ugly and thieves could use them too easily. This gizmo consisted of two round units fitted by the window. The top one had a clutch system inside and a rope ran through this and was coiled around the bottom unit.

If there was a fire, you threw the bottom reel out of the window and that uncoiled the rope, measured for the distance, down to the ground outside. That left the other end of the rope, complete with a belt, running over the upper clutch and inside the bedroom. You put the belt over your head, tightened it, and jumped out of the window. For the first few seconds it was terrifying but then the clutch grabbed the rope and the system lowered you to the ground, bringing up the bottom end of the rope with another belt on it for the next person. Well, that was the theory and my mother just happened to be there when the gentleman was fitting it all to the wall. He explained how it worked and my mother looked out of the fifth floor window and shuddered. She has a fear of heights.

'You wouldn't get me jumping out of there with that thing wrapped round me,' she said.

'You would if your arse was on fire,' he said. Did I say 'gentleman'?

Early one Sunday morning, there was a ring at the doorbell. I went downstairs and opened the front door. Nowadays, with all his American experience Michael Crawford has a rich, rounded voice, but in those days he really did have more than a hint of his famous comedy part, Frank Spencer, when he spoke.

'Good morning,' he said, and continued with the trademark phrase, 'I've got a problem.'

My eyes scanned the street. This had to be a wind-up. Where were the cameras? I pulled him in and shut the door so that I would be safe from prying lenses. He came up to the lounge and explained that he was about to tell me something that I mustn't tell anyone. The whole of showbusiness was buzzing at the prospect of who was going to play the Phantom in Sir Andrew Lloyd Webber's new musical.

'I'm going to be the Phantom,' he said and I nearly fell through the floor. I had to stop myself saying what would have come out as a rude and unbelieving – 'YOU?'

The first time I'd seen Michael he was singing in a high, nasal American voice in the wonderful film *Hello, Dolly*. Later, I saw him singing in the equally nasal, but now Northern tones in *Billy*. When he came to see me he was appearing as Barnum in the musical of the same name. I just couldn't believe he was going to produce the deep lustrous, opera-like voice needed for the part of the Phantom. In everything that he did, Michael was marvellous and I was about to find out why. While performing the arduous role of Barnum he was also taking singing and voice-training lessons. What a pro. I had been to see him in Barnum and, apparently, afterwards had said that if ever he needed help with any stage tricks, all he had to do was ask me.

'We are having problems with some of the stuff we want to do. If you will do it, I need you to create some effects for me.' He explained the various needs and I went to work to make them happen. I made him come through the mirror, his image first and, because he wanted fireballs to fire from his hands, created a tall walking stick that fired the balls for him, much safer. I showed him how to find the trapdoors for him 'to descend to the underworld' and, of course, made him vanish at the end. That latter was a real problem because they wouldn't let me have a trapdoor cut into the stage where the chair was situated so, if you see the show, he doesn't go down a trapdoor. Where does he go? He vanishes!

Every time I called in to check a design, Michael Crawford would be there, on the stage, watching them build sets, looking at where the lights were, talking to technicians and the director. He was more than an actor, more than a singer and knew more about the theatre and the sets than anyone. He was the Phantom.

To my design, Dad made one wonderful trick that was never put into the show. The Phantom was to walk down the staircase at the start of the second act, singing 'masquerade' and strut around the stage. At the end of the song, the crowd on stage 'recognise' him and go to attack him. The stick and the costume suddenly shoot up into the air and fall to the stage in pieces. The Phantom has vanished. The director merely wanted him to be seen descending through a trapdoor to his underworld. Shame.

Various girls had drifted in and out of my life during the early years in Royal Crescent. Caroline, the glamorous solicitor, was the foremost of these. We really had quite a turbulent fling but I was growing more and more towards Debbie. I sold the house and moved in with Deb. We decided that I needed one property that covered all my needs. On a map of London I drew a large circle with the studios at the centre. That circle represented a half-hour drive to work. In the circle I drew a segment, pie chart fashion, to the west of TV Centre and in that segment I drew a small circle around a small penny.

With a photocopy of that I sent a note to all the estate agents in the area, saying that I was looking for something in the region of £750,000, a big increase on Giffard's Barn. Debbie went to view dozens of the houses that were sent to us and picked a few for me to visit. None were really suitable. Everyone goes through this, don't they? You can't put your finger on exactly what you are looking for but you know it when you see it. Debbie even saw a house complete with its own zoo in the back garden which I didn't bother viewing, but I did go to see one owned, allegedly, by the son of a Middle Eastern prime minister, which had an armoury in case the resident came under attack. The décor in this house was horrible. One of the bathrooms was entirely decorated in a delightful shade of cat-sick green. It would have cost a fortune to put right and it already cost a fortune to buy. Another no-no, but as I was leaving the property, the estate agent said that there was another house nearby that was not on the market but, as it was rarely used, who could tell? The property had been purchased over a year previously and decorated and furnished to the highest standards, but no one had moved in.

Arriving in Denham, West London, I drove up Tilehouse Lane and turned into the drive of Sherwood House. There was no 'if'; this was what I had been looking for. Set in 12 acres of grounds, divided equally between natural woodlands and formal gardens, it was perfect. Designed by Gilbert Scott, the architect of Battersea Power Station and the original red post office telephone boxes, it boasted five bedrooms and one of those had its own lounge, six bathrooms (nobody would be able to call me filthy rich), eight toilets (there would never be a panic, one was bound to be vacant), and the ground floor had everything that a home should have. More than that, there was a balance in the house that a Feng Shui designer would have loved. Incidentally, have you ever wanted to go to the counter in WH Smith and complain that the Feng Shui books are in the wrong place?

At the end of the drive there was a lodge cottage, bigger than the flat Mam and Dad had at Giffard's, so they could be part of the experience. Large garages would make perfect workshops.

There was only one problem. It was over £1 million. Mervyn – manager, accountant, keeper of the Daniels purse – was with me on that first viewing. I asked if it was possible to find the resources to buy it. He said it would be a stretch, but it would certainly be feasible. The negotiations went on with the American owner for months and I thought I would never get the place. Debbie saw it and thought it was wonderful. I couldn't be there when Mam and Dad came down to view the property. The groundsman and housekeeper had been living in the lodge cottage and were preparing to vacate when my parents turned up to view. They had a good look at all the rooms where it was proposed they would live and at their garden and where they would park their car and so on. As they drove away Mam asked, 'What do you think, Hughie?'

'Well, I don't think it's big enough,' he replied.

'Well, it's bigger than where we are at the moment.'

'Is it? When our kid moves in with all his stuff, it'll be a very tight squeeze.'

'He'll be living in the other house, Hughie.'

'What other house?' Dad asked.

Dad had assumed that the Gatekeeper's cottage was where we were all moving into. He hadn't seen the huge main residence and couldn't believe it when he did. I purchased the whole package lock, stock and barrel, complete with furniture, and my solicitor, on the day the deal was struck, held out a cheque for over £1 million for me to sign. It's a really funny feeling when you do that. He walked away and all I had to buy for Sherwood were a few mirrors. Fine, but that meant I had two houses and all their furnishings to sell. Once again we moved in just before Christmas. We were even further away from South Bank.

Sherwood House had once belonged to Roger Moore, he of *Ivanhoe*, *The Saint* and, of course, *James Bond* fame. When I eventually bought the place, the villagers were very confused because Roger and I looked so much alike!

One of the main reasons for buying such a grand place was that I had planned to ask Debbie to marry me. I had given up asking her to go away and find someone else. We were together and, above all else, really good friends. I made her laugh a lot and I still do. It's a bit off-putting when you're trying to be a sex symbol. We had an 'arrangement' and knew we would get married one day. One day, in late August 1987, it was sunny and in the early evening Debbie and I were seated on a swing seat on the patio. I had a bottle of champagne hidden in case I got lucky. I had decided to propose. I was now nearing 50 and Debbie 30. Surely the press wouldn't be interested in the story now? At 30, Debbie was mature enough to have made her own decisions about life, so where was the scandal?

'Debbie, I may not be very tall, I'm not very good looking and I'm going a bit bald, but the one thing I will promise you is this; it will never be boring. Will you marry me?'

She cried and I said, 'does that mean yes, or does that mean no?'

She said, 'Yes.'

We kissed. I opened the champagne and considered that I had got lucky.

It was a time for weddings, apparently. My best friend at the time, Ken Jones, the musical director from the BBC and the man responsible for all the backing music for my television shows was a man who lived life to the full. He told me that he was getting married but as he was a bit strapped for cash at the time could I suggest what he could do about his honeymoon. I offered my house in Spain. He was overjoyed.

It's funny how your values change. While I was out looking for a place to live I had come across a golfing complex at La Manga, in Spain. At that time I only played holiday golf, once a year or so, but the houses were magnificent. Debbie and I decided to have a villa built on the course and we were full of excitement. We had all the trimmings and I altered the design of the house to give better aspects and all that jazz. Between ordering it, planning it, visiting other similar properties and seeing it nearly finished, we bought the truly wonderful Sherwood House. When we went back to La Manga, good though it was, it wasn't the dream home any more. That title was held by Sherwood.

Ken came up with a strange request. 'Will you come on honeymoon with me? We could play golf and that would give me something exciting to do while we are there.' Ruth, his wife to be, hit him.

Eight of us went on Ken and Ruth's honeymoon – Ken and Ruth, of course; Debbie and I; Mervyn and his wife, Sylvia; and a couple who were to become great friends, Peter and Jean Hodson. We arrived at the villa in the evening and all of us fellas, but not Ken, had raided sex shops and catalogues for toys and goodies. This had to have been the most hilarious wedding night of all and you should have been there. We had video cameras pointing at their bed, floating sex manuals in the bath, an inflatable sex doll was sat on the loo and a mountain of sex toys on their dressing table, stool and bed.

One of the 'kits' was a honeymoon kit for men and Ken kept going into the bedroom and coming out wearing all this kinky gear over his normal clothing, which somehow made it look worse but at the same time very funny. Eventually, we all went to bed and then we heard Ruth shriek as she found the sex doll. Mervyn and Sylvia gave up and went to bed as Ken came out into the corridor carrying the doll. How men are turned on by these things I don't know, we found it hilarious. I stood it up against Mervyn's door so that when they opened it in the morning the doll would fall on them. As we stood talking, Ken suddenly started to laugh again. The doll had a slow leak and the legs were buckling. 'She' slid down the door and appeared to be looking through the keyhole. Mervyn heard the screams of laughter, opened the door and the doll fell forward, but much lower than we had intended. From that moment on Mervyn and the doll were inseparable. We laughed all week.

As our wedding got nearer we planned it down to the last

detail. I couldn't be two-faced and I felt it was inappropriate for me to get married in a church. Sadly, there seemed no alternative to a church service, other than a registry office. I suggested to the authorities that we had the ritual in our garden, but they said it had to be in a place of worship.

'But this woman worships me!' I said, but they wouldn't accept that. Luckily for us, our local register office in Beaconsfield seated 200 and that was where we decided to hold the wedding. Having hired a glass horse-drawn coach, I was determined that our celebrations would be as grand as possible. If Debbie wasn't to have a church wedding, then I had to make it as special as I could for her. We asked guests to wear the full formal outfit of tailcoats and top hats, while Debbie was to be in a fairytale white wedding dress and veil.

Five months before, when Ken had married Ruth, the registrar had performed a Derek Nimmo version of a vicar as he recited the vows. His 'floaty' voice caused some giggles at a time that was supposed to be very solemn. I thought it best to have a word with the guy beforehand to see if I could persuade him to be a bit more 'normal'. I also needed permission to get married on a Saturday afternoon.

Over lunch, I approached the subject of a late wedding and was told that it was out of the question. I asked why this was so.

'We close at twelve.'

'The problem is, you see,' I said, starting to wear my diplomat's hat, 'this is going to be an awfully big wedding and there will be a lot of press there. I know it sounds odd, but if we had ours in the morning, it would interfere with everybody else's weddings on that day. Also, if we can have our wedding in the afternoon, you'll get an invitation to the reception.'

'You're on,' he said.

Then I carefully addressed the subject of his voice.

'Do you know that when you talk to me now you sound

quite normal, but when you speak at the wedding you sound a bit strange?'

'Oh yes,' he smiled. 'That's because I think it gives me a little more authority and importance at a key moment.'

'Oh no! You're much better when you talk normally. You don't need to change your voice at all, in fact I'd like our wedding to be more relaxed and friendly.'

'Do you really think so?'

'Oh yes!'

Mission accomplished. My reasoning for an afternoon slot was that I didn't like the idea of having to get married first thing in the morning and then having to celebrate all day long with it all petering out at the end. I wanted the whole event to have the atmosphere of a steady build-up followed by a big-bang finale and carriages at eleven.

Big bang was appropriate terminology, as I employed a fireworks company to provide the climax to the day. Le Maître was a French-based company that concentrated on giving the very best displays possible. A youngish man on a vintage motorbike, encased in leathers, helmet included, turned up one day and introduced himself as the firework designer. The young chap was frightfully well spoken and we went on a walk around the garden. He was a real character.

He explained how the fireworks were all fired by computers that played the music and moved the ignition back in time for the duration of the fuse so that the explosions matched the music. He liked the Georgian windows in the marquee so that even if it was raining, the guests would still see them. He would put small fireworks close to the guests and the marquee, larger ones would rise from behind the first hedge and off the main lawns and then the really big ones would be fired from down near the woods. The speakers would go into the hedges so the music surrounded us as we watched. This was a long way from 'light the fuse and retire'. My uncle did that – lit a firework and never worked again. Boom boom.

He counselled against having the fireworks spread out; rather, he suggested, it was better to have them all go off within ten minutes or so. It would be much more exciting and create a bigger impression, he believed.

Once again I asked how much it would cost. This time he ducked the question with a discussion on my choice of music. I picked 'Zadok the Priest' from the Coronation Suite by Handel and any reference to my Dad's name was purely intentional.

'Great, that's five minutes and seventeen seconds!' he announced. 'We'll throw them all up in that and you'll get a superb display, for £2,500.'

'So, what would I get for £5,000?'

He paused, his eyes lighting up. 'You'd get another walk round the garden!'

Three days before the wedding, Debbie and I were walking around our garden hand in hand when a car pulled up in our drive. A woman emerged and introduced herself as a journalist from the *Daily Mirror*.

'We've found your first wife, who is living in a council house in the north-east and is prepared to sell us her story,' she said.

'Are you really telling me that people are interested in a junior clerk and a typist of 30 years ago? I've been divorced for 20 years. If you don't get out of my drive within two minutes, I'll call the police.'

The reporter got back into her car and drove straight up to Jackie declaring that I didn't care if she talked to the *Mirror*. Jackie was paid a few thousand pounds and the story, by now distorted, was spread across the tabloids on the day we got married. From that moment on, we decided never to buy, or read, another newspaper.

The press still haunt me for stories about my private life, but what is there to say? When I refuse to answer their questions, they write answers themselves about distorted, out-of-date stories that I can't believe people actually want to read. The most recent one which has been following me around for the last few years is that I am supposed to have said that if the Labour Party got into power, then I would leave the country. That is not what I said. My true words were that if the Labour Party got into power and changed a whole list of things, *then* I would leave the country. As it was, the Labour Party did get into power, but just carried on with Conservative policies. So what's the point of leaving now?

The *Mirror* didn't just run the story for a day. They dragged it out for a week. They talked about Jackie, in the early days, living on the breadline, but never mentioned that I was sleeping in the back of a car. They never mentioned the cars and the money that I did send, which was always more than the court order. They even cut up and then featured a letter in which I was quoted as saying to my ex-wife, 'there is no court in the land that can make me buy you a house.'

Now that was absolutely true, but it was in reply to Jackie asking me to buy a house for her and her boyfriend. I didn't blame Jackie; she just wasn't used to what the hacks can do to the truth.

I don't understand why the press thinks that slagging people off is a good idea. Surely there are enough newsworthy stories without needing to resort to that.

A worse, but then much funnier, thing happened. Ken Jones, he of the hilarious honeymoon, came to see me. Absolutely po-faced, which wasn't like him at all, he asked, 'Have you seen these?'

There is a classic old gag of a man being approached by a 'wide boy' and asked whether he has any 'dirty pictures' of his wife and when the man, angry at the question, says 'no', the guy asks him if he wants to buy some. Ken had 'dirty pictures' of Debbie. These weren't just dirty, these were disgusting. My face must have been a picture and then I looked up to see him in convulsions. I don't know who had done the job and, now that I am into computers, I know you can do magical things with images, but on these you really couldn't see the join. Having doctored the images using photos from God knows where, they had then taken the trouble to transfer them to Polaroids. I could've killed him. I guess he got me back for leaving the inflatable sex sheep in his bed on the honeymoon night. It was his Welsh origins, you see.

The big day, 2 April, arrived and Debbie was driven from her hotel in her coach with the large glass windows so that the crowds who were lining the streets and hanging out of the windows could see her. She looked absolutely stunning. Her dress was made by one of the costumiers at the BBC who specialised in designing spectacular costumes for film dramas. The pure white silk bodice was covered in tiny beads and silver wires and looked magnificent.

My brother drove me to the wedding in the Ferrari. He was over the moon as it was the only time he ever got to drive it.

The register office was on the first floor. Hundreds of people were gathered on the front lawns and cheered our arrival. This was great for us, but I couldn't help wondering why they were there. We were only a couple getting married who just happened to be on TV. Still, it was very nice of them all to come to the wedding.

As Deb alighted from her carriage and walked up the steps into the register office, a newspaper reporter jumped out at her and shouted, 'Is that dress supposed to be special, Debbie?'

The prat had hidden in a broom cupboard all morning and Debbie's dad showed enormous restraint in not hitting him. It was the last thing we wanted on what was a very special day.

We were determined that this press invasion wouldn't spoil our big day, though, and once the reporter had been removed, everything went ahead as planned. As we drove back from the church in the glass carriage, the sun shone down upon us and we waved at the crowds lining the road from Beaconsfield. People were leaning out of their windows and cheering and it felt just like a Royal wedding. Even the Blackpool Spotters had driven down to wave and cheer.

It had taken three days to build the tent in the garden, which Debbie insisted should be called a marquee. I wasn't showing off, I just wanted it to be the best I could possibly manage. One of our friends, Jess Conrad, a very funny guy, said, 'the food in that tent was better than in any restaurant I have ever been to.' A dance band, guests doing cabaret and then the fireworks brought the evening to its peak.

We had written to all our neighbours warning them to keep their pets indoors at this point, but to join us for this part of our celebration. The whole village turned out to see the remarkable pyrotechnics and we all 'ooohed' and 'aaahed' together.

Just as the fireworks climaxed, a full moon rose over the trees in the clear night air and Mervyn asked, 'And how much did that cost?' Ever the accountant.

It was truly magical.

As Mickey Mouse showed our guests to their cars at 11.00pm, Debbie and I prepared for our honeymoon and for the rest of our lives together. We went on honeymoon to Los Angeles where the Magic Castle Club guys gave us a party, to Las Vegas where our friends gave us a party and then had three wonderful weeks in Hawaii and we didn't take Ken, Ruth, Peter, Jean, Mervyn or Sylvia. I wish we had taken Ken and Ruth. They went skiing and in the last week of our honeymoon I got a message to say Ken had died, quickly and painlessly, but he was gone. I didn't tell Debbie. I couldn't. We were staying in a room built on the beach and I walked down to the water's edge and threw a flower into the ocean. 'Bye, Ken.' I told Debbie when we got back.

The other sad message I received while we were away was a call from Joyce to say that John Fisher, the Producer who had said he would never leave the BBC, had left and gone to Thames Television, an ITV company. I immediately got the BBC to sign up the rest of the team on sole contracts. It was interesting that when we got a producer for the next series, who didn't know anything about magic, the show appealed more to the general public and less to the magicians. TV life was not over yet.

It wasn't until I came home that I saw what the *Daily Mirror* had done to us and I heard how my mother had cried. Looking at the diary, I noticed that I had been booked to perform at Robert Maxwell's birthday party, at his house near Oxford. I telephoned Mervyn to ask how strong the contract was and told him that there was no way that I could work for them after the way his newspapers had treated me after the wedding. I knew that if I was allowed on stage in front of that lot, I would not be able to resist letting fly.

'I promise you, I will ruin that birthday party.'

Mervyn broke the contract.

The years at Sherwood were very happy. We loved the people in the village of Denham and everyone was very friendly. I had also taken on board a wonderful family, the McGees. Debbie's mam and dad are great and became good friends with my mam and dad. Robert, Deb's brother, sadly supports Chelsea, so there's no hope there. Donna, Deb's sister, is gorgeous and full of life. For years, she and her husband, Simon, tried to have children with no success. They went in for the treatment, you know, the bottled stuff (I did offer her draught, if you know what I mean, with no success either), and one wonderful, wonderful morning I was driving along and I got a call to say Donna was pregnant. I filled up and I had to stop the car. Funny that, isn't it? Normally you stop the car and then fill up. Now they have two fabulous boys.

Then we got mice. Dad offered to rid us of our infestation. Debbie was a little cautious about the use of baited traps at first, but reluctantly agreed after Hughie's insistence that it really was the only way. The traps went down, and the next morning Debbie came running upstairs screaming that there was a squashed mouse in the cupboard in the kitchen. I was getting shaved at the time so I just passed a comment that Dad would be pleased. She phoned the Lodge cottage and asked for the 'mouse murderer' to come and remove the poor thing. A few moments later and the doorbell rang. The open door revealed Dad standing there dressed in top hat and mourning tails, ready to perform a funeral ceremony complete with tiny casket.

The last I saw of this ceremony was Dad walking funereally down the back garden with Debbie shuffling along behind him. She was as daft as him!

Dad was always incredibly fit and very strong. Standing 5ft 4in, he had a tendency to be a little on the stout side, all due to Mam's fabulous home cooking. He worked for me into his seventies, not just on illusions, but also around the estate, mending this and fixing that.

It was just a few hours after arriving for a convention in Lausanne, Switzerland, that I got the bad news. Dad had suffered a heart-attack. The good news was that he was still alive and in hospital, so I grabbed the next flight home and within a few hours I was standing at his bedside. The attack had been mild, but he was very shaken. None of us, including Hughie, had expected such a healthy, active man to suffer such a heart problem.

I had recently read how, in America, doctors had put sensors on to individual cells of the human body. If the eyes could see the oscilloscope, the brain was able to detect the sensors very quickly and make the cell react. There was obviously some power in the brain to make the body react positively, if it could see the result. I explained all this to Dad and asked the nurse if the heart monitor could be moved so that he could see it. I told Dad that he could control his heart by looking at the oscilloscope and being positive and that's what he did, sitting up in bed watching the little green screen. Whether it helped or not, I don't really know, but it gave him a focus and a hope and the doctor said that his heart steadied very quickly.

A few days went by and I walked into the ward on my usual visit only to discover that Dad's bed was empty. It gave me a shock, until a nurse informed me that he was further down the ward mending something. Dad was underneath a bed with a screwdriver, fixing the mechanism. As we trotted back to his cubicle, I heard him say to a guy with a Zimmer frame, 'What are you using that for?'

'It's helping me to walk,' came the reply.

'No, it's not. You're leaning on it,' Dad reasoned. 'Not leaning on it would help you to walk.'

Years before, Dad had developed an arthritic hip and when the doctors had told him to go to bed and rest it, he said, 'if I do that, I'll never get up again. I'll do more exercise instead.' This he did and slowly worked his hip back into full use again. I think the cod liver oil tablets also helped a lot.

Dad came home after his heart was shown to be in full working order and it was ten years before Dad suffered a stroke. I was so disturbed by the news, I can't remember where I was at the time, but I dropped everything and ran to the hospital to find him once more. He had lost the use of his left side and was obviously very frustrated. I was distressed at seeing him in such a sorry state and wished I could do something to help, but no magic wand in the world could change things. It was down to Dad's strong willpower again.

The hospital worried me though. It seemed that anybody over 70 was not worth taking the trouble for. Some of the staff saw my dad simply as a piece of meat in a bed. Thank God for the few who didn't and who took the time to really be caring. And the constant stream of doctors and nurses wanting the same information astonished me. Why weren't these statistics written down, or computerised and made available to all who needed it? I found the whole place terribly inefficient.

When we eventually got Dad home, I built a contraption to help him stand up. I designed it in such a way that if he fell over while attempting this, it would always deposit him safely back into his seat. Dad was totally unaware of the side where the stroke had robbed him of all his senses. It wasn't a case of it not working any more; as far as his brain was concerned, his left side simply didn't exist. Hughie was desperately keen to recover his proper functions and his drooping facial muscles improved a little, but it was an uphill task. Roy, our stage manager, used to massage him for hours.

Dad also started to have fits and I would get a call from Mam, run down the drive and try to control the incredible strength that people in such a state develop. Both Trevor and I had real problems recognising that this man was the same father who had been so fit and active. Trevor probably found it a bit more difficult than me as, being the older of the two of us, I had to make myself get on with the situation.

Mam surprised us all with her strength to cope, even learning to drive again and took Dad out on various errands. When he started to speak fewer words, Mam got very irritated and tried to bully him into responding. Eventually, I had a quiet chat with Dad on my own.

'For some reason, Dad, you're being bloody rude to Mam who is caring for you. What's the matter?'

It took ages to get the answer out of him. 'I sound funny.'

As a result of the paralysis and perhaps because his hearing had been affected, his voice sounded peculiar to him and this was making him too embarrassed to talk. I wondered why the experts at the hospital hadn't warned us, or given us some guidance on what must have been a common problem for stroke victims.

I brought an extension telephone into the room and called an old mate of his. They chatted on the phone for about half-an-hour.

'Now, Dad, if you can chat to your friend a couple of hundred miles away and he can understand you, then so can Mam. You only sound funny to you.' His face lit up with the revelation and we never had any further problems, though he always hated sitting around.

Ordering an electric wheelchair, I hoped it would provide him with some mobility. What I had forgotten was that because he couldn't remember right from left, the first time he sat in it, he turned it on and wiped out Mam's rose border.

In the middle of all this, I got a call from the Combined Services Entertainment group. These were the people who organised the entertainment for the British troops stationed all over the world. Debbie and I have done a lot of shows for the troops, having been to Germany, Cyprus, Belize, the Falklands and Belfast. This time they wanted us to go to Saudi Arabia. At the time, Saddam was creating a lot of trouble and Desert Storm was brewing. I knew Debbie was always a bit wary about the Middle East, having been trapped there once, so I said I would go alone and I intended to tell her when the time was ripe.

The right time never seemed to come along and the trip was getting nearer and nearer. Christmas was also not too far away and I didn't know how to tell her at all. The telephone rang and Debbie answered it. A *Daily Mail* reporter asked her how she felt about her husband going into the desert. I heard Debbie say something about him having it all wrong and that I wasn't booked to go anywhere so I crept out of the room. She crept after me and I had to tell her.

The Saudis didn't mind us going in and protecting them but they banned all alcohol and entertainment. If we were in their country we had to live by their laws, which seems very strange to us free-thinking and liberal people, doesn't it? To get around this, I flew in with a large camera bag into which I had stuffed a lot of tricks, small in size but big in their effect.

First we had to undergo gas-suit training, which I remembered from my army days so I got through that very quickly. Then, with Tom Spencer from CSE as my 'bodyguard', we flew out to Riyadh. That was quite a trip. I finished up doing shows on top of tanks, in tents, in sheds, on the decks of ships, in fact absolutely anywhere. I remember being amazed when taken out to lunch in one of the towns to see British children sitting in the restaurant. Their mother asked if they could have my autograph and I expressed my surprise. 'Oh, it's nothing. It's all being puffed up by the newspapers,' was her reply.

I had just left the greatest amount of firepower I had ever seen a few miles away in the desert. How anybody could be that sheltered from the truth I couldn't figure out at all.

At one venue I landed by helicopter to be told that the Americans were going to scramble their helicopter force in an exercise. Suddenly, klaxons blared out and men came running, pulling on their gear as they did so. Row upon row of engines kicked into life and the first wave lifted into the air in a checkerboard fashion. If you can imagine all the black squares taking off first then you have the idea. No sooner had they cleared the front row than all the 'white squares' took off. In a couple of minutes, there was no sign they had been there other than huge dust clouds swirling in the air.

On one occasion, a television crew caught me being transported across the desert on a tank. At home, I hadn't told

Mam and Dad I was going abroad as they would have worried. Dad was watching TV and, despite still suffering from his stroke, was bright enough to spot me.

'Where did our kid say he was working this week?' he asked Mam, and Debbie had to do a lot of waffling to get out from under that one.

An armoured vehicle took me for a ride in the desert. We zoomed out of the camp, went a few hundred yards and the young commander swung the vehicle around a few times.

'Right,' he said, 'where's the camp?'

As far as the eye could see in every direction were tracks. I didn't have a clue.

Again, I was asked for an autograph and it turned out to be for his very young children. He showed me their pictures.

'I hope I see them again,' he said. The madness of war.

I think that the biggest surprise to me was to find out that Saudi Arabia exported vegetables. As we flew over the desert, we could see large round fields being irrigated from the centre, the force of water rotating the long horizontal sprinklers. They told me that they had plenty of water that came from desalination plants. We had just gone through a long season of sprinkler bans at home.

Tom had promised that we would be home for Christmas and so, a couple of days beforehand, we made our way back to Riyadh. Our plane had left early. Nothing else was going home. I couldn't fly back as a civilian because I had come in as military and had no visa. Tom and I went along the runway in the dark, literally thumbing a lift on anything going back to Europe. We went to Germany and I phoned Debbie from there. 'What are you doing in Germany?' she asked.

I told her, 'You have no idea how big this desert is!' We did the same thing again and thumbed a lift to England. Home for Christmas.

When we went to Croatia, we got a huge shock. The authorities were talking about getting the various factions back together. They never will. It would take a huge re-education over several generations to make them realise the stupidity of their dislike of each other. We went to one village where one faction, at about 2.00am, crept out of their houses with their hands over the mouths of the children. They didn't use their cars as it would have made too much noise and woken the neighbours. These were neighbours that they had grown up with, gone to school with, gone shopping and played with. They left them to take a pasting from an attack they knew would come with the dawn.

On our last night in this awful environment, where we had seen drunken 14-year-old kids with automatic weapons shooting into the sky and tried to sleep with rats running around our hotel room, we got involved in a charity show that the troops themselves were performing. Our troops were raising funds in Croatia for a hospital in Southampton because they didn't think there was any point in raising funds for people who lived so far in the past. The biggest auction fundraiser that night was Debbie's knickers!

Wars and arguments that are the result of something way back in the past always get right up my nose. Why can't we live in the Now and the Future, learning from our mistakes and creating a better world, instead of perpetuating the disagreements? If we lived in the past then we should never go to Italy for our holidays because the Romans invaded us, didn't they?

It is all so silly. To show you how silly it is, when we went to Croatia, the British troops were under the overall command of an Argentinian general! Who won that war, then?

One winter it snowed very severely and our lawns were covered with glistening white, perfect for tobogganing. Dad wanted to go out. I borrowed a sledge, mounted a sun lounger on it, stuck Dad on that and pulled him around the garden. Dad sat like Father Christmas on his sleigh and laughed like hell.

He struggled on for some time before he had another major stroke and was rushed into hospital once more. This time it didn't look good and we sensed that the end was at hand. Remarkably, he had told Mam that the last two years had been the happiest of his life, which made a mockery of the euthanasia question. I believe if most terminally ill patients are given enough love, care and laughter, they can have a great time.

As Mam and I stood over Dad, he started to have another fit. Mam, having been a nurse, knew the signs and ran out of the room. My dad, having been forever my hero, was finally leaving me. I couldn't help him so I ran after Mam.

I was very upset at the funeral, but I have never really cried for him since. We were great mates, Dad and I, and we had a grand life together. There seems no point in grieving because it is the law of nature that we are all going to die. When Dad died, I was aware of the fact that life had moved on and I had to move with it. I believe that life continues in our genes, our chromosomes and DNA, and I feel sometimes that Dad lives on in me. I am a continuance of his life and believe that he, and I, will travel on in my sons and grandchildren, too.

This really came home to me one night when I was working a short season at the Prince of Wales Theatre again. The night before, I had some shrimps in a restaurant and I must have had a bad one, a really bad one. The show started and I felt a bit queasy. Martin was to close the first half and I made it up to my dressing room but by now I felt really ill. As I entered the dressing room I felt faint and dropped to the floor deliberately so that I wouldn't hurt myself if I fell over. I crawled to the toilet bowl and tried to be ill. Waves of dizziness came swirling around me and *I became my father*. I know that sounds weird. It wasn't a dream. I was still me, but filling me were all the feelings of my father.

Early in the second half of the show, I passed out in the wings and they took me to hospital where, for a while, life stopped for me but they brought me back again – obviously, or I wouldn't be writing this. That was the only time I missed a show through illness.

We sold the house in Spain and Debbie bought me a boat. We called it *Not a Lot* and it was a very fast petrol-engined Bayliner capable of over 40 knots. She really could fly. The problem was that although she was only berthed in Port Solent, near Southampton, I could rarely get down to see her. We loved it when we did but there was a period of about 18 months when we couldn't. Regular performances, as well as charity work, filled the days, the weeks and the months.

Charity work takes up so much time but it is good to give something back. We once kept every charity request for a period of 12 months and it added up to an average of 27 requests a day. You can't do them all so I homed in on a few. I am a Water Rat of the Grand Order of Water Rats. This charity is over 100 years old and originally was put together to look after people in showbusiness, but now looks after a wider range of charitable needs. Great names of the past – Laurel and Hardy, Charlie Chaplin, Maurice Chevalier and the like – were all Water Rats. As I write this, we have Bob Hope, Jimmy Tarbuck, Bruce Forsyth, Sir Harry Secombe and so many more amongst our membership. From film stars to pop stars to Punch and Judy men, the Water Rats work for charity. I am proud to have been elected King Rat twice. I also work for the Royal Theatrical Fund, an even older showbusiness charity. More publicly I am involved with the Yorkshire Cancer Campaign, a Barker of Variety Club, the Children's Charity and a patron of Dystonia and the Multiple Sclerosis Centre in Reading. It's all go sometimes.

Debbie and I decided it was time that we had a rest and went down to the boat for at least a long weekend. I telephoned an engineer that I know down there and asked him to clean her up, top to bottom and back to front. 'It'll be nice to see you again,' he said.

Port Solent has fantastic facilities for sailors and we drove down to arrive in the early evening. *Not a Lot* looked great and I looked forward to taking her out the next day. That evening we dined in the marina, went to the pictures and used the shower and toilet facilities, always immaculate, on the dockside. We went to bed on board and fell sound asleep.

At about 6.30am I got up and used the toilet. Thankfully, as it happened, I only had a 'jimmy riddle'. The toilet had a small handle by the side with which you pumped water into the bowl to flush it. No water came through. I peered at the various instructions stuck on the walls because it was a long time since I had used this loo. I pumped and pumped and twisted and pumped and nothing came through.

I went back to bed. I lay there for a couple of minutes and my nose started to twitch at a particularly bad smell that was coming from somewhere. After a while, I couldn't take it any more, got up, went back into the loo and pumped and pumped and pumped the handle. Nothing.

I went back to bed again. Debbie, who normally has a terrible sense of smell, snuggled in and asked, 'What's that smell?'

'I don't know,' I answered, 'but it is getting worse.'

I got up, pumped a lot more; I ran taps to see if we had water on board and we had; I took up the floorboard that gave access to below deck and stuck my head down the hole. Below decks was immaculate, as new, and I offered the suggestion, after a few more pumps of the handle, that maybe the smell, now vile, was coming from outside.

Shorts were pulled on and I went out into the morning

sunshine. Not many people were about to see the half-naked conjurer sniffing the morning air like a Bisto kid. No smell out there. Several times I tried to go back to bed but couldn't go back to sleep,. Eventually we got some Jeyes toilet fluid and poured that down, pumping all the time but it would go away.

The back end of this boat (back end is a very nautical term) was very streamlined and where it sloped towards the water there were two locked screw caps, fitted flush with the bodywork. One was for fresh water and the other was for pumping out sewage. Not the best design, putting those two alongside each other, I thought.

Debbie passed me the special tool for opening the caps, a double-pronged key. I should point out at this stage a couple of things, one I knew and one I didn't. What I knew was that, even though we were tied up, Debbie was always very careful about getting on and off boats, once on the Norfolk Broads, she had fallen in while jumping ashore. What I didn't know was that for hours I had been pressurising the toilet compartment. The pressure under the cap prevented me from unscrewing it, jamming it fast.

I got Debbie to pass me a towel and increased the leverage on the key handle. It wouldn't budge. I hit it hard and the cap spun very, very quickly out of its socket in the bodywork. In a replica of an oil gusher, a shower of shit shot into the air over the Solent, just missing my ear as it rose high into the air. Debbie, Miss Careful, leapt off on to the quay and was 50 yards away instantly. We have a law of nature that applies everywhere but which, unfortunately, did not come to mind at the time. As I looked up, gravity took over and the gooey, evil-smelling fountain changed direction.

I was covered, head to toe. The stuff hung off me like thick cobwebs. Debbie was rolling about on her back screaming with laughter. Why do women find this stuff funny? Where's the sympathy? All I could think about was, 'I haven't been here for 18 months. This stuff isn't even mine!' Sorry.

Debbie hosed me down with icy cold water from the supply normally used for re-filling your tanks. She stayed upwind.

We have a very funny, happy life, which again seems to upset some reporters who expect all showbusiness people to get divorced. We are always pulling gags on each other and as a comedian I have to express regret that, so far, Debbie is ahead. She pulled a superb gag that finished up with me literally rolling on the floor.

When I write or design, I hate being interrupted. It stops the 'flow'. One day, in an old drawer, I found a small leather tag, rather like a bookmark, with 'do Not Disturb' imprinted in gold. I put this on the back of my collar so that Dierdre, my then secretary, and Debbie, my then wife (that'll keep her on her toes), would leave me alone. It didn't work. They thought it was hilarious.

Hours later, I went upstairs and God only knows how long she had been waiting, but Debbie was lying stark naked on the bed. Eat your heart out, fellas! She was wearing the sort of sleeping blindfold that you get on long haul flights. Printed on it was 'DO NOT DISTURB'. Further down her body she had a sign that said, 'DISTURB'. Perhaps 'rolling on the floor' was not a good choice of words.

Every year of my life was getting better and better. It's time I namedropped and, OH BOY, can I name-drop.

I was invited to do a Royal Variety Show for the Queen Mother and I knew how Prince Charles adored her, so I wrote to the Prince, who is, after all, a member of the Magic Circle and a Companion of the Grand Order of Water Rats and I had the nerve to ask him whether he would like to appear out of a box, on stage, as a surprise for his grandmother, who wouldn't know he was going to be there.

A 'standard' letter came back expressing regret that Prince Charles would be unable to assist. I just assumed that some member of the Royal Household had given the idea the brush off. On the night, I did an act and Prince Charles and Princess Diana were in the Royal Box with the always lovely Queen Mum.

After the show, they all walked around the cast, complimenting them as they do, and eventually Princess Diana came to me and said, 'I am so sorry that my husband couldn't help you, Mr Daniels. We thought it was a wonderful idea but I am afraid that it was turned down by security.'

I had a wonderful picture of the royal couple sitting at the breakfast table, her in curlers as they ate their cornflakes and opened the post.

'Ooh, look at this, Charles. That funny little man off the telly wants to stuff you in a box.'

Princess Michael of Kent asked me to do a children's party for her. How do you say 'no'? I hadn't done a children's party since Newquay but I got some props out and went down to the house. When it was my turn to perform I gathered the children around me and everything was fine except for one child who was a terror. There's always one. Nothing seemed to work to keep him down. I invited him up to do a trick with me, the classic Chinese Linking Rings. This routine never lets me down and a lot of the credit must go to my son Martin, who wrote the routine with me when we were at the Prince of Wales. This routine had been a major factor in my television show winning the Golden Rose and was a total baffler because, unlike most routines, in this one all the rings are handed out and in the possession of the helper at some stage.

This child had some knowledge.

'There's a hole in one of them.' I showed him in great detail there wasn't. He grabbed one end of the chain as I held on to the other, leaned back and he yelled, very loudly, and despite being able to see that if there was a 'hole' the chain would fall apart, 'I KNOW THERE'S A HOLE IN ONE OF THEM.'

He was starting to spoil the party. Not his fault, he was just over-exuberant. I pulled him towards me. 'What's your name?' I asked. 'William,' he said.

Someone in my eyeline nodded and I can clearly remember thinking, 'Oh, that William.' Too late to stop now, Daniels, I grabbed him by the lapels and held him nose to nose with me.

'Well, now listen, your Royal Highness,' (it's very strange saying that to a child), 'one day you may well be King of England and have my head chopped off, but in the meantime you will sit down there, shut up and BE GOOD.'

The latter was shouted louder than he'd been shouting. He looked at me in amazement, sat down, shut up and was good. What he didn't know was that if he had bitten me, I'd have bitten back. Been there, done that.

As a fund-raiser for charity, Prince Edward organised three other members of the Royal Family to be team captains in a television show called *It's a Royal Knockout*. How he got them to agree to this I don't know. I was asked to play the part of a judge, a sort of super referee. It seemed like fun but I already had a booking for that evening. No matter, I was told, the event would start rehearsing early and be over by midafternoon. Even so, the Knockout was in the Midlands and my show was at the Savoy Hotel in London. I said I would do it and went off on the day, with Debbie, to join in the madness.

Because it was for charity and even more so because it involved the Royals, the stars came out of the woodwork to take part in games that you normally couldn't have got them to do for money. The morning rehearsal took place and the most senior Royal asked for a special meeting to discuss the rules.

I had studied all the rules most carefully as, if I got them wrong, perhaps I would be exiled, or worse. Perhaps Prince William had gone home and told his family. Ted Daniels, now Paul, from a two-up, two-down in South Bank, sat down at the head of the table. On my right was the Duchess of York, popularly known as Fergie, and next to her was Prince Edward. Directly opposite Edward was Prince Andrew and on my immediate left was Princess Anne who would become the Princess Royal a few years later.

Most of the items were trivial and easily dealt with, but suddenly Princess Anne asked that the rules be changed completely for one of the games and it didn't make a lot of sense. The other captains had no real objections, but I had. I refused to change the rules and the Princess looked deep into my eyes. You never think of the Royals as sexy, do you? Well, I am here to tell you that Princess Anne can make your hair curl, and I think I was wearing a wig at the time.

'I'm sorry, Ma'am, but I think that you only want the rules changed because at rehearsal this morning Tom Jones couldn't pull himself out of the water and climb the rope. You picked your team and I am afraid you are stuck with it.'

I got the look again and wondered if William had squealed on me to his auntie. Her Royal Highness let the matter drop and I walked away.

The recording ran late – very late – and it was early evening when it finally wrapped. I ran across the field to say my goodbyes and to apologise for having to dash off. Princess Anne asked what the rush was and I explained that I was late for a private cabaret at the Savoy. Without hesitation she took command.

'Edward, get Andrew.'

He ran away and while he was gone she asked whether I had anyone to take my car back to London. The job fell to Debbie, who has never really forgiven me for that. Prince Andrew ran back.

'Have you still got the Queen's Flight helicopter?'

'Yes.'

'Then take Mr Daniels to Windsor, he's late for an appointment. I'll telephone ahead for a car to take him to the Savoy.'

Quick thanks and goodbyes were said and he ran for the helicopter while I ran to get my clothes and my act box out of my car.

We loaded the helicopter (the biggest, reddest helicopter I had ever seen) and, as Prince Andrew climbed the ladder into the cockpit, I climbed into the luxuriously upholstered lounge area with a couple of bodyguards and the Duchess of York. The bodyguards, in case you were wondering, were for her, of course. We flew to Windsor and landed in the grounds. On the way, I showed the Duchess and 'the boys' some card tricks.

As we landed, corgis ran out yapping and there was a very clean black limousine waiting for me. More quick thanks and I was whisked along the M4 to London, changing in the back of a Royal car. As the doorkeepers saw the car approaching the river entrance they went into a right panic. They were not expecting a Royal and it caused a major fuss. I wish I'd had a camera to snap their faces when they opened the door and the conjurer got out!

I was due on stage at 9.30pm and I was spot on. My opening line was, 'Now you're not going to believe this ...' and they probably didn't.

I also went to St James's Palace for a cocktail party to honour charity workers. It's a really nice palace with lots to see inside. Standing there, drink in hand, a young boy came up to me. Everyone else was an adult. Very confidently he held out his hand, which I shook as he said, 'Gosh, Mr Daniels, are you going to do some magic?'

I explained that I was only there as a guest and not as a performer and his face fell.

'Look,' I said, 'I'll get shot if someone finds out but come over here.' We went to a slightly screened-off area of the room and I took out a pack of cards. He saw some tricks for about ten minutes and then said, 'I wish I could do magic.' I asked him if he had ever had a magic set or book, and he said that he hadn't.

This boy had been so polite and so excited by it all that I said that I would send him one of my marketed sets of magic.

'I'll have to ask Mummy,' he said and shot away through the crowd. He wasn't long.

'Mummy said it's OK.'

I took out a pen and pad. 'What's your name?'

'Frederick.'

'And your surname?'

He looked at me as if I was bonkers. 'Windsor.'

I tried to act as if I had known, 'Oh, of course, silly me. Where do you live?'

I was not doing well.

'Here,' he said.

So that's where I sent it.

CHAPTER 14

AND NOW, THE BALLET

So many people write to me, email me, fax me and stop me on the streets, all with the same question: 'Why aren't you on the telly?' It came about like this. The BBC started to change. New 'gods' took over and tried to turn the huge broadcasting company into a commercial concern. It was to become much more 'news'-orientated and where once the corridors churned with programme-makers, more and more accountants moved in. It all seemed very strange.

During breaks in the shows we made there, I would ask the audience who was unhappy with the licence fee. Most would raise their hands and I would offer up an alternative point of view.

'Consider the price of a ticket for a night out at the theatre, or even the cinema. If I was to tell you that the seats would only cost you 50p to come and see my show, would you think that was an amazingly good offer?'

All the audience would agree.

'So I would get 50p off all of you. Of course, you would have to get dressed up to come and either drive in or take transport.

There may be parking fees involved and, at the very least, a snack or drinks. The price goes up and up, but 50p is not bad at all. Our last show got 15,000,000 viewers and, at 50p per person, I should have been paid £7,500,000 for performing.'

This comparison always surprised the audience. I went on to point out just how much they were getting for their licence fee in terms of hours of broadcasting both on television and radio and I know a lot of them changed their minds about the cost of the licence. Nowadays people are paying three times that amount to watch a wider range of channels showing exactly the same range of stuff they got from the BBC.

Once you have covered sport, films, comedy, cartoons and the like, there isn't anything else. The terrestrial channels already covered our range of available interests.

The concept of the BBC was brilliant. All the viewers would pay a little towards the service and the volume of income would pay for a totally independent service, free of having to kowtow to commercial interests and free of politics. It was never supposed to be commercial, it was supposed to serve us, the viewers who were paying for it.

Over the years, the money bought great studios, great wardrobe and props facilities, easily the best rehearsal rooms in London, and so on. The place buzzed as day after day, night after night, producers and directors, lighting and sound, wardrobe and make-up, writers and artists, painters and builders would all be rushing about involved in artistic endeavour, and all trying to outdo each other in the quality of an amazingly wide range of programmes for all ages. It was exciting to be there.

Suddenly, a couple of things happened at the same time. You have to understand that in America the advertisers control the broadcasting to such an extent that they practically control what the viewers are given to watch. Advertising agencies in America decided that they couldn't change the buying habits of older viewers so they started to plough their money into programmes specifically aimed at the young audiences. To me, this is a declaration that they couldn't do their job properly. They should have been able to create adverts to suit and to sway the older audience, but no, they gave in. This is even more surprising when you realise that the older audience is growing very rapidly and I don't know about you, but when I was young I didn't want to stay in watching television.

As is usual in this country, we followed suit. I could understand, possibly, the commercial stations following the advertising trend, but so did the BBC, abandoning traditional shows and transmitting 'young' comedy with 'naughty' words that drove away their older audience.

Then they started to sell off the facilities and lose their professional production staff and crews. The new system required having nothing in stock and 'buying' in anything that was needed, including production crews. It is true that the old way did need a major pruning and streamlining, but the new regime missed the point. They pruned the wrong end, keeping the already top-heavy management and losing the people who actually made programmes.

There was an end result that perhaps they had never considered – all the terrestrial channels started to look the same. Whereas the BBC used to have its own style, its own 'look' and its own quality, by using the same lighting, sound and set designers who were being used by all the other channels we, the viewers, lost choice and the other channels had nothing to try to live up to.

Also, more than ever before, the terrestrial channels started to show the same type of programmes opposite each other. If the BBC had a game show, then ITV had a game show, police drama opposite police drama, and football opposite football, *ad infinitum*. Such a move was bound to reduce the number of viewers for each type of programme and we were being offered less and less choice. I began to wonder if the people who planned the schedules had shares in satellite television companies.

There was a lot more. There was the moment when one of the 'bought in' make-up girls, approaching my face with Polyfilla in hand (I need a lot of make-up!), said, 'Ooh, I've never made a man up before.' I asked where she had learnt about make-up and all her experience had been gained on a Selfridges counter. She knew nothing about wigs, beards, moustaches or prosthetics that are used to change the appearance of a performer. She knew nothing about the different types of studio lights and the effect on make-up.

We were assigned an Australian girl who was in charge of, and controlled, our entire budget for the series. In her early twenties she had never worked in any kind of broadcasting before. Madness ruled.

One of the new accountants asked a producer why he needed the studio all day, which of course was expensive, when the programme was only half-an-hour long. The accountant knew nothing of rehearsals or camera choreography or lighting requirements or even the amount of time it takes to build a set.

All around us money was being spent on stuff that had nothing to do with putting a better product on the screen. I was unhappy and I was far from being the only one. The corridors that once buzzed, now moaned. The 'freedom' that built a great broadcasting company was the thing that was now bringing it down. It was not answerable to the people who were paying for it. It was not answerable to anyone.

One day, a couple of us were talking about how hard it was to make programmes. The whole building was talking about redundancies being grabbed by all the good creative people who knew they could get jobs anywhere. A man joined us and took part in the conversation. It turned out he was a journalist and he published everything I said. The bosses didn't like the publicity. The crews who worked in the building all said I was right.

So I had to go. The method was obvious, if you are in the industry. It has been done many times. Both the magic series and the game shows were suddenly very difficult to follow if you were a viewer. Their time slots were altered, not only on the same day, but also the days were changed. If viewers can't find their favourite programmes regularly, then the audience breaks down. Then the Controller can say that nobody is watching and close the programme down. It is difficult for them to do that if you are always in the ratings, so they 'plan' you out of the ratings. Even I couldn't find out when I was on.

Some months after the last series was recorded, I was at a dinner function and Isabell Kristensen, the designer of fabulous dresses, was sitting opposite me. She said to Debbie, 'When I saw you on television recently, I said to myself, "I *have* to dress that woman." You looked so good, your figure is great. So I telephoned my agent and she telephoned the BBC. We were so sorry to hear that you are not making any more television shows.'

And that is how I found out that my time at the BBC was over.

The next day, I got Mervyn to telephone the BBC and it was confirmed.

I have just re-read what I have written and it may seem to you that I am bitter about what happened. The opposite is the truth. Without knowing it, they did me the most enormous favour. Over the years I had been there, I had often wondered how I would feel if I was told I wasn't wanted any more. Every artist I have talked to about this has the same fears – 'Will they want me back again?' The moment I got the call from Mervyn, however, all I felt was a great sense of relief. It's a cliché I know, but I really did feel as though a great weight lifted off me and I was free. Brilliant. Maybe I was under a greater strain than I was aware of making the last couple of series, but all I know is that I felt great. I couldn't have left the BBC at a better time and, as a working entertainer, I have had the most wonderful time ever since.

I was in Television Centre recently and it was dead – hardly anyone around during what used to be the busiest time, the evenings when the programmes were recorded. Perhaps it comes to life during the day when the accountants roam the corridors. I hope that one day someone realises it is supposed to create its own productions and brings it back to life again.

Now that I was free to accept contracts a long time in advance (in the past I lost a lot of work waiting for the BBC to determine its recording schedules) Debbie and I worked all over the world in theatre and cabaret, on both public and corporate work. It was not only the range of different countries, it was the wide range of work that made life interesting and a challenge. We took on a couple of cruises a year.

If you go on a cruise then the big tip is to join in with absolutely everything that is happening on the ship, even the things you don't think you'll like. If you are worried about being seasick, take a tip from Dr Daniels: with your doctor's approval, get some seasickness tablets. That's a funny name really because they should be anti-seasickness tablets. Three or four days *before* you sail, take one in the morning and one in the evening every day until you embark. If you wait until you get on board to start taking them, it will be too late.

I do hope this next story will not put you off cruising, which is a fabulous way to have a holiday.

Debbie and I sailed off on the *QEII* on a return trip bound for New York. We had heard that there were a couple of hurricanes around but thought that, if we were sailing, there had to be a way around them. After a couple of days of peaceful, but cloudy, cruising, I did a cabaret show on the ship and life was good.

The next day, the captain warned that we would be in the centre of a storm that night at around midnight. 'Storm' was an understatement. We had an early dinner and, by 9.00pm, the ship was starting to pitch up and down. Thankfully, for me, she wasn't rolling from side to side. I can't stand that.

We decided to go to bed early and the waves were really starting to roll in by then. All passengers were warned not to go out on deck – they would have been crazy to do so. The wind was howling fiercely and eventually got up to speeds of 130mph before the anemometer literally blew away. Considering how well they are fixed down, it must have been some wind. The big storm over England a few years back had wind speeds of 100mph.

I went to sleep while the ship battled through 40ft waves and occasionally half-awoke when a door or drawer in the cabin flew open and banged shut.

At 0205 there was a huge explosion and I was wide awake immediately. There was a feeling of a major accident, that we might be going down, that we had hit something. Debbie was very frightened so, to appease her, I, Sleepy Daniels, got out of bed and looked out of the window. Waves were going by at an impressive height and I was being thrown up and down. Doing my best impression of a naked string puppet, my legs bending when I least expected it, I went to the door and walked out into the corridor. There was nobody there and so I went back to bed mumbling, 'No alarms so we must be all right,' and I went back to sleep.

I think Debbie felt that I should have done more to protect her, but she's the one who can swim, not me.

The next morning was still rough but it had all calmed down by lunchtime. The ship had been hit by a 93ft wave. That would have gone over the top of the BBC's Broadcasting House. It certainly went over the top of the *QEII* and you have to stand alongside her to realise how big it must have been. The water had gone over the top of the bridge and some had even gone down the funnel.

None of the crew had ever seen anything so big at sea and the damage must have cost many thousands of pounds. We had lost life rafts, the front mast, winches, foghorns and the supporting beams under the foredeck had been bent at right angles despite being extremely thick metal. The foredeck itself was wok-shaped.

Amazingly, no one was hurt. In a rolling sea I have known people to break limbs, but in this head-on collision no one was even bruised. That was even more amazing when you realise that Hurricane Luis was the worst recorded storm in the twentieth century. It was a tribute to the great shipbuilders of the Clyde that the Queen sailed through it. The British press headlines read that she 'limped' into New York, but that wasn't true. This great ship went in at normal speed and did us proud.

Because of the delays during the repairs, I couldn't stay on board for the return trip. I had four TV shows to record on the Monday so I disembarked in New York and flew back. Some trip. Debbie stayed on board with our friends for the return trip and gave me one of the best laughs I have ever had. The fax read, 'Darling, do you remember all those waiters we thought were gay? Well, it's amazing how many of them aren't.'

★ ★ ★

Every year we have managed to fit in a tour of the UK and,

whenever possible, Ireland. This large illusion show is mostly based around comedy and both Debbie, who is now even doing illusions, and Martin joined in the fun. Touring is damned hard to set up and damned hard to sell, but it is great fun to do. Mervyn thinks we are all mad because there are much easier ways to make money in this business. What does *he* know, we ask.

When he is not touring with us, which is most of the time, Martin is off doing the comedy clubs, the corporate work, summer seasons and all the jobs that make our business tick over. You don't have to be on television to make a career in showbusiness. In truth, most of the business is done away from broadcasting anyway. He and his wife, Jo, are very happy and even more so now that they have Lewis to look after and to play with. Lewis is walking. That happened when he was one year and one day old, on Boxing Day. Martin had a video camera pointed at him as he played near the settee. Lewis looked up, saw the camera, and walked. Show-off! I wonder where he gets that from.

My youngest son, Gary, left ICI and went to work in computers for NHS hospitals in the Middlesbrough area. From being a podgy lump (we always use terms of endearment in our family) he suddenly got into aerobics and is now a streamlined hulk, he tells us. He is living near Middlesbrough with a lovely, funny, happy girl called Lisa, whose father runs a pub. If only the pub had been on a golf course it would have been perfect.

Paul, the eldest, is still my biggest worry in life. Hey, it can't all be good, can it? For years he drifted in and out of our lives, sometimes for months and wouldn't bother getting in touch to tell us how he was getting on. He meandered from job to job and seemed mostly to be out of work. In his personal habits he wasn't too clean and preferred the scruffy look of the streets. Still does, as far as I know. He just did not want to be part of the family, and yet kept coming back as if he did. It is all very disconcerting.

For years, I blamed myself – the going away, the divorce and all that messy stuff in my early life. Psychiatrists would go down that route maybe, but there comes a time in your life when you are old enough to look around and realise that not all relationships are perfect. If the early life disturbed Paul, surely by now he has the experience of his own failed relationships to build on? Me? I was always the cock-eyed optimist, always hoping that he would pull through and start contributing to society in some positive way.

I did all I could for many, many years. I hung on to any shred of hope that was visible, but there was none. He was an excellent magician, although he told the newspapers that he didn't like the art at all. I suspect that he was frightened of the comparison with me and I can understand that. He was constantly uncontrollable and I never knew what he was up to. When Paul turned 30 I had to realise that he was now a man. This was the time when I decided that I had put up with enough; I could no longer 'bail him out'.

I worried, cared and thought about him constantly. For years, he was the last thing I thought about at night and the first concern that hit me every morning. He still is.

The worst moment came one day when I was having a meal with friends and I got a phone call.

'Paul is in prison,' the voice at the other end said.

'For what?' I needed to know but feared the worst.

'Some kind of fraud.'

Paul, being a biker, had realised it was very difficult to get insurance cover and had formed his own insurance company. Whether it was deliberate or not I will never know, but he got it wrong, didn't set the system up correctly, and a government office closed him down. The press made a meal of him standing in court alone as he was sentenced. He went to court alone because he had never told any of the rest of the family he was going. We'd have all been there for him.

Legally, he had committed fraud. It was a serious offence and he got 12 months. According to Paul, he had been told that, as a first offender, there was no chance of him getting a jail sentence and that is why he never bothered calling us. Who will ever know?

It's not easy to get into prison to visit someone. There were days of telephoning to find out how to get permission to visit. Eventually, I drove to Pentonville and went through the procedures of forms and what you could and couldn't take in, door after door locking behind me. It's a good job that I had been to have my claustrophobia cured the year before or I would probably never have made it inside. There are times when you don't want to be recognised and this was all of them. There is a strange embarrassment in the other people who are visiting and even in the warders. I didn't care, I just wanted to see my son.

There should be school tours of the worst side of prisons; they are bloody awful. Hopefully, it would scare them to bits and they might think twice about committing their crime.

Paul was sitting in a long room of tables, the aisles of prisoners separated from the aisles of visitors by low partitions. He was noticeably frightened and obviously unhappy. The sentence had hit him hard and he had woken up with a jolt from his 'it'll never happen to me' attitude. He told us that he was in the 'mildest' part of the prison, but he still hated it. I honestly believe that if they had put him into the worst part for two weeks, with him expecting to be there for a year, and then told him to go home with a warning that if he ever came back they'd put him in for three, it would have made a difference. As it is, anyone going inside does what every human being does in any situation, they just get used to it. I could do nothing. I left Pentonville gutted.

As often as I was allowed to, I visited him. It never got better. His girlfriend Sam visited him and even Debbie made the trip 'inside'. Martin and Gary came down. All of us hated seeing him trapped.

A few weeks later, he was transferred to Ford Open Prison where he boasted that he had played in the same football team that George Best had been part of. As I sat and listened to him while on a visit, he said how much he admired some of the things the other lads had done and told me how easy it was to fiddle money out of a telephone box. What schooling.

During this period, we decided to refuse any interviews for the gaggle of press constantly sneaking around us. Publicity was the last thing he needed at this time while he was doing his best to get himself back on his feet. The tabloids were only interested in him because of me and I was keen to protect him.

In the meantime, I wrote almost every day. I wrote my diary, told him what the family was up to and generally let him know that we all cared and were still rooting for him. If I was working abroad, I sent postcards. He answered a couple of times and I was thrilled to receive his letters in reply. Together, we started to formulate a plan to help him when he came out. After being in prison for fraud, he stood no chance of getting a decent type of office job, so I suggested he became a local, self-employed handyman. He was a very skilled tiler and could turn his hand to anything. We considered general gardening, plumbing, decoration, electrical work and even small building work. He had the talents; we had to find a way to exploit them.

Together, and please note that I say 'together', we came up with a total plan that would swing into action on his release. Nobody knows when they are starting out in life for the first time, or in Paul's case, the second, exactly what is going to be best for them. We put together a package of occupations that Paul could do all at the same time until he found which was the best for him. We listed what we knew he could do and he agreed to each one in turn.

First, the name had to go. If he used his own name then he would always be associated with me. He carries the family name of Newton, so we called him Paul Newton. It is very difficult nowadays to work, especially in the areas we were discussing, without transport, so I said that I would buy him a van and a mobile phone to get him started. Every function that you go to nowadays has some table-hopping magicians and, as that was his forte, I knew that he could easily get work doing that with the big advantage for him of not being associated with me. During the day he would do tiling and light deliveries and any other job that came up needing a light van. This was all agreed and we mapped out everything in great detail. He asked for some magic props and everything was fixed.

It was 'yes' to everything and suddenly I felt we were starting to get him back on the right track. Maybe the blow of being in prison all those months had shocked him into surrender. I was pleased, relieved and extremely hopeful. The plan was ready and together we waited for the day of his release, which was to be some time near the end of 1998. Sadly, they did not let him out for Christmas with the family. That would have been a fantastic celebration. At 7.45pm Paul became an uncle, Martin became a father, I became a grandfather and Debbie insisted on being a Debbie. As the trouble and strife with Paul appeared to be coming to an end with all the plans laid out for his release, something else that was wonderful happened. Lewis was born on Christmas Day. Now that's what I call a Christmas present. All day the whole of my family and Debbie's family were on standby with the champagne ready. If there was a hitch, then it was because Deb and I were stuck in pantomime and I couldn't get up to see him for over a week as we had shows every day. The pantomime was in Tunbridge Wells and I was playing a schizophrenic Sheriff of Nottingham (Don't ask!) I could hardly wait to see my first grandchild and give him a magic set. Just kidding. Only just.

Paul was finally released on New Year's Eve. Who decides this stuff? A group of men, Paul among them, were all released from an alcohol-free zone into the biggest night of the year for getting drunk. Certainly in Paul's case, it wrecked his chances of making a clean break before he even got started. Although I don't even think that he realises it, I have noticed that it only takes a couple of drinks to change his personality. Alcohol seems to kick in fast with him. Predictably, he went straight home to his girlfriend in London and got smashed out of his brains. A couple of nights later, she kicked him out. I don't blame her; he deals a tough hand. Strangely, later, he blamed me for having been kicked out, and I realised that he blames everybody for his misfortune except himself. He telephoned Sam threatening suicide.

That same night, straight after the evening show, I set off for Doncaster to see Lewis. The next day there were to be no pantomime shows. I had just left Tunbridge Wells when I got a call from Jackie to tell me that Sam had telephoned to say Paul had taken an overdose. I went icy cold and then very calm. As I drove, Debbie dialled Sam and the police and other services. The police phoned me back to say they had found him in a park and had seen him into a pub (where else?) but couldn't do anything, as he hadn't committed a crime. All that we had planned, designed and arranged, removed in one fell swoop.

I made for London and telephoned Martin to say we weren't coming. The scene was incongruous as I arrived in my Bentley to pick up Paul who was dirty and smelly. I had no choice and I felt so sorry for Debbie. He's not her worry and she got lumbered. I took him back home, got him cleaned up and he went to bed.

In the six months that he had been inside, all he had learnt was to be bad. There had been no training as to why crime was wrong. There had been little investigation into his mental health. The system isn't working to make things better. It is not enough just to lock them up; someone should be teaching them a better way and a better understanding, even if it is against their will. They are prisoners, aren't they? On the night that we were supposed to be celebrating a New Year and a new birth, Paul had messed it up again and he was causing stress between Debbie and myself. It says a lot about the strength of our marriage that we survived the next couple of weeks.

For the next few days, Paul and I retraced our steps; We went back over the plans. It was very much along the lines of, 'OK, you're out and you've had your fling. You have to swallow the fact that you have spoilt your relationship with Sam, but there's always a chance that if you get straightened up, you might see her again.'

We got him a phone. I went to the printers and had a few thousand postcards printed with his new 'businesses' advertised on both sides ready for a 'leaflet' drop. Local newspapers were scanned for flats or houses that he could live in locally. I would finance the operation and he would pay me back from his income. A week or so later, Paul and I went out for a drink and, when he promised to be home soon, I stupidly left him there.

He returned very late that evening and was immediately very abusive. Swearing and shouting at me in an alcoholic state, he climbed the stairs and went to bed. The following day, I awoke to find that he had packed his bag and left. I haven't seen him since.

What hurt even more were the occasions when he went to the press, in order to make some extra money by selling stories about me. They swallowed it the first couple of times but then the reporters started to phone me and tell me that he was so obviously lying that they wouldn't print anything. They are not all bad, then. He still telephones the newspapers when he gets drunk and says he has a great story to tell, but it's all old news and they ignore him now. I'm not sure if his problem is alcohol or schizophrenia, or a mixture of both, but I have had to shut him out of my head and realise that now, after all the chances he has had, it ain't my fault. Even after all the pain, though, he will always be in my heart. He has a wonderfully close family waiting for him and it distresses me to think that he is missing all the fun that we share.

No one can help him now, but it is heart-breaking to think how bad he has become and I fear for his future. Paul is the only person who has the power to put an end to his programme of self-destruction, but I don't think he ever will.

Apart from losing Dad, which is a natural part of life, and losing Paul, which needn't have happened at all, I have very little to complain of in my long and full life. Every moment of every day is taken up with doing shows, planning shows, designing shows, chasing Debbie around the house (one day I'll catch her) or driving north to see the family as often as possible. Whether I'm out walking down the street, driving or even in planes, there isn't a day that goes by without someone coming up to me and asking if I am coming back on TV. I find that amazing, because I haven't done a series now for several years.

Television does affect people. In all the arguments I have heard about the use of 'bad' language and violence on the screen, there has always been the 'far-out' producer or the voice of the do-gooder arguing for total freedom to show anything they wished. It is true that most people will not be affected and some will totally ignore what is on the screen. It must equally be true, therefore, that some people will be affected and some will be affected very strongly. Just as I copied Errol Flynn when I was young, the young people of today will copy the heroes they are offered.

Any entertainer should realise that responsibility and if they cannot, then the controllers of television should realise it for them.

A couple of examples. I've had people writing to me to say thank you for saving their marriage: 'We were going to get divorced and we went to your show and found out that we could still laugh together.'

Or one that I found funny: a guy stopped me in the street one day and said, 'Well?'

'I'm sorry?' said I.

'Is it better then?'

'I'm not sure I'm with you,' I said, trying not to look totally perplexed.

'It's gone, what do you think?' he announced, pointing to his face. He could see I was not on the same planet.

'At the club last week you saw my beard and said that I looked like a mouse coming through a lavatory brush, so I shaved it off.'

I'm just a conjurer and if I have the power to change lives, what power do the others have?

Now that anyone in anything can show a sex scene, have you noticed how long the directors drag them out instead of getting on with the plot? In the right place, I have no objection to it at all. Apart from when it involves children, I don't understand why we spend millions trying to stop people looking at naked people. If that's what they want, fine. In a film or a play where it takes a minor role to the main plot, however, let's get on with the movie.

Probably the best reason for some sort of control was offered by the late Joyce Grenfell, a rare comedienne and character actress, who said on a chat show about sex scenes, 'Oh them, I don't know why we have to watch them. When Clarke Gable swung the leading lady into his arms and carried her up the stairs, the director would cut to waves crashing on the shore the next morning. We all knew what they had done, but we didn't have to watch every sweaty moment of it.'

A producer sitting in the front row leapt to his feet. 'We show it because it is there. We show it because it exists. We show it because it is real.'

Joyce Grenfell came back with, 'diarrhoea is there, it exists and it is real, but I don't want to pay to watch it.'

A couple of years ago we sold Sherwood House and I thought that I would miss it. Not at all. In the two years since moving, I have not given Sherwood a single thought. Debbie went out on the house search again and found a completely different house and it's right on the river. It is so 'on' the river that there is even a creek running underneath the bedrooms. Every day I look out of the wall-to-wall windows and watch the coots, moorhens, ducks and swans gliding past. This is heaven. Yes, Mervyn, I know it has taken us two years to refurbish it, just pay the bills.

Mam is still living in Denham, surrounded by fabulous neighbours who all seem to call in and look after each other. She loves it when Trevor and his wife Rosie call in with the 'brood'. They have two sons, Callum and Owen, and two gorgeous twins, Kelly and Nicola, who are going to be stunning when they get a little older. Trevor has two other sons, Mark and David from his first marriage. It's a lot of children, but he has found out now what was causing them, so they won't be having any more.

A couple of years ago, in order to force myself to do something other than work, I took up golf more seriously. I now know that I will never be any good at it but I hear that it is like sex – you don't have to be good at it to enjoy it. We met a professional golfer, the best I ever saw, called Peter Robinson, at Rockley Resort in Barbados, when he was on honeymoon with his wife Sandie. He asked if I would like to play golf and memories of Ken's honeymoon came flooding back. He showed me a few things but he gave Debbie lessons as well. Sadly for me, Debbie is rapidly becoming better than me. You will probably see her in those celebrity matches. If you do, have a good look at the little caddy and give me a wave.

This year, 2000, will probably see my last theatre tour with the Magic Show. There are other things I want to do instead. Thankfully, I feel good and I am having a great life. The other day I walked past an 'over 60s' club.

I have never been a 'club' person, so I looked at it and wondered why anyone would want to join it. Then I realised I could join it and actually stopped in the street to consider this. How could I be over 60? I don't feel any different. Since then I have talked to much older people who tell me they don't either, so what's all this ageism stuff about? Once, on a game show, we had a couple fill in the application forms and I looked down it as I was about to interview them on a recording. Under 'ambitions' they had written one of the saddest comments that I have ever seen. It said, 'None left'.

I still have loads of things I'd love to do. Thanks to the actress Carmen Silvera, I got to do one of them not too long ago when I appeared in Moliere's comedy in the West End. Me! A nearly straight actor! Now I'd like to do a musical, or another play, or be in a film. I guess the last one goes back to my early days in the cinema. I'll blame Errol Flynn for that one.

I am having a great career and I am surrounded by loving friends and family. I work hard and play hard. Most exciting of all is that, in the last few months, Debbie has been working towards having her own classical ballet company, which we hope will open in September this year. There wasn't a lot of ballet in South Bank and I grew up thinking it was a bit lahdi-dah and posh. I was wrong and now I really enjoy it. Adding to Debbie's choreography, my contribution is to have designed the set concepts and to build in the special effects that will enhance the dancing. This is going to be good. This is a whole new career.

Now, where did I put my tights? I must practise my pirouettes.

So here is the first trick that I ever learned.

The Age Cards

That is the name of the trick because a lot of magicians ask a member of the audience to think of his or her age and then find it on some cards that are handed out. Me? Over the years I have learned that not everyone wants to give away their age so instead I introduce them to a simple computer that can locate any number they think of up to 63. Try this yourself: Think of a number up to 63 and look at the cards. Select the cards that have your number on them. Well, if you were to point at those cards I could tell you immediately what your number was out of all the numbers printed on the cards.

1	3	5	7	9	11	13	15
17	19	21	23	25	27	29	31
33	35	37	39	41	43	45	47
49	51	53	55	57	59	61	63

2	3	6	7	10	11	14	15
18	19	22	23	26	27	30	31
34	35	38	39	42	43	46	47
50	51	54	55	58	59	62	63

AND NOW, THE BALLET

4	5	6	7	12	13	14	15
20	21	22	23	28	29	30	31
36	37	38	39	44	45	46	47
52	53	54	55	60	61	62	63

8	9	10	11	12	13	14	15
24	25	26	27	28	29	30	31
40	41	42	43	44	45	46	47
56	57	58	59	60	61	62	63

16	17	18	19	20	21	22	23
24	25	26	27	28	29	30	31
48	49	50	51	52	53	54	55
56	57	58	59	60	61	62	63

32	33	34	35	36	37	38	39
40	41	42	43	44	45	46	47
48	49	50	51	52	53	54	55
56	57	58	59	60	61	62	63

Even though there is only one secret to the trick, there are lots of ways that you can present it to the audience.

So, if you haven't already done so, think of one of the numbers on the cards. Next find out which cards the number is on by looking at all the cards ...... the numbers are always in sequence so it is easy to find.

Now look at the top left hand corner numbers on the cards that you have picked and ADD THEM TOGETHER. The total will equal the number that was in your mind at the beginning.

So, suppose you thought of the number 5. It would only be on two of the cards. The numbers in the top left hand corner of those cards are 1 and 4. Add 1 + 4 and you have 5.

If you have thought of the number 63 then it is on all of the cards and adding the top left hand corners of all the cards equals 63 (but then, if all the cards are named you know it is 63 anyway).

The numbers in the top left hand corner are known as Key numbers. You will come across the word Key again in other tricks. It means that they are the important part of the trick.

In this case the numbers 1, 2, 4, 8, 16 and 32 can be added in different ways to make up any of the numbers on the cards.

So now you know the secret of the trick, but the entertainment has to come from YOU.

How can you improve upon the effect?

The first thing that you must do is to know the trick VERY WELL and I mean VERY WELL. Just because the secret is simple does not mean that it is not a good trick, the best tricks are simple BUT you have to be able to do them almost automatically.

Spend at LEAST one evening doing it yourself, to yourself firstly, over and over so that you practice the simple additions to create any of the numbers. Then try it out on a family member who won't give the game away if you get it wrong.

You must not let ANYONE see that you are adding up.... Don't use your fingers or paper and pen..... Calculate in your mind only and hang onto the totals whilst you are talking about the trick ..... I KNOW THAT THIS PART IS DIFFICULT BUT I WANT YOU TO BE A BETTER MAGICIAN. I have seen so many people, young and old, hesitate and obviously be adding up and that spoils the trick and makes it obvious.

So how can you perform this differently. On the face of it you just give out six cards and ask the person to think of one of the

AND NOW, THE BALLET

numbers and tell you which cards have their number printed on them. You look at these cards and then tell them the number that is in their mind. OK. Not bad, BUT it could be better.

Consider this as an alternative presentation: On the table you have some coins, a mixture of values and preferably about ten of them......

'I am going to try to read your mind. To do this I am going to use a very simple form of computer and some coins. Firstly think of any number that is printed on the cards. Make sure that it is fixed in your mind. Now take one of these coins and put it onto the card that has your number. Have a look at the other cards and if your number is on any of the other cards take a coin and put one onto each of those cards.'

As they are looking and doing this you can add up the left-hand corners as they are putting the coins onto the cards. In this way they will be busy whilst you are busy. If they stop putting coins onto the cards......

'Are you sure that none of the other cards have your number on them? Well, now, you have used up 57p....' (or cents, or whatever) '....so you must have thought of the number.......' and you tell them what their number is.

Think about this. By using something that is NOTHING at all to do with the trick you have thrown them a piece of misdirection. They will be thinking about the money and not the real method. The next time that you do the trick....not at the same time, remember, the money will be a different total amount, who cares? Not you, YOU have a SECRET.

A LAST WORD

Paul Daniels died on 17 March 2016, aged seventy-seven,
after a short illness.

This autobiography, originally titled *Paul Daniels: Under No
Illusion*, and first published in 2000, is long out of print,
although an ebook edition was made available in 2012. It may
be that its author has left the secrets of his many brilliant
illusions to posterity, or at least to his family, for magicians as
rare as he was tend to keep the tricks of their trade to
themselves. He published no more about his life, but for sixteen
years lived by the precept he set out at almost the very end of
this book: 'I still have loads of things I'd love to do.'

When he was diagnosed with an incurable – indeed,
untreatable – brain tumour, he remained in hospital for some
two weeks. Even facing, as he was, his inevitable end, not only
with no hope of remission, but with foreknowledge of the very
little time left to him, he remained concerned about others, not
just his wife and family, but patients in the hospital with him.
His son Martin recalled: 'A couple of days after I arrived to see
Dad in hospital he was up and walking about trying to cheer
up all the other patients. He said to me, "Right, I am going to
have a wander round now and see if everyone is all right." He
went round the beds saying hello, making jokes. He sat at the
nurses' stations.' He might have descended – it would have been
entirely forgivable – into self-pity, have adapted his own famous
catchphrase to say, as one fan did of his death: 'Don't like this.
Not even a little.'

Instead, he faced the dying of the light with his thoughts
turned to others. He leaves behind a life and a career and a body
of work that will continue to endure, long after his death. There
is nothing illusory about that.